MW01068998

# Trithemius and Magical Theology

SUNY Series in
Western Esoteric Traditions

David Appelbaum, Editor

# Trithemius and Magical Theology

## A Chapter in the Controversy over Occult Studies in Early Modern Europe

Noel L. Brann

STATE UNIVERSITY OF NEW YORK PRESS

Cover illustration: Gravestone image of Trithemius, Würzburg, Neumünster, from workshop of Tilmann Riemenschneider. Author's photograph.

Gratitude is expressed for permission to reprint the following:

- Title page, John Dee, *Monas hieroglyphica*, Antwerp, 1564. Reprinted by permission of The Huntington Library, San Marino, California.

- Title page, Robert Fludd, *De macrocosmi historia*, Vol. II, Oppenheim, 1619. Reprinted by permission of The Huntington Library, San Marino, California.

- Title page, Gustavus Selenus (Augustus II), *Cryptomenytices et cryptographiae*, Lüneburg, 1624. Reprinted by permission of The Huntington Library, San Marino, California.

- Title page, Gaspar Schott, *Schola steganographica*, Nuremberg, 1665. Reprinted by permission of The Huntington Library, San Marino, California.

- Title page, Gaspar Scott, *Physica curiosa*, Würzburg, 1667. Reprinted by permission of The Huntington Library, San Marino, California.

- Trithemius presenting *Octo quaestiones* to Emperor Maximilian. Title page, Oppenheim, 1515. Reprinted by permission of the Rare Books Division, New York Public Library, Astor, Lenox and Tilden Foundations.

- Engraving by Albrecht Dürer, *Melencolia*, 1514. Photo: Warburg Institute, University of London.

Marketing by Fran Keneston
Production by Ruth Fisher

Published by
State University of New York Press, Albany

For information, address the State University of New York Press, State University Plaza, Albany, NY 12246

**Library of Congress Cataloging-in-Publication Data**

Brann, Noel L.
  Trithemius and magical theology : a chapter in the controversy over occult studies in early modern Europe / Noel L. Brann.
    p.  cm. — (SUNY series in Western esoteric traditions)
  Includes bibliographical references and index.
  ISBN 0-7914-3961-5 (alk. paper). — ISBN 0-7914-3962-3 (pbk. : alk. paper)
  1. Trithemius, Johannes, 1462–1516—Contributions in magic.
2. Magic—Religious aspects—Christianity—History of doctrines.
I. Title.  II. Series.
BX4705.T77B73   1999
261.5'13'092—dc21                                                98-14898
                          *Copyrighted Material*                     CIP

10 9 8 7 6 5 4 3 2 1

*To my wife Joy, with love*

# Contents

# Acknowledgments

Of the specialist libraries to which I am indebted for expediting the present study, I single out for special thanks the offerings and staffs of the Warburg Institute and British National Library, London; the Bibliothèque Nationale, Paris; the Folger Shakespeare Library, Washington, D.C.; and the Huntington Library, San Marino, California. Also helpful were certain generalist collections, most notably the Library of Congress and the libraries of Stanford University, the California Institute of Technology, the University of California at Los Angeles, and Hofstra University. For relevant visual illustrations and permission to publish I thank, in addition to the Huntington Library and Warburg Institute indicated above, the New York Public Library.

Among individuals who significantly contributed, both indirectly and directly, to the eventual appearance of this study I single out for special mention Irwin Abrams, Roger Williams, Lewis Spitz, and Lawrence Ryan, all of whom guided me in the earliest phases of my academic career at Antioch College and Stanford University; Wayne Shumaker, with whom I conversed over this topic in the beautiful environs of the Huntington Library and who gave a critical reading to an early version of my manuscript; and the late Charles Schmitt, with whom I shared many hours on the subject of Renaissance magic within the highly conducive walls of the Warburg Institute. I likewise express my indebtedness to a number of anonymous readers, among whom Professor Shumaker and Professor Jeffrey Russell subsequently identified themselves, who had the patience to pore through this study at various earlier stages of its preparation and to furnish me with helpful comments for revision.

Finally, Trithemius scholars everywhere, myself included, owe a special acknowledgment of gratitude to Professor Klaus Arnold, who has so diligently worked to prepare the bibliographical ground for a study like this one. Though, in my own Trithemius inquiries, I have always been borne along by ideas crystallized by my own independent reading of the primary sources, first in my book on the monastic humanism of the abbot and then in this one on his magical theology, I have never lost sight of how Arnold's preliminary spadework has facilitated my task.

Last, but far from least, I mention the indispensable support of my wife Joy, to whom I dedicate this book. Without her constant nurturing and help of more practical kinds, such as giving me the needed push to replace my mechanical typewriter with the word processor, this study might not have made it past its difficult prepublishing stages.

# Chapter 1

## Introduction: The Theoretical and Biographical Ingredients

### The Theological-Magical Nexus

One of the more prominently featured themes in the history of ideas, extensively spelled out by Lynn Thorndike in a multivolumed study, is the association between magic and science. "My idea," explained Thorndike at the outset of his vast scholarly undertaking, "is that magic and experimental science have been connected in their development; that magicians were perhaps the first to experiment; and that the history of both magic and experimental science can be better understood by studying them together."[1] Refining this thesis for the early modern period is Frances Yates, who, by claiming that the Hermetic expression of magic in particular played a substantive role in the evolution of modern science, has raised a virtual hornets' nest in the midst of Renaissance studies.

The intellectual breakthrough setting the stage for the modern scientific temper, according to Yates, required a critical change in the conception of man's relation to the universe, the key of which lay in the shift from a geocentric to heliocentric cosmic outlook. Instrumental in promoting this revolutionary shift, Yates has argued,

1

was a revived Hermeticism. With Giordano Bruno her main focus, whose Hermeticized world view reputedly resonated with and helped to confirm the heliocentric cosmic outlook of Copernicus and Galileo, Yates forced a reevaluation among Renaissance historians concerning the proper connection between the Hermetic revival and the seventeenth-century scientific revolution. While intrinsically fascinating in its own right, however, it will not be our object here to enter into the controversy surrounding the so-called Yates thesis concerning the origins of modern science.[2] The subject of the present study, the abbot Trithemius (1462–1516), rather highlights the affiliation of magic with another discipline more basic than science, since even science was traditionally said to hinge from it. Reference of course is to theology, which represents the intellectualization of religious attitude and practice.

One of the founders of modern anthropology, Bronislaw Malinowski, concluded after a lifelong investigation of the magically conditioned Polynesian Trobrianders that, in their primitive beginnings, magic and religion are essentially indistinguishable. Magic, Malinowski determined on the basis of his Trobriander study, springs from an instinctual and emotional need of the human being to press forth "into impasses where gaps in his knowledge and the limitations of his early power of observation and reason betray him in a crucial moment." An important social consequence of this inner drive to resolve the enigmas of existence, Malinowski maintained, is the formation of a system of "rudimentary modes of behavior and rudimentary beliefs," with the function of magical ritual being to fix and standardize such behavior and beliefs into permanent forms.[3] Inasmuch as these are traits which also inherently belong to religion, it followed for Malinowski that magic and religion, at bottom, are essentially one and the same.

When such primitive impulses to bridge the gaps of knowledge and overcome human limitations are organized by religion into an intellectual system, the result is theology. To the extent that religion, as Malinowski would persuade us, can be identified with magic, the result is "magical theology"—*theologia magica*. It will be the object of the present study to go one step further. When a conscious attempt is made, as in the case of the abbot Trithemius, to recapture the religious origins of magic and to harmonize its precepts with Christian dogma, the outcome is more properly termed "Christian magical theology"—*theologia magica Christiana*. Though himself only marginally immersed in practical magic (his specialty lay in the techniques of cryptography, or secret communication through magical means), Trithemius, first at Sponheim and later at Würzburg, was not content to leave the matter there. He devoted considerable time and effort to the problem of how to rationalize the theory of magical theology upon which his practical operations rested.[4]

Living to the threshold of the Lutheran revolt from Rome, Trithemius was immersed in a Christian tradition of magic that linked him with occultist strains in the scholastic and humanist movements of the past and the reform movements of the future on both sides of the Catholic-Protestant divide. Much as Trithemius could scarcely uphold the legitimacy and benefits of magic without reference to certain of its leading champions of the Middle Ages, so did the sixteenth- and seventeenth-century exponents of magical theology commonly call upon the name and ideas of Trithemius among their forerunners to justify their magical speculations and operations. Indeed, as we will subsequently note, some were so taken by his magic, originally deemed to constitute a bridge from the ancient pagan and Jewish theologies to the theology of Christ, as to perceive in it a further bridge to reconciliation between Catholics and Protestants.

If, as will be conceded, Trithemius shares some blame for the ensuing witch persecutions by authoring certain writings which played a part in their justification, it will be pointed out that he also helped set the stage for the Renaissance and seventeenth-century movement, spearheaded by the Paracelsians, to preserve a legitimate place for magic within the orthodox theological schemes of Catholic and Protestants alike. There were predecessors and even contemporaries, it is true, who, assuming a more thoroughgoing and systematic approach to the revival of the ancient arcane traditions than is represented by Trithemius's sporadic outbursts in the same vein, may have exercised a more decisive influence on later occult theory. Among the latter were the Italian Platonists Marsilio Ficino and Giovanni Pico della Mirandola and Trithemius's German acquaintances Johann Reuchlin and Agrippa of Nettesheim.[5] The point of the present study, however, is not to uphold a dominant influence by Trithemius on the history of magic. Rather, on a more modest scale, it is to present the theological rationale for magic of one of its more provocative Renaissance spokesmen, and to show how that rationale was diversely received during the highly volatile two centuries after the abbot's death commensurate with the Reformation, the witch hunts, and the onset of the scientific revolution.

Needless to say, Trithemius's theory of magical theology did not arise out of a vacuum. It was forged out of a particular life experience which embraced, in conjunction with the occult studies, a strong desire to effect spiritual reform both in its author and in the wider Christian Church to which he devoted his monastic way of life. Prior to entering into the theoretical intricacies of the magical program formulated by Trithemius, accordingly, we need first, in a concluding section to this introductory chapter, take stock of the concrete circumstances within which that program was forged.

## The Biographical Setting

Trithemius, according to a story put into circulation during the latter half of the sixteenth century, was once summoned into the presence of Emperor Maximilian I where, in a dramatic demonstration of necromantic powers for which he had earned widespead notoriety, he conjured from the dead, together with sundry ancient heroes, Maximilian's own deceased wife Mary of Burgundy. That a similar tale was contemporaneously afloat concerning a certain Doctor Faustus, who was said to have performed a comparable feat for Maximilian's son Charles V, was not lost to the demonological critics of both men. As one among these, Christoph Zeisseler, observed in relation to the Faustian anecdote: "Some men relate that this same act was performed by Johannes Trithemius."[6]

How, then, did the magical legend of the abbot Trithemius, coalesced as it came to be with the legend of Faustus, take shape? Unlike the historical Faustus, Trithemius came to his magical studies from what initially was an entirely different slate of interests. Trithemius was first and foremost a Christian monk, a member of the Benedictine order, who dedicated his life to fulfilling the requirements of monastic piety. Secondly, Trithemius was an exceptionally erudite monk who, as the abbot of two monasteries during his lifetime, zealously advocated in the pursuance of his monastic goals, not piety alone, but *learned* piety. This feature of Trithemius's career led him not only into more traditional ventures expected of the monastic career, such as mystical theology and ecclesiastical history, but also into the not so traditional venture of humanistic studies which were in a state of widespread revival in his day. Thirdly, Trithemius joined forces with other learned theologians of his day in taking the offensive against those he considered to be foremost human conveyors of the demonic arts, the witches and sorcerers. Only fourthly did Trithemius himself enter into the arcane field of magic, centering on the techniques of cryptography for his special interest but furnishing them with a solid foundation of occult theory which also drew on affiliated magical studies such as astrology, Pythagorean number theory, alchemy, and Cabala.[7]

What, then, are the biographical particulars that led Trithemius from his uncontroversial beginnings to the controversies of his final decades? Christened Johann Heidenberg, Trithemius acquired his Latin name from his birthplace of Trittenheim on the banks of the Mosel. Following the premature death of his father, his mother eventually remarried and, adopting the new family name Zell, produced several more children, of which only one, Johann's half-brother Jacob, survived to maturity.[8] Convinced by a "miraculous" dream at the age of fifteen that he was destined to a life of letters, and frustrated at every turn in this regard by a stern stepfather who had a very different idea about his future, the young Johann was anxious to leave home as soon as possible to pursue his education. Upon breaking away from his parents Trithemius at first adopted an itinerant way of life, spending a short spell in nearby Trier, moving on into the Netherlands, and at last making his way to Heidelberg where, enrolled in the *studium generale*, he came into association with some of the foremost German humanists of his day. In the company of these, who included in their number Johann von Dalberg, Conrad Celtis, Jacob Wimpfeling, and Johann Reuchlin, Trithemius helped to form the Rhenish Literary Sodality.[9]

After completing his Heidelberg studies, in 1482, Trithemius set out in the company of a friend on a journey back to the Mosel valley. He did not, however, reach his goal, being caught up in a snow storm on his way home and taking shelter in the nearby

Benedictine monastery of St. Martin at Sponheim, located in the diocese of Mainz. In obedience to what he construed to be a providential hand guiding his way, Trithemius, once the storm ceased, chose to remain within the cloister's walls as a novice. By the age of twenty-one he was elevated to the Sponheim abbacy, which office he occupied for the next twenty-three years.[10]

In his abbatial role Trithemius vigorously pursued the career of letters which he believed that God had marked out for him. His avowed ideal was "true monastic erudition"—*vera eruditio monastica*, conceived as the union of learning with piety, of the intellect with the will, of pagan philosophy with the "philosophy of Christ." In keeping with this ideal he gathered on the shelves of his abbey library a large collection of texts, "of about two thousand volumes, both handwritten and printed," as he later nostalgically recalled after being compelled to forsake them following his move to Würzburg. To promote this venture he pressured his monks into handwriting texts in the monastic scriptorium even as the printing revolution was making that task seemingly superfluous.[11] And at his writing desk he undertook his own private literary career, concentrating for most of his Sponheim period in the areas of monastic reform, mystical theology, ecclesiastical history, and Christian humanism in keeping with the principles of literary elegance he shared with his associates of the Rhenish sodality.[12] In both functions, as bibliophile and literary scholar, Trithemius became renowned throughout Europe, in which dual role he served as an attractive magnet for some of the most illustrious men of his age. Among these were not only leading literary scholars of his day, but also a number of princely patrons. Of the topics of interest championed by Trithemius which increasingly drew these visitors to his cloister, not the least noteworthy is that of magic.[13]

If Trithemius gave much to his many studious visitors, he also took much from them. This held true especially in the area of language study, concerning which, he later acknowledged, he owed his earliest lessons in Hebrew to an unnamed Jew he had met in Heidelberg, his first Greek lessons to Celtis, and his advanced lessons in both languages to Reuchlin. It was especially as a Greek scholar that Trithemius earned fame in humanist quarters, with one visitor to Sponheim revelling in this regard: "The abbot was Greek, his monks Greeks, and likewise Greek were his dogs, stones, and vineyards.

And that entire monastery seemed as though it were located in the middle of Ionia."[14] Both the proficient Greek and the less proficient Hebrew of the abbot, as it turned out, directly played into the formulation of his magical theories, since, through Greek, he gained access to the obscure mysteries of Pythagoras and Hermes Trismegistus, and through Hebrew, to the mysteries of Cabala.

Until 1499 the visible scope of Trithemius's intellectual activity was largely circumscribed by the conventional boundaries of the medieval liberal arts curriculum. Then, as if out of the blue, Trithemius in that year declared himself to be an exponent of the occult arts. The form in which this announcement took place was a letter addressed to a Carmelite monk of Ghent, Arnold Bostius, the object of which was to inform the correspondent of a treatise the abbot was currently composing. The subject was steganography, that is, the art of writing secret messages and transmitting them over long distances through the mediation of angelic messengers. Unhappily for the future reputation of Trithemius, Bostius was not in a position to receive the abbot's letter, having died shortly before its arrival. As a result, words intended for Bostius's eyes alone fell into the hands of the unsympathetic prior of the cloister, who, expressing shock by what he beheld therein to be an admission of illicit demonic magic, circulated the abbot's words to the general public. Thus was born Trithemius's magical legend.[15]

Reinforcing the abbot's notoriety as a black magician was a sharply negative response to the cryptographic tract in question by a visitor to Sponheim a few years later, the French scholar Carolus Bovillus, who, during a fortnight stay at Sponheim, was requested by his host to read and comment upon the completed portions of his steganographical tract. To the abbot's surprise and consternation Bovillus was far from pleased by what he gleaned therein, and at some later date, after pondering the experience, wrote a letter to a mutual friend of the two men in which he recounted his Sponheim visit and acrimoniously stigmatized his host as a demonic magician.[16] While not discouraged by these traumatic events from further engaging in his magical speculations, Trithemius was chastened by them into being more circumspect about their disclosure, one facet of which lay in his decision to retain the completed portions of the steganographical handbook in manuscript form accessible only to specially selected disciples.

In the ensuing years Trithemius and his Sponheim monks developed increasingly strained relations, and by 1505 they mutually agreed to a parting of their ways. There is no direct evidence that Trithemius's emerging magical interests played a part in this decision, the more probable bone of contention lying in the abbot's imposition of highly demanding scholarly standards upon his monks which even included the hand copying of texts as if the art of printing had never come into existence. As the years of his Sponheim abbacy wore on, Trithemius evidently became looked upon by his monks as an uncompromising taskmaster whose exactions from them went well beyond what they believed to be the just requirements of their vows. However, while Trithemius's rapidly proliferating reputation as a magician may have played no direct role in the quarrel with his Sponheim monks, it may well have played at least an indirect role. For very likely exacerbating the tension between the resident abbot and monks was the disturbing intrusion into their cloistered tranquillity of many visitors. While some of these were certainly attracted by the conventional monastic subjects of Trithemius's scholarly expertise, others were undoubtedly attracted by his reputation for unconventional subjects in the arcana and by the many magical offerings on his monastic shelves.

In any case the bad rapport between Trithemius and his Sponheim monks reached a breaking point, and in 1505 the abbot was handed a convenient means to finalize the break by accepting an invitation from the margrave-elector Joachim of Brandenburg to meet him during an assembly of the German princes in Cologne. Trithemius's official resignation from Sponheim came the following year when, after spending a period itinerantly (part of the time as Joachim's guest in Berlin), he succeeded in finding a new post at the head of the monastery of St. Jacob in Würzburg. Here Trithemius was to last out the remainder of his life, dying in 1516 at the relatively young age of fifty-four.[17] It is true that, in his new Würzburg home, Trithemius often found cause to lament the loss of his Sponheim cloister and the magnificent library which he had collected there. The trade-off, however, was that his changed environment provided him with much-needed peace and quiet. Being no longer besieged by the strife characteristic of his Sponheim years, Trithemius at last felt free to pursue untrammeled the ambitious literary program to which he had dedicated himself years before.[18] Among the works completed during this seminal period were some, such as the Hirsau annals, which might be expected of a monastic scholar. Other writings appearing during this period of intense literary activity, however, did not so easily fit the contours of monastic custom, pursuing as they did a theme of occult causation laid down earlier in the aborted *Steganographia*.

The special significance of Trithemius for the present study lies in more than his effort to justify the occult studies. It lies in the specifically theological mode in which he chose to express that justification. While still at Sponheim, primarily through a series of letters to friends, Trithemius began a protracted campaign to rationalize his invention of steganography, crucial to which was was the reconciliation of magic with the theological dogmas defining Catholic orthodoxy, and after arriving at Würzburg brought to fruition a number of further writings in the same vein. Following the guidelines of this theologically conditioned program Trithemius concentrated on two separate genres of occult writings, the first consisting of extended demonological warnings and the second of positive defenses of magic.

Trithemius's removal from Sponheim to Würzburg afforded him the time and psychological respite he needed to bring to fruition this bipartite magical program. Belonging to the first category, demonology, were his *Antipalus maleficiorum* and *Liber octo quaestionum*, the latter of which, directed to certain theological queries posed by Emperor Maximilian, was considerably taken up with the issues of demonic influence. In addition he outlined a projected encyclopedia of demons, *De demonibus*, for which he completed a preface, and composed a query, no longer extant, into the association between demons and epilepsy, *De morbo caduco et maleficiis*. Belonging to the second category in turn, the theory and practice of magic, were an apologetic of magic inserted into the autobiographical *Nepiachus*, the second major cryptographical tract titled *Polygraphia*, and the *De septem secundeis*, an amalgamation of astrological with Cabalistic theory about occult influences upon human behavior which drew on the same system of planetary angels enlisted in the controversial steganographical tract and identified by critics such as Bovillus with the demonic servants of Satan. In addition Trithemius used this opportunity to pen a more complete answer to Bovillus than was hitherto possible, a *Defensorium mei contra Caroli Bovilii mendacia*, which, like the *De morbo caduco*, has been lost to posterity.[19] Trithemius's intention in all of these arcane writings, to be spelled out in the following pages, was to stem the tide of accusations against his magic triggered by the waylaying of his 1499 letter to Bostius and augmented by the unsympathetic response of Bovillus to his reading of the *Steganographia*.

The format for the remainder of this study is organized according to the following scheme. Being mindful of the need for an historical context within which Trithemius could credibly plead for adherence to his magical program, we will proceed in chapter 2 to a presentation of the patristic, medieval, and early Renaissance magical heritage from which Trithemius drew sustenance for his occult speculations. Following this preparatory step we will move, in chapters 3 and 4, to a systematic exposition of the occult theory forged by Trithemius in his Sponheim and Würzburg cloisters, with one part consisting of his demonology and another of his positive magical program. That mission accomplished, we will proceed in chapter 5 to an examination of how Trithemius came to serve as a kind of hub for the further debate over occult studies in the context of such subsequent events as the Protestant and Catholic reform movements, the culmination of the witch persecutions, and the emergence of the scientific revolution and accompanying "new philosophy." In the concluding chapter 6 we will take note of sundry post-1700 scholarly responses to Trithemian magic and elicit from the foregoing five chapters what this author has perceived to be a basic theme of consistency underlying what sometimes appears to be its divergent and even self-contradictory goals.

Unlike Doctor Faustus, with whose magical legend his own became popularly entangled, Trithemius furnished to apologists of magic in the next two centuries a thoroughgoing Christian rationale for engaging in the occult arts. The posthumous image of the magical abbot for some was of one who had consorted with demons, whereas for others, just as committed as himself to the proposition that true magic represents a divinely sanctified branch of Christian theology, Trithemius helped reinforce the conviction that magic can just as easily obey the commands of God as those of the Devil. Finding in the great medieval scholastic Albertus Magnus one of his own favored paradigms for the union of magic with theology, Trithemius in turn became a foremost paradigm for others dedicated to the same goal.

# Chapter 2

## The Magical Inheritance

### Patristic and Medieval Demonology

Patristic and medieval thought was conditioned by a demonological view of the world. Presuming demons to be capable of perpetrating their iniquities directly, the church fathers were also persuaded that demons sometimes seek out human confederates exceptionally fitted for receiving secret instruction in the magical arts. A typical representative of this outlook was Lactantius (fl. 300), who declared that "through demons have been discovered astrology, divination, the practice of augury, and those very practices which are called oracle-giving, necromancy, magic, and whatever other evils that men practice either openly or secretly."[1]

An early Christian like Lactantius had good reason to shun magic. For of the slanders leveled against Christians by their pagan critics, thrown into sharp relief by the third-century Platonist Celsus, especially upsetting to them was that Jesus and His apostles had performed magical operations in the guise of divine miracles. Famously rebutting, point by point, Celsus's attack on Christianity was Origen (ca. 185–254), who responded to the charge that Christ and His disciples performed their miracles through demonic means with the rejoinder that their resort to miracle working was of

secondary importance to their rare piety of soul and inspired powers of persuasion. This was not to say, however, Origen further
insisted, that the miracles of Jesus and the saints were superfluous.
Through their miracle-working powers, he contended, their authority could be viewed as deriving from a more elevated source than
their own persons. Otherwise, the Platonically educated Origen
chided Celsus, their sermons would have been viewed as holding
no greater claim to truth than "Grecian dialectics."[2]

As also revealed by Origen's reply to Celsus, a miracle-working
Jesus and his apostles were not the only target of Celsus's
antimagical excoriations. So was the miracle-working Moses, elic-
iting the charge, sharply refuted by Origen, that the Jews "worship
angels and are addicted to sorcery, in which Moses was their instructor."[3] For Origen, in contrast, the miracle-working powers of
Jesus lay on a supernatural continuum with those of Moses and
sprang from the same providential design. Not so persuaded to this
smooth continuity of passage from the miracle working of Moses to
that of Christ, however, was Origen's Western contemporary
Tertullian (ca. 160–230), who declared the Jews to be foremost
propagators of the false charge of magic against Christians. The
source of Jewish misunderstanding about the meaning of Christ's
miracles, Tertullian contended, lay in their belief that the promised
Messiah had not yet arrived. Having failed to perceive the fulfillment
of their own prophecies in the birth of Jesus, the Jews had also
failed to grasp the crucial significance of the miraculous events
that came to pass in conjunction with the incarnation of Christ.
For this reason it followed for Tertullian that the Jews "should hold
Him a magician from the powers which He displayed, expelling
devils from men by a word, restoring vision to the blind, cleansing
the leprous, reinvigorating the paralytics, summoning the dead to
life again, making the very elements of nature obey Him, stilling
the storms and walking on the sea."[4]

However, given their resolve to preserve a clear-cut distinction
between genuine miracles and demonic magic of the type charged
against them by their enemies, the early Christian fathers were
confronted by a dilemma posed by their own biblical testimony. For
if truly miraculous religion and magic are not to be confused with
one another, following their own line of argument, how are we to
account for the positive role played by the three Magi in the drama

surrounding the birth of Jesus? Facing up to this vexatious question in the Christian East was St. Chrysostom (ca. 345–407), who maintained that the Magi, having earlier studied their craft under the aegis of the "gentile demons," discovered in the Christ child a pathway out of their errant ways to a more sublime, magic-free faith. Adhering to an identical religious standard in the West was St. Jerome (ca. 340–420). Conceding that the Magi "were taught their art by the demons," Jerome contended that it was not by virtue of their magic that they were led to the Christ child, but by a supernatural revelation originating apart from their magic. Instead of legitimizing the demonic art to which they had subscribed, declared Jerome, the miraculous revelation guiding the Magi to Jesus "completely destroyed the power of their art."[5]

Similarly anxious to maintain a clear-cut boundary between Christian miracle working and gentile marvel working was St. Augustine (354–430), whose version of a magic-free Christian Platonism in many ways resembled that of Origen before him. Likewise putting him into common cause with Origen, Augustine interpreted the miraculous feats of Jesus as springing from a supernatural power of the kind which was also granted to the Hebrew patriarch Moses. Whereas Pharaoh's magicians "worked by the kind of sorceries and incantations to which evil spirits or demons are addicted," declared Augustine, Moses performed his miracles in a state of holiness "and helped by the angels."[6] At a further stage in the providential plan of world history laid down by God, according to Augustine, the miracles of Jesus and of His apostles "occurred in order to encourage the worship of the one true God and to put a stop to polytheistic practices." To still any suggestion that they might have anything in common with sorcery, Augustine added that "they were wrought by simple faith and pious trust, not by spells and incantations inspired by the sacrilegious curiosity of the art of magic—vulgarly called *goetia* and, more politely, theurgy."[7]

The arguments of the pagan Neoplatonist Porphyry (233–304), who in the name of theurgy had sought to preserve the good name of magic by emphasizing the necessity of holiness in the magician, was soundly rejected by Augustine, as were also the occult principles ascribed to a figure whom Lactantius earlier had praised as even more ancient than Pythagoras, the Egyptian wonder worker

Hermes Trismegistus. Whereas, for Lactantius, Trismegistus was a marvel-working gentile sage who both had foreshadowed and prophesied the coming of Christ, Augustine viewed Trismegistus as a dangerous demonic magician.[8] While conceding that many effects exceeding ordinary human capability are attributable to the magical arts, Augustine cautioned that "all such predictions and prodigies, which seem miraculous and divine . . . are merely the tricks and traps of malignant demons, which can only be countered by true religion."[9]

A further stage in the movement to distinguish Christian miracle working from its magical counterfeit is represented by St. Isidore of Seville (ca. 570–632), who devoted an entire chapter of his *Etymologiae* to "this vanity of the magical arts."[10] Among those adopting Isidore's unyielding hostility to magic in the Carolingian period were Hincmar of Rheims (ca.806–882), who declared the occult arts to be accomplished, without exception, through "a diabolical operation,"[11] and Rabanus Maurus (ca. 776–856), who developed antimagical vituperation into a full-scale *De magicis artibus*.[12] In the post-Carolingian period two separate but closely intertwined demonological developments, following the attitudes represented in these writings, came into play. The first was a legal campaign against sorcery carried out by the secular and ecclesiastical authorities of Europe, and the second, a systematic rationalization of the demonological world view lending theoretical support to this campaign by the mystical and scholastic writers. The key to the shift of the query into occult studies from the secular to the ecclesiastical courts lay in the evolving belief that magic was a crime not only against man, but also against God. As such, magic increasingly became construed by its enemies, in preparation for the later witch hunts, as a form of religious heresy.[13]

At the height of the Middle Ages, in the twelfth and thirteenth centuries, punishment for acts of sorcery and witchcraft remained exclusively within the sphere of the secular courts. Moreover, the church of the time was determined to keep it that way. For example, Pope Alexander IV promulgated a canon in 1258 prohibiting overly zealous inquisitors from intruding "into investigations of sorcery without knowledge of manifest heresy involved."[14] It was not Pope Alexander's intention, of course, to sanction the practice of sorcery, but only to clarify the boundary dividing witchcraft, a secular crime, and heresy, a religious crime. So far as the crime of sorcery seeped over into the arena of religion, canon law prior to the fifteenth century declared it to be, not heresy, but infidelity. According to the canon lawyer Gratian (fl. 1140), the kinds of infidelity to which witches and sorcerers were particularly prone were idolatry and apostasy, inasmuch as they forsook the true faith of Christ for Devil worship and the adoration of demons. But though these were offenses calling for ecclesiastical discipline, they still fell short of the extreme impiety of heresy justifying the penalty of death. Indeed, far from encouraging the persecution of witches, Gratian's treatment of the sorcery question reveals a way of thinking which could do more to hinder than to assist a widespread persecution of witches.

Following the lead of his canon law predecessors Burchard of Worms and Ivo of Chartres, Gratian incorporated into his decretals a ninth-century "canon," the so-called *Canon episcopi*, implying that many acts of sorcery, together with the alleged congregation of their practitioners in a "witches' sabbat," might well lie more in the imagination that in the real world. But this did not preclude the supposition for Gratian, as for other heirs of the *Canon episcopi* tradition, that witches were still deserving of severe punishment, the reasoning being that the Devil still lurked behind their hallucinations. However, rather than going to the extreme of urging the execution of convicted witches, a characteristic feature of the witch persecutions in their later stages, Gratian rather settled on a more moderate penalty of expelling them from their parishes.[15]

Similarly conveying the skeptical *Canon episcopi* legacy was John of Salisbury (ca. 1115–1180), who, however, elicited somewhat different implications from its underlying premise that the marvels of sorcery are located more in the mind than in the real world. In agreement with Gratian that the Devil "inflicts the excesses of his malice on certain people in such a way that they suffer in the spirit things which they erroneously and wretchedly believe to experience in the flesh," John perceived witches more as passive victims than active perpetrators of demonic maleficence. "Who could be so blind as not to see in all this a pure manifestation of wickedness created by sporting demons!" proclaimed John, adding that "it is only poor old women and the simple-minded kinds of men who enter into these credences."[16] Reflected in these words is an attitude closer to that of later skeptics seeking to put an end to the witch persecutions than to that of true believers, including the abbot Trithemius among them, promoting their persecution and death.

The hint of indulgence toward witches displayed by John of Salisbury, however, was the exception rather than the rule at this stage of the Christian attack upon magic, though the trend was one which still fell short of the full-scale witch hunts of the later centuries. While often obscured in the literature of this period, the thin line dividing sorcery from heresy was not entirely effaced even with the coming of the more blatantly demon-fearing popes of the fourteenth and early fifteenth centuries: John XXII, Benedict XII, and Eugenius IV. Although the Avignon pope John XXII took a significant step toward the later witch hunts by promulgating a canon of 1326 declaring sorcery to constitute sufficient grounds for excommunication, he stopped short of abrogating the 1258 canon of Alexander IV by placing the pursuit of witches and sorcerers beyond the bounds of the Inquisition. Similarly, while allowing that the heretics included many sorcerers among them, Eugenius IV, in a 1434 letter to an inquisitor, refused to proclaim witchcraft a form of heresy.[17]

As it turned out, the distinction between sorcery and heresy first began to dissolve, not within the framework of canon jurisprudence itself, but within the theoretical speculations of the medieval mystics and scholastics who formulated the theological underpinnings of canon law. This ominous development prepared the intellectual ground for Pope Innocent VIII's bull of 1484, *Summis disiderantes*, officially reversing Alexander IV's 1258 canon by declaring witchcraft to be a heresy and thus subject to the Inquisition, which in turn prefaced the notorious "Witches' Hammer"—the *Malleus maleficarum*—of 1486 serving as a cutting edge of subsequent witch hunts.[18] Turning now to some leading mystical and scholastic writers of the high Middle Ages and early Renaissance representative of this reactionary shift, we should keep in mind that theirs was a way of thinking with which Trithemius would have far more in common than with the skeptical view encouraged by the spurious *Canon episcopi*. What would make Trithemius's mission especially thorny, we will see, is that a principal thrust of the demonological position which he adopted from his medieval predecessors was increasingly directed at the kind of learned magic to which he himself subscribed and which he commended to the use of other pious Christians.

Unless strongly fortified by the grace of God, proclaimed the twelfth-century Cistercian abbot Richalmus (d. ca. 1220), "no man can avoid the frenzy of the demons."[19] Much like his Benedictine contemporary Caesarius of Heisterbach (ca. 1180-1240),[20] Richalmus believed that a demon could be lurking behind every door and under every bed. Nor, as the typical judgment went along these lines, did the demons only exert their "frenzy"—their *furor daemonicus*—directly upon their intended victims. They also prompted certain of these victims to serve them as human intermediaries, instructing them in the precepts of their black arts so that they might lead others into the perdition already reserved for themselves.

According to the twelfth-century apocalyptic visionary Hildegarde of Bingen (1098–1179), a foremost feature of the dreaded Antichrist was that he would excel "in all the diabolical arts." Being in turn instructed in these same black arts, his human disciples "call the demons their gods, and worship them in place of God. And with their help they pursue the vanities and the harmful powers of the sorcerers."[21] A principal strategy of such diabolically inspired magicians, if we are to believe Hugh of St. Victor (1096–1141), was to insinuate their diabolical arts in the Christian educational curriculum. Sharply rejecting the claim that magic, as an ally of philosophy, deserved a place among the blessed *artes liberales*, Hugh caustically retorted that, in contrast to true philosophy, magic "seduces souls from the divine religion, promotes the worship of demons, engenders corruption of morals, and impels the minds of its followers toward every crime and abomination."[22]

While the medieval monastic writers were testifying to a demon-infested world and the willingness of certain human agents to act in confederacy with the evil spirits, so were the scholastic theologians of the universities. The author of the *Sententiae*, Peter Lombard (ca. 1100–ca. 1164), struck a familiar chord in this respect when he referred to "certain consultations and pacts...with the demons, which are concerns of the magical arts, of the soothsayers, and of the augurs."[23] In the following century the Franciscan Alexander of Hales (d. 1245) anticipated yet another prominent motif of the witch hunts, misogyny, when, in reply to the question of why the crime of witchcraft seemed to abound more among women than men, he explained that "just as the instruction of sin was first transferred to a woman, so likewise in our own day does the deceitful instruction of witchcraft transfer more frequently to women than to men."[24]

To be sure, the Aristotelian philosophy characteristic of the rise of medieval scholasticism also contained a strong naturalist component which conceivably could have worked against the witch persecutions. According to this philosophical outlook, possibly in conjunction with the skeptical *Canon episcopi*, enkindled natural melancholy better than supernatural demons could explain the apparently supernatural exploits of the sorcerers. However, as illustrated by such scholastic thinkers as Peter Abelard (1079–1142) and St. Thomas Aquinas (1225–1274), Aristotelian naturalism could just as readily play into the hands of the persecutors of witches as of their opponents. For the demons, according to this way of thinking, although originating in a place above nature, were experts in employing natural means, including the means of melancholy, to aid in their deceptions.

According to Abelard, who enlisted the help of St. Jerome and Isidore of Seville to make his point, the demons, "being skilled by the subtlety of their art and by long experience in the things of nature . . . , understand the natural powers of things."[25] For Abelard, then, the defense by self-proclaimed magicians that they were only working in the harmless realm of nature was no defense at all. St. Thomas, despite access to a still broader spectrum of Aristotelian offerings in the century following that of Abelard, further reinforced this position in the context of restating St. Augustine's fundamental distinction between the miracle and a merely magical marvel.

St. Thomas, it is true, appears to have been attuned to an inner, hidden arena of nature which, though inaccessible to ordinary reason, is accessible to imperceptible influences from the stars. Such is illustrated in a brief treatise, by scholarly consensus held to be a genuine product of his hand, under the title *De occultis operibus naturae*.[26] But for St. Thomas the concealed marrow of nature, the realm of magical marvels, still corresponded to that mutable part of the human being which passed away with time, setting it radically apart from from the realm of true miracles transcending the natural arena which corresponded to the immutable part of the human being persisting after the encrusting body had fallen away. For St. Thomas the distinction between the true miracle and the natural marvel hinged upon a simple rule of hermeneutics. If a marvel is understood by some and not by others, its cause can be relegated to nature at a level exceeding the threshold of ordinary consciousness. But if the same marvel cannot possibly be understood by any human being save through supernatural revelation, it can safely be taken as a true miracle. "Properly speaking," wrote St. Thomas in this regard, "miracles are works done by God outside the order usually observed in things."[27]

If St. Thomas had left the matter here, we might construe his words as still allowing the possibility of certain forms of magic which are as permissible as any other natural science. But in truth, echoing Abelard's earlier declaration that the demons "understand the natural powers of things," St. Thomas viewed natural magic to be more of a complementary aid to demonic magic than its licit alternative. Admittedly, his *De occultis operibus naturae* has been taken by some as arguing against this claim, one result of which has even been the spurious attribution of an alchemical writing to his authorship.[28] As St. Thomas well understood, however, it is one thing to apprehend occult powers of nature and quite another to seek esoteric access to those powers through magical means. Being so easily manipulated by the demons, natural magic was no less suspect to St. Thomas than outright demonic magic.

Happily for the future course of magic, however, the verdict of St. Thomas on this subject was not the last to be expressed. An alternative verdict, indeed, was already discernible within Thomas's own scholastic guidelines, which distinguished demonic magic not only from the true miracle, but also from a favorable form of natural magic—*magia naturalis*. Only detestable demonic magic, according to this way of thinking, is to be judged a consort of religious infidelity and heresy, whereas natural magic, in contrast, is deemed to be inwardly harmonious with both religious fidelity and sound theological orthodoxy. For medieval scholars of this persuasion the celebrated scholastic dictum "faith seeking understanding" (*fides quaerens intellectum*) could legitimately be extended to include the pursuit of esoteric knowledge about the world, the proper subject of natural magic. Thanks to a stubbornly persisting esoterist strain within the medieval scholastic tradition, as we will now see, it was not necessary for the Renaissance Platonists, in their campaign to fuse magical with philosophical themes, to break completely new ground. For in taking up the cause of magic, the Renaissance Platonists worked within guidelines already laid down by certain of the medieval scholastics before them. The abbot Trithemius, an enthusiastic defender of the occult studies even as he sought to expunge demonic influences from their midst, by his own acknowledgment owed his magical ideas and program as fully to this medieval scholastic heritage as to the Platonic renascence of ancient magic going on in his own day.

## The Medieval and Early Renaissance Defense of Magic

Like his Italian contemporary St. Thomas, William of Auvergne (= of Paris, ca. 1180–1249) assumed the existence of a demon-infested world and took seriously the threat demons posed for salvation. Also in agreement with Thomas, William accepted that demons sometimes enlist willing human agents on their behalf, instructing them for this purpose in the magical arts. Such illicit studies, William admonished in his *De legibus*, are excessively concerned "with curiosity, which is the lust of knowing things which are unnecessary."[29] In his strictures against the demonic arts, however, William distinguished himself from St. Thomas in a crucial regard. For whereas St. Thomas, by assigning demons to the natural realm, in effect had condemned natural along with demonic magic, William retained a place for natural magic in his licit curriculum of studies.

By confounding good natural with demonic supernatural magic, complained William, we do a disservice to God, who occultly planted wonder-working "seeds of nature" (*seminae naturae*) at the moment of creation. For this reason, he observed in his *De universo*: "Many occult and marvelous virtues reside in things which we are unable to comprehend."[30] What distinguished William from St. Thomas in this regard, who similarly acceded to the existence of an occult natural realm, is that William made it accessible to those specially equipped for its penetration. In this way William revealed himself to be in touch not only with ancient demonological traditions, but also with ancient occult traditions premised on a belief in a form of magic free of demonological encroachment.

Likewise revealing familiarity with the occult traditions was a German scholar with whom Trithemius identified above all others in his later campaign to legitimize the occult arts, Albertus Magnus (1193–1280). This is not to say, however, that Albertus dismissed the view, upheld by his student Thomas among others, of an absolute gulf of separation between miracle and magic. Addressing himself, for example, to whether Jesus' feat of walking upon the waters could be explicated in terms of natural causation, Albertus, after weighing the arguments on each side, concluded that the exploit in question "indeed was not natural but miraculous," with his line of reasoning running as follows.

"A miracle," Albertus explained, "is said to lie, not only beyond the capability of the knower (*non solum supra facultatem cognoscentis*), but also beyond the capability of the known object (*supra facultatem rei cognitae*)." Conversely, "inasmuch as we observe many natural things to lie beyond the scope of the understanding of the ignorant rustic, those things which merely lie beyond the capability of the knower are not miraculous."[31] Following the same logic Albertus differentiated the miracles of Moses from the merely demonic marvels of the magicians of Pharaoh, noting that demons like those in the service of the Egyptian sorcerers "effect nothing which exists beyond the order of nature . . . ; therefore, such work is properly termed marvelous, and not a miracle."[32] But while limiting the powers of demons to nature, Albertus did not on that account, as Thomas, go the next step of consigning all natural magic to demonic machination. For evidence he again went to scripture, this time calling on the illustrious example of the three Magi to verify tht "the magician (magus) is properly so-called from the word 'great' (magnus), because, having knowledge of all things from their necessary causes, . . . and conjecturing from the effects of natural things, he sometimes exhibits and produces marvels of nature."[33]

Given, however, that he had simultaneously restricted the scope of demons to the natural realm, Albertus, if he were successfully to make a case for the legitimacy of natural magic, needed to resolve a philosophical dilemma. If demonic magic is confined to the limits of nature, how are we to distinguish good natural magic of the type employed by the three Magi from wicked demonic magic of the type employed by Pharaoh's demonically inspired magicians? Albertus's solution to this dilemma, suggesting the influence of the skeptically conceived *Canon episcopi* on his thought, was to maintain that the demons produced their marvels, not in reality, but only in the imaginations of their spectators. Because of this insidious ability of the demons to enter into the imagination and produce amazing phantasms having the shape of reality, "it sometimes appears to a man that he is an ass weighted down by a sack, sometimes that he is an eagle in flight, and sometimes that he is transferred from place to place with Diana and her female followers."[34] The power of authentic natural magicians to perform marvels, on the other hand, was held by Albertus to rely, not on the gullible imagination, but on a genuine knowledge of how to tap the arcane forces of nature.

Another scholastic thinker to recognize a potential of good as well as evil in magic was the English Franciscan Roger Bacon (ca. 1214–1292). From his demonological perspective Bacon revealed the kind of misogynist sentiment which would become a distinctive mark of the witch hunts to come, contending that "both women and demons have taught many superstitious practices with which the nation is filled."[35] Bacon's primary motive in making this important concession to demonology, however, was not to urge the rounding up of suspected witches, but rather to point up why magic had been so bitterly vilified through the ages. Its defamers, he complained, by erroneously commingling demonic and natural causes, had condemned many legitimate studies along with illegitimate ones, so that those working in quite valid but little understood fields of investigation, "the very wisest who know these things," felt the need to hide their discoveries from public view. Bacon's counsel to Christians, therefore, was not to expunge all arcane sciences from their studies, but rather "to separate the true from the false."[36]

The fact that a particular science concerns itself with seemingly strange or uncanny occurrences, Bacon declared, is not of itself sufficient grounds to label it wicked magic, for "there are innumerable things that have strange virtues, whose potencies we are ignorant of solely from our neglect of experiment." If the viewer only looked more closely he would realize that these occurrences are really no more supernatural than, say, the occult power of the magnet to attract iron. In taking up this cause, however, Bacon confessed that the "experimenters" themselves sometimes contributed to the misunderstandings about their activities. Directly anticipating a criticism which would later be commonly made against Trithemius, Bacon sharply took to task those who have "abused characters and incantations written by the wise against harmful things and intended to be very great blessings;" these misguided men, he charged, not only have misapplied enigmatic characters and invocations received from past students of nature, but have added some of their own.[37] While conceding that the inscription of magical characters and the voicing of chants sometimes accompany such arcane wonders, Bacon contended that the same marvelous occurrences can be expected to take place in exactly the same way without such magical rites. As for himself Bacon had "disregarded the incantations and . . . discovered the wonderful action of nature, which is similar to that of the magnet on iron."[38]

In a passing reference Bacon acknowledged that Antichrist, as a step on his way to subjugating mankind, would not hesitate to employ the arcane sciences "in order that he may crush and confound the power of the world."[39] By words like these, reflecting an apocalyptic climate recently revitalized by the prophetic Calabrian visionary Joachim of Fiore (c. 1130–c. 1202), Bacon revealed acquaintance with the theory, uttered before him by Hildegarde of Bingen among others, that magic would play a key role in announcing the appearance of Antichrist. Needless to say, the apocalyptic aura surrounding the subject of magic, already a constant of Catholic thought before Bacon, came into still sharper relief as the relatively stable thirteenth century passed over into the more unstable fourteenth. It is not by chance that there coincided with this transition the forging of an astrological-angelogical distribution of historical periods which was to serve Trithemius in good stead. Subsequently dubbed "the Conciliator" after the major work setting forth this cosmic overview of history, its author, the Paduan physician Pietro d'Abano (1250–1315), subsequently acquired a magical notoriety in close association with that of the later abbot in his debt.[40]

It is understandable, however, that the highly volatile conditions which might encourage the practice of magic in certain cases might well have the contrary effect of discouraging magic in other cases. Assuming an extreme antimagical position, for example, was the Oxford Dominican Robert Holkot (d. 1349), who proclaimed that all magic, without exception, is perpetrated "with the aid and counsel of demons, effected either by prayers or by a pact either express or implicit on the part of the invokers."[41] Attesting to the apocalyptic state of mind behind such asseverations was the Parisian scholastic Pierre d'Ailly (1350–1420), who rebuked the many false prophets of his day for putting the true prophecy of Christ in such bad repute that "the unfaithful declare our miracles to be performed by the magical art." In response D'Ailly pleaded, "especially in these times of ours, which seem to be very near the end of the world" (*maxime his temporibus, quae fini mundi propinqua esse videntur*), for his readers to develop a proper skill "of discerning and being on guard against these types of seducers and their seductions."[42] Despite the tensions of apocalyptic expectation impinging on his speculations in this area, however, evidenced by a pronounced attraction to astrologal theory in association with his theological inquiries, D'Ailly revealed that he stopped short of proscribing occult study altogether. His attack on false prophecy was as applicable to nonastrological, inspired vatication as to its scholarly astrological form. Just as good Christians are faced with the difficult task of distinguishing divine from demonic prophecy, he reasoned, so are they faced with the corresponding task of distinguishing divinely inspired from demonically inspired astrology.[43]

The same kind of anxious conditions that lay behind D'Ailly's apocalyptically inspired warnings against false prophecy also lay behind the condemnation of magic by the theological faculty of the University of Paris in 1398, the twenty-eight proposition *conclusio* of which was recorded and enlarged upon by Jean Gerson (1363–1429) in his *De erroribus circa artem magicam*.[44] Yet Gerson too, a friend of D'Ailly, followed up his warnings against black magic with the concession that certain kinds of arcane studies are permissible. While upholding the Parisian condemnation and taking his own firm line against "the pestiferous superstitions of the magicians and the foolish superstitions of soothsaying old women," Gerson left a loophole for those who argued for the legitimacy of the occult arts, conceding that "that certain men have all too often lightly attributed things to demons which more rationally are said to be from material and natural causes." Or putting this concession in terms more directly to the point of the present subject, Gerson allowed that "many marvelous and efficacious virtues exist in sensible things, . . . the knowledge of whose operations can be termed natural magic."[45]

In acquiescing to the possibility of a natural alternative to demonic magic, Gerson may well have had his astrology-loving friend D'Ailly in mind. Whatever his specific motives, by this acknowledgment Gerson furnishes us with a convenient bridge to the systematic revival of ancient magic by the Renaissance Platonists. For it was but a short step from Gerson's avowal of demon-free "marvelous and efficacious virtues" occultly residing in nature and the systematic revival of the magical studies by Ficino and his followers at Florence in the later fifteenth century. As Professor Kristeller has persuasively demonstrated, it was Ficino's intention, not to depart from the medieval scholastic traditions, but to recover the ancient sources nurturing those traditions in their philological and philosophical purity. For Ficino those sources included, as forerunners to his beloved Plato, such legendary ancient magical sages as the Persian Zoroaster, the Greek Pythagoras, and the Egyptian Hermes Trismegistus.[46] As we will observe in its place, the occult ground shared by medieval scholastics like Albertus Magnus and Renaissance Platonists like Ficino and Giovanni Pico would also come to be shared by Trithemius.

"I have not made use of so much as one expression of that profane type of magic which relies upon the worship of demons," proclaimed Marsilio Ficino (1433–1499) in defense of his occult interests, "but have made mention only of natural magic, which assumes its benefits from natural investigations into the propitious disposition of the heavenly bodies."[47] The precise point of intersection between Ficino's magic with his Platonic philosophy lay in the notion, derived not from Plato himself but from the early Neoplatonist Plotinus (205–70), of "seminal reasons" (*logoi spermatikoi*; Latin: *rationes seminales*), which establishes structural correspondences between generative forms in the material world and generative ideas in the human mind. Being a dynamic process, generation in both of these spheres—of the subjective mind and of the objective world—requires an energizing principle, identified by Ficino both with the force of love (*eros*), which Plato had discoursed upon in his *Symposium*, and with the principle of an occultly sympathetic *spiritus*, the Latin equivalent of Greek *pneuma*, claimed by ancient Neoplatonists such as Proclus, Iamblichus, and Porphyry to infuse, animate, and bind all things from the highest star to the lowest prime matter.[48] But a further feature of Ficino's scholarship also encouraged this direction of his thought, to wit, his occupation with ancient texts which he believed to have come down from the ancient Egyptian magician Hermes Trismegistus.[49]

A notable product of the occultist revival fostered by the Medici patrons of Ficino was the cult of the three Magi. The serviceability of this scriptural prototype to the defense of occult studies is highlighted by Ficino's reminder that the foremost magicians of their time "adored the born Christ child." With this scripturally sanctioned paradigm in mind, Ficino rhetorically inquired: "Will you then be so foolish as to fear terribly the name of the magician?" As Holy Writ itself attests, insisted Ficino with reference to these illustrious exemplars, the study of magic, far from offending God, "was very pleasing to the Evangel, which does not thereby signify the sorcerer or witch, but the wise man and priest."[50] In this way Ficino put himself on record as departing from that version of the Magi, upheld by Jerome and Augustine among others, which embarrassingly explained away their occult activities as prenativity indiscretions in favor of one upholding the Magi as scripturally based validations of magic.

Likewise assuming a favorable attitude to magic in conjunction with a thoroughgoing training in the scholastic method was Ficino's young associate Giovanni Pico della Mirandola (1463–1494). Among his nine hundred theses Pico declared, with the three Magi as illustrious cases in point, that "natural magic is licit, and not prohibited"; that "magic is the practical part of science"; and again that "to perform magic is nothing else but to marry heaven to earth."[51] Moreover, being fluent in Hebrew, Pico joined Cabalistic precepts to his Platonic and Hermetic ones,[52] the effect of which was to add an important dimension to the occult theory directly anticipating a principal feature of Trithemian magic. Conceived by its adherents as having originally been transmitted to human beings through the mediation of angels, the secrets of Cabala in turn could be viewed as justifying the invocation and manipulation of angels for the further transmission of those secrets.

It was not, however, solely by the implication of angel magic in Cabala that Pico can be said to have prepared the way to the magical theology of Trithemius. Other Cabalistic features brought out by Pico also contributed to this end. For one, the rituals of Cabala were based on combinations of divine names believed to contain marvelous magical virtues, and, for another, the letters of Hebrew were invested by the Cabalists with numerical values which allowed their art to become readily associated with the ancient Pythagorean tradition with its corresponding numerological emphasis. Finally, Cabala itself employed a cipher alphabet which in many ways resembled the kinds of cryptological operations for which Trithemius would become famous. In this sense, then, Cabala can be said not only to have constituted a central ingredient of Trithemius's cryptography, but prefigured it as itself an enciphering system.

While the basic features of this occult amalgam are discernible in medieval magic, Pico is to be credited with framing those features in their most cogent intellectual formulation before Trithemius. Adopting the celebrated Hermetic characterization of the human being as a great magical miracle—a *magnum miraculum*—Pico went on to draw a fundamental distinction between good natural and Cabalistic magic and wicked demonic magic. Whereas, conceded Pico in his celebrated *Oratio de hominis dignitate* with which he intended to preface the nine hundred theses, one form of magic admittedly "depends entirely on the work and authority of demons," another form, "when it is rightly pursued, is nothing else than the utter perfection of natural philosophy."[53] Whereas the first, unfavorable form of magic is "a thing to be abhorred," the latter form "brings forth into the open the miracles concealed in the recesses of the world, in the depths of nature, and in the storehouses and mysteries of God." In explicating this view, moreover, Pico can be said to have anticipated Trithemius not only in the substance of his views, but also in the defensive way by which he made his views known. Those who failed to grasp this lesson, carpingly protested Pico against his critics, can be compared to "ignorant dogs." For just as dogs bark at strangers, so do these detractors of good magic "often condemn and hate what they do not understand."[54]

The resemblance between the occult precepts of the Italian Platonists and those of the German abbot Trithemius need not depend on mere historical analogies. For a direct personal link

existed between Trithemius and his Florentine analogues in the
person of the abbot's humanist friend Johann Reuchlin (1455–1522),
who visited Florence on two separate Italian journeys in the latter
decades of the fifteenth century.[55] Taking his lead in the arcana
above all from Pico, with whom he shared a command of Hebrew,
Reuchlin also shared with his Italian acquaintance the presumption that the Hebrew tongue contains miracle-working powers in
its very words, which Cabala is especially equipped to capture. The
larger effect of this presumption, also adopted by Reuchlin's friend
Trithemius, is further to obscure the distinction between miracle
and magic.

While recently visiting in Rome, Reuchlin reported in his
Cabalistically inspired *De verbo mirifico*, Pico had proposed to him
"that no names in magical and lawful enterprises possess a virtue
equal to that residing in the Hebrew tongue or in languages most
nearly derived from it." The reason, Pico instructed Reuchlin, is
that at the beginning of creation all the names given to existent
entities "were formed from the Voice of God; therefore, that in
which nature exercises its most potent magic is the Voice of God."
This was not to say, however, Pico further apprised Reuchlin, that
the Jews were granted an exclusive monopoly in this regard. Also
granted access to the secrets of Cabala were certain specially prepared gentiles. Admittedly, the case for this contention was made
harder by the appearance of magical counterfeiters in the ranks of
the gentiles; when these pretend to effect miracles, Reuchlin agreed,
"it proves to be an illusion (*praestigium*) rather than a true miracle,
and takes place, not with the help of God, but by a pact with
demons." A very different interpretation, however, could be applied
to a few gifted gentiles who "mingled Hebraic names with their
arcane vows or secret operations." According to Reuchlin, following
the instruction of Pico, "in Orpheus, Pythagoras, and Plato there
were no other secrets so occult and hidden as their divine Hebraic
names of virtue, which they did not wish to make accessible by
writing down."[56]

In this doctrine, expressly associating the marvelous powers of
divine names spoken of by the Cabala with the marvelous occult
virtues attributed to nature by the gentile occult traditions, Reuchlin
set forth in essential terms the concept of magical theology—of
*theologia magica*—which was also to be a distinguishing mark of

the occult philosophy professed by his fellow German Trithemius. Magic, in keeping with this conception, is not merely to be tolerated, but is to be energetically espoused as a fitting adjunct to Christian theology. At its most exalted level of expression, according to this Cabalistic version of magical theology, the magical marvel is indistinguishable from a miracle instigated by voicing a divine name. While having practical application, its essential function is to facilitate a mystical-magical drive for unmediated knowledge of God.

Through his demonological writings Trithemius believed that he was laying down a safely orthodox line of defense behind which he might more effectively carry out his magical program. It is thus to the subject of Trithemius's demonology that we will first turn, preparatory to our subsequent treatment of the abbot's theoretical justification of the occult studies. After fathoming these separate but interrelated thrusts of Trithemius's magical theology we will then be in a position to assess how its Janus-like features played out in the two centuries following the abbot's death, a period coinciding with ecclesiastical schism, the witch hunts, and the scientific revolution.

# Chapter 3

## The Demonological Vision

### The Monastic Rudiments

The year before his death Trithemius received an urgent request from a friend. Currently incarcerated in his town, the Nuremberg humanist patrician Willibald Pirckheimer (1470–1530) informed him, were certain heretics who, "accused of various errors in the Catholic faith, have repeatedly summoned very terrible demons to their aid." Having heard that the abbot had composed a tract "against these people and against their damned, superstitious, vain, and diabolical arts," Pirckheimer expressed a desire to borrow it "so that I may learn how to extirpate, eradicate, and exterminate such wicked men . . . from our midst."[1] The work to which Pirckheimer referred was probably Trithemius's *Antipalus maleficiorum*, one of the tracts kept on hold during the the abbot's harried last years at Sponheim and finally completed in the newly found tranquillity of his Würzburg cloister, though other titles from his pen testifying to his demonological credentials also fit Pirckheimer's description.

In his role as monastic theologian and reformer Trithemius consciously sought to revive the pristine ideals of the Christian

fathers within the contemporary Benedictine monastery. This ambitious task necessarily entailed the renewal of a demonological
view of the world which lay at the core of patristic and monastic
theology. It was Trithemius's conviction, brought out in his monastic homilies and sermons before he embarked on more formal expositions on the subject, that demons do not intrude into human
affairs uninvited. Their necessary inroad is human wickedness. In
a homily warning monks against breaking their vows and aban-
doning their cloisters, for example, Trithemius warned that "just as
the lamb which goes walking alone in the desert is eaten by the
wolf, so is the negligent and impure monk who withdraws from the
sight of his pastor devoured by the demons."[2] Or again, Trithemius
admonished monks at the outset of a section of his *De tentationibus
monachorum* specifically given over to the subject of demonic temptation: "It is the part of demons to insinuate evils, and it is our part
to refuse consent, because the more vigorously we resist their assaults, the more surely will we overcome them."[3] These and many
similar statements in Trithemius's religious writings testify to the
kind of theological subsoil out of which his demonology grew.

At times, it is true, the picture of demons drawn by Trithemius
was one of little more than roguish mischief makers, a characterization especially evident in his ecclesiastical histories. Under the
year 860 in his Hirsau annals, for example, Trithemius recorded
the visit of an exceedingly troublesome demon to the town of Mainz
whose disconcerting antics were reported to have ranged from
shaking the walls of buildings and casting their loosened stones on
unsuspecting pedestrians below to steathily creeping into the beds
of women at night.[4] Sometimes, as later indicated in the the same
work, a given demonic prankster could become such a familiar
fixture in a town or region as to become widely known to its inhab-
itants and referred to by name as if it were human. A certain
demon called Hudekin, according to a detailed narrative furnished
by Trithemius under the year 1132, took up residence in the Saxon
diocese of Hildesheim where it performed numerous outrages against
the populace of that region.[5] Anecdotal narratives like these were
intended by the abbot as relatively light didactic lessons in which
demons figured as little more than temporary annoyances to men
and women as they went about their daily business. On a more
serious note, however, setting the stage for his demonological writ-

ings proper, Trithemius also portrayed demons in his hortatory writings as putting at risk the very possibility of salvation. After all, as he pointed out in the *De tentationibus monachorum*, the prince of demons has one overriding end in view: to seduce others into the same state of damnation as is his own lot in the eternal scheme of things.

What Trithemius did not expressly state in the foregoing cases, but still implicitly assumed, is that demonic visitation does not take place without human cooperation. The indispensable avenue into the world for demons is the debased will, which in turn becomes still more debased under their influence. Having themselves forsaken God, according to this more solemnly construed demonological precept of Trithemius, demons seek to lure human beings into doing the same. Their presence in this capacity is manifested in two main forms. The first form, generally responsive to the counteractive powers of exorcism, is simple possession, whereas the second form, far more resistant to exorcistical techniques, involves the association of demons with willing human confederates, the witches and sorcerers. In this way a campaign started by Trithemius in his cloister to admonish his monks against fraternizing with demons developed in time into a full-scale demonological program as readily applicable to the laity as to clergy.

It is true that a predisposition toward the second, more wide-reaching deployment of demonology was evident in the earlier stages of the abbot's career, as revealed by an entry for the Dominican inquisitor Jacob Sprenger, a coauthor of the notorious *Malleus maleficarum* of 1486, incorporated into his catalogue of illustrious Germans (completed 1491–1495). However it was not until he arrived at his new monastic home in Würzburg that Trithemius found the opportunity to produce a significant demonological output of his own reflecting the views of the *Malleus*.[6] For with a pronounced shift at this phase of his career to a magical agenda of his own, Trithemius concurrently evinced a demonological shift to accompany it, the principal results of which, as previously brought out, are his *Antipalus maleficiorum*, *Liber octo quaestionum*, and a preface and outline for an encyclopedically conceived *De demonibus*.

In the wake of the controversy instigated by his uncompleted *Steganographia*, Trithemius strenuously argued that his perfectly legitimate cryptological brand of magic should not be confused with the illegitimate demonic brands he so extensively assailed in his demonological writings. However, as we will now observe, Trithemius's demonological digressions also took on a life of their own which would significantly play into the witch hysteria characterizing his age. In this context demons were not simply taken for granted by Trithemius. In a further application of the scholastic maxim "faith seeking understanding," Trithemius first of all addressed himself to understanding why a good God allows evil demons to intrude into and disturb the divinely instituted cosmic order. On that foundation Trithemius could then proceed to the next step of clarifying the many ways, including the way of magic, by which the demons set about luring human souls into their grasp.

### Sorcery, Sin and Divine Providence

A clue to the important part demonology came to play in the literary career of Trithemius is found in a letter to a friend soon after his arrival in Würzburg. Informing his correspondent of a list of writings he had already been able to complete in his newly found tranquil surroundings, Trithemius added that he had also begun, with the encouragement of friends, "a large work in twelve books, to be titled *De demonibus*, in which I have determined to demolish all the profane arts of the magicians, both in genus and in species, and to assess their causes, inventors, books, modes, and deceptions, individually and by name."[7] To another friend about the same time, Trithemius related that his motive in composing this encyclopedic work was "with all my might to explode and refute all the superstitious arts, both of the demons and of men, and to show how very vain, pernicious, and detestable they are—and this in various ways from the very books of those foolish men who have transmitted these arts."[8] While failing to bring to fruition the ambitiously conceived work indicated to these correspondents, Trithemius did leave behind a preface and outline of its projected contents, and further incorporated many of its ideas into the more manageable confines of the *Antipalus* and *Octo quaestiones* (see title page, plate 1).

A belief in the existence of demons, reasoned Trithemius, is inextricably bound up with a belief in the existence of God and of the immortal soul, the triadic interconnection of which he promised to develop in a chapter heading of his *De demonibus* affirming "that God, the demons, and immortal souls exist."⁹ A further chapter, declaring that "we are able to prove the existence of demons by three reasons," testifies to Trithemius's belief that scholastic rationalism could be utilized to undergird the demonological credo.¹⁰ A chapter declaring the demons to be of many different kinds is followed by a series of chapters specifying eleven known species—demons of the air, water, earth, and fire, demons of dark caverns, light-bearing demons, and so on. That such demons are not merely harmless cohabitants of the world aloof from human affairs is also indicated in the outline to the *De demonibus*, with one heading maintaining, for example, "that demons often visibly serve men," and another reputing to answer the question of "why some demons gladly converse with men."¹¹

As an extension of his view that the main avenue for the entrance of demons into the human sphere is moral turpitude, Trithemius held demonic sorcery to enter the world by the same means. As noted in the *Antipalus*, "accessibility to sorcery is given through sin," the explanation discovered in the observation that "when the Devil is about to do injury to a man, he is never wont to assail him very arduously unless he perceives that his victim, by reason of sin, is deprived of heavenly help." It followed for Trithemius, accordingly, that "whoever wishes to keep himself safe from the sorceries of the demons should always very zealously guard his conscience from the pollution of sin, especially of the mortal kind."¹² Although perceiving all of the human vices to be conducive in some degree to the invitation of demonic sorcery, Trithemius viewed two vices in particular as being especially inviting in this regard, both traditionally listed among the *vitia capitalia*. The first is accidia, a combination of sloth and sorrow, and the second, lust (*luxuria*).

Accidia (a variation of the Greek *acedia*), according to the conventional moral theory worked out in the early Christian monasteries and further amplified by the scholastics, is the vice par excellence of physical and spiritual idleness (*otium*), in which capacity it produces the kind of debility and vacuity in which the demons are likely to find their least resistance. Not only is lust often found to accompany such idleness, according to Trithemius in reference to this vice, but also sorcery. As put in the preface to the

*De demonibus*, accidia "incites lust, teaches the depraved arts, encourages superstitions against the faith, pursues prophecies of the future, and prompts the dreadful actions of the sorcerers."[13] And concerning the vice of lust in accidia's attendance, Trithemius further admonished his readers against "incontinence and consorting with deceitful women, for the power of doing injury is conceded to the perfidy of witches above all through the prohibited vice of lust."[14]

The sequence from cause to effect which Trithemius envisaged between lust and sorcery also worked for him in reverse, with demonic incubi and succubi seducing lascivious human beings into a state of ravenous sexual desire. Paradoxically, however, while viewing one prominent consequence of sexual commerce with the demons to be an intensification of erotic voracity, Trithemius viewed another as the elimination of sexual desire altogether. Needless to say, Trithemius was not without a resolution to this apparent self-contradiction, answering that "since men very often sin through the lust of the flesh, with God's just permission, whether they be [heretical] Christians, Saracens, or any other unfaithful persons, they are, with the maleficent cooperation of demons, swiftly and readily punished in their genitals."[15]

This is an analysis of bewitchment, nevertheless, which confronted Trithemius with a certain dilemma. For if sin prepares the ground for bewitchment, why is demonic affliction so often visited on innocent infants? Trithemius did not evade this dilemma, addressing it in both his *Antipalus* and *Octo quaestiones*. Invoking the pronouncement of sacred scripture in his *Antipalus* that the sins of the fathers are able to be visited upon the sons, Trithemius contended by the same token that the demons of the fathers attracted by their sins are equally able to be visited upon their sons. It follows that if a child should suffer the effects of sorcery as a result of inheriting his parents' sins, his parents, should they wish to cure their child of his demonic afflictions, must repent of their sins as if they themselves are the target of the sorcerous deed.[16] Another possible cause of demonic affliction in an infant is the wrong choice of a midwife. For this reason "let parents beware that they do not welcome witches and those strongly suspected of sorcery into the duties of midwifery. For a maleficent midwife, that she might please her demon, sometimes exercises incredibly wicked acts against those being born."[17]

Trithemius's inclusion of non-Christian "Saracens" among those predominently subject to demonic affliction raised an analogous dilemma concerning those unprivileged to be born and raised as Christians. Not inconsistently, Trithemius confronted this dilemma with the same headstrong inflexibility with which he confronted the dilemma of demonically afflicted infants. Thus, in response to the question of whether non-Christians can be saved, Trithemius answered not only in the negative, but added that the condemnation by the Church of "Jews, pagans, gentiles, Saracens, heretics, and infidels" also entails the condemnation of the demons inspiring them.[18] Following this guideline, the involuntary infidelity of non-Christians is just as conducive to the attraction of demons as the voluntary infidelity of heretical Christians. It is therefore no wonder, mused Trithemius, that witches and sorcerers are especially plentiful among "the unfaithful pagans, Saracens, and other worshippers of idols, whose damnation is not in the least to be doubted."[19]

This latter consideration answered the question for Trithemius of why so many marvel workers were to be found among the infidels, and where the essential difference lay between their astounding magical marvels and the kinds of miracles attributed to Christ and His saints. Whereas infidel magi were beheld by their credulous observers as performing miracles, in truth, he contended, they were performing demonically induced marvels under the auspices of the Devil, "who like an ape desires to imitate whatever he has perceived; deceives the minds of men, especially those of the infidels, by various illusions; and seduces the faithful to himself by a certain resemblance between his marvels and miracles."[20] Adopting a comparable approach to heresy, that is, infidelity seeking to undermine Christianity from within rather than attacking it from without, Trithemius did nothing to discourage the thesis of the more zealous among the witch hunters that heresy constitutes a danger more serious than one of merely inviting demons into the human sphere. Demonic sorcery and witchcraft practiced within the Christian community, he agreed with this more radical proposition of the demonologists, are themselves forms of heretical expression.[21]

Although his theology required the existence of demons, and furnished them inroad into the world by means of moral and spiritual depravity, Trithemius nevertheless was bothered by the question of why a benevolent God had allowed maleficent demons into His cosmic scheme. For if it is true that wickedness in its various manifestations invites demons into the world, it is also true, as he well understood, that the havoc stirred up by demons is visited upon the innocent as well as upon the guilty. In a digression on this subject in his *Octo quaestiones* Trithemius reminded his readers that the inscrutable Creator knows far better than mere mortals how to order a just universe. Though we might suggest possible hypotheses, such as the one, earlier presented, that "infants not infrequently perish from bewitchment because of the sins of their parents," in the last analysis we must accept our ignorance of God's unfathomable ways.[22]

All the same, a response of "learned ignorance" to thorny theological questions like this one was Trithemius's last rather than first resort. In keeping with the rationalist tradition of medieval scholasticism, Trithemius tried to make sense of divine providence before relegating it to the darkness of unknowing. His plan to conclude the *De demonibus* on this subject came to nought through his inability to get beyond its preface and outline of its contents. But he did capture the main points of its projected discourse in the final questions posed to him by Emperor Maximilian.

A troublesome point raised by Trithemius in the sixth of his *Octo quaestiones* concerns the requirement of divine permission in the performance of sorcery. Deprived of God's permission, attested Trithemius, witches and sorcerers "can attain their ends neither by themselves nor with the help of demons; for all power is from the Lord God."[23] The seventh question addresses itself more fully to this paradox, asking "why the omnipotent God, inasmuch as He is the just judge of wicked acts, permits sorceries to come into existence to the ruin of mankind, by means of which not only sinners are cruelly tormented, but also many innocent victims perish?"[24] Trithemius's reply to this query is divided into two sections, the first comprising eight reasons (rationes) why God acquiesces in the demonic vexation of mankind as a whole, and the second, eight reasons why God acquiesces in the demonic vexation of Christians in particular.

Six of the eight reasons given by Trithemius for a universal presence of vexating demons, as it happens, are technically addressed, not to demons per se, but to the underlying existence of evil upon which they frequently depend for sustenance. With the

seventh reason, however, the subject of demons themselves, together with the sorcery said to be taught under their tutelage,
directly enters the picture. According to this explanation for demonic intrusion into the world, a kind of just retribution is effected
whereby those who take pleasure in deceiving others by demonic
means, "the enchanters and witches, contemptuous of following the
salutary example set by Christ," might themselves be deceived by
the same means. Added to this worldly retribution of sorcerers for
their demonic activities, moreover, is one reaching to the afterlife.
For by striving, in collusion with the demons, to acquire worldly
approbation "while at the same time despising the Saviour of the
world Whom they ought to have adored," the sorcerers, Trithemius
judged, are justly plunged into Hell through the agency of those
very same demons.[25]

The last reason for general demonic vexation offered by
Trithemius, foreglimpsed in the abbot's earlier *De tentationibus
monachorum*, is that demons are justly employed by God to test
free will. While allowing that demons in this capacity are rightly
termed "agitators (*incentores*) of evils," Trithemius insisted that "in
no way can they be called their true instigators (*impulsores*),"[26] a
designation to be reserved for God alone. However, in keeping with
the requisite of free will, Trithemius further acknowledged that
one is permitted to choose between obeying the just mandates of
God and becoming seduced by demons into violating those mandates. The excuse that one or more demons might lie behind a
given outrage against God, as viewed by Trithemius, was no excuse
whatsoever, for, demons aside, "that evil which a man wills is willed
out of his own private disposition." To relegate to demons a moral
responsibility properly belonging to oneself, Trithemius determined,
is to fail the test placed by God upon his soul. Following this reasoning, the existence and attending vexations of demons are no
more incompatible with the providential plan of God than is the
evil upon which the demons feed. Accordingly, "even if the will of
the demons is always iniquitous, that power can never be unjust."[27]

Moving from the demonic vexation of mankind in general to
that of Christians in particular, Trithemius reiterated its probatory
function with the contention that demonically instigated suffering
represents "a test of Christian faith and a trial of our integrity."[28]
Further reasons given for the demonic vexation of Christians, he
continued, are that it tests the capacity of Christian patience,

induces humility, experientially assists the soul in distinguishing good from evil, furthers, through its attending tribulations, the purification of the soul, and promotes penitence and other sacramental aids "which possess considerable power against all the sorceries of the malignant spirits." The last-named reason in particular, certified for Trithemius by the articles of Christian faith, was purportedly reinforced by the testimony of the witches themselves who, upon being interrogated by their inquisitors, were often pressed into the admission "that listening to the Mass and availing ourselves of objects which have been blessed by the church greatly debilitate the powers of the demons."[29]

Regarding the kinds of incentives that attracted sundry sinners, heretics, and infidels into consorting with the demons, Trithemius in the outline for his *De demonibus* listed a virtual catalogue of mysterious powers which perverse individuals hoped to acquire from demons in exchange for their services. According to one chapter heading, for example, "the superstitious arts promise good knowledge"; according to another, with special relevance to the abbot's own clerical calling, "superstition promises to give and take away preferments"; and according to still another, "superstition destroys the power of copulation between men and women." And if these seductive promises were not sufficient to attract many superstitious personages into the service of the demons, other still more inflated ones were that, by following the proper procedures, they could become invisible or fly though the air at lightning speed.[30]

Much as the Devil despoiled our first parents through their excessive curiosity in matters exceeding the proper bounds of their understanding, according to Trithemius, so did the demons continue to appeal to overweening curiosity among sorcerers to effect their cooperation. Of these excessively curious types, following traditional guidelines, Trithemius differentiated two basic categories, the first consisting of unlettered women, and the second, of lettered men. With this distinction in mind Trithemius reproached for coming under the influence of demons "not only the simple and unlearned, but also the great, the powerful, and the learned."[31] But while making a technical distinction between the two kinds of sorcerer, illiterate and literate, Trithemius further insisted that "in their pernicious and truly damnable curiosity they are all as one," sharing as they do a desire to achieve with demonic assistance "that which they are unable to do naturally."[32]

To cajole prospective human agents into doing their wills, maintained Trithemius, the demons often deceive them into believing the opposite, planting in them the illusion that they are ministers to their bidding. In any event, though sometimes hovering invisibly over human actions and entering into them free of human mediation, the demons also sometimes choose select human beings to serve as special intermediaries for their sorceries. Accordingly, his aim in the work at hand, Trithemius declared in the preface to his *De demonibus*, was to furnish a useful aid not only against the demons themselves, but also against their human confederates. In his own words, it was his objective to provide a guide "on behalf of the Holy Mother Church and against the wicked and very impious necromantics, enchanters, prophets of the demons, and soothsayers."[33]

Indicating in one of the chapter titles following these words that the primitive church applied great diligence to the task of extirpating the demonic arts, Trithemius in a further title, implying that the work of expunging the black arts from the Christian populace was far from complete, lamented on "how difficult it is in these times of ours to purify the church of these errors."[34] One chapter bemoans the lack of vigorous opposition by the bishops of the church to the spread of superstitious magic, and another complains that, as a direct result of this superstitious abuse of the true faith, "the church is gradually made infirm and diminished in her powers." Further chapters declare that all the magical superstitions "were proclaimed as evil by Christ and by the apostles" and that the church in Trithemius's day "is more afflicted by this bitter enemy than during the time of the martyrs."[35]

The irony of comments like these scattered throughout the demonological writings of Trithemius is that their author was himself widely held to be an excessively curious contributor to the problem he diagnosed. Highlighting this irony is the complaint made in the *Octo quaestiones*: "Alas, how many Christians exist today, indeed, how many clerics and how many priests (may I spare the majority?) who employ many different superstitions in their daily behavior, by means of which they pursue implicit covenants with the demons." Without the least hint that he fell under the same cloud of suspicion as he here assigned to others, he added that these superstitious souls deserved not only whatever secular punishment they received from the authorities, but also eternal damnation in Hell.[36] Regrettably for his future reputation, with

Bovillus pointing the way, Trithemius would find others similarly disposed who would do their best to turn this harsh counsel upon himself.

Significantly, the aforementioned attack by Trithemius on Christian "superstition" appears in the context of a protracted discussion of the distinction between genuine miracle working and demonic marvel working. Clearly, Trithemius had a special interest at stake on this subject which necessarily put him at odds with those, taking the lead of Augustine and Thomas Aquinas, who strictly adhered to the premise of an absolute antithesis between miracle and magic. Whereas, on the basis of the identical premise, some demonologists banned all magic from the Christian curriculum as another name for sorcery, Trithemius was confronted by the more knotty problem of proscribing some forms of magic while allowing others. If Trithemius were successfully to make this case, he needed to resolve a dilemma which, now to be addressed, is raised in his own writings. This is how the Christian magician is successfully to overcome the ontological barrier separating the realm of divinely instituted miracle from that of demonically instigated magic.

### The Problem of Accommodating Magic to Miracle

One of the queries broached by Trithemius in his *Octo quaestiones* asks: "If it is true that no one is saved outside our faith, from where do the miracles attributed to the unfaithful arise, since we know from the narrative of many men, even among the incredulous, that these are awesome feats?" In reply Trithemius maintained that the word *miracle (miraculum)* is inappropriately applied to such feats, which amaze their spectators, not because they arise through divine agency, but because they are "novel and unusual, taking place contrary to custom." Not to be excepted from this opinion, moreover, are special kinds of marvels effected "through contracts, both implicit and explicit, with the demons."[37] Just as demons cannot actually perform miracles but only simulate them, likewise are human beings under their spell, the witches and sorcerers, faced with the same limitations. It followed for Trithemius, accordingly, that "the marvels of the unfaithful, either those which occur today or those which we read to have occurred in the past, either are artificially fabricated or are produced by an illusion of demons."[38]

In systematic exposition of this thesis Trithemius listed four principal causes of marvel working—God, the angels, the demons, and human beings, of which he determined that only the first-named, "the first and greatest author of marvels, Who has illuminated the whole world by filling it with signs, miracles, and virtues,"[39] authentically deserves the label of miracle worker. So far as miracles are said to be peformed by representatives of the other categories, such as angels and saints, they are necessarily accomplished, not through powers residing within themselves, but through powers imparted to them by God, in the mediating role of which they are charged with administering exclusively to the Christian faithful. Human accessibility to the powers of true miracle working, according to Trithemius, are furnished via two main avenues. By the first avenue, of which Christ's apostles were prime exemplars, a man draws directly on the miraculous power of God, "provided that he has received the merit of holiness in the faith of our Lord Jesus Christ, by an invocation of the Divine Name." By the second avenue a man is enabled to produce marvels "by virtue of his approximation to angelic purity," the cause being that "to men who are pure and fervid in their love of God the holy angels reveal arcane matters which are hidden to others, and manifest many things to them at the command of the Creator."[40]

In both of these avenues to genuine miracle working Trithemius offers valuable clues to how he envisaged a transformation of mystical into magical theology, with a Christianized Cabala constituting a key to its effectuation. Two primary features of Cabala spoke for its appropriateness in this regard. The first feature lies in the presumption that miraculous powers reside in the very words employed in the act of prayer, the equivalent, as it were, of a divinely sanctioned form of encantation, and the second feature, in the presumption that the encantations of prayer legitimately invoke angelic assistance to achieve proximity to God. Conspicuously unsuitable for this mediating function, however, is the entire category of demons, together with that vast portion of mankind which, existing outside the pale of the faithful, is especially vulnerable to demonic influence. Those, accordingly, who effect their marvels in commerce, not with God and the angels but with the demons, cannot properly be termed miracle workers but counter-feiters of miracles. For it is the disposition of the prince of demons, the Devil, lamented Trithemius in a passage earlier cited in a related context, that he "seduces the faithful to himself by a certain resemblance between his marvels and miracles."[41]

Of the various ways in which the demons, together with their sorcerous human allies, opted to express their apish ways, Trithemius emphasized two disciplines in particular readily lending themselves to their deceptive aims. The first is the art of prophecy and the second, the art of medicine. So far as the demons show themselves capable of accurately predicting the future, Trithemius contended that they do so, not with absolute certainty as in the case of divinely inspired angels and prophets, but by mere conjecture. Moreover, in the act of communicating those conjectures to human beings, "sometimes they tell the truth, and other times they deceive and dupe those to whom they have transmitted their conjectures." To the question of why demons do not always lie in their prophetic utterances, Trithemius answered that if they did so they would eventually be found out and thus be deprived of instilling further confidence in their pronouncements. Concerning the second art claimed by the abbot to be especially vulnerable to demonic appropriation, corporeal medicine, Trithemius maintained that demons "sometimes proffer a cure for infirmities because they have acquainted themselves with the natures of all the herbs, and are easily able to apply their skills to those who are ill, and to bear away the diseases which they themselves have instigated in the first place, at the timely moment withdrawing from the senses those calamities which they have inflicted upon their victim."[42]

But while, as viewed by Trithemius, astounding prophecies and astounding cures to bodily illness are two of the leading ways by which demons gain mastery over the human soul, they by no means exhaust the range of possibilities. Anything which might take on the appearance of a miracle is grist for the demonic mill. So skilled are the demons in this regard, noted the abbot, that, in caricature of the miraculous resurrection, they even sometimes feign to raise the dead, to which the writer responded that they "do not really revive those who have died, but only, in various ways, deceive the senses of man." In these and many other ways, proclaimed Trithemius, "the demons are able to display, by a certain false similitude, semblances of miracles which the saints manage to accomplish in truth."[43]

Inasmuch as such aping abilities of the demons cannot be referred to a heavenly origin, Trithemius was left with only one other possible matrix out of which they might arise. Whether simulating their "miracles" through an actual interraction with the world or through mere alterations of their observers' minds, contended Trithemius, the demons, while pretending to surpass nature, are necessarily circumscribed by the finite bounds of nature. No matter how amazing their feats, "all the miracles of the demons either are phantasms or are effected by a certain natural industry." In enlarging on this thesis, however, Trithemius can be said to have clarified one constituent of his magical theology only to obscure another. Observing that certain men "experienced in the occult mysteries of nature" are able to produce marvelous natural effects independently of the demons, it followed for Trithemius "that the demons, of a still subtler nature and with more experience, are able to effect many marvelous things naturally which are not understood by any ordinary man."[44] The prickly question of course raised by this observation, thrown into sharp relief by Trithemius's simultaneous role as an exponent of licit natural magic, is how we are to distinguish between nature put to the use of the demons and nature put to the use of God.

Concerning the particular ways by which sorcerers call demons into their service, Trithemius specified three principal methods: the first by an explicit invocation of demons; the second, by insinuation (*implicatione*); and the third, by forgery (*suppositione*). By the first-named method, we are told, "necromancers and the wretched little women whom we commonly call witches (*mulierculae, quas vulgo maleficas nuncupamus*) effect marvelous deeds by a visible invocation." Utilizing the second method for demonic assistance, Trithemius continued, are those who, without expressly invoking demons, enlist their implicit cooperation through such means as "sacrifices, fumigations, and vows."[45] It is not by chance, he observed regarding these first two modes of diabolical intrusion into human affairs, that demonic invocations and rituals resemble the prayers and rites employed in the church, the explanation being that the demons, being expert mimickers of miracles in general, are equally expert in mimicking the specifically miraculous powers which reside in the sacraments of the church. The third-named method of enlisting demonic assistance, on the other hand, that by forgery, differs in a fundamental way from the previous two. Whereas, noted Trithemius, those who perform their awesome feats by the invocation and insinuation of demons appeal to the external simularities existing between their sorcerous symbols and rituals and the divinely sanctioned ones of the church, those who perform their feats by forgery appeal to the gentile expressions of magic without an overt attempt to identify them with Christian ritual and symbolism.[46]

A number of points made by Trithemius in conjunction with the above-stated three methods for soliciting demonic collusion lend them further refinement. In connection with the method of explicit invocation, for example, Trithemius pointed out that sorcerers might expressly contract with demons, exchanging certain services (including sexual services), for such malefic powers as inciting storms, wasting crops, inflicting illness, and the like through occult means. Giving literal meaning to their characterization as necromantics, moreover, Trithemius charged them with powers of conjuration whereby they "recall into their presence, by pernicious incantations, whomsoever they wish from the infernal regions."[47] Similarly, in connection with the more indirect method of insinuation, Trithemius noted that "certain exceedingly curious men," without actually calling demons into their presence, achieve similar results "by using characters, signets, figurines, and necklaces in accompaniment with strange-sounding words."[48] In both of these ways, Trithemius pointed out, an analogy can be detected between the rituals and symbolic language of the sorcerers and those of the church. "For just as in the Church of God the sacraments are signs (*signa*) of the invisible grace of the Holy Spirit," as this analogy goes, "so there are known to be certain characters and modes of invocation, taught in the school of the demons, which mediate in the pact between a man and his malignant spirit."[49] As for the third way offered by Trithemius for gaining demonic assistance in the fabrication of miracles, forgery, this issues, he maintained, not out of an intent to mimic the rites of the Christian Church, but rather out of an intent to place the infidel religions on a par with Christianity.

In the latter regard Trithemius declared that "if Jews, Saracens, pagans, and gentiles, who do not believe in our Lord Jesus Christ, perform miracles here on earth, we believe that these are accomplished, not by the virtue of God, nor by the ministry of angels, nor by the merit of holiness, but by a forgery produced by demons (*sed daemonum . . . suppositione*)."[50] Inasmuch as true miracles are a sign of true religion, false or forged miracles are a sign of false religion. Since that very Being Who has imparted true religion, the omnipotent God of the Christians, "also causes miracles," it should not surprise us to find that the founders of false religions, to lend their impieties an appearance of authenticity, are often wont to feign miracles to accompany their deceptive words.

A prime example for Trithemius of one who fabricated miracles to lend supernatural authority to his religious injunctions was Mohammed. The diabolically inspired founder of Islam, the abbot was convinced, counterfeited miracles to promote his counterfeit of religion. "Upon being inspired by evil demons," charged Trithemius, "Mohammed went on to embellish it with false miracles, not from God, but in commerce with demons."[51] But while having no problem in characterizing the Islamic religion, together with its "miracles," as a diabolical forgery, Trithemius had greater difficulty applying the same principle to that other religion competing with Christianity, Judaism, whose founder, Moses, had often been depicted by Christian writers as a genuinely miracle-working forerunner of Christ.

For Trithemius Mohammed's offenses were chiefly unpardonable because they occurred in the Christian era, when he and his followers might have accepted, but instead voluntarily rejected, Christ's role as the exclusive source of true miracles. The same could not be said, however, for pre-Christian Jews, who, "after receiving the law through Moses before the incarnation of the Son of God, were frequently illuminated by divine miracles." However, to be consistent with the foregoing indictment of Islamic religion, Trithemius extended no such exoneration to those Jews who had come after Christ's resurrection. As for the miracles attributed to Moses by scripture, Trithemius fully accepted their validity, but only in their capacity as preludes to the still greater miracle working of Christ. By the same token he condemned out-of-hand, as counterfeit, all Jewish "miracles" that had taken place since the resurrection. If marvel-working effects were witnessed in Trithemius's own day at the hands of Jews, their spectators could confidently infer that "these are the works of demons and visible signs of their errant ways."[52]

Formally, Trithemius here can be said to have completed his query into whether infidels are capable of effecting miracles. In a kind of addendum to this subject, however, he called attention to a form of natural wonder working considered by some to deserve separate treatment from the foregoing demonic, angelic, and divine forms. In rebuttal to this proposition, Trithemius determined that such marvelous powers as are said to be extracted by a magician from the hidden recesses of nature "cannot be exclusively natural" (*non potest esse simpliciter naturalis*), a result of the requirement "that something come into it from an outside power, that is, that either a good angel or a malignant spirit at least partially occupy the meditating person." Under the assumption that the "outside power" can be divinely as well as demonically constituted, then, according to a theory of wonder working shared by Trithemius himself, "he who learns how to detach himself from every accidental thing and enter into the unity of his own self above the senses is able to effect marvels naturally."[53]

For Trithemius, then, the idea of a natural magic operating in a realm of its own, separated from the divine, the angelic, and the demonic realms, was an absurdity. Natural magic, he determined, cannot posssibly function by reference to material nature alone, but must always depend on supernatural forces lying outside itself. At one extreme these forces might belong to God and to the good angels in His ministry, and at the other extreme, to the Devil and to the wicked demons in his ministry. The natural magician, accordingly, cannot avoid, in the name of a neutral or value-free art, making a hard choice between divine and demonic intervention in his operations.

Unhappily for those who might look for perfect consistency in this query by Trithemius into the miracle-magic problem, the argumentative threads of its fabric still show a number of loose ends. One such lies in the apparently self-contradictory presumption that supernatural demons are restricted to the bounds of nature for the source of their marvel-working powers, and another is Trithemius's blurring of the traditional miracle-magic distinction by allowing some forms of magic to be performed under divine supervision while rejecting others as demonically inspired. According to the occult theory formulated by Trithemius, to be described at length in the next chapter, only magic in its wicked demonic form stands at radical variance with the divinely instigated miracle, whereas such magic as is performed under divine auspices, while admittedly placed in a subordinate relationship, is capable of being assimilated to the miracle. Whereas in the first instance miracle working and magic diverge, in the second instance they merge. For Trithemius, despite the sustained effort indicated above to distinguish genuine Christian miracles from the merely magical marvels of infidels, the authentic miracles of the Christian saints lay on a continuum with the magical feats of the ancient gentile and Jewish theologians. This is the positive side to Trithemius's doctrine of magical theology which bears its harsh negative side in his demonological rantings.

Regrettably, as will now be brought to our attention, the demonological outpourings of Trithemius, while arguably geared more to insulating his own magic from diabolical contamination than in promoting the witch hysteria, betrayed a decidedly misogynist streak of his personality that could only add fuel to the fires ignited by the witch hunters. In the section closing out the present chapter it will be shown that Trithemius was willing to purge witches by exorcistical means, if at all possible, of their demonically inculcated pollutions. As will first be made clear, however, putting him in basic complicity with the authors of the *Malleus maleficarum*, Trithemius also accepted that some people, among whom women comprise the greater number, are so inveterately corrupted by demons as to warrant their execution. As a first resort Trithemius sought to apply the appropriate corporeal and ecclesiastical remedies to those claimed to be witches. As a last resort, however, he was prepared to surrender up convicted witches to the inquisitors for possible execution.

## The Witch Issue

One of the queries posed by Trithemius in the *Octo quaestiones* asks why wicked and impious human beings, "such as those women whom we vulgarly call witches" (*ut sunt mulieres, quas vulgo maleficas noncupamus*), are endowed with powers to rule over evil spirits denied to good and zealous upholders of the Christian faith.[54] Trithemius's answer, consistent with his explanation for the existence of sorcery in general, was that these powers have been permitted to witches for the same reason that sin is permitted. For, he reasoned, just as sin, together with the demons drawn to it, poses a test of Christian faith, the same can be said for the malefic powers of witches.

That Trithemius's occupation with the witch question was not merely a minor rivelet in the wider stream of his demonology is demonstrated by his plan to address a number of separate chapters of his projected *De demonibus* to the subject. One chapter, for example, declares in its heading "that the arts of the demons are conferred upon maleficent women," and another seeks to explain "why a larger number of maleficent women are found than men."[55] In the epistolary preface to his *Antipalus* Trithemius similarly set forth as a major topic of the text to come "a certain wicked type of evil-doers, especially women (*praecipue autem mulierum*), who inflict countless destructions upon mankind with the cooperation of demons and witchcraft."[56] A further query of the *Octo quaestiones* specifically addressed to the malefic power of witches (*de postestate maleficarum*), constituting the sixth of the eight topics posed to the abbot by Maximilian, lends further testimony to the not insignificant role played by specifically female sorcery in Trithemius's demonological outlook.

Of the kinds of demons especially drawn to witches, one singled out for special mention in the last-named tract is identified as "the light-shunner (*lucifugum*), because it has a special horror of and repugnance toward the light." As to why this demon is more attracted to illiterate female witches than to their learned male counterparts, Trithemius furnished the following explanation. By avoiding the aerial condition necessary for the transmission of light, the abbot noted, this demon also avoids a condition necessary for the transmission of sound, therefore making it unsuitable for the conveyance of voiced chants characteristic of learned male sorcery. The same demonic trait which is of little use to learned sorcery, however, is of great benefit to unlearned witchcraft not dependent upon incantations. Since this demon, Trithemius observed, "is more subtle than all the other varieties, and is distinguished by an exceedingly impudent rashness, it is especially wont to enter into the sorceries of women."[57]

Further reflecting a misogynist bias on Trithemius's part is an explanation in the *Antipalus* of the various ways in which witches visit injuries upon their targeted victims, with some doing so close at hand and others at a distance. In the first instance we are informed that witches administer poisons specially concocted from secret recipes furnished them by their demonic masters—sometimes, to make them more enticing, disguising them as medicines for infirmities which they earlier had inflicted upon their victims through other means. And in the second instance, the injuries are reputedly perpetrated from a more remote location without the possibility of physical contact between the witch and her victim. Should this distance not exceed the limits of visual contact, noted the abbot, a method favored in the latter connection is fascination (*fascinatio*) whereby "a suggestion (*iniectio*) . . . passes from one's affected eyes to those of another with the object of doing him injury."[58]

The kinds of injuries thus inflicted, catalogued in various chapter headings of *De demonibus*, are extensively enlarged upon in the *Antipalus*, with the list reading like just about anything that is destructive to both the worldly contentment and superworldly aspirations of the human being. With occult knowledge acquired from the demons, witches are claimed to kill newborn children; to cause physical impairments such as lameness, dizziness, deafness, and blindness; to provoke epilepsy and various forms of insanity; to induce sterility and impotence; to enchant domestic animals and foment crop-ravaging storms; to sow discord; and so on down the line. And if all of this were not enough to point up the great danger posed by these lost souls "whose impiety is the greatest possible, and whose frenzied desire to do injury to mortals is incredible," Trithemius found to be especially deserving of his maledictions their lustful tendencies, which has the effect both of destabilizing the institution of marriage and of undermining the clerical vow of celibacy. As perceived by the abbot, witches not only "enkindle a foul and very disquieting kind of love in the hearts of mortals, by means of which they seduce them into perdition," but themselves engage in "exceedingly defiled sexual relations," sometimes between themselves, sometimes with victims of their maleficence, and sometimes with demonic succubi and incubi nocturnally materializing in their beds.[59]

An apparent contradiction arises in the latter connection of how a trait indicated as capable of inducing sterility and impotence in the witch is simultaneously to be charged with instigating sexual voraciousness. Through sorcery, declared Trithemius in the *Antipalus*, witches "remove the generative power from both men and women, and render them sterile and impotent in the act of intercourse."[60] As further pointed out in the pages of the same writing, however, such sex-related consequences of sorcery, far from contradicting the supposition of an inordinately stimulated erotic drive in witches, rather helps to confirm it. Thus, posing the question of "why demons are so prone and ready to impose the bewitchment of impotence upon men," Trithemius answered that "these bewitchments do not befall good and wicked men indifferently, but precisely those who are defiled by fornication, by adultery, and by illicit associations with women."[61] This perception of sorcery also underscores Trithemius's belief that its victims are not mere innocents, his reasoning being that the more sinful they are, the more vulnerable they are to the malevolent intentions of the demons.

Further on in the *Antipalus* Trithemius posed the question "whether the virile members are truly removed by sorcery, or only appear to be so?" In reply Trithemius disputed the claim that witches can literally remove male genitals, but did allow the witch an ability to so influence the imagination of the observer as to effect this illusion.[62] The same power of deceiving the imagination was also assigned by Trithemius to other apparently stupendous exploits attributed to witchcraft, such as the making of storms or transforming human beings into beasts. An entry in the Hirsau chronicle, under the year 1010, illustrates this principle of Trithemius's demonology, where reference is made to the apparent transformation of a young man into an ass by two old women of his village. Granting that the alteration did not take place in reality but only in the imagination of its onlookers, Trithemius did not intend thereby to mitigate the seriousness of the crime. On the contrary, he admonished his readers that "a malignant spirit, with divine permission, is able to delude the eyes of men by its marvelous ludifications."[63]

Thus, while accepting that witches are able to inflict genuine damage on their intended victims by occult means, Trithemius was also persuaded that injury is sometimes more imagined than real. This, he maintained, is made possible through a capacity of witches to produce delusion (*praestigium*) in the minds of their spectators, defined in the *Antipalus* as "a certain deceptive power (*quaedam illusoria vis*), acquired either through art or through usage, which so blunts the senses of a man, especially his sight, that he may see a thing otherwise than it truly is."[64] And how is this accomplished? By an agitation of the bodily humors in her victim by the witch, explained Trithemius, "various apparitions are caused in the confused sensual powers."[65] In this way Trithemius transferred to the victims of witchcraft certain characteristics, such as the disturbance of the imagination by melancholy, also widely held to reside in the witches themselves, with the deceptions she instilled in others viewed as but a secondary consequence of her own demonically inspired self-deceptions.

Concerning the conditions necessary to a successful perpetration of bewitchment, Trithemius, in a lengthy discourse on the subject in his *Octo quaestiones*, established three primary requisites. The first is "one who is frenzied and depraved in the mind by a maleficent will"; the second, "an intimate diabolical cooperation"; and the third, "divine permission." If one or another of these requisites is lacking, declared Trithemius, "the bewitchment will not be able to be performed." Working backward through this order, Trithemius assured his readers that should God refuse permission, a demon cannot possibly gain control over a given victim. Secondly, solely one in whom a demon insinuates himself is capable of performing sorcery. Finally, when a malevolent will is lacking, a demon cannot find an appropriate medium though which it can produce sorcery. However, once it has found an appropriate human being to suit its foul purposes, it "uses the frenzied witch in the same way as an artisan uses a tool for the performance of his craftsmanship."[66]

The last-mentioned point, appearing to make a witch more of a passive than active agent of demonic malfeasance, raises a sticky issue touching upon the very legitimacy of the witch persecutions and attending trials. For it could be argued from this acknowledgment pertaining to Trithemius's third requisite of bewitchment—and, indeed, *was* strenuously argued as the witch persecutions intensified and widened their scope—that accused witches, being passive instruments rather than active perpetrators of diabolical malfeasance, should not be held responsible for their crimes. This alleged passivity is expressed in two ways. By the first way witches are passive implements of the demons, and by the second way, they are the passive victims of their own disordered and melancholic imaginations. In either case, following the reasoning of those opposed to the witch persecutions, witches are more to be pitied than feared.

In both of these respects Trithemius made clear his belief that the case for the inculpation of witches is far stronger than that for exculpation. In the first instance witches are endowed with the capacity to withstand direct demonic intrusions, and in the second instance, with the capacity to withstand indirect intrusions through melancholy frenzy. In one case as in the other, the appropriate means of defense is a vigorous exercise of the free will. While accepting that witches are more prone to melancholy and related corporeal disturbances than the usual run of human beings, Trithemius disputed the inference that humoral imbalance is a cause of witchcraft. To maintain this thesis is to put the cart before the horse, inasmuch as, although it may be granted that a humoral infirmity like melancholy is often found to accompany bewitchment, it does so as its effect rather than its cause. The material humor, Trithemius determined, is not a source of that mental alienation commonly observed in witches, but rather is a natural result of a supernatural affliction. Responsibility for the malfeasances of witches should be located, not in their humoral disorders, but in their "exceedingly truculent depravity."[67]

Far from deserving absolution from punishment for being mere passive instruments of the demons, protested Trithemius against this argument, witches, owing to their free will, should be made fully accountable for their iniquities. For this reason Trithemius extended little mercy to these "maleficent women who, out of a depraved will and by their free consent, have passed over into a league with the demons, receiving from them certain notations and symbolic signs by means of which, after they have been summoned, the demons scurry into their presence." If the upshot was death for their more serious offenders, so be it. As enjoined by sacred scripture (Ex. 22:18), witches "should nowhere be tolerated, but rather, as the Creator of all things commanded . . . , they should be utterly exterminated."[68] Or, as the same opinion is stated elsewhere with equal force: "Inasmuch as the crimes of these people are exceedingly offensive to God, to nature, and to mankind, they are justly punished by the ultimate penalty of fire."[69]

References like the above in his demonological writings establish that Trithemius was not a merely innocuous bystander of the witch persecutions. Admittedly, shortly to be addressed, Trithemius appears to have been at least as interested in exorcising the evil-working demons of witches as in exhorting the punishment of their human confederates. But this did not mean that, upon encountering resistance to his less stringent exorcistical methods for purging accused witches of their demons, he was not also amenable to the harsher methods of the inquisitors. His voice not only played a significant part in encouraging the witch persecutions of his own day, but also, as will be shown in its place, continued to work its strident effects upon the witch hunts during the following two centuries.

Nevertheless, even as we concede to Trithemius's responsibility in contributing to the witch hysteria, we must also emphasize that the motive behind that responsibility was largely a secondary rather than primary outgrowth of his demonological outlook. For on the whole it was Trithemius's desire in his demonological writings, not so much to inculpate witches and sorcerers as to exculpate his own brand of magic from the accusation that it was demonically inspired. Or, put another way, his aim was to envelop his own magical speculations in a cloak of demonological respectability, for which purpose the subject of male professional sorcery was even more to the point than that of unlettered witches. With this in mind we need now to assess the attitude of Trithemius to the generally male counterparts of the unlettered witches, the educated professional sorcerers, the demonically inspired powers of whom, upon superficial scrutiny, might mistakenly be confounded with the abbot's own divinely inspired and divinely sanctioned magic.

## The Problem of Learned Sorcery

Trithemius's treatment of professional sorcery played on the same kind of cultural prejudice informing his attacks on witchcraft. Much as his sharing of a prevailing antifeminist sentiment helped to condition his views of witchcraft, his sharing of a prevailing prejudice against "infidel" Jews, Moors, heretics, and the like helped to condition his views of professional sorcery, with the presumption made that those generally in league with the Devil are also more particularly open to instruction in the demonic arts. Sometimes, in recounting the stories of those succumbing to this temptation, Trithemius offered up in his historical writings little more than light anecdotal lessons geared to warning his readers against the folly of trafficking with demons, whereas other times he implied that truly sinister motives were at issue. Moreover, apart from the didactic motives implicit in such historical accounts, Trithemius also revealed differing responses on his part to the outlandish stories reported, ranging, as it were, between naïve credulity, narrative detachment, and skeptical incredulity.

Typifying the prejudicial attitude that lay behind Trithemius's admonitions against sorcery is the account, under the year 1059 in the Hirsau annals, of the abrogation, with the help of magic, of an order for the expulsion of Jews from the Trier diocese by its archbishop. For being lent the services of a certain Rabbi Moses, as this account goes, "a sorcerer, an enchanter, and a necromantic" who effected the death of the offending bishop before his own altar by shaping his waxen image and melting it in synchronism with the appropriate incantations and rituals, the Trier Jews were thereby magically saved from the order of expulsion.[70] But while holding non-Christians like the Trier Jews to be especially vulnerable to the demonic arts, Trithemius also enlarged his notion of infidel to embrace faithless Christians, which in his mind included not only heretics but also nonheretical albeit misguided members of the church, especially princes, who thereby hoped to enhance their worldly powers through diabolical means. Thus, much as he intended the above-cited story about the sorcerous talents of the Jewish sorcerer Moses to warn about the dangers of associating with demons, so did he utilize a story to the same effect, entered under the year 1323 in the same volume, relating to an aborted attempt by the Habsburg prince Leopold to enlist a sorcerer to help rescue his brother Leopold from incarceration by their enemy Lewis of Bavaria.[71]

More problematic in its implications for Christian demonology is a story related in the abbot's compendious history of the Franks of how Lochthild, the mother of the king Clodion (or Clogio), employed demonic sorcery to gain victories for her son on the battlefield. "With her charms and incantations she defeated and rendered demoralized whichever enemies to her son she wished," related Trithemius, "and no matter how far removed they were, she destroyed them and brought victory to the Franks with the aid of demons, and by her sorcery procured fear, terror, and flight in the enemy."[72] Since Trithemius simultaneously held the Frankish empire to have evolved in accordance with a providential plan laid down by God,[73] we must assume from this narrative that even the evil-working activities of the demons and their human confederates are ultimately bound by, and subjected to, the demands of divine preordination.

In another historical anecdote reported in his Hirsau annals, however, this time under the year 1134 relating to the reputed magical exploits of Henry the Lion, Trithemius reveals that he did not always lend credence to the outlandish feats he was describing. Relating a number of the marvelous exploits ascribed by legend to Henry, including his conveyance across the seas, with demonic help, upon the beast from which he had acquired his sobriquet, Trithemius put them down as no more than imaginary inventions of his devotees propagated for the purpose of investing him with the semblance of supernatural support. While indicating sympathy with the motives of Henry's overly zealous admirers, the abbot nevertheless felt compelled to take them to task for exaggerating the prince's prowess whereby, "placing the truth of their narrative under the guise of a mystery, they eagerly utter the deeds of a mortal as though he surpasses the limitations of mortals."[74]

Aside from whether such sorcerous exploits as indicated in the above anecdotes actually happened, Trithemius, by relating them, underscored the great appeal of magic to princes as a device to further their political objectives. If the magic attributed to princes did not actually do all that was claimed, it all the same endowed them with the aura, with or without demonic assistance, of exceeding ordinary human limits. This aspect of his demonological writings placed Trithemius in a ticklish position, since, at the same time, he was making a concerted effort to enlist regal support for his own magic. This meant that, in his simultaneous roles as magician and demonologist, Trithemius was faced with the daunting task of persuading his princely patrons to take up some kinds of magic while avoiding other kinds at the peril of their souls.

In the preface to his *De demonibus* Trithemius nostalgically recalled the days of the primitive church when the Christian princes rightfully displayed much intolerance toward the black arts. So adamant were they in their detestation of demonic magic, he exulted, "that they would not permit a Christian to gaze into the astrolabe or the astrologers to possess any of these [forbidden] instruments." Currently, in contrast, the vanities of the black arts were freely and widely taught and practiced with little fear of punishment by the authorities. Unhappily, lamented the abbot, "there is no one to contradict this development, no one to prohibit it." Rather than repudiating these arts as they ought, their practitioners, "having given themselves over to the arts of the demons," promise far more than they can possibly deliver. In so doing, charged Trithemius, they "noisily catch the attention of kings and princes, corrupt the orthodox faith, destroy the purity of our religion, and reintroduce idolatry."[75]

The censure by Trithemius of those who, through their proficiency in demonic magic, "noisily catch the attention of kings and princes" points up the slender tightrope on which he was balancing. As will be brought out in the next chapter, the abbot's own forthright appeal to royal support in his magical activities appeared to many of his critics to constitute corroborative evidence that he himself should be included among the noisy attention getters of princes whom he had so harshly condemned. In his resolve to discourage illicit magic by one among these princes, the emperor Maximilian, Trithemius clothed his replies to the eight questions posed by his imperial patron in the language of demonology. It was with the identical objective that Trithemius dedicated his *Antipalus* to the margrave-elector Joachim of Brandenburg, a choice highly understandable in light of the portrayal of Joachim in his Hirsau annals, under the year 1484, as "an austere judge and censurer of wicked reprobates and a supreme cultivator and lover of justice."[76] Significantly, highlighting the double-edged motive behind his arcane speculations, these same princes would serve Trithemius as addressees of his principal magical tracts.

The contents of these prince-dedicated demonological tracts, however, also indicate a wider appeal of magic, beyond their promises to enhance the ruling powers of the prince, to the wider public at large. For they pretended, charged Trithemius, to instill such special knowledge in those who gained access to their demon-imparted secrets as to thrust their minds to a place transcending mundane reality. For these, magical knowledge was more than a means of enhancing worldly power. It represented an end in itself, furnishing them with access to that arcane realm inhabited by their demonic instructors.

A trait singled out by Trithemius as greatly contributing to the current fad for illicit magic, pointed up in the preface to the *De demonibus*, is "the injurious and exceedingly pernicious curiosity of mankind" which, starting with the transgression of the first parents, has always been in close league with sin and, by extension, with the demons. It is not by chance, therefore, speculated the abbot, that among the excessively curious of the world are found an inordinate number of "sorcerers, enchanters, necromantics, diviners, demoniacs, superstitious men, fortunetellers, astrological prophets, soothsayers, and augurs, together with all others who serve the cause of the arts of the demons and who zealously obey their master in all things, promising great things to the curious and shamefully deceiving all who believe them."[77] The very composition of this projected encyclopedia of demons, Trithemius acknowledged to a friend in a letter announcing its birth, was spurred by his determination that curiosity in the occult arts had gotten out of hand. Such a work was needed, he decided, because he and his correspondent were now living in a time "in which some learned as well as unlearned men are all too curious, inquiring after those things of which they would be better off ignorant."[78]

So far Trithemius's attack on demonic magic, aside from scattered anecdotal references in his histories, has been a nameless one. But Trithemius's writings are also replete with specific references to key offenders of the magical arts in the ancient and medieval past, some of whom authored theoretical texts in support of their occult activities. A crucial distinguishing feature of their intellectualized form of sorcery is that, through their writings, the maleficent act is able to be conveyed not only over long distances, but also over a long period of time—indeed, even to future generations. With this added danger in mind Trithemius wondered in one chapter heading pertaining to professional sorcerers "whether it is more expedient to burn than to preserve their works?"[79] While we cannot be sure from the chapter title alone on which side of this question Trithemius fell, by looking elsewhere in his writings we can find support for both of these contradictory positions. At times

Trithemius called for the banishment of sorcerous writings if not their outright incineration, whereas other times he made the case that if the Christian scholar is to overcome the errors of the sorcerers, he needs first to familiarize himself with the writings in which those errors are inscribed. Accordingly, despite scattered pleas for the banning of sorcerous writings in his demonological speculations, many of the texts against which he warned were most assuredly lying on his own monastic shelves. For how else, Trithemius argued, can one know the true unless he is able to compare it to the false?

Posing the question in his *Octo quaestiones* concerning the provenance of the current vogue for magic, Trithemius replied that it was originally an Eastern import, the ancient propagators of which "seduced almost all of Asia Major and Minor from the Christian faith." In the course of time, he alleged, this alien Eastern practice seeped into the Christian West, so that "today there are many among us Christians who have surrendered to the works of the demons—enchanters, sorcerers, and reprobates in the faith who deceive many people by reason of an excessive curiosity and promise impossible things by means of their arts." Given, Trithemius reasoned, that the writings of these necromancers "are filled with superstitions and impiety, they are justly banished from the bounds of the faithful."[80] Understandably, however, to be brought out in the next chapter, when Trithemius turned to the defense of his own magic revealing familiarity with many of these same proscribed writings, he assumed a far more indulgent position than is here indicated.

An ancient prototype for the kind of magic against which Trithemius warned his readers, reinforcing his presumption of an Eastern origin of the magical vogue, was a first century Neopythagorean of Cappadocia, Apollonius of Tyana. The abbot's verdict upon Apollonius's feats, as revealed in his reply to a query about them from an interested correspondent, was an acerbically negative one, though he had difficulty making up his mind as to whether the marvels ascribed to Apollonius owed to actual demon conjuring or simply to a remarkable ability to feign marvels through sleight of hand. "Either the miracles, signs, and prodigious activities attributed to Apollonius in the eight books of Philostratus are to be looked upon as invented and false fables," Trithemius responded to his interrogator, "or else, if they actually occurred, I proclaim without hesitation that they were perpetrated with the cooperation of demons."[81]

If Apollonius truly performed the uncanny feats attributed to him, Trithemius elaborated, he engaged neither in legitimate natural magic, as some of his admirers had held, nor in genuine miracle working, as others had contended. To the first claim Trithemius answered that Apollonius "did not comprehend any natural science, nor does the virtue of natural magic apply to the types of things which are related about him." And to the second claim he responded that "Apollonius was a mortal and corruptible man, one whose power should not be supposed to have surpassed the permissible order of nature, which alone merits the name of miracle." Given that "the divine power alone accomplishes true miracles," Trithemius could not bring himself to concede that the miracle-working ability reserved exclusively for the holy was delegated to a man "who lived as a worshiper of idols, was full of much superstition, and in his knowledge was exceedingly alien from the true God." The unavoidable conclusion to be drawn was that if Apollonius truly accomplished the marvels as recorded, they were effected "by no other means than by the cooperation and power of demons."[82]

That Apollonius had successors in the Christian era is confirmed in Trithemius's histories, though, in many of these cases, the abbot was less inclined to read an overtly demonological motive into their activities than one of attention-getting charlatanism. A story appearing under the year 1256 in the Hirsau annals, for example, tells of an unnamed false messiah who, after performing many prodigious marvels before crowds of spectators and thereby "infecting a few kingdoms in Asia by his errors," in the end was unmasked for the impostor he was.[83] Along similar lines, but showing greater detail about the subject's exploits, is the story related by Trithemius of a certain Theodo who, in various public appearances in the region of the upper Rhine in 1262, feigned to effect such marvels as amputating the head of his servant and afterward restoring it, and traveling through the air, accompanied by his dogs, as though he were a flying hunter. While admittedly astonishing those of his spectators "ignorant of his subtleties," he did not astonish the present writer, who personally had encountered individuals with similar pretenses. Whether they did so with or without demonic assistance, he was convinced that their marvels were performed "by means of a certain natural ludification."[84]

As for whom Trithemius may have had in mind when he indicated personal experience in this area, one figure above all stands out in his writings. He was the notorious magical doctor Faustus, whom the abbot encountered by chance when the two figures passed a night at the same Gelnhausen inn in 1506. Replying to an epistolary inquiry the following year concerning his reaction to the meeting, Trithemius painted a highly unflattering portrait of the man whose magical legend, as time would tell, subsequently became popularly merged with his own. Identifying him as a certain George Sabellicus who also went by the name of Faustus, Trithemius declared the individual in question, "who dared to call himself the prince of necromancers," to be, in contradiction to his inflated claims, "a vagabond, an utterer of vain repetitions, and a wandering monk who, lest he have the temerity to profess further in public places things so abominable and contrary to the Holy Church, is deserving of chastisement by whips." Proclaiming himself "fountain of necromantics (*fons necromanticorum*), astrologer, propitious magician, chiromantic, agromantic, pyromantic, and one skilled in the hydromantic art," Faustus, in Trithemius's far more unflattering characterization, proved himself to be, not a truly wise man as he claimed, but a foolish dolt deserving more of pity than admiration from his curious spectators. Accordingly, cautioned Trithemius, the unwary were advised to be on guard against this charlatan, "one who in truth, being ignorant of all good letters, ought rather to be called a fool than a master."[85]

Conceding to his correspondent that he was not able to verify in that one chance meeting with Faustus the full truth of this harsh judgment, since "as soon as he heard that I was present he fled from the inn, and could not be persuaded by anyone to be introduced to me," Trithemius reported that he had subsequently received much information about the self-proclaimed *fons necromanticorum* from reliable first-hand witnesses. For instance, according to an eyewitness report reaching him from Gelnhausen after his departure, Faustus "proclaimed, in the presence of many men, that he had acquired such great knowledge and memory that if all the volumes of Plato and Aristotle, with all their philosophy, completely perished from the memory of man, he by his genius, as if he were another Ezra the Hebrew, could restore it with an even more superior elegance." Moving on to Würzburg, Faustus publicly promised still more remarkable feats, even going so far as to state the blasphemy "that the miracles of Christ our Saviour were not truly marvelous acts, and that he himself could perform, every day and wherever he wished, all the things which Christ performed." Finally Faustus reportedly wandered into the town of Kreuznach, near Sponheim, where he boasted of possessing many marvelous powers, one of the more conspicuous being that "he was the most accomplished man in the art of alchemy who has ever lived, and that he knew and could perform whatever men desired."[86]

Trithemius did not indicate whether he viewed Faustus as having modeled himself after the ancient magical paragon Apollonius of Tyana. But he left no doubt that this was the case concerning another contemporary magician of the day whose exploits reached him by ear and through letters, the Italian Giovanni Mercurio da Correggio. Under the year 1501 in his Hirsau annals Trithemius recorded the visit of Mercurio to France where, openly declaring himself to be Apollonius's modern heir, "he promised great, strange, and exceedingly marvelous (indeed, should I say incredible?) things." Compared to himself, boasted this self-proclaimed *Mercurius secundus* (the first being Mercurius Trismegistus), the ancient sages "were unlearned men, and there was no figure among them truly wise in the arcana," whereas he, in contrast, "was conversant with every science of the world, understood all the mysteries and arcana of natural things, was capable of investigating the profundities of all writings, and was ignorant of none of those things which man is able to know in the world." All of this, Mercurio boasted, was evidence that he was "born for the highest things" and "filled with a divine spirit." But while Mercurio outwardly displayed a solemn and virtuous demeanor to reinforce this image of himself, even distributing to the poor of Lyons the honorarium which he received from the king, Trithemius speculated that this was most likely only a mask of righteousness to hide what was really malice of intention.[87]

Like that of the contemporary Faustus, the magical reputation of Mercurio, if we are to believe Trithemius's account, appears to have rested more on braggadocio and self-aggrandizement than on outright demon conjuration. Anxious to dispel any suggestion of the latter explanation for his extraordinary powers, Mercurio is said to have maintained, in terms resembling those adopted by Trithemius under the brunt of similar suspicions, that his marvels were performed "not with the help of demons, but by that art of natural magic which the ancient kings and wise men held in great esteem." But while happy to countenance such a rationale for his own magic, Trithemius was unwilling to cede it to Mercurio. Moreover, while appearing to perceive in Mercurio more of a harmless quack than a dangerous manipulator of demons, Trithemius also used the occasion of his narrative to warn that the distance separating the two kinds of marvel working—empty charlatanism and demonic magic—was not always a great one. While indicating some ambivalence in this regard, reluctantly granting at one point in his presentation of Mercurio's exploits that "whether he truly held such powers from God or not I am unable to say," Trithemius on balance concluded that Mercurio was likely in at least implicit league with the demons, a magical impostor whose feats were given the appearance of veracity by the demonic ability to influence the imagination of his spectators.[88]

Having left behind no literary legacy of their own, such adepts of the magical arts as the foregoing have led more by example than by precept. To the extent that they have played a part in the formulation of precepts, their principal role in the history of ideas has been to dramatize the powers of magic apart from the occult theory with which they were evidently conversant. Others similarly disposed, however—in this, more directly comparable to Trithemius himself—left behind a written record to lend buttressing to their magical operations. Unlike Trithemius, however, at least as construed by himself, these voluntarily subjected their magic to wicked supernatural spirits in violation of God's laws.

Sometimes, observed Trithemius, the reputation of a given scholar for engaging in demonic magic depended more on rumor than on hard evidence discovered in the scholar's literary legacy. An example was the erudite tenth-century ecclesiastic Gerbert of Aurillac (subsequently raised to the papacy as Sylvester II), who is said to have enlisted demonic aid in his pursuit of the papal dignity. Lacking such hard evidence, Trithemius noncommittally responded to the Gerbert legend that whereas some historians "have maintained that this man was a necromancer and entered into a pact and covenant with demons," he himself could not confirm this opinion, "for I am only repeating these assertions from others."[89] In other cases of scholars who were held by popular acclaim to truck with the demons in exchange for marvel-working power, however, Trithemius harbored no such doubts, noting that they had foolishly left behind a literary trail of their demonic machinations. Our task now is to call attention to the more specified listing by Trithemius of those whom he considered to be dangerous scholarly purveyors of the Devil's work.

Of the treatises listed in the *Antipalus* as having been composed for the instruction of the demonic arts, thirty-nine titles treating explicit demonic magic and thirty-seven titles treating the implicit form, Trithemius noted that many were spuriously attributed to otherwise highly respectable authors. Heading up the less perilous group of writings, "which, although they hold no manifest communion with demons, nevertheless, by reason of their mode, composition, and use, must be vehemently feared," are tracts ascribed to Hermes Trismegistus, Geber, Ptolemy, Arnaldus of Villanova, Alkindi, and Albertus Magnus. Among these the name of Albertus Magnus in particular elicited a vigorous protest from the abbot's pen, one who, the writer insisted, far from countenancing the kind of wicked magic sometimes advocated under his name, "always condemned books of such a nature."[90] Following up on these texts instructing in the implicit manipulation of demons, Trithemius continued, is a second series of texts, also often erroneously attributed, instructing in the arts of explicit demon conjuration.

The first title revealing itself in Trithemius's list of patently demonic texts is the *Clavicula Solomonis*, the contents of which, Trithemius assured his readers, "the king of Jerusalem never composed, nor, for that matter, even saw."[91] A further work in this category, again of specious attribution, is the Hermetically inspired *Picatrix*, containing "many things that are frivolous, superstitious, and diabolical, . . . even though certain natural things seem to be interspersed."[92] Other writings in this group had also appeared under some of the same names found in the first group, added to which are treatises ascribed to Aristotle, Virgil, Simon Magus, Mohammed, Michael Scot, and Pietro d'Abano. The respectability of many of the authors to which these texts had been attributed,

Trithemius advised, should not deceive us into letting down our guard. For, in keeping with the Devil's commonly observed strategy to clothe his evil ways in the likeness of virtue, the vicious magical writings of those working under diabolical impetus often appeared under the names of virtuous pagan and Christian scholars.

If it is true, as earlier shown, that Trithemius displayed great harshness toward the unlearned witches, even going so far as to counsel their death in extreme cases, it is clear from this section of his *Antipalus* that he displayed equal harshness toward learned sorcerers. For it was the abbot's verdict that those "who invoke demons through the books and the arts of the necromantics, and who conjure them so that they will appear in a circle, in a glass, in a mirror, in the remains of the dead, in a ring, in the hand, in a fingernail, in an image, in water, in fire, or in anything else whatever, procuring through them visions, dreams, revelations, or judgment . . . , are rightfully punished, first temporally by flames, then, after death, eternally tormented."[93] Among the suspect tracts deemed by Trithemius to have earned their authors this extreme penalty appeared under the name of the thirteenth-century astrological physician and "Conciliator," Pietro d'Abano.

D'Abano it was, as earlier pointed out and to be more fully spelled out in the next chapter, who, through a vision of planetary intelligences governing history in cyclic repetitions, provided Trithemius with the cosmic framework for the containment of his magical precepts and operations. Trithemius's appreciation of certain aspects of D'Abano's occult speculations, however, did not mean that he uncritically accepted everything appearing under that author's name. Moreover, setting D'Abano apart from, say, Albertus Magnus, Trithemius was not altogether certain that some of the suspect writings ascribed to him were not of genuine attribution. When touching on D'Abano's name in his ecclesiastical catalogue, it is true, Trithemius adopted a rather noncommittal approach to his subject's magical notoriety, confessing that, with regard to the question of whether D'Abano "effected many marvelous feats through the superstitious art," he was not in a position to render a definite verdict since, "if I recall correctly, I have never read nor seen anything among his treatises."[94] By the time he composed his major demonological tracts, however, coinciding with the composition of the *De septem secundeis* and the beginnings of the

*Steganographia*, Trithemius could no longer plead ignorance of D'Abano's literary output.

It is above all in the *Antipalus* that Trithemius demonstrated his willingness to relinquish his earlier pretext for neutrality and come down resolutely on the side of D'Abano's demonological critics. Of the reasons he gave for doing so, one in particular draws our attention by its resemblance to the kind of criticism also commonly leveled against his own magic. D'Abano, charged Trithemius, "feigns to conjure new demons and spirits into his presence for years, months, days, and particular hours, calling both upon their names and upon their works."[95] Conveniently ignoring the similarity of this accusation to that made against his own handbook of steganography, Trithemius went on to castigate a number of other writings bearing the name of D'Abano in similar language. While conceding that some of these suspect tracts might be spuriously ascribed, Trithemius suggested that others truly issued from D'Abano's hand, thereby making it easier to pass off the various forgeries appearing under his name as genuine articles.

What, we might ask, are the kinds of activities in which those who author and read such "superstitious volumes" are engaged? The answer is—just about anything which seems to require more ability or time than is available to the ordinary human being. Whether prompted by an implicit or explicit manipulation of demons, the magical impulse, as perceived by Trithemius, is conditioned by a desire not only to reach higher than the average human being, but also to arrive there more quickly and efficiently than a conventional discipline will allow. The irony of course is that Trithemius made the identical appeal in his own magic, adding the crucial proviso, of course, that the assisting occult force issue out of a divine rather than demonic origin.

Two of the more prominent pursuits of those professionally attracted to magic, the author of the *Antipalus* noted, are an enhancement of the memory and an improvement of the capacity to acquire and retain new knowledge. Serving as a notable shortcut to the first end is the Lullian *ars combinatoria*, the precepts of which, Trithemius judged, "are partially truthful and partially vain,"[96] and to the second end, the *ars notaria* which, "by the use of characters and a mixture of Greek, Hebrew, and Arabic names . . . dares to promise knowledge of all the arts."[97] Of the pursuits facilitated by the notary art, Trithemius singled out two occultly based ones as being of particular interest to professional magicians. The first is alchemy and the second, astrology, sometimes considered apart from one another and sometimes in mutual interconnection.

A principal motive behind the fad for alchemical investigation in his day, as Trithemius emphasized in a number of anecdotes incorporated into his histories, was simple greed. Yet despite their inflated claims, as he typically pointed out in the morals to these stories, the foolish alchemists inevitably ended in squandering rather than augmenting their wealth. For this reason Trithemius likened alchemy in his Hirsau annals, with a cluster of examples to back himself up, to a "chaste whore" (casta meretrix) who, he chided, "has many lovers but, by deluding them all, is successfully embraced by none among them." Promising to make its foolish suitor wealthy, warned Trithemius, alchemy in the end only impoverishes him, the result being that "from foolish men it makes insane ones; from rich men, paupers; from philosophers, fatuous men; from deceived men, very garrulous deceivers—all who, though they know nothing, profess to know all things, and, although they are very poor, promise to endow their followers with the riches of Croesus." While starting out with the single-minded goal of finding a shortcut to great wealth and power, the abbot wryly mused, the adepts of alchemy find themselves at last to be not only poorer and less powerful than before, but also "full of confusion."[98]

This unflattering portrait of the alchemical art also creeped into the pages of a work by Trithemius where it might be less expected, the Polygraphia, where the writer again vituperated against counterfeit alchemy which, "though she is loved by many, is yet chaste." Further enlarging on the character of this false paramour, he listed among her handmaidens "vanity, fraud, duplicity, deception, sophistry, cupidity, falsity, counterfeit trust, foolishness, indigence, poverty, despair, cowardly flight, ill repute, and mendacity," all of which, he charged, "feign loyalty to their beloved mistress, promise to keep her inviolate, and willingly prostitute themselves in her stead to pecunious, greedy, cupidinous, and foolish curiosity seekers."[99] That so unfavorable a depiction of alchemy would be set forth in a work which itself was at least partially conditioned by the Hermetic traditions out of which many Western alchemists had drawn for an explanation. The motive behind Trithemius's warning against the *casta meretrix*, to be extensively brought out in the following chapter, did not grow out of an abhorrence to alchemy as such, but only to what the abbot considered to be its widespread abuse.

That there might also be an incentive behind alchemical investigation more sinister than mere monetary avarice was also signaled by Trithemius in certain of his writings, suggesting that either implicit or explicit demonic inspiration could well lie behind its follies. Pointing up this more ominous turn to his admonitions against the "chaste whore" are the lives of two of her reputed lovers recounted in the Hirsau annals, Arnaldus of Villanova and Johannes of Rupescissa, who, claimed the writer, combined alchemical with heretical chiliastic speculations. Arnaldus, we are told, after predicting the end of the world in 1356 with the help of the book of Daniel and certain prophetic utterances of Joachim of Fiore, was condemned by the Parisian faculty and went into exile in Sicily to escape the inquisition. The Franciscan friar Rupescissa, a fellow Catalan of Arnaldus, "was induced—or rather, I should say, seduced—by I know not what spirit into abandonment of the Catholic Church and, after predicting certain dreadful things in the guise of a prophet, was cast into prison by the authorities of his order, where a deceitful spirit was found upon his lips."[100] That both Arnaldus and Rupescissa had also been seduced by the art of alchemy made perfect sense for Trithemius, who perceived one kind of diabolical deception to be closely bound up with the other kind. Left dangling in this account of a purportedly alchemical-chiliastic connection, however, is an explanation for what men like Arnaldus and Rupescissa, with their sights on the impending end of the world, possibly stood to gain from any material riches acquired from their arcane investigations. It follows, without being explicitly stated by the abbot, that the alchemical aspirations of magi like Arnaldus and Rupescissa had deeper meaning for them than a desire for mere worldly wealth, the fruits of which would be expected to be obliterated with everything else in the moment of apocalyptic finality.

Trithemius also did not indicate whether Arnaldus and Rupescissa employed astrology as an aid in their prophetic utterances. But since astrology was considered to be an indispensable ministrant to alchemy, we can logically make that inference. Astrological prophecy presented a serious problem for Trithemius. Having himself adopted an astrological conception of the cosmos, most patently illustrated by the system of planetary angels lying behind his *De septem secundeis* and incorporated into his *Steganographia*, Trithemius found it encumbant to distinguish as best he could between legitimate and illegitimate astrology. In keeping with the Christian liberal arts tradition he held nonfatalistic astrology, a branch of astronomy compatible with the dogma of free will, to be a legitimate and chaste handmaiden to orthodox Christian theology. But his Christian convictions would not allow him to extend the same indulgence to fatalistic judicial or divinatory astrology, which contradicts the Catholic dogma of free will. Whereas, he decided, the first form of astrology is thoroughly compatible with the teachings of Christ, the second form, taught to man by the demons, is incompatible with those teachings.

Some chapter headings of the projected *De demonibus* furnish us with a good index of how the prospect of astrological prophecy played on the abbot's fears. Thus, in a chapter warning against divinatory astrology, Trithemius observed that "demons impiously and rashly cooperate" with such superstitious credulity as is manifested in the astrological art.[101] Devoting another chapter "to the many vanities dependent upon astrology,"[102] Trithemius went on to list a long sequence of examples expressly outlawed by the church, fifty-one in all, among which are found necromancy in its narrowly original sense as divination "from the graves and bones of the dead"; pyromancy, or divination from fire; aeromancy, or divination "from the air, winds, and clouds"; hydromancy, or divination from water; geomancy, or divination "from a projection of points upon the earth"; chiromancy, or divination "from the lines of the hands"; and so on down the line, concluding with astromancy or divination "from the study of the stars."[103]

The primary motive behind astrological divination, Trithemius acknowledged in the preface to the *De demonibus*, is a desire to foresee the future, prompting the diviner (*mateomanticus*) to claim, through specially endowed powers of clairvoyance, to discern with perfect clarity of vision "all past, present, and future things." However, as this discourse also establishes, the strictly vaticinal pretensions of the astrological diviner are part and parcel of a broader range of inflated claims by virtue of which he is often summoned to the courts of princes. For in his role as "an imitator and disciple of the Devil," charged Trithemius, the diviner hopes, by gaining the ears of princes and their ministers, to give the demons inroad into their most secret councils. Employing strange-looking symbols and characters said to signify the names of ancestors and the images of planets, Trithemius charged, in truth he is displaying "the characters of the demons, together with the rings, sceptres, crowns, and various other instruments of demonic mathematical calculation."[104] Vested with such demonic aids, attested the abbot, the astrological diviner is so puffed up by a belief in his magical powers that he promises far more than he can possibly deliver.

Among his bombastic vauntings, according to Trithemius, the demonically inspired diviner claims, in addition to more mundane abilities such as discovering hidden treasure and inducing the surrender of a hostile army before the battle is fought, "that he will easily produce and bring into view all things, both those things upon which man is able to ponder and those things which Hell keeps concealed, and furthermore that he will conjure all the shades (manes) and heroes." To lend credence to vain promises like these, Trithemius sarcastically rejoined, is tantamount to declaring that virtually nothing is beyond the reach of the demonically driven diviner. If requested, "he will fly though the air to Arabia, will resuscitate Hercules and Alexander the great from the lower regions, and, if you wish, he will call up to you from the lake of Avernus your own father or mother."[105]

It should be clear from this excursus on the dangers of astrological divination that Trithemius's view of its pretensions goes well beyond a claim to mere prophetic acuity. The divining function is conceived to be but a specialized aspect of a larger profession of learned sorcery—learned, that is, in principles imparted to the sorcerer by the demons. By magical means, according to Trithemius, the diviner-sorcerer, if not actually able, with demonic assistance, to perform such marvels as flying through the air, resuscitating the dead, and predicting the future with thoroughgoing accuracy, is capable of implanting that impression in the minds of his observers with demonic help.

The irony of the abbot's attack on shams like the above, as will be made clearer as this study progresses to its next stage, is highlighted by attacks of others on his own magic for similar pretentiousness. Trithemius's difficulties were compounded by the fact that some of the claims which he criticized in other theorists of the arcana resembled, at least on the surface, his own claims on behalf of steganographical magic. As will shortly be observed in greater detail, that resemblance most certainly was not lost to Bovillus and other like-minded critics of Trithemius's arcane investigations, who assigned the abbot to the same camp of demon conjurors as he assigned others. That Trithemius furthermore sought out the support of princes for his magic, a practice he characterized in others as gauged to insinuate demonic influence in their courts, only confirmed in the minds of many that he was a perpetrator of the very demonic magic he so righteously had condemned.

Given the discomforting resemblance of his magical practices to those of other professional magicians whom he declared to be under the sway of demons, Trithemius was faced with an imposing—according to his critics, even insurmountable—problem to solve. This was how to distinguish occult procedures which he condemned in his demonological writings from other occult procedures sanctioned in his magical writings. Before turning to Trithemius's effort to resolve this dilemma, the subject of the next chapter, an aspect of his demonology still remains to be considered which shares certain ground with his campaign to distinguish good from bad magic. This is how to distinguish those specially vested with the power to expunge demons, the exorcists, from the demon-conjuring sorcerers whose powers they are pledged to counter.

It followed as a logical consequence of Trithemius's demonological train of thought that the exorcist, if he is successfully to rid a given human ambience of demons, must possess a power over the demons superior even to that of the sorcerers themselves. In the latter case, we have seen, it is not always clear whether the sorcerer is doing the bidding of a demon or the demon is doing the bidding of the sorcerer. Theoretically, at least, no such uncertainty can be charged against an exorcist, since his sole obedience is to God and to the church. To the untrained eye, however, which is not easily able to penetrate the veil of outward appearances, the exorcistical power to expunge demons can appear to be indistinguishable from the magical power to conjure demons, leading those unable to appreciate the divine source for the authority of the exorcist to confound him with sorcerer. Trithemius, as we will now see, did not leave a need for this clarification unaddressed. In concluding the present cortant component of his demonology, moreover, we will underscore the point that Trithemius by no means consigned the "miraculous" power of exorcism to the monopoly of clerics. He declared its essential potency to reside in the soul of every virtuous and faithful Christian.

## The Distinction between Sorcery and Exorcism

For Trithemius the exorcistical function of clerics was an extension of their curative function. But while judging clerics to be better trained than most in carrying out these two functions of their profession, remedial and exorcistical, he considered their ecclesiastical office to be an expedient rather than requisite for the cure of souls. Much as every Christian of sufficient purity of soul is capable of acting as his own spiritual physician, so is he capable of acting as his own exorcist. As pointed out in the preface to the *De demonibus*, immunity to demonic corruption is optimally accessible to one who, regardless of his social station, is "touched by the zeal of divine piety" (*tactusque zelo divine pietatis*).[106] Drawing his antidemonic powers from the same divine source as does the officially designated exorcist, the lay as well as the ordained Christian, when armed with the necessary knowledge and talismanic aids, is deemed to be capable of acting as his own expeller of demons. Extensive evidence for this contention is furnished by the abbot's *Antipalus*, which in effect placed in the hands of the laity techniques of demon expulsion that might otherwise be considered to be in the exclusive province of clerical exorcists.

Thus, in relation to a question previously touched on asking why witches and other wickedly disposed individuals are granted powers over demons denied to faithful Christians,[107] Trithemius could argue that the premise on which this question is based is a faulty one. Just as pious Christians have been appropriately armed to defend their sanctity against the corruption of sin, Trithemius reasoned, so have they been appropriately armed to defend their sanctity against the corrupting demons and their human agents, the witches and sorcerers. The identical supposition conditioned his plan for the *De demonibus* and composition of the *Antipalus*.

In some cases of demonic sorcery, as we have seen, there was a fine line in Trithemius's mind between eliminating the evil and

eliminating the evil doer. But the abbot also accepted that, prior to
the application of extreme measures by the courts, less extreme
remedial ones should be applied by the physicians and theologians.
In response he assembled a number of remedial aids, beginning
with some he believed to be authorized by the early Christian
saints. One of the more common exorcistical aids pointed up by
Trithemius is the sprinkling of holy water throughout the house of
the afflicted and in the surrounding yard. Another aid is the so-
called powder of the hermit Pelagius (*pulver Pelagii eremitae*),
described after a recipe invented by a monk of Mallorca and transmitted to the abbot through his teacher Libanius Gallus. As this
recipe goes:

> Obtain as much as you might wish of the substances from the
> candles blessed at Candlemas, from Easter wax and incense,
> from herbs ground into powder on the feast of the Assump-
> tion, from pulverized Offertory bread blessed in the Lord's
> Supper, and from the powdered soil of the cemetery, adding to
> these holy water and salt! Put the powdery substances through
> a sieve until they are finely ground! Then place the mixture
> made from these powders and from the wax into warm water
> which has been blessed until all the constituents are com-
> bined as thoroughly as possible into a single mass! After this,
> standing above the result, proceed to utter the Lord's Prayer,
> the Ave Maria, and the Apostles' Creed.[108]

The purpose of this complicated operation, we are told, is to obtain
the crystallization of "tiny crosses" (*cruces parvulas*), which are
then to be scattered, together with holy water, in the house, yard
and stables.[109]

If these exorcistical aids are not sufficient to do the job,
Trithemius also prescribed another for possible use, the "exorcist's
bath." As this antidemonic procedure is specified: "Let the water be
fresh and clean from a river, and let all those things which are
necessary be held in the hand, that is, a small container filled with
soil from the cemetery after it has been blessed, ashes sanctified in
the Church at the conclusion of fasting, wax bessed at Candlemas,"
and so on for several pages reminiscent of the "powder of Pelagius."
Interweaving this exposition are many prayers and chants, accom-

panied by the admonition that the exorcist not allow to be mingled with them "anything of a superstitious, vain, or suspect nature, since the demons are frequently attracted by such things."[110]

Of the possible antidotes against witchcraft and sorcery, however, Trithemius upheld as the one holding the greatest chance of success, indicated in a chapter heading of the *De demonibus*, "a right faith, holy behavior, and certain trust."[111] For, as Trithemius reasoned, all physical aids to the exorcistical function are necessarily in vain unless employed in conjunction with spiritual ones. "It should be noted," wrote Trithemius in his *Octo quaestiones* with the officially designated ecclesiastical exorcists in mind, "that the demons, together with their maleficent human confederates, are more readily repelled by one priest than by another, and also in one time and place more readily than in another time and place."[112] The same rule of course also applies to those under the regimen of the exorcists, with efficacy in the exorcistical function depending on the spiritual status of victim and exorcist alike. Needless to say, the appropriation of exorcistical powers by the demonically assailed victim does not alter this basic talismanic principle.

Speaking specifically to the problem of afflictions visited by witches in the preface to the second book of his *Antipalus*, Trithemius designated, on one hand, "three classes of men who, with God's protection, cannot be injured by the mischief of these women," and, on the other hand, "three classes who are very frequently and easily injured."[113] Treating the latter group first, Trithemius, as we would expect, considered those most vulnerable to the maleficence of witches to have placed themselves in this position by their sinful behavior, thereby voluntarily drawing demonic afflictions upon themselves. At first place in this list are those who, "in despising the sacraments and the keys of the Church, persist for a long time in their mortal sins without seeking true penitence"; in second place, those who, "in spending all their time with their lust and voluptuous pleasures rather than with God and being especially wont to partake of the venereal act, transgress the laws and just measure of nature"; and in third place, those who, "neglecting and underestimating the blessed instruments of the Church, do not make good use of their presence or honor their institution."[114] Over and against these wretched victims of sorcery are posed three other classes of men who have learned how properly to protect themselves against malefic vexation by constructing an insulative spiritual barrier around themselves.

The first class of those optimally impervious to sorcery, according to Trithemius, is comprised of "judges and ministers with public jurisdiction who, out of their love of God and of justice, pursue these women, take them into their custody, punish them, and exterminate them." Having specifically been charged by God with the commission of seeking out witches and passing sentence upon them, the official inquisitors are also vested with the power to prevail over the witches and to compel them into fearful submission. A second class of men deemed by Trithemius to be maximally fortified against the afflictions of sorcery are the officially designated exorcists of the church, "good and faithful Christians who, as ministers venerating the rites of the church, legitimately employ benedictions and exorcisms against the attacks of the demons, at the same time always guarding over their own consciences to keep them free from mortal sin." Finally, a third class of Christians optimally immune to malefic vexation is made up of those who are extraordinarily pious and holy, of those, that is to say, "who by a particular perogative of divine compassion are in various ways protected and directed, inwardly and outwardly, by the holy angels."[115]

Concerning the functions officially assigned by the church to the first two groups indicated above, the inquisitors and exorcists, Trithemius's emphasis, we have established, was on banishing the demons before the more extreme measures of the inquisitors were necessary. Moreover, as stated in the *Antipalus*, Trithemius viewed the mandate of the exorcists to be not only of removing demonic affliction once it occurred, but also of assisting prospective victims in building up their defenses against the demons before affliction could be visited upon them.[116] In setting forth this prophylactic charge of the exorcist, the abbot with good reason underscored fidelity and holiness as crucial features of his character. For the exorcists, he judged, act as more than merely passive inhibitors to demonic assaults. In fulfilling their vocation they necessarily assume the highly active role of conjuring and compelling demons in a manner not easily distinguishable from that of the witches and sorcerers themselves.

The decisively probatory test of discrimination between sorcerer and exorcist, Trithemius consistently held throughout his demonological writings, lies in the stark contrast between their spiritual characters. Declaring demon-conjuring sorcerers to be inveterately corrupt, Trithemius saw a very different case to hold for the demon-expelling exorcists. Concerning their virtues, exhorted the abbot, "it is paramount that the priest and minister of Christ be completely faithful, chaste, pure in conscience, neither ridiculing nor despising the operation he is about to perform, but honoring and constantly advancing it in the faith of the universal Church."[117] A contemporary illustration of the qualities essential to the exorcistical task, whose exploits were drawn out to great length by Trithemius in his Hirsau annals, was a certain abbot Adam who had succeeded in clearing two different convents of demons in Trithemius's own time (1499).[118] How, the reader of the abbot's histories might well ask, is an exorcist like the abbot Adam to be distinguished from sorcerers similarly endowed with powers to command demons? This possible confusion between sorcerer and exorcist is one that Trithemius endeavored to unravel for the emperor Maximilian in the *Octo quaestiones*.

The bare power to conjure and compel a demon, Trithemius assured Maximilian, does not in itself consign one in whom it is vested to the ranks of the sorcerers. For it can be that his power derives from a divine source lying at the opposite pole from demonic evil, namely, the Holy Spirit, the institutional manifestation of which is the Christian church. More specifically, the power to compel demons can issue from a said person's rare piety, from his ecclesiastical office, or from a combination of piety and office. In the early church the Christian saints, commissioned "to crush under their heels the head of the ancient serpent," were endowed with the ability to cast out demons in emulation of their master Christ. With the institutionalization of the church this commission became formalized in rites of exorcism performed by clerics expressly mandated for this function. To these "has been conceded by the approved authorities of the church of God that, once they have been invested with prerogatives of the ministry, they are permitted to expel demons from the bodies of men."[119]

The therapeutical office of the cleric, Trithemius observed, is distinguished from that of the corporeal physician by placing its focus on the spiritual causes of such malaise as is commonly associated with demoniacs. But Trithemius also let it be known that, since spiritual infirmity induced by demons also often triggers accompanying physical infirmity, the exorcistical function must take into account material along with spiritual remedies. "It is to be understood," Trithemius exclaimed in the same regard in his *Antipalus*, "that natural diseases and illnesses sometimes coincide with sorceries." It logically followed that the successful exorcist "is necessarily skilled in both kinds of medicine, corporeal and spiritual."[120]

Trithemius's concession that exorcism entails expertise in corporeal along with spiritual matters sprang from more than a desire on his part to alleviate the physiological consequences of demonic possession. It also sprang from his understanding that the exorcist should be able to distinguish supernatural causes of affliction from natural ones. Thus, in a concluding summary of twelve principal rules by which "the operator of this medicine" can successfully perform his commission, Trithemius listed as his seventh rule that, before the exorcist begins his procedures, he should first carefully assess the symptoms of the afflicted victim "so that he may know whether the infirmity is from sorcery or from a debilitation of nature." In this regard Trithemius took to task inexperienced or overly zealous inquisitors who, in their rush to judgment in such matters, "maintain that all the diseases over which they have been consulted have proceeded from sorcery."[121]

Unfortunately, Trithemius's own failure to establish a clear-cut criterion for assessing when natural infirmity is present independently of demonic possession and when it is the effect of a demonic cause fed into the very diagnostic confusion he professed a desire to clarify. A particular bone of contention in this regard centered on the subject of humoral melancholy, viewed by Trithemius, in keeping with its well-known demonological reputation as "the Devil's bath" (*balneum diaboli*), as an especially serviceable way into the world for the demons. According to this demonological notion seconded by Trithemius, the demons, drawn to melancholy, are in turn able to enlist melancholy to the end that they might more effectively alter the imaginations of their victims, thereby deceiving them into mistaking their internal phantasms for external reality.[122] It is just such a muddling of two separate explanations for eccentric behavior that lay at the crux of the witch persecutions, the principal movers of which condemned to the stake many diagnosed by the physicians as natural melancholics.

The dual office of the exorcist as, simultaneously, spiritual and corporeal physician, Trithemius determined in his role as ecclesiastical historian, can be traced to the very origins of the Christian Church, with Christ and His apostles, who "cured many sick men by the words of holy prayer," serving as emulative models. "At one time in the primitive Church," Trithemius observed in the *Antipalus*, "not only the sorceries of demons, but also any other infirmities whatever issuing from them as their effect were cured by the exorcisms and prayers of the ministers of Christ." From that time to the present "the priests and holy men of Christ, by their exorcisms and prayers, have cured many people not only from demonic enchantment, but also from other infirmities of the body."[123] For this reason, Trithemius continued with an eye to some of the titles he undoubtedly had assembled on his own bookshelves, we should not be surprised to find in the libraries of the ancient cloisters numerous texts concerned with physiological together with spiritual remedies for bewitchment. The exorcistical function, he insisted, is aided by access to many writings authored "by the physicians and wise men" (*per physicos et sapientes*), for only by first eliminating all possible natural explanations can the exorcist be assured that a given demonic supernatural explanation is the true one.[124]

Given this dual facility of the exorcist—as corporeal and spiritual physician to the demoniac, Trithemius recognized a danger in the application of the exorcistical method which he sought to forestall. If the classical ideal of optimal health can be said to be summarized in the famous Juvenalian motto "a sound mind in a sound body" (*mens sana in corpore sano*), a corresponding motto, filtered through the ascetic sieve of the Christian Middle Ages, is epitomized by Trithemius in the slogan "a pure soul in a sound body" (*anima pura in corpore sano*). But whereas the Juvenalian motto is premised on the presumption of equilibrium between mind and body, Trithemius's conception of the exorcist's duties belies a presumption that a pure soul does not always coincide with a healthy body. In this regard Trithemius expressly cautioned the exorcist to take care "that the health of the body is sought in such a way that the integrity of Christian purity is not corrupted."[125]

The temptation to seek the cure for a physical infirmity even when a prescribed medicinal regimen might threaten the spiritual health of the patient also lay behind another caveat Trithemius incorporated into his demonological writings. In a chapter heading of his *De demonibus* Trithemius inquired "whether it is permitted to repel sorcery by means of sorcery?"[126] Though he never found the opportunity to answer this question in the work at hand, references to the same query in his completed demonological writings clearly reveal what it would have been.

Thus, in a digression on this subject in the *Octo quaestiones*, Trithemius charged that those who employ sorcery to cure the malefic effects of sorcery "prefer the health of the mortal flesh to God, and seek their safety, not from Christ, but from the Devil and from his ministry." In making this choice they in effect show that they "prefer living in a state of [corporeal] health in the name of the Devil, even if unhappily, to enduring a modicum of suffering here on earth out of a love of Christ, and afterwards exulting with Him forever."[127] Reiterating this position in the *Antipalus*, Trithemius counseled therein that "infirmities should never be cured by the invocation of demons." On the contrary, inasmuch as only good can successfully counteract evil, "the ecclesiastical remedies must first be summoned, that is, those of penitence and the emendation of sins, followed by exorcism, prayers, devotional exercises, and the support beseeched from the saints." While it is granted to the exorcist, if necessary, to conjoin natural remedies to his spiritual ones, this is always to be done "without the bewitchment of demons or superstition contrary to the rites of the Church."[128] To sum up: "Sorcery is never licitly cured unless its cause is removed, which is sin."[129]

Trithemius's theory of exorcistical remedies is based on a concept of spiritual correspondences. "Between contraries or dissimilar things," he exhorted in this regard, "there can be no familiarity, but only continuous repugnance and hatred." Consequently, since great disparity and antipathy exists between a good Christian and a wicked demon, "there can likewise be no expression of trust of one toward the other, nor a mutual concurrence in the operation of marvels."[130] But the lack of intimate familiarity with demons, Trithemius emphasized, does not mean that a pious Christian lacks the capability of dominating over them. Among the righteous, the privilege of command over the demons is most conspicuously available to one who, at the opposite extreme from those having similitude to the demons, reveals his similitude to the holy angels. The force of this command, moreover, is greatly strengthened when a Christian combines likeness to the angels with an official ecclesiastical designation as exorcist.

This aspect of Trithemius's demonology throws valuable light on what he was about in his own magic. For while expressly rejecting demonic magic out-of-hand, even showing a willingness to send its perpetrators to the stake, he implied at the same time that angels, with whom pious Christians seek both approximation and similarity, can legitimately be invoked to produce results foreclosed to demons. "Whoever, then, will become a true worshiper of God and similar to the holy angels," Trithemius maintained in support of this point,"is able to effect many marvels in the presence of those who entreat them."[131] One such marvel consists of the rite of exorcism. Accordingly, reasoned Trithemius, it is not through the power of the demons that men are able to perform their supernatural marvels, including the marvel of exorcism, but through the angels whom they resemble. Or rather, more accurately put, it is the omnipotent Creator, working through angelic mediators, who is the source of genuine exorcism. "Inasmuch as God is more powerful, by infinite degrees, than all the demons," as Trithemius pressed home this point, "His virtue is greater for saving men than is the impiety of the demons in doing them injury."[132]

Given his appeal to possible angelic help in the practice of exorcism, Trithemius left his readers in a hermeneutic quandary which he did not very successfully clear up. It is the same quandary which, as we will shortly see, played a key role in obfuscating the intentions of his patently angel-driven art of steganography. Not every spirit found in one's proximity, Trithemius pointed out, is necessarily of the evil demoniacal variety. "For accompanying us are more good angels by whose virtues we can be helped," he averred, "than there are demons accompanying witches whose insolence is able to molest us."[133] But what was lacking in Trithemius's analysis was a practical criterion for distinguishing between the two kinds of spirit, angelic and demonic. Failing as demonologist to work out a clear-cut technique for differentiating the two types of supernatural spirit, which would thereby permit him to expel one with the help of the other, Trithemius carried the same failure into his steganographical magic, where he similarly obscured the distinction between good angels and wicked demons. His inability to come to terms with this daunting task, we will now observe at closer range, would seal his subsequent notoriety as a demonic magician in the very mode of those he so acridly assailed in his demonological writings.

# Chapter 4

## The Occult Vision

### The Making of the Magical Legend

"I am currently holding in my hands a great work," Trithemius boastfully wrote to his Carmelite friend Arnold Bostius in 1499, "which, if ever published, will be marveled at by the entire world." Having conceived the said writing in four books, of which he had completed two and part of a third, Trithemius apprised his correspondent that it would "teach very profound, marvelous, and incredible things to all who are ignorant of them, things which have never been heard of by this age."[1] Intended for the eyes of Bostius alone, the 1499 letter announcing the birth of steganography, as earlier noted,[2] arrived at the Carmelite's Ghent cloister to find its addressee no longer among the living. Confiscated and circulated by the astonished prior of the cloister against the abbot's wishes, this letter initiated the legend of Trithemius as a demonic magician.

What, then, are some of the "very profound, marvelous, and incredible things" which Trithemius claimed to be able to effect by his steganographical art? The first book, he informed Bostius, "contains over a hundred ways of secretly writing whatever you wish without any suspicion, without the transposition of letters, and

85

without fear of detection." If Bostius were to receive a message from him composed according to its instructions, "there is no man in the world who, by his natural industry alone, can know or suspect what might be contained in my letter, but only he who is conversant with the art, taught to him either directly by myself or by one whom I have taught." The second book in turn reveals how to transmit a message just as secretly, but this time over great distances, sometimes exceeding a hundred miles, "without words, without writings, and even without signs." Using this phenomenal technique Bostius would be able to communicate with a far-removed acquaintance, even one who was a prisoner locked away in a dark dungeon, "no matter how closely he is guarded, even if he is held three miles below the ground." The third book, Bostius was further apprised, demonstrates "how to teach an uneducated man in only two hours, though he be knowledgeable only in his mother tongue and have never known a word of Latin, to write, read, and comprehend whatever he is meditating upon in Latin, and this with sufficient elegance and skill that those who see his writing will praise his words and understand his Latin composition." Finally, the fourth and last book instructs how a thought can be clandestinely transmitted to one who is in the company of others. No matter in what activity either party to the communication might be engaged—conversing, eating, singing, or the like—the sender, "without words, without nodding signs, . . . even with the eyes closed," can conjure a secret thought and have it covertly transferred to the mind of another.[3]

Having concluded that he had made a mistake in the Bostius affair by dispatching the announcement of his magical invention in an overt form, as distinct from the covert form called for by his cryptological method (necessarily the case, since he had not had an opportunity to indoctrinate Bostius in its principles), Trithemius resolved thereafter to require the personal presence of anyone who might wish to receive knowledge about his occult investigations. Illustrating this decision is a letter from Trithemius to a friend who had already spent some time under the abbot's magical tutelage, the Dutch canon regular Cornelius Aurelius (d. ca. 1500). Thus, soon after the Bostius misadventure Aurelius thanked Trithemius for having "kindly unlocked to me, the humblest of your friends, all the arcana of your heart and the secrets of things (*omnia cordis tui arcana rerumque secreta*), which I hold dearer than all the riches of Croesus," and indicated a desire to resume his occult studies under Trithemius's instruction.[4] Chastened by his recent experience in the matter of the Bostius letter, Trithemius consented to Aurelius's petition, but attached to that consent a condition. If Aurelius were serious in recommencing instruction in the magical arts, Trithemius wrote from Sponheim, "it is necessary that you be personally present here."[5] Only after the student was proficient in the secret language of steganography could the risk be taken of translating private oral into written instructions.

As Trithemius shortly learned, however, as brought home to him by the subsequent visit of Bovillus to his Sponheim cloister, this method of preserving his good reputation had its limits. Declaring to a correspondent and mutual friend of the two men, Germanus de Ganay, that he had arrived at Sponheim expecting to engage in many hours of profound philosophical discussion with his host, the writer complained that instead, to his dismay, he found that he was dealing with "a magician who is not in the least degree distinguished in philosophy."[6] If the unforeseen disclosure of the Bostius letter can be said to have delivered the first serious blow to Trithemius's magical reputation, a second severe blow was inflicted by the widely publicized negative reaction of Bovillus.

No sooner did he meet with Trithemius in the abbot's Sponheim cloister, Bovillus informed Ganay, than his host "proposed that I peruse his *Steganographia*, which, so he claimed, was ordinarily made available only to very few men." Acceding to this request, Bovillus expressed shock at what he therein beheld, and indignantly cast it aside "inasmuch as such wonders and unaccustomed names of spirits (should I not rather say demons?) began to terrify me." His suspicion that the writing under consideration had exceeded the lawful bounds of speculation was whetted by the strange nomenclature in which it was cast, for its names, Bovillus complained to Ganay, "are either Arabic, Hebraic, Aramaic, or Greek, yet there are few, indeed, almost no Latin ones; moreover, countless characters are used by means of which each conjuration is singularly designated." While noting that the contents of the work were interspersed with "very holy and pious prayers," Bovillus had determined the piety signified thereby to be insincere, and the tears of devoutness provoked by its prayers, "crocodile tears." Far from embracing heavenly wisdom as it claimed, the tract at issue "undertakes to exchange divine wisdom for wisdom which is worldly and vain."[7]

Nor did Bovillus leave his ungenial response to Trithemius's tract in generalities. Upon examination of the text, he informed his correspondent, he discovered that its author "designates the names of the spirits, arranges their conjurations, and inscribes the character of each in its turn; afterwards he distinguishes their figures one from the other, from which, as long as necessity dictates, he can extract and voice the appropriate names of the spirits in accordance with each of the conjurations." The spirits are said to comprise four main types: emperors, dukes, counts, and servants. "Much as the winds are divided by the philosophers," scoffed Bovillus, the heavens are divided up by Trithemius into twelve regions ruled by emperors; to each emperor is assigned, "so I think, thirty or forty dukes"; to the dukes, a larger number of counts; and to the counts a still larger number of servants.[8]

As for how all of this can be expected to expedite the art of secret communication, Bovillus elicited the following sequence of steps from the suspect writing. When the steganographer "wishes to reveal his counsels (which he calls his secrets) to a distant friend," so Bovillus gleaned from its pages, "he writes, instead of the usual letter, a certain prayer which, being disguised with sanctity and devotion, he impresses with the character of one of the twelve emperors." Upon receiving the cryptic yield of this activity, the friend, having first been instructed in the principles of the art, "opens it and immediately looks to the bottom of the letter to take note of the character corresponding to the emperor." If, say, the said emperor is located in the East, the recipient of the secret messages "turns toward the east, holds the letter open in the direction of that region, and then searches in his books for the appropriate conjurations which compels its prince to send him someone among his servants."[9]

In adopting such unlawful practices as the aforementioned, charged Bovillus, Trithemius demonstrated that he stood far closer to an ancient demon-conjuring pagan like Zoroaster than to the demon-shunning Christian saints. But even putting aside the question of demonic participation in the abbot's magic, Bovillus was astounded by the absurdly inflated claims made by the tract. One of these was that Trithemius could quickly teach a foreign tongue to an unlettered man and, just as quickly, cause him to forget all that was learned, and another, that he could magically augment one's riches through "that inane and exceedingly fallacious consumer of wealth, alchemy."[10] Implied in this latter accusation was that Trithemius believed himself to have stumbled upon an occult means for financing his vast Sponheim library and other expensive appurtenances of his cloister.

To his chagrin, then, Trithemius discovered that his decision to initiate Bovillus into the secrets of his magic had been a serious blunder. It was not, however, an entirely naïve presumption on the abbot's part that had led him to miscalculate Bovillus's response to his magic, since Bovillus to that point had given Trithemius good cause to trust that he would act as a sympathetic witness to the abbot's occult ideas. For one thing, Trithemius prefaced the *Steganographia* with a theoretical defense of the occult arts not far removed from that set forth by Bovillus's self-acknowledged master Lefèvre d'Etaples in his unpublished *De magia naturali* (1493). And for another, Bovillus himself previously had shown some sympathy toward ancient magic, having earlier sung the praises of the occult-minded Druids, along with Zoroaster, Hermes Trismegistus, and Pythagoras, as gentile forerunners of the theology of Christ.[11] It was evidently this shared interest in the arcane wisdom of antiquity that had prompted Trithemius into making his invitation to Bovillus in the first place, and misled him into expecting from his guest a sympathetic response to his pioneering cryptographical venture.

Further complicating our understanding of what took place at Sponheim during the visit of Bovillus was the considerable delay of the Frenchman's reaction. But even if the 1509 dating of the Ganay letter is incorrect, as only an examination of its missing handwritten original could prove,[12] evidence is at hand that Bovillus was less openly hostile to Trithemius during the course of their meeting than he conveyed to Ganay. For in a letter to Bovillus written soon after his departure, Trithemius referred amiably to their recent time together in which they had conversed, among other subjects, upon "very profound questions of the Holy Scripture."[13] And about the same time Trithemius received a letter from Ganay noting that, upon his return to France, Bovillus "has made frequent mention of the fact that he has come to look with envious eyes upon your superior powers and, if I may confess the truth, admitted that he has become a beholder and admirer of your virtues."[14] These epistolary testimonies to Bovillus's Sponheim visit suggest that either the principal participants were unabashed hypocrites or that the indignation of Bovillus jelled only much later.

In any event Bovillus's letter to Ganay, instead of deterring Trithemius in his commitment to a magical program as might be expected, rather had the contrary effect of motivating him to enlarge upon and sharpen its theoretical rationalization. Notable testimonies to this response are found in a defense of his magic inserted by Trithemius into his autobiographical *Nepiachus*; extensive prefaces to his major cryptographic texts, the *Steganographia* and *Polygraphia*, the major ideas of which are reiterated in further prefaces to their keys; and lengthy explicative epistles to selected correspondents. Trithemius's histories in turn, as in the corresponding case of demonology, furnished a number of anecdotal illustrations for fleshing out his occult principles on the stage of everyday life.

As we will now come to see with the help of these writings, the apologetic strategy adopted by Trithemius went beyond arguing for a mere toleration of magic by Christians, going a crucial further step, after removing magic from the exclusive domain of the demons, of putting it to the service of Christian theology. At the crux of the issue raised by Trithemius in this matter, it will be established, lay a resolve not only to legitimize magic, but to celebrate magic, on the model of mystical theology, as a suitable vehicle for moving the soul from earth to Heaven. "Mystical theology," Trithemius once wrote, "can be persuaded by man, but is not able to be taught in any way except under the auspices of divine erudition."[15] And just as mystical theology had to be squared in the abbot's mind with the tenets of his Catholic teachings, so did magical theology which is its derivative. In this more sublime sense, Trithemius determined, the essential affiliation of magic is not with the secular arts and sciences, but with the religious quest for God.

As suggested by the heading of the special segment addressed to this subject in the *Nepiachus*, "an apology on behalf of myself against those who believe that I have given myself over to the magical arts" (*apologia pro memetipso contra eos, qui me magicis artibus operam dedisse existimant*),[16] Trithemius felt called upon not only to defend the magical arts in principle, but also to defend his personal reputation as their advocate. Accordingly, our examination of Trithemius's magical apologetic will display two distinctly separate but interconnected features. The first feature pertains to his campaign to uphold the integrity of his personal reputation, and the second feature, to his campaign to uphold the reputation of the magical arts through an articulation of their theoretical underpinnings.

While not always easy to disentangle, these two features of Trithemius's magical apologetic are still distinguishable in the same way that the principles of any abstract science are distinguishable from the character of the person enunciating them. In the case of Trithemian magic, however, setting it apart from the secular sciences, these distinguishable features are united in the presupposition of its advocate that the vindication of a human art is fundamentally bound up with the spiritual worth of the person doing the vindicating. Pleading for this basic principle of his magical theology to be applied to select forerunners of the past, among whom he singled out his fellow German Albertus Magnus for special mention, Trithemius likewise pleaded for it to be applied to himself.

### The Personal Defense

In the not too distant past, lamented Trithemius, lived a very learned man notable for his pursuance of "natural magic, that is, the wisdom of nature (*magiam naturalem, id est, sapientiam naturae*), who, by reason of his marvelous knowledge of occult natural virtues, has fallen into suspicion among the vulgar until the present day."[17] The figure to which Trithemius referred was Albertus Magnus, who shared with the abbot underlying intellectual as well as geographical ground for the meeting of their minds. It is not by chance that this plaint appears in the abbot's autobiographical *Nepiachus*. For Trithemius discovered in Albertus a kind of alter ego whose occult speculations directly foreshadowed his own magical theory.

The function of Albertus as a stand-in for Trithemius in this regard was highlighted even before the abbot set pen to paper in the *Nepiachus*, being earlier alluded to in his miscarried 1499 letter to Bostius.[18] It again cropped up in the abbot's catalogue of illustrious Germans, where, with the same sense of righteous indignation as though it were he himself being so accused (as indeed it was), Trithemius avowed that if Albertus "in any way effected the marvels attributed to him, I am satisfied that these were accomplished, not by sorcery, but by hidden powers of nature which had been made accessible to him."[19] Still again, this time in the Hirsau annals, Trithemius commemorated Albertus's death in 1280 with the observation that "many things which appear stupendous to the ignorant are able to come into being through naturally occult causes, the perceptions of which throw into stupor those spectators who are of weak judgment."[20]

But while looking with favor upon Albertus's arcane investigations, Trithemius admittedly did not condone every writing appearing under his name. As we have also seen him arguing in his *Antipalus*, some superstitious works were currently circulating under the name of Albertus which, the abbot confessed, should remain outside the purview of all good Christians. But these, he hastened to add, had spuriously been attributed to Albertus by wicked men who had sought to lend his name to illicit magical operations.[21] Yet laying aside these counterfeit works ascribed by popular acclaim to Albertus, Trithemius was still faced with a potentially embarrassing feature of the Dominican friar's authenticated reputation that also necessarily redounded upon his own, namely, Albertus's familiarity with many of the writings he condemned.

Though accepting that Albertus "sometimes cursorily read the books of necromancers and [demonic] magicians," Trithemius vigorously denied that, in his own magical theories and operations, "he made use of them or held trust in them." Albertus consulted such despicable works, Trithemius was certain, "not to imitate their teachings, but so he could know by what method they might be refuted." In following this procedure Albertus no more sinned than did St. Augustine when he read the works of the heretics so that he might more effectively counteract them. Albertus read the tracts of the illicit magicians, Trithemius determined, "not to become adept by their reading, or to effect a result, or to enjoy them, . . . but to be able to disprove, at their foundation, the foolish and perfidious claims of those ignorant men who believe such things."[22]

His considerable admiration for Albertus aside, however, it appears that Trithemius was much more taken with the portrait of Albertus delivered to him by posterity than with any specific magical doctrine to be discovered in the learned scholastic's actual writings. The main value of Albertus for Trithemius did not consist of a transfer of theoretical principles from one to the other, but rather of a transfer of an aura of Christian respectability surrounding Albertan magic. As will now be brought out, the personal defense of Albertus by Trithemius was but a prelude to that of his own. For Trithemius understood, in his own case as in that of Albertus, that if he were to succeed in persuading his readers of the worth of his occult theory, he first needed to persuade them of his own personal worth as a Heaven-bound Christian.

"I confess," half-boastingly conceded Trithemius in his *Nepiachus*, "that my love for study and books has been immoderate," following up this admission with the even more startling one that "whatever in the world is knowable, I always desired to know" (*quicquidem in mundo scibile est, scire semper cupiebam*). Not by chance, this acknowledgment of bibliomania by Trithemius, and its role in his drive for what since has popularly come to be known as a "Faustian" will to learning, shortly precedes the abbot's apology of magic. At the same time Trithemius was also compelled to acknowledge, in connection with his insatiable drive for knowledge, "that, as God well knows, there are certain men who unfairly calumniate me, maintaining that I have debased my mind by the evil arts and by the vanities of necromancy—nay, should I rather say, by acts of sorcery (*ne dicam maleficiis*)."[23]

Trithemius was not oblivious to the widely circulated rumor, "I know not for what reasons, that I am familiar with, and have performed, marvelous things by arts with which I am not acquainted, and with the help of spirits which I did not know existed." If the ugly gossip about his powers were to be believed, with the help of demons he had managed, among other marvelous feats, to raise the dead, recover stolen goods, and accurately predict the future. Standing in refutation of these charges was not only Trithemius's word, but his entire life. With God as his witness, he vowed, "neither in my will nor in my power has there ever existed the practice or display of such fatuous deeds." As anyone who knew him well could testify, he was not only a faithful Christian solidly steeped in Catholic orthodoxy, but also "a priest and servant of Jesus Christ, one who has never held commerce with the wicked arts nor taken part in the society of, or made a pact with, the demons." If anything of novelty were ever to be detected in either his writings or deeds to provoke suspicion, it was accomplished by virtue, "not of the works of demons, but of nature, of industry, and of permissible philosophical speculation." Concerning these unfounded rumors "it remains for me only to console myself by my conscience, which knows itself to be blameless of the contagion of these iniquities."[24]

Revealing a similarly defensive tone were certain comments placed in a 1503 letter to Count Johannes of Westerburg urging his correspondent to be on his guard against any rumors reaching him about the abbot and, in the face of them, "to defend my reputation against the brazen audacity of my enemies." The honor of the writer had been unjustly sullied by scandalous gossip, he informed Westerburg, because "among the general populace there are very few to be found who understand the mysteries of the occult natural arts" (*paucissimi . . . mysteria occultarum adinventionum naturalium intelligant*). The writer could pinpoint the initial impulse leading to these false rumors—the Bostius letter. His notoriety was a direct result of a misunderstanding of this letter by ignorant men who were not meant to be exposed to its precious contents. If Bostius had lived to receive the ill-fated letter himself, or if the prior of his cloister had discreetly retained the letter in confidence as he should have, "there would not now be circulating among your acquaintances such a report about me concerning my marvels."[25]

Concerning such damaging rumors Trithemius reassured the count that "there lies nothing within me beyond the limits of nature—save our Christian faith, which Grace, not nature, has given." While not denying that his magical studies sometimes led him to dip into certain suspect or patently illicit writings along with the legitimate ones necessary to his art, he did so, he insisted, with no more culpability than Albertus Magnus before him who "read without guilt many superstitious books authored by depraved men, yet was himself neither depraved nor superstitious." Though, like Albertus, Trithemius was painfully aware of "how many vain, ridiculous, and abominable fabrications are superstitiously concealed in books of magic," and that such volumes sometimes contain "things concerning the conjurations of demons," he also shared an understanding with Albertus that one can only successfully refute that which he understands. The writer only asked that the same rule applying to Albertus be also applied to himself: "Wickedness is not the knowledge of evil, but its practice."[26] Inasmuch as "natural magic, which once rested on the principles of nature in their pure simplicity, had of late become mingled with so many impurities and deceptions," it logically follows that "no one, unless he is well instructed in [magic of] both kinds, is able to tell one from the other."[27]

The personal sense of indignation revealed in writings like the above also came to the surface within the text of the controversial *Steganographia* itself, the preface of which spiritedly rebutted the rumor "that I am a necromancer and [black] magician, or that I have contracted a pact with demons or that I have made use of . . . superstition." In developing this point Trithemius moved back and forth between pleading his Christian righteousness and attacking his critics for their ignorance. At one extreme he reminded his derogators that "I am a Christian who, of my free will, have devoted myself to the monastic way of life," reassuring them in this regard that "I do not desire to live and dwell otherwise than befits a true Christian and a monk committed to the rule of blessed father Benedict." At the other extreme, however, he accused those slandering his good name of criticizing that which they did not understand, reminding them that just as "a judge shows himself to be rash who passes sentence concerning something before he has learned the truth of its cause," by the same token a judge of the art of steganography "should first learn this art and only afterwards pass sentence upon it." Deserving of blame, he retorted, was not his wholly licit and highly useful technique for secret communication, but rather "your own obtuse minds."[28]

Apparently, however, as conceded by the abbot in a 1506 letter to the French scholar Johannes Capellarius, the controversy stirred up by such "obtuse minds" was enough to throw a serious roadblock in his way to the completion and publication of the *Steganographia*. Informing Capellarius of his discovery at last of needed peace and leisure for study at Würzburg, Trithemius presented his correspondent with a list of writings he had found time to complete in his new surroundings. Among the titles included in this list, suggesting his retreat to what he considered to be a safer version of cryptography than steganography, was "a great work which I have entitled *Polygraphia*, in six books."[29] Noticeably absent from the list, however, was the earlier cryptographic writing with which the correspondent had already been made familiar, passages of which the abbot had copied out for Capellarius the year before and the finished portions of which he had shown him when the two men met during an assembly of the German princes at Cologne.

"I don't know if I will ever publish my *Steganographia* which you saw in Cologne," Trithemius fretted to Capellarius, submitting three main reasons for this reluctant decision. First, he worried that the work might be abused, "inasmuch as wicked men may use our inventions for wicked ends just as good men may use them for good ends"; second, he had expended great labor on the project, yet with "a return of small reward"; and third, the work in question had provoked adverse opinions by "ignorant and vulgar men, since whatever they don't understand they attribute to the wicked arts." The last-cited reason in particular for leaving the tract stillborn called for elaboration. For maliciously disposed critics of his art, complained the abbot, "assert that I have raised the dead, that I have called up demons from the depths, that I have predicted the future, and that I have escorted brigands and joined thieves with my charms," slanders to which Capellarius should give no credence. "All of these charges," the writer avouched, "are fabrications and outright lies which I not only have never carried out, but have not even contemplated." Though Trithemius admittedly did not deny that "I have read many things of the magicians," he had done so, he assured Capellarius, "not so that I might imitate them, but so that I might confound them by now and then refuting their worst superstitions."[30]

Echoing many of the concerns expressed in the above-stated letter to Capellarius is the dedicatory preface to the *Polygraphia*, addressed to Emperor Maximilian, demonstrating that the rancorous barbs of his critics continued to vex him well after he had shifted his attention to a less controversial method of cryptic communication. Recounting therein the episode of the misappropriated letter to Bostius instigating the slanderous campaign against his magic, Trithemius complained about the no-win situation in which he had found himself. On one hand, should a man in his position, whose goal appears to exceed the limits of nature, demonstrate that he is able to bring his promises to fulfillment, "he is said to have accomplished this not otherwise than with the aid of demons." If he cannot do so, on the other hand,"who doubts but that he is a liar and ought rightly to be rejected by all good and learned men?"[31]

Of those placing him in this uncomfortable position, Trithemius complained to Maximilian, one critic in particular called for special mention. Recently paying him a visit at Sponheim, he informed the emperor, was the French Piccard Bovillus, "whom I treated, as best I could, with humanity, and to whom I extended with a pleasant countenance, as long as he was with me, all the benefits of my hospitality." Unhappily, his guest was not of a mind to appreciate his generosity, ferociously turning on him over the issue of an earlier cryptographic writing which he had partially composed and presented to his visitor for evaluation. Casually leafing through its pages with his mind seeming to be occupied elsewhere, related Trithemius, Bovillus by all appearances favorably responded to their contents. If he secretly harbored doubts about the work in question, the only hint was that he did not request a key prepared by the abbot for unraveling its codes and ciphers. His hypocrisy, we are informed, was not revealed to the world until his return to France, where he "shamefully violated our covenant of Christian friendship, inflicting evil on me in exchange for the good which I had bestowed on him." For queried by their mutual friend Ganay about what had transpired during his Sponheim visit, Bovillus "replied with false answers instead of true ones, and gave out lies in return for the benefits which I had extended to him."[32]

Bovillus's surprising allegation to Ganay, Trithemius learned to his astonishment, was that he had given himself over to the "depraved arts" and had become, on that account, "a magician and necromantic." Though convinced that the tribunal of history—and, more importantly, the tribunal of God—would prove him to be innocent of the charges leveled against him by Bovillus, and their spokesman "to be impious, cruel, rash, and a liar in this matter," Trithemius in the meantime felt himself to be unduly plagued by a spate of malicious rumors about his arcane activities triggered by Bovillus's accusations, no less harmful because they were unfounded. Lest Maximilian himself lend credence to these baseless rumors, Trithemius felt called upon to reaffirm "that I have never held

commerce with depraved or pernicious demons or with the magical
or necromantic arts; rather, each and every thing which I have
written, or which I have promised to write, is pure, sane, natural,
and in no way or form inwardly at variance with the Christian
faith." If anyone wished to test this oath, "I do not fear to place
these promises of mine, whenever and as often as necessary, before
good and learned men for examination, whose judgments I would
not attempt to oppose."[33]

As to why, if Bovillus's accusations were unsubstantiated,
Trithemius had elected to suspend further work on his suspect
tract and keep its completed portions under wraps, the writer vigorously denied that this was the behavior of a guilty person. To
quell any such inference, Trithemius assured the emperor that he
had adopted this course, "not because I fear the rash opinions of
Bovillus, but so that I might not seem to give cause of suspicion to
many others relating to my activities." The innocent victim of these
calumnies would rather "placate my enemies by my silence than
enrage them into a state of insanity by my letters and writing."
Accordingly, with resort to an unflattering play on his chief accuser's
name, Trithemius apprised Maximilian: "Let the *Steganographia*
stay hidden in the shadows, and let it not be made accessible to the
society of cows (*bovelline societate*), which is accustomed to make
judgment concerning things of which it is ignorant and to despoil
the reputation of a good man by reason of its own desire for depravity." As consolation, however, "I consent to bring to light, with
the *Steganographia* still remaining in the shadows, the adjoined
work which I call the *Polygraphia*, divided into six books."[34]

In coming to this decision, however, Trithemius also let be known
his apprehension that the reverberations set in motion by Bovillus's
attack on the prior cryptographic tract could also redound on its
polygraphic successor. To forestall any such possibility, Trithemius
swore in the preface to the *Polygraphia*—in words, not by chance,
closely resembling those of its steganographic forerunner—that all
matters to be treated within its pages "are genuine, pure, and
natural, and are remote from every study of wicked superstition."
While, confessed its author, this work too could be expected to be
faulted by some critics, it should be censured, he pleaded, not for
those uses for which it was intended, but only for its abuse by
those improperly instructed in its precepts. Like the proverbial
*Copyrighted Material*

sword in the hand of a madman, this polygraphic brand of magic in the possession of a malevolent person can conceivably be utilized on behalf of the demons; in the possession of a good person, on the other hand, it can be effectively utilized to help counter and defeat the nefarious assaults of the demons. Understandably assigning himself to the latter category, Trithemius assured his imperial dedicatee, in language virtually unchanged from his earlier defense of steganography, that his entire monastic career and reputation as a lover of Christ furnished unassailable testimony that "there is not now, nor has there ever been, nor (with God as my protector) will there ever be, commerce between myself and the demons, nor are any of my studies, occupations, or lessons steeped in the sorcerous, necromantic, or profane arts." Whoever judged otherwise "thinks wrongly, causes me injury, and thereby lends credibility to the impudent lie of Bovillus."[35]

So irksome did Trithemius find the Bovillus affair that he even found a place for its treatment in a section of his historical writing far removed from current events. "May God be merciful to you, Bovillus," Trithemius berated his most prominent disparager in a passage inserted into the entry for 1388 in the Hirsau annals, "for you are a feigner of lies who, in a letter addressed to your fellow Gaul, Germanus de Ganay, have falsely accused me, Trithemius, at the time residing at Sponheim, of being a magician or necromantic."[36] In making these false accusations it was Bovillus, rather than the undeserving target of his vicious attacks, who had proved his superstitious credulity by granting far greater powers to the magical arts than were warranted. "You who are ruder than a cow, Bovillus," the abbot chided his nemesis with the usual vilifying play on his name, "have been deceived, for you in effect concede to the depraved arts that which not even a discerning art can effect through the powers of nature." And if that were not enough, Bovillus had defamed Trithemius's Sponheim monks by insinuating that he had seduced them into participating in his black arts, joining alchemy to steganography among the arts in which he had reputedly furnished instruction. To this contention Trithemius vehemently replied that not only he personally had never engaged in superstitious magic "nor entered into the theater of alchemy," but neither had any of his monks. Besides, he sarcastically reminded his antagonist, it would not be the tribunal of Bovillus to which Trithemius would be called at last to answer these unjust charges, but the "tribunal of God."[37]

The Bovillus affair commemorated by an "historical" entry like the above, as it turned out, placed in jeopardy more than the magical reputation of Trithemius himself. It also imperiled the abstract magical theory the abbot had formulated to justify his cryptological operations. If Trithemius were to make a successful case for magic before the judgment of history, it would not be enough to persuade his readers of his merely personal worthiness as an advocate of its precepts. He would also need to persuade them to the worthiness of the precepts themselves apart from the spiritual status of their sponsor. This second stage in his strategy is illustrated not only by the prefaces of both of his major cryptographic tracts, the *Steganographia* and the *Polygraphia*, but also by a number of other writings from his pen broadening the justification of cryptological magic in particular to one of magic in general.

The starting point for Trithemius's justification of magic, making it a fitting prelude to the pages that follow, is the rule of esoterism. If Trithemius had anything to regret about the events surrounding his magical speculations, it was not, as critics like Bovillus had charged, that he had succumbed to demonic influence. It was rather that he had failed to take the proper precautions to preserve his precepts from contamination in obedience to the imperative for esoteric confidentiality, whereby instruction in magic is exclusively reserved for those spiritually and intellectually fit to receive it. After all, according to the abbot's own testimony, a primary motive behind his invention of his cryptographical techniques lay in their utilization for this very purpose. Only after such secretive confidentiality was established, it will now be observed at closer hand, did Trithemius feel secure that the sanctity of his magical principles would be protected from the kind of demonic corruption charged against him by his enemies.

## The Divine Revelation and the Esoteric Rule

"All the things which I have stated or am about to state in this work," proclaimed Trithemius in the preface to his *Steganographia*, "rest upon Catholic truths and natural principles (*veris catholicis et naturalibus principiis innituntur*)." Far from being incompatible with true religion as charged by his misinformed critics, the author of the work at hand declared, the precepts of the present volume "both in their entirety and in their singular parts, are in accord with God and with a good conscience, without injury to the Christian faith and in support of the integrity of the ecclesiastical tradition, without any superstition, without idolatry, without any explicit or implicit pact with malignant spirits, without suffumigation, adoration, veneration, worship, sacrifice, or oblation proffered to demons, and without any stain or sin either venial or mortal." On the proviso that these precepts be cautiously applied in keeping with the dogmas of the church, "the knowledge and practice of this invention is aptly put to good use, and is not unseemly for a wise man and for a good and faithful Christian."[38]

As for himself, as Trithemius had called to the attention of Bostius in the notorious letter informing him of his marvelous cryptographical invention, he required no such exculpatory plea to bring him to the same position. "I have learned these things neither from man nor through man," Trithemius assured Bostius, "but through a revelation (*sed per revelationem*)." Thus did the magical abbot, in explanation of how his art of steganography came into being, suggest affinity to a procedure generally associated with inspired prophets claiming illumination from a divine source. After pondering long and hard on the problem of steganographic communication, Bostius was informed, Trithemius was handed a key to the art, not in the thralls of his conscious labors, but while dozing in temporary respite from those labors. Appearing before him in a dream, he reported, was a shadowy figure who addressed him by name and declared to him: "Those things upon which you have been speculating, Trithemius, have not been in vain, although they are impossible to you alone, and neither you nor another in your company will be able to discover them by your own powers." Thereupon revealing to him "how those things upon which I meditated in vain for many days were easily able to be accomplished," the spectral visitor proceeded to instruct him in the secrets of steganography.[39]

A modern skeptic versed in Freudian psychology might well assign this explanation of the birth of steganography to the natural powers of the subconscious. But Trithemius, in a theological mode of thinking, preferred to refer his vision to a place transcending mere nature. And since he was convinced that it did not arise out of a diabolically induced vision, he was left with only one possible alternative explanation. It was inculcated in his mind, he believed, by God. Moreover, he further attested, having been specially selected by God to receive this vision, he was required by divine mandate to impart its principles solely to others spiritually and intellectually worthy of receiving them. In carrying out this divine mandate for esoteric confidentiality, as pointed out in the preface to the *Steganographia*, Trithemius was following a precedent established by the ancient sages.

"It is the opinion of our most erudite men," observed Trithemius in introduction to his steganographical handbook, "that the ancient sapients whom we call by the Greek name 'philosophers,' if they happened to discover any arcana either of nature or of art, concealed them by various modes and figures so that they would not fall into the clutches of depraved men." Nor, Trithemius added, were the ancient gentile sages alone in their adherence to this esoteric guideline. Also subject to its demands was the Jewish sage Moses, who, "in the description of Heaven and Hell, concealed the ineffable secrets of these mysteries in simple words," followed by the early Christian St. Jerome, who "understood that St. John's revelations were written down, not in the form of what he literally saw, but in cryptic symbols." Taking their cue from these great philosophical and religious thinkers, Trithemius further noted, have been learned poets who have found it advisable to mask their recondite speculations in myth and fable.[40]

The call for esoteric secrecy characterizing the preface to the *Steganographia*, as might be expected, also appears in the follow-up *Polygraphia*. In words closely resembling those of its steganographical forerunner, Trithemius introduced his polygraphical handbook with an appeal to the extreme antiquity of the art about to be presented and a caveat (*cautela*) to keep its sacred precepts, just as did its revered adepts of long ago, "safe from the incursions of depraved men."[41] Reiterating the identical caveat at the conclusion of the text, the writer exhorted that "all things do not need to be communicated to all men, especially those things whose use is as easily applicable to evil as to good." If the student of polygraphy pays careful heed to these admonitions, he will find that no matter how great are the secrets which he discovers through these methods, "even greater are those secrets which still await discovery."[42]

The preface to the art of polygraphy also testifies to how, in support of his imperative for esoteric secrecy, Trithemius sought to deflect the accusation of demon conversance back upon his incriminators. Many of those directing their carping criticisms at his magic, claimed Trithemius, in fact were under the sway of the same demons they unjustly had assigned to himself. The polygrapher, on the other hand, by veiling his occult precepts from his vulgar accusers, also perforce veils them from the demons attracted into their company. As he put this call for recondite expression in his own characteristically recondite way: "Lest the arcana of owls be revealed in any way to the demons, these mysteries are concealed under enigmas."[43] When the true meaning of these enigmas was understood it would be recognized, in rebuttal to the slurs directed against him by his demonically inspired detractors, that the motives lying behind his magic were utterly pure and holy.

As the example of Bovillus painfully taught Trithemius, however, a general call for high standards of selectivity in the choice of disciples in the magical arts did not foreclose the possibility of misjudgments in particular cases. A further instance of misjudgment, but for different reasons, is revealed in a letter from the abbot to a young disciple, Johann Steinmoel, rebuking him for selling his secrets for money. "This is not the way of true wisdom, nor is it seemly at your age to place your hope in vanity or, in search of a reward of vile worth, to cast pearls before the swine," Trithemius reproached Steinmoel, pointing out to him that, by disregarding the vow to secrecy to which he had sworn, he had inflicted injury upon the reputations both of himself and of his teacher. "It is not the part of all men to understand the arcana of nature, and to bring to light something which lies hidden and beyond ordinary usage in familiar areas of concern," Steinmoel was reminded, the privilege of which is reserved exclusively for the spiritual worthy. Unhappily, despite ill-advised attempts to flatter his teacher with empty adulation, by his simony Steinmoel had voluntarily exempted himself from this privileged status.[44]

Trithemius's irate reprimand of Steinmoel reflected admonitory advice the abbot had received from his own master in the arcana,

Libanius Gallus, who had reiterated it in a letter sent to the abbot less than two months earlier with the injunction: "Guard well your objective, and care not either for wealth or for the excessively vain honors of the world!" The art in which he had been instructed, Libanius reminded his monastic disciple, was to be turned to the acquisition, not of earthly riches, but of heavenly ones. To further this injunction the "thrice-great" abbot, "blessed in the name of Christ," was charged with taking care to preserve the secrecy of the precepts conveyed to him, imparting them solely to those proving themselves to be worthy of their reception.[45]

The dark manner in which Libanius drove this counsel home to the abbot mirrored the dark manner in which he believed that all instruction in the arcana should be communicated from teacher to student. Listed among Libanius's strictures for esoteric concealment, for example, is the injunction: "Cover your investigation with silence, and do not send forth a dove before its time!" Or again: "Do not offer your bread to cows and goats, nor set your spirit free through inferior doors!" Or still again: "You should not feed birds in the sun but in the shadows, and you ought not reveal a glass or mirror in its entirety to dogs because it is dangerous."[46] In reply to Libanius's enigmatic counsel Trithemius reassured his "sole preceptor" (*praeceptor unicus*) that he had always endeavored to be faithful to his precious teachings, above all to the imperative for esoteric secrecy. "I have removed my hay from the cows and goats," he assured his teacher in comparably abstruse language, "and have fought a great battle with the apes from which I so far have emerged the victor."[47]

As will brought out in the following chapter, accent in the last sentence should be placed upon the words *so far* (*sed hactenus*), since the verdict of posterity upon the magic of Trithemius is a mixed one. It is not our object here to determine whether he ultimately succeeded or failed in this regard. It is rather to understand the deeper theological motives that lay behind his effort.

In making his case for esoteric exclusivity, Trithemius addressed its potential benefits to one exclusively membered group in particular. Given their obviously practical application to secular activity, it is no wonder that princes were among those who were most likely to be attracted to Trithemius's cryptographical inventions, and to invite their inventor into their presence for the kind of personal instruction he commended as a corollary of the esoteric rule. In making a special pitch to such princely patrons as Emperor Maximilian, Joachim of Brandenburg and Philip of the Palatinate, however, Trithemius can be said to have made himself vulnerable to an accusation which, in his demonological capacity, he had directed at other magicians, namely, that they were predominantly attracted to the courts of rulers. In making his special plea to princes, therefore, Trithemius was placed in the discomforting position of convincing his critics that it sprang from an entirely different motive than that driving the wicked sorcerers, as he put it in his *De demonibus*, to "noisily catch the attention of kings and princes."

## The Special Appeal to Princes

So far, Trithemius informed Bostius in his misappropriated letter, only Philip of Wittelsbach had been apprised of his steganographical techniques, one "whom I have shown the possibility of this craft with a clear demonstration."[48] And why was Philip so interested? Who better than a prince like Philip, Trithemius answered his own question, might make use of an art designed to relay messages secretly over long distances, while at the same time resting assured that their guarded contents, unlike those of their conventional epistolary counterparts, could not be extracted from their bearers by either persuasion or duress. But while acknowledging that a prince like Philip might be more attracted to his art than than the usual run of men, Trithemius also let his correspondent know that that this was not without certain conditions, the key one being a piously virtuous character of the prince to whom the art is taught. "Otherwise," Trithemius explained to Bostius, "many unwanted things may come about through them—evils, betrayals, deceptions, fornication, and all the other things which wicked men pursue."[49] Or as he made the same point in the preface to the *Steganographia*: "Although this science, in itself, is very virtuous and quite useful to the state, nevertheless, when it comes into the possession of depraved men (may God forbid such a thing) the entire order of the state in time will be not a little disturbed, the public trust put into peril, and all the letters, documents, and treatises of men—indeed, their very discourses—be brought into the gravest suspicion."[50]

In the wake of the turbulent eddies stirred up by the premature dissemination of the Bostius letter, Trithemius sought to shore up support for his cryptographic magic by direct written appeals to his princely acquaintances. Thus, to Joachim of Brandenburg Trithemius wrote that "the firm, stable, and licit" science of natural magic not only "adorns and embellishes princes very excellently," but also is of very practical use in their political duties. "What," he rhetorically inquired of Joachim, "is more honorable, what more useful, than that the eminent and invincible prince, with his birthright, wealth, and wisdom intact, should take delight in studies by the employment of which kings and princes in former times, wise and powerful men, were feared by all others upon the earth?" With the aid of magic modern princes are promised results not unlike those of their celebrated regal ancestors, who "not only were made powerful by their studies, and were also endowed with riches, honor, and felicity, but also acquired eternal fame."[51]

Similarly, in the dedication to his second major cryptographic work, the *Polygraphia*, Trithemius declared to the emperor Maximilian that he was offering him "mysteries wrapped in enigmas" (*aenigmatibus involuta mysteria*) which are not meant for just anyone. Above all they were meant for those, like Maximilian, who combined royal dignity with an acute mental capacity, virtuous disposition, and exceptional education. The work at hand, Maximilian was to be assured, treats of very obscure matters which, "in my judgment, can be very useful—nay, are outrightly necessary—to princely men."[52] And in the preface to this work Trithemius further expatiated on why princes were exceptionally adapted to initiation in the cryptographic secrets which he was about to disclose.

Of the princes of old singled out by the writer as coming to appreciate the value of cryptic communication in the transmission of their state secrets were the pagan Augustus and his Christian imperial successor Charlemagne. But an edifying example could also be found among Maximilian's own contemporary rulers, King Matthias of Hungary, "Hammer of the Turks," who was not adverse, so claimed Trithemius, to employing occult means as a weapon to overcome the Islamic "enemies of Christ's cross." But Matthias's remarkable military successes against the Turks, Trithemius emphasized, were not explainable by reference solely to his knowledge of the arcana. It was also paramount that his motives were pure, and that the victory he sought over the infidel Turks was motivated more by spiritual than by secular concerns. Matthias "preferred wisdom to gold," Trithemius insisted in support of this point, "and therefore always triumphed as the glorious conqueror."[53]

In this way Trithemius gave a distinctly occult turn to the ancient Platonic ideal of the philosopher-king, transforming it, as it were, into that of the magus-king. Just as the word *magician* (*magus*) can legitimately be substituted for the word *philosopher* (*philosophus*) in the parlance of students in the arcana, Trithemius counseled Maximilian, by the same token the call for a philosopher-prince (*philosophus-princeps*) by the Platonists can also be construed as a call for a magician-prince (*magus-princeps*) in resonance with the occult precepts of the ancient Pythagoreans and Hermeticists. Moreover, if one outcome of Trithemius's special appeal to princes was to recast the Platonic philosopher-king as a magus-king, another, at a still more sublime level, was to recast him as a magical theologian-king. For a loftier goal lies behind a prince's magical pursuits, Trithemius urged his prospective regal patrons, than one of mere practical expediency and magisterial adornment. It is, Trithemius maintained, to furnish the prince with an inner passage to God. Thus, in words to Joachim of Brandenburg, Trithemius declared that licit natural magic "not only performs visible effects, but also marvelously illuminates the intellect of the man skilled in it with knowledge of the Deity and furnishes invisible fruits to the soul."[54] In a like vein he urged Maximilian to unite a pure heart to an illuminated mind in his magic, assuring him that "a devout mind is able to perform great things, and he who attaches himself to God will be loftier than the world in his understanding."[55]

It goes without saying that a subject of study which, as stated to Joachim, "marvelously illuminates the intellect . . . with knowledge of the Deity," and by virtue of that illumination, as stated to Maximilian, promises to endow its devout adept with the capacity to "perform great things," would likely be of interest to a larger circle than that of princes. It would entice anyone desirous of acquiring extraordinary knowledge and its attending power in any discipline whatsoever. While pursuing royal support of his magic as a practical matter, Trithemius by no means intended to limit its study to secular rulers. For the cryptic transmission of messages, he understood, could readily be applied to any enterprise whatsoever, whether carried out by princes or by select members among their subject, calling for disguising a hidden idea or intention with a surface meaning.

Further expanding the relevance of steganography to the larger populace were certain of its ancillary promises, such as the occult inculcation of knowledge in a diversity of languages. By resort to the steganographical art, Trithemius had boasted to Bostius, "I am able to teach all there is to know in the world in every possible language, even in languages I have never heard."[56] Given the busy schedule of princes forced on them by their office, it is no wonder that the abbot's promise of a shortcut to universal knowledge might have considerable appeal to them. But this "Faustian" conceit is one whose allurement clearly stretches to a far larger audience than secular rulers, applying to anyone who might aspire to far-ranging knowledge without being required to pass through the strenuous stages of conventional education.

The underlying precondition Trithemius consistently laid down for the conveyance of his secret art is that its beneficiary be spiritually worthy of its reception. Magical proficiency, Trithemius insisted many times in his writings, is not to be made accessible to just anyone. Whether he be a prince or belong to a lower echelon in the social and political hierarchy, the magical adept must be spiritually worthy of receiving the sacred secrets of the arcana. This worthiness of character, Trithemius cautioned, pertains to both the mind and the affections, with the successful magician on that account combining a studious approach to his subject with a piously virtuous disposition. Moreover, once the intellectual and moral rectitude of the magician is established, rules of esoteric instruction are necessary to protect his occult operations from the possibilities of contamination from the outside.

Being compelled to explicate his magical theory while simultaneously parrying the thrusts of his demonological critics, Trithemius was faced with the knotty task of exempting himself from his own theologically grounded admonitions against consorting with demons. Accordingly, an understanding of what Trithemius was about when he defended his steganographical art must address the philosophical and theological presuppositions on which he based it. Such a query logically begins with Trithemius's own acknowledged starting point in magic, his secret instruction in occult precepts imparted to him by his foreign teacher Libanius Gallus in the last decade of the fifteenth century. Or, put more technically, that starting point can be said to begin with Libanius's own teacher in the arcana, the Majorcan monk Pelagius, whose precepts indirectly reached Trithemius through Libanius's personal mediation.

## Pelagius and Libanius

The circumstances allowing for Trithemius's instruction in the arcana by the man he later dubbed his sole preceptor in its principles, Libanius Gallus,[57] were furnished by a visit of Libanius to Sponheim in 1495. After passing time as an observer of the German princes at Worms, recorded the abbot in his *Nepiachus*, Libanius made his way to Sponheim where the two men jointly entered into principles of magic earlier conveyed to Libanius by the pious Majorcan hermit Pelagius. In the course of this autobiographical excursus Trithemius made clear that his receptivity to Libanius was greatly enhanced by the high regard in which he held his visitor. In a further excursus in his Hirsau annals Trithemius put Libanius's teacher Pelagius in the same favorable light.

As recounted by Trithemius, Pelagius, under his given name Fernando of Cordova, earlier had traveled the world and astounded many people with his remarkable powers of mind, which he had enhanced by occult means. Among these powers was a remarkable memory that could draw in an instant not only on holy scripture, but also on the great physicians, philosophers, and theologians. Fernando's rare acumen, Trithemius further exulted, extended not only to past things, but also to those of the present and future, a quality which, combined with his incredible memory, made him virtually unbeatable in debate. Further impressing his audience were his polylinguistic abilities. "He knew how to speak fluently, as well as how to write, read, and understand, the Hebraic, Greek, Latin, Arabic, and Aramaic languages," noted Trithemius, "which in one so young was greatly to be admired."[58]

If all of this seems vaguely familiar, resembling traits attributed by Trithemius to, among others, Faustus and Giovanni Mercurio, it is not by chance. For admitting that he was spurred to a recollection of Fernando's exploits by the superficially parallel case of Mercurio, Trithemius nevertheless concluded, with little more than his own inner conviction to back his assessment, that at bottom the two marvel workers worked at cross purposes. For whereas, averred Trithemius, Fernando's arcane principles arose out of Christian virtue and piety, Mercurio's arose out of empty braggadocio, out of a wicked collusion with demons, or out of a combination of these.

But if Trithemius did not harbor suspicions of Fernando rivaling those of Mercurio, his account makes it clear that others did. Referring to a visit of Fernando to Paris around the middle of the fifteenth century, Trithemius acknowledged that "the opinion about him was diverse, with some judging him to be a demon-filled magician, whereas others held a contrary opinion." Certain of Fernando's detractors even went so far as to claim that he was Antichrist, a view flatly contested by Trithemius, who called attention to "the pursuit of the man for all things Christian." Indeed, so intensely and compellingly did Fernando feel a drive for Christian virtue and piety, Trithemius observed, that he found that he could no longer satisfy its demands in the usual secular channels. Accordingly "out of love for Christ," Fernando renounced all temporal affairs and sailed to the island of Majorca where, under the new name of Pelagius, he assumed the habit of a solitary hermit.[59]

In this example, of course, Trithemius saw a parallel, not to the vaunted Mercurio, but to himself in his own monastic humility. Also in conspicuous resemblance to the career staked out by Trithemius, the reborn Pelagius is recorded to have discovered in his solitary and celibate way of life, not a cause to forsake his earlier investigations into the arcana, but needed peace and quiet for their pursuance optimally unimpeded by worldly distraction. To facilitate his scholarly program, Trithemius emphasized with further parallel to his own situation, Pelagius surrounded himself with an exceptional library, including many codices in cryptic subjects. It was under these conditions that Libanius Gallus, attracted by the illustrious reputation of Pelagius, made his way to Majorca to receive private instruction in his occult principles. Being Pelagius's sole disciple, continued Trithemius, Libanius, "easily the most learned of all the doctors of our time whom I have known," was made heir both to his teacher's esoteric secrets and to the books relating to them assembled on his shelves.[60]

The account by Trithemius of his initiation in the arcana by Libanius thus reveals him also to be beholden, at a second stage of transmission, to the instruction of Pelagius. The recipe for the so-called powder of Pelagius cited in the previous chapter, a talismanic concoction effective in exorcistical rites, represents one way in which Trithemius was able to draw, through Libanius's mediation, upon Pelagius's legacy.[61] In a more basic way, however, Pelagius, through the agency of Libanius, helped Trithemius to fill in the details of his magical theory, comprised, he acknowledged in the pages of his *Nepiachus*, "of many things in arcane philosophy and in Christian faith concerning the nature of both good and evil spirits and concerning the mysteries of nature, and many other things which were not commonplaces indiscriminately taught in the schools of society during that time." Inasmuch as Libanius, following Pelagius's lead, was widely venerated "for his renowned instruction in every doctrine, and admired no less for his Christian faith and holiness of behavior than for his erudition," the abbot had no more reservation about receiving lessons in the secret arts from him than did he from Pelagius. Thus,"having been aroused by my fame," Libanius was pleased after his arrival at Sponheim to find his host exceedingly receptive to his arcane speculations.[62]

"On apprehending the disposition of my mind and my indefatigable passion for studies," Trithemius continued, Libanius greatly exulted and, in the process of communicating his occult precepts to the abbot, disclosed not only the name of the obscure Pelagius behind their inspiration, but also that of an Italian polymath of far greater fame. For upon discovering how ably and enthusiastically his Sponheim host responded to his teachings, "whom Minerva has found fit to grace with her luster," Libanius freely opened up to his magical disciple his full repertory of occult knowledge, holding nothing back "among those things which I have been able to acquire with great labor over a period of thirty years, first from Pelagius and then from Count Giovanni Pico della Mirandola and many others." Above all, as a result of his instruction in things "which until then had been unknown to me," Trithemius was led to an understanding of the critical distinction between licit natural magic, "which, as Pico declares, teaches us how to perform marvelous works by means of mediating natural virtues," and illicit demonic magic, "whether this be by necromancy residing in the corpses of the dead, or by pyromancy, or by the invocation of exorcised demons, or by erotic magic, or by whatever other name you might wish to call it."[63]

Concerning the evil magic "effected with the cooperation of evil spirits," which Libanius was anxious to differentiate from the good kind divulged to him by Pelagius and Pico, Trithemius did not deny that Christians should be on their guard against its dangers. But a very different story held for the art of natural magic, which, he pleaded, far from merely deserving of toleration by the ecclesiastical authorities, should be actively encouraged for its ability to assist the soul on its heavenly pilgrimage. For this reason Trithemius was not ashamed to be dubbed a "lover of magic" (*me philomagum appellari non pudet*), the explanation being that the magic of which he was so passionately enamored was but another name for wisdom, "whether it be divine, human or natural" (*quoniam amator sum sapientiae divinae, humanae ac naturalis*). "This is the magic which I follow," proudly proclaimed Trithemius, a far cry from that other magic which is "superstitious, diabolical, and permitted to none of the faithful, since it is condemned by the Holy Church."[64] In further writings attesting to his proud role as a *philomagus*, as will now be the focus of our attention, Trithemius expounded in more specific terms the philosophical constituents of his magical theory on which, so he maintained, all licit magical operations, steganographical ones included, necessarily depend.

## The Theoretical Precepts

In his *Nepiachus* Trithemius raised a question that, so he hoped, would help to clarify the difference between his own magic and that of the demonically inspired sorcerers. Does magical illusion (*praestigium*), he asked, necessarily owe to a demonic origin? In reply Trithemius distinguished between four different kinds of illusion, three of which can be attributed either directly or indirectly to demons, and a fourth, his own kind, to a divinely instilled power to tap the occult powers of nature

Expectedly declaring the most serious form of magical illusion to be accomplished by an explicit conjuration of demons, Trithemius followed up with a second form of illusion which, while not relying on overtly direct demonic assistance, acquired that assistance by indirectly covert means through the use of "words, charms, incantations, and objects." A third form of magical illusion distinguished by Trithemius in its turn, outwardly appearing more harmless than the previous two but theologically suspect all the same since demons could still be lurking behind its chimeras, consists of "such deception as those wanderers employ who are known as jugglers." Finally, he identified a fourth form of illusion which, rather than posing a threat to the soul's salvation as the previous three, he deemed to be wholly congenial with the demands of Christian faith. Terming this last-named form natural illusion (*praestigium naturalis*), Trithemius contended that it alone of the four categories cited "pertains to natural magic, under whose auspices marvelous effects (the causes of which those who admire them do not understand) are produced by proficients through the occult application of natural virtue."[65] Regrettably for his future reputation, Trithemius left his readers in the dark as to how they might distinguish, in any particular case, the last-named category of illusion from its demonic look-alikes. The failure to do so would haunt all his efforts, beginning with the misappropriated Bostius letter, to clear himself of the charge of demonic sorcery.

All the remarkable feats herein described, Trithemius assured Bostius in his synopsis of the *Steganographia*, are accomplished "naturally, without any superstition or help from any spirits whatever." Granting to Bostius that "many noble and very learned men believe either that these things are impossible or that they are entirely supernatural," Trithemius replied that "many things are naturally possible which seem to those ignorant of the power of nature to be impossible or contrary to the state of nature." If a rumor by chance had reached Bostius "that I am knowledgeable in, and am able to perform, marvelous wonders," the writer entreated his Carmelite friend directly to discount it and continue to think of him "not as a magician, but as a philosopher" (*non me magum dico existimares, sed philosophum*).[66]

In truth, however, as also brought out in the Bostius letter, Trithemius was not content with reducing his magic to a mere phenomenon of nature. Something of the supernatural, albeit belonging to a place other than that inhabited by the demons, also entered into it. Enhancing this theological feature of his "natural magic" was Trithemius's melding of its Hermetically based precepts with those of the Jewish Cabala, "preferred," he proclaimed in the preface to the *Steganographia*, "because of its exceedingly hidden mysteries."[67] It is the special property of the "profound and secret art" known as Cabala, Trithemius maintained, "that it easily renders the pupil incomparably more learned than the master." But advancement in this regard, he further cautioned, should not be taken to be automatic, requiring as it does both a natural disposition and diligent study on the part of the practitioner. More specifically, it succeeds only in one "inclined by his nature to progress, and studious in those things which he learned in the tradition of Cabala."[68]

The overall magical theory formulated by Trithemius constituted a fusion of several different ancient traditions—Pythagorean number mysticism, alchemy and natural magic, astrology, and Cabala—into a grand occult vision of the universe linking earth to Heaven. The key roles played by astrology and alchemy in this vision issued out of the abbot's Hermetic background, which likewise depended on an invisible interplay between alchemical powers lying within the earth's bowels and astrological powers originating above the earth. With the addition of Cabala, Trithemius expanded the scope of magic beyond the terrestrial and planetary spheres to the spheres of the angels, seven of which, following a scheme adopted by Trithemius from Pietro d'Abano, are presumed to govern over the seven planetary orbits. Each link in that occult cosmic chain, as the abbot further expounded, corresponds to numerical sequences laid down by the Pythagoras. These occult cosmic powers, as envisaged by Trithemius, further link up with still higher supernatural emanations issuing from God, which work their effects upon the world both directly and indirectly through astrological and angelic mediation.

In connection with this hierarchical theory Trithemius further presumed that every external effect produced by occult means must be accompanied by a corresponding internal effect within the soul of the operator. The common denominator of inward and outward magical transformation, theorized Trithemius, is purification (*purgatio*), interpreted externally as the purification of material substances through the medium of planetary influences and internally as the purification of the soul through the medium of angelic influences. While the primary goal of these *verae scientiae*, as Trithemius envisaged it, is to transport the soul of the adept to God, an important secondary feature of their use is to produce such terrestrial marvels as Trithemius's own ingenious methods of cryptic communication. For this reason, attested Trithemius in his *Nepiachus*, Pico della Mirandola rightfully answered the critics of his occult studies that "many very learned ecclesiastics have approved of, and pursued, natural magic, which not only has never been condemned by the Church but cannot conceivably ever be condemned."[69] The occult arts, determined Trithemius in agreement with this tenet, are wicked only when utilized for wicked ends, whereas when they are utilized for good ends they warrant the highest praise. The truth of this precept was confirmed by Holy Writ itself in its sympathetic depiction of the three Magi.

"The word magic (*magia*)," noted Trithemius, "is the Persian term for what in Latin is called wisdom (*sapientia*), on which account magicians are called wise men, just as were those three men who, according to the Gospel, journeyed from the East to adore, in his crib, the infant who was the Son of God in the flesh."[70] In this way Trithemius effectively reversed an interpretation of a decisive moment in the Christian drama commemorated by the Feast of the Epiphany, traceable to St. Jerome and St. Augustine, distinguishing between the wicked arts of the Magi and their divinely guided mission to witness Christ's birth. Now an interpretation could be assigned to this pivotal event of the Christian calendar that not only cast the Magi as witnesses to Christ's miraculous birth, but also vindicated the magical principles to which they adhered.

The underlying motive at issue in this magical restatement of Christian theology is aptly captured in an earlier-cited letter from Trithemius to Libanius, the intent of which was to enlist his magical instructor's assistance in an important matter. Would Libanius, beseeched the abbot, favor him with his prayers and offerings "so that my perverse mind might be reformed (*ut mens reformetur inversa*) and be made one in the love and knowledge of the highest Good, that is, of the Father, the Son, and the Holy Spirit, and that, having pursued the agreeable state of its origin, from which it fell into multiplicity, it might carry out this reform in accordance with its initial unity?"[71] The call for *reformatio* in these telling words to Libanius, while certainly resonating with a general trend of the religious reformers to cleanse Christianity of its diabolical accretions, assumed a specialized meaning of its own by calling for the admission of magic into its prescriptive instructions. The reformation to which Trithemius referred in his letter to Libanius is a *reformatio magica*, entailing a passage of the soul, on the model of alchemy, through a series of purgative stages to a state of godlike sanctity and "enlightenment."

In presenting his notion of enlightenment, evidenced by the earlier-cited references to occultly conditioned illumination conveyed to Joachim and Maximilian, Trithemius was far from prefiguring the future age, dominated by mathematical rationalism and quantifiable mathematical science, with which later historians customarily came to associate that term. What Trithemius envisaged had far more in common with the received illuminations of the Christian mystics than with the mathematically quantifiable intellectual constructions of the scientific age to follow. For the more rigorous of the scientific rationalists the term *occult enlightenment* would represent an absurd oxymoron. For those in rapport with the thinking of Trithemius, on the other hand, it would represent a magical reworking of the mystical "dark night of the soul." It was, in the final analysis, a magical way to mystical enlightenment that Trithemius intended the rule of esoterism to unlock.

In the preface to the *Steganographia* Trithemius declared that the mysterious principles he was about to divulge were to be made accessible only to those who met two primary conditions: first, the union of a piously virtuous disposition with zealous study, and second, knowledge in an abstruse body of enigmatic symbols upon which to draw for the transmission of secrets.[72] This dual requisite is restated in the preface to the follow-up *Polygraphia*, which, while granting that "our labor in these things is great," insists that arduous labor will be in vain if it is not infused by a light originating from above. "Many have tried to seek the light in the shadow deprived of light," as he put this principle in typically enigmatic form, "but nevertheless they have not been able to gain their object, because it lies buried in the ashes of the fire." Comparing the polygraphic "lover of light" (*amator lucis*) to an owl who "guards over the arcanum," Trithemius cautioned that such a priceless treasure is accessible solely to one who, being sufficiently purified and illuminated by the heavenly fire, is equipped to delve into its dark depths. Having penetrated the visible world to the invisible world lying behind it, "the mind of a man which has been illuminated is able, without impediment, to strike familiarity with, and to ascertain, marvels."[73]

The illuminative virtue of magic is restated many times in the course of the abbot's literary output. Just as the union of Christian virtue and revelation is a mainstay of Trithemius's mystical theology, so is it a mainstay of his magical theology. A pure heart and illuminated mind—these are the core requirements set forth by Trithemius for successful and legitimate magical proficiency. The pivotal role this insight played in the magical theory of Trithemius is pointed up by four letters written to select friends in the period 1503 to 1505 presenting sustained expositions of his magical principles, with the theory informing them, as we will now have occasion to establish, professing to effect a synthesis of Hermetic alchemical doctrine, Pythagorean numerology, astrological correspondences, and Cabalistic word magic. The first two of these letters were composed for the instruction of the princes Johannes of Westerburg and Joachim of Brandenburg, and the second two, for the instruction of French friends of the abbot, Johannes Capellarius and Germanus de Ganay, the latter who, as earlier noted, also played a key part in the subsequent magical notoriety of Trithemius by his reception and circulation of the vindictive Bovillus letter.

Writing to Johannes of Westerburg in 1503, in a letter earlier cited in another connection, Trithemius expostulated for the instruction of his correspondent "three principles of natural magic without which no marvelous effect can be performed." From start to finish in the course of this explication Trithemius established that the foundation for his "three principles" lay in the numerological speculations of Pythagoras. The first principle, Westerburg was apprised, consists of the One or unity, the deprivation of which necessarily frustrates every magical operation. By the second principle in turn, "distinct from the first in order but not in dignity," unity (also termed the monad) evolves into the binary, and by the third principle, the binary leads, via the ternary and quaternary, to the denary and multiplicity.[74] With recourse to a philosophical simile recently given popular currency by one similarly steeped in the mathematical symbolism of Pythagoras, the German cardinal Nicholas Cusanus (ca. 1400–1464), Trithemius added that this second principle occupies "the center of natural magic, whose undivided circumference can be depicted as a circle of such immensity that it extends into infinity." By the third principle in turn, explained Trithemius, the marvelous powers of magic are made manifest, for locked within it "is the consummation of the number of the grades and of the order through which all the philosophers of the secrets of nature and inquirers of the truth of God have pursued their marvelous effects."[75] In the third and consummating principle, that is to say, Trithemius perceived the transformation of theoretical into operational magic.

As for the kinds of marvels able to be effected through the application of the foregoing three principles, Trithemius listed as examples "the miraculous cures of infirmities and of all the illnesses," the putting of demons to flight, and, aided by a reading of the astrological charts, the pronouncement of accurate prophesies. While acknowledging variations in the outward forms of these magical marvels, Trithemius emphasized to Westerburg that they share a common trait. Success in the operation, he insisted, is dependent on a spiritual transformation, via a series of spiritual stages from denarium to unity, within the soul of the operator. "Whoever has been elevated to the uncompounded and pure state of utter simplicity," as he put this idea to Westerburg, "may be perfect in every natural science, may bring marvelous works to pass, and may discover amazing effects."[76] Or as the the same idea can be alternatively expressed, this time suggestive of alchemical imagery: "If a man is reduced to his own unified simplicity by a suitable cleansing through purifying fire, he is permitted to plumb the depths and perform all the mysteries of possible knowledge."[77]

Echoing a corresponding theme of his mystical theology, Trithemius urged Westerburg in the last-named regard to move his mind well beyond the material sun to "that true Sun which is God," where, being invigorated "by the fervor of a most holy love," his soul might be simultaneously purified in its affections and enlightened in its knowledge.[78] "Just as Holy Scripture testifies concerning the inward knowledge of God, that is, that no one understands it who does not receive it," as Trithemius memorably capsulized this idea for Westerburg, "likewise no one is able to initiate us in these mysteries unless he has received, by a divine gift, the incomparable light of understanding" (*lumen singulare intelligendi*).[79] While many had sought the clarifying powers of this light, few had found them, since God alone decided who was to be worthy of their reception. "The spirit of God," the writer expatiated, "blows where it will, illuminates whom it wishes, and, by virtue of its divine authority, conducts him upon whom it has been breathed into the complete knowledge of the truth."[80]

From his Benedictine standpoint, moreover, Trithemius gave a special twist to this simile, allowing that while the illuminative "spirit of God blows where it will," some were better prepared to receive it than others. In particular, those best suited to admit the arcane secrets of God were, like himself, devoted to the solitary way of life. Given, Trithemius pointed out to Westerburg, that "the philosophy imparted by this instruction is secret and heavenly," it followed that "a man truly desiring to know and understand it must flee the tumult of men, desert the world, and contemplate Heaven, this not only with his eyes but also with his mind."[81] In this way Trithemius not only underscored the theological foundations of magic, but also implied that the specifically monastic mode of theologizing was its quintessential vehicle.

The obverse side of the call to Westerburg for magical enlightenment consists of a number of caveats, the neglect of which necessarily dooms any attempt at marvel working to failure. In the case of astrology, for example, Trithemius warned that the best efforts of the magicians, "even if they possess books about, and know perfectly, the courses, powers, operations, and properties of the stars, and understand fully their images, seals, and most secret traits," are bound to miscarry unless their operants pay careful heed to these three principles "whereby they are permitted to proceed from the beginning and to return to the beginning." A like caveat applies to the art of alchemy, for when observance of these principles is lacking in an alchemical operation, "neither is the knowledge of the art acquired nor the effect of the operation discoverable." Concerning those who fail to pay proper heed to these caveats, Trithemius regretted to say that he had encountered not a few men "who, while otherwise very learned, err in this natural magic." More specifically, "some waste both their time and fortunes engaged in alchemy; others allow their lives to slip away from themselves together with their possessions; others, wishing to elicit medicine from their art, achieve nothing from their tedious labors; and still others endeavor to predict the future but speak false instead of true things." Very different from this false and unproductive magic, however, is the true and highly productive magic of Trithemius, based as it is, he assured Westerburg, on the "three principles" constituting the subject of the present letter.[82]

In a conception of magical marvel working representing the exact converse to that indicated in his demonological writings, which holds miscarriage in the procedures of magic to be integrally bound up with sin and "infidelity," Trithemius counseled Westerburg that magical success is integrally bound up with a combination of Christian faith and virtue. "Whatever the astronomers promise, whatever the astrologers, the magicians, the followers of the alchemists with their envy of nature, and the necromantics (who, in truth, are worse than their demons) promise," Trithemius assured Westerburg, those properly anchored by faith and virtue will truly bring to pass. But while faith and virtue are indispensable to success in the magical act, Trithemius emphasized, no less indispensable is knowledge of magic's underlying principles, since "without knowledge, through their numbers, degrees, and orders of the middle, end, and origin, the magician cannot, without scandal or impiety, effect his images, nor can the alchemist imitate nature, nor can a man conjure spirits, nor can a prophet of nature predict the future, nor can any curious person grasp the meaning of his experiences." Provided that he rigorously keep his magic free of diabolical insinuation, Westerburg could rest assured that his "uncompleted operation cannot, of itself, be seduced into error."[83]

Thus, while allowing that error can conceivably enter into magic to be mingled with its divinely elucidated truths, Trithemius contended that this was an accidental rather than essential accretion resulting from their often faulty temporal transmission. Further contributing to this faulty understanding of magic, he cautioned Westerburg, traceable to the very early days of the occult studies, was the fact that "certain sages of ancient times entrusted with secrets of nature either were completely silent about these or else enwrapped them in an exceedingly great obscurity so that they could not be truthfully known except through similes."[84] The discerning student of magic, however, is able to overcome this obstacle by learning, through instruction in the aforementioned three principles, how to penetrate the surface simile to the profound reality lying behind it.

Largely reiterating the ideas contained in Trithemius's 1503 letter to the count of Westerburg is a letter to Joachim of Brandenburg, composed only weeks later, declaring that magic properly performed in accordance with the previously cited pure principles (*puris principiis*), "not only performs visible effects, but also marvelously illuminates the intellect of the man skilled in it with knowledge of the Deity and furnishes invisible fruits to the soul." As in the counsel to Westerburg, this proud claim to Joachim is also accompanied by an aviso. "Today we see that the name of magic is detested and made hateful to almost all men," Joachim was alerted, "so that, as if under the sway of a single judgment, they condemn all who pursue it in their studies and believe that its very use is wholly adverse and contrary to the Christian religion."[85] Trithemius offered Joachim two reasons for the current stigma attached to the name of magic, both of which, he was certain, owed not to its legitimate use, but to its abuse.

The first reason for the widespread notoriety of magic, Trithemius informed Joachim, was that certain of its practitioners, in truth more foolish than diabolically insidious, had attempted to accomplish feats lying beyond the scope of their limited capacities. Paradoxically, it was out of this group that also arose some of magic's severest vilifiers, a result of their frustration in failing to achieve the marvels they were unwisely promised. "When these had read of the marvelous experiences of the sages in magical subjects and had become attracted to them by their desire and curiosity (a trait which they unfortunately still display today)," observed the writer, "they began to carry out their operations only in keeping with the surface meaning, not comprehending those things which they read." Thus falling short of their coveted object, "they ignominiously rejected and condemned many excellent books, commended by both experience and intellect, as inane, deceitful, and frivolous."[86] The second reason imparted to Joachim for the widespread opprobrium directed against magic, viewed more gravely by the writer, was that, in their zeal some of its practitioners, "not being content to deceive men in the aforesaid manner, . . . have added instruction in things of the Devil." Owing to this second type of abuse above all, a prime subject of Trithemius's demonological writings, the texts of natural magic have become widely despised for being "wicked, reprobate, superstitious, diabolical, and contrary to our holy faith."[87]

For these two reasons above all, lamented Trithemius to Joachim, "sacred and good magic (*magia sancta et bona*), once written down by its authors in a just and pure manner, has subsequently become so confused, disfigured, and spoiled that the bare hearing of its name seems to be abhorred among Christians, and to be everywhere all the more hated, it seems, as it appears to be impenetrable." Given, therefore, that "there is scarcely anyone today who can differentiate natural magic from the superstitious and vain variety," and that "what is sacred lies together with that which is shamefully despised and profane," the trend among the authorities has been to show intolerance to one kind of magic as to the other. As Trithemius put this complaint to Joachim in no uncertain terms: "The preachers of God's word and confessors, acting as physicians of the soul, compel and prohibit all of the Christian populace, under the threat of severe censure and excommunication, from observance or reading, either publicly or privately, in this subject, completely forbid its use to all Christians, and give over however many of the books of this science they can find to be burned by fire." It was of course with the object of reversing this lamentable state of affairs that Trithemius inscribed the enclosed principles to Joachim. "For if natural magic might be reduced to its initial purity" (*ad primam puritatem suam reduceretur*), he reiterated this object to Joachim, "it once again can not only become beloved by all men, but also can be made especially serviceable to princes."[88]

To help steer his correspondent along the right path Trithemius supplied Joachim with a list of eleven rules or guidelines. The first rule enjoins the student of magic to be naturally disposed to the art in which he seeks instruction, and the second rule, with astronomy serving as a foremost repository, to possess "adequate knowledge of its vocabulary" (*linguae sufficientem noticiam*). The third rule in turn requires the adept "to possess many books in this science," though cautioning him to make sure that they are emended, if at all possible, according to injunctions of the church, and the fourth rule, that he enlist a skilled preceptor in his art, the sole exception being when, "by a special gift of grace, the Omnipotent One wishes to illuminate the mind unaided, which very seldom is wont to occur."[89] By the fifth rule, continued Trithemius, the adept is enjoined "to know the distribution of the entire universe, both at its superior and inferior levels," and by the sixth rule he is urged to familiarize himself with "the way of life appropriate to this art, its required order of laboring, the right hour of the day, the process and the lord of the process (opus operisque dominum), that is, its planet, the suitable location, the form, and the composition of the material, . . . and, after all these things, the measure of his own soul, and the virtue and goodness which reside in the power of his activity." By the seventh rule, closely related to the previous one, the adept is exhorted to know to which planet a given spirit enlisted in an operation is subject, together with its optimal material conditions; "for inferior things are subject to superior ones," as he explained this precept, "and only by means of similitude, agreeing with substance, accident, power, virtue, number, degree, and property, . . . does the operation of marvels in natural magic become more advantageously put into effect."[90]

The ninth rule of arcane investigation specified by Trithemius for Joachim's instruction lays emphasis on the worthiness of all those, starting with his instructor, with whom the adept associates himself in his magical operations. "In those things which he alone is not able to perfect," Trithemius notified Joachim, "he must have associates who either are worthy by nature or have been made worthy by instruction." The tenth rule further enjoins the magical adept to be "firm in confidence," being careful never to hesitate in his "pursuit of the effect," and the eleventh and last rule, reconfirming the demand for esoteric confidentiality, declares that "he who wishes to perform fruitfully in the art of natural magic must keep to himself all those most secret matters and must not reveal to anyone other than to his master and to his disciple either the completion or the failure of any operation, or the nature of the operation itself, or his intention, or his art, or his appointed time." This last-named rule issues from the principle, Trithemius noted for Joachim's profit, that "this science flees the public sector; and so that its effects may be brought to completion, it is very rarely divulged."[91]

Two years later, in 1505, Trithemius addressed a further epistolary exposition of his magical principles to a Parisian correspondent with known astrological interests, Johannes Capellarius, the occasion of which was Capellarius's request for access to a portion of the abbot's controversial steganographical manual. Having the solicited pages recopied by one of his monks and dispatched to Capellarius "on condition that it be kept concealed," Trithemius in the accompanying letter advised his correspondent to approach the enigmatic work in question with more than a blind zeal for knowledge. If knowledge is not to degenerate into vain curiosity, Trithemius counseled Capellarius, it must be informed and invigorated by love. For only by joining love (*amor*) to knowledge (*cognitio*), Trithemius instructed Capellarius, is the magician to be assured of insulating his discipline from demonic intrusion, the reasoning being that "evil demons indeed know, but because they do not possess love, they do not attain to that fruition which is born, not from one of these alone, but from both."[92]

In calling for the passion of love in the magician, it goes without saying, Trithemius did not mean a mere earthly affection of the kind touted by "certain gentile philosophers, and many today located outside the bounds of Christianity." The love to which he referred is Heaven-bound Christian love, and the knowledge infused by it, Christian knowledge. At a deeper level of analysis, accordingly, Trithemius's two-term formula *cognitio-amor* can be said to expand to a three-term *cognitio-amor-fides*. "The primary road to God," Trithemius instructed Capellarius with this expanded formula in mind, "is science or knowledge through faith (*scientia sive cognitio per fidem*), without which no man can be saved." Explaining to Capellarius that "true knowledge arises out of faith, and love out of knowledge," Trithemius drew the logical conclusion that "a man who does not have faith does not have knowledge, he who lacks knowledge lacks love, and he who does not have love cannot experience the final enjoyment." Accordingly, "to this true knowledge (*scientia vera*), my mathematical friend, must all your sciences and studies be referred, because unless you bring this to pass, you will consume yourself in empty and foolish labor." It is an inborn feature of such "true knowledge," Trithemius apprised Capellarius, that, "instead of extolling the knowledgeable person, it rather instills him with compunction and love, and instead of inflating its possessor with pride, ~~Copyrighted Material~~ with humility."[93]

The occasion provoking the somewhat later letter to Ganay was Ganay's discovery of an earlier epistle from Trithemius to his disciple Steinmoel—the same Steinmoel, it will be remembered, earlier berated for abusing his instructional privileges—asking for clarification of an obscure reference to "a very rare and admirable philosophy, shrouded in numbers, elements, and enigmas, and abstruse with arcane words, so that its meaning is entirely lost to me and far exceeds the present capacity of my mind."[94] Not to our surprise, Trithemius clothed his reply to Ganay's query in the numerological idiom of Pythagoras characteristic of his earlier letters to Westerburg and Joachim. What distinguishes the 1505 Ganay letter from its 1503 forerunners, however, is the abbot's combination of Pythagorean precepts with those of another "ancient theologian," Hermes Trismegistus.

The Hermetic work constituting the mainstay of the expository response of Trithemius to Ganay is the alchemical Emerald Table— the *tabula smaragdina*. Beginning with a typically Pythagorean rendering of his "very rare and admirable philosophy," Trithemius counseled Ganay that for the mind to achieve a perfect understanding in these matters, "the ternary must be completely reduced to unity, for though unity is not a number, every number arises out of it." However, this time around the same idea also received an alternative alchemical mode of expression, corresponding to the second of thirteen alchemical precepts comprising the Hermetic Emerald Table: "What is superior is like that which is inferior, and what is inferior is like that which is superior (for only by unities does every number persevere), so that there can be accomplished many miracles of one thing." In clarification of what now in effect consituted a Pythagorean-Hermetic composite, Trithemius inquired of Ganay: "Is it not true that all things flow from one thing, from the goodness of the One, and that whatever is joined to unity cannot be diverse, but rather fructifies by means of the simplicity and adaptability of the One?" Significantly, Trithemius found helpful to illustrate this principle the same kind of play on his name which, corresponding to the twelfth precept of the Emerald Table, was also commonly applied to "thrice-great" Trismegistus. Explained the abbot, evidently with encouragement by his teacher Libanius: "I, Trithemius, am not comprised of three minds, but, while exulting in the ternary, endure within one integrated mind giving birth to a marvelous offspring (*qui parit mirabilem foetum*)."[96]

Elaborating on the generation of the Hermetic *mirabilis foetus*, Trithemius reiterated the Emerald Table's fourth precept that "its father is the sun, its mother the moon; the wind carried its seed in her belly, and the earth nourished it." Declaring the progeny of this marvelous magical birth in turn, in keeping with the fifth precept, to be "the father of all perfection throughout the world," Trithemius further brought out its cathartic powers by the seventh precept that "if its seed is cast upon the earth you will separate the earth from the fire, the gross from the subtle." The illuminative powers instilled in this marvelous progeny in turn are highlighted by the pronouncement, relating to the eighth precept, that "when the ternary has finally returned to itself, . . . it will thus be made potent and glorious in the clarity of unity, demonstrate its ability to bring forth every number, and put to flight all obscurity." Such is the "one thing" spoken of in the second precept, so assiduously sought by all bonafide magical adepts, who understand that only after cleansing their minds of the impurities and contaminations of the world are they enabled "to comprehend, without contradiction, all the mysteries of the excellently arranged arcanum."[96]

The expressly alchemical basis of Trithemius's magical theory of course raises a potentially embarrassing question about his motives, thrown into prominence not only by Bovillus in his later letter to Ganay accusing the abbot of demonic magic, but also by various allusions in his own writings placing the art of alchemy in a distinctly negative light. In a word, how could the legitimacy of one suspect art, steganography, be reinforced by appeal to another suspect art, alchemy? This is a strategy, it seems, which could easily backfire, compounding rather than resolving the predicament posed by the abbot's magic.

In his letter to Ganay Trithemius revealed that he was aware of this apparent contradiction, and sought to reconcile it by differentiating the spiritual form of alchemy prescribed in this letter from the vain form which he derided elsewhere as a "chaste whore." In his earlier letter to Capellarius, as we have seen, Trithemius had sharply distinguished true science (*vera scientia*) from its false look-alike. In his follow-up letter to Ganay, by the same token, he sharply distinguished true alchemy (*vera alchymia*) from its empty and ineffectual counterfeit. What he so far had professed, Trithemius conceded to Ganay, "the alchemists also promise with respect to compounded bodies." However, these false adepts, "wandering from the true course," not only deceive themselves, but also deceive others into the bargain. These alchemical charlatans, "since they do not understand the source of the power of nature, try to imitate nature by breaking into discrete parts that which is indivisibly universal."[97] Or put in terms more closely suggesting the modern way of expressing this opposition, they seek to reduce to particulars that which, when observed from Trithemius's larger occult vision, constitutes a holistic unity.

In stark contrast to the false claims of the alchemical impostors, Trithemius exhorted Ganay to remember that, at bottom, "our philosophy is heavenly, not worldly, that we might faithfully behold, by a direct intuition of the mind through faith and knowledge, that Founder (*principium*) of things Whom we call God— Father, Son, and Holy Spirit—one Founder, one God, and one Highest Good existing in a Trinity of eternal Persons, and also that we may believe in His existence with conviction and become intimately acquainted with Him from Whom all things present to us derive, always adoring Him with a very fervid display of love and service." But while ardent love of the Triune God is essential to success, Ganay was apprised by Trithemius, it must be coupled with zealous intellectual study, the necessary starting point of the magician's arduous spiritual journey. To put this "alchemical" sequence in succinct form: "Study generates knowledge; knowledge prepares love; love, similarity; similarity, communion; communion, virtue; virtue, dignity; dignity, power; and power performs the miracle."[98]

By paying close attention to the precepts underlying this sequence, Trithemius assured Ganay, *alchymicus Christianus* not only will be guaranteed success in his magical operations, but will also be protected from external diabolical interference. For in those precepts, Trithemius insisted, resides "the sole path to the goal of magical perfections both divine and natural, by the virtue of which it is protected and propagated far from deceptive, diabolical, and superstitious influence." The adept guided by this proper understanding of alchemy will realize that, while made capable of effecting remarkable worldly transmutations, his primary goal is a transmutation carried out within himself. If knowledge of natural things is critical to such magical success, still more critical is knowledge of divine things—knowledge necessarily infused by divine

love and informed by Christian faith. As Trithemius cogently summarized this idea for Ganay: "For truly we would have magic to be
understood as nothing else but wisdom, that is, the discernment of
things both physical and metaphysical, which knowledge is dependent upon a power resident within both divine and natural things."[99]

Closely bound up in Trithemius's mind with a defense of "true
alchemy" was a defense of "true astrology," which he considered to
constitute a valuable ally of alchemy. Accordingly, in distinguishing
legitimate from illegitimate alchemy for Ganay's instruction, he
also felt the need to do the same for astrology in alchemy's service.
Thus, in addition to disparaging the alchemical impostors as "fatuous men, disciples of the apes, and enemies to nature," Trithemius
also characterized them as "despisers of the heavens, without whose
intelligible consonance there can be no alchemy." After all, he asked,
"how can he who fails to understand worldly affairs discover celestial ones?"[100]

Planetary harmony, Trithemius instructed Ganay, is the outward celestial manifestation of an inward occult harmony suffus-
ing and binding all things. Moreover, exhorted the writer, "the
celestial harmony to which we must raise our eyes is not material
but spiritual consonance, in which number, order, and measure
converge, via the ternary, in the One." But while acknowledging
that inferior things necessarily conform to astrological consonance,
Trithemius did not hold the same for "superior things" subsisting
in the spiritual realm, among which is to be counted the immortal
soul. Inasmuch as "stellar harmony has neither brought forth the
mind nor influenced it," he reminded Ganay, the human soul can
never be said to be subject to celestial compulsion.[101]

As early as 1487 Trithemius had indicated the centrality of this
axiom to his theological outlook when he advised a correspondent
that "it is not nature which compels a man to evil, but only his own
will."[102] The excursus into astrology in the Ganay letter offered
Trithemius the opportunity to enlarge on that theme. Thus, while
admittedly having no problem accepting the proposition, upheld by
a certain unnamed "lover of the occult" (*philocryphus*), that "whoever possesses knowledge of the condition of celestial harmony may
be made familiar both with past and future events," Trithemius at
the same time wanted Ganay to understand that this should not be
confused with a belief in fatalism. On the contrary, he admonished,

fatalism should be vehemently rejected with the avowal that the stars, "inasmuch as they do not know or feel anything, neither confer wisdom to our minds nor have any control over us."[103] Should God permit an especially gifted observer of the heavens to predict the future, this is not because the human will is subject to celestial determinism, but because the astrologer is better fitted than most to grasp the providential laws of nature—laws from which, nevertheless, the immortal soul is inherently exempt.

For this reason Trithemius could commend to Ganay a form of "true astrology" (vera astrologia) which, in service to "true alchemy" (vera alchymia), sharply contrasts with a false form of astrology, premised on the assumption of fatalistic determinism, which administers to false alchemy. Those belonging to the latter group are put down by the writer as "rash, vain, and mendacious deceivers of our minds and chatterers of frivolous things," whereas those belonging to the former group are heralded for properly discerning that "the disposition of the stars lends nothing to the immortal mind, nothing to natural knowledge, and nothing to supercelestial wisdom—except insofar as body holds sway over body." Or, to put this antifatalist credo another way: "The mind is free, being neither subordinated to the stars, nor receiving their influences, nor following their motion, but communicating only by a supercelestial principle, by means of which it has been created and made fruitful."[104]

The foregoing epistolary expositions of occult doctrine reveal the appearance of a certain discrepancy between Trithemius's theory and his practice. In both cryptographical writings on which his fame as a practitioner of magic chiefly rested, the Steganographia and the Polygraphia, Trithemius expounded a theory of magic that did not fully concur with the cryptic operations it was intended to justify. In the case of the Steganographia, the tract triggering this spate of theoretical statements, this discrepancy hinges largely on a distinction between natural and angelic magic. In the case of the Polygraphia, however, the corresponding discrepancy appears to hinge principally on the distinction between natural magic and purely mental operations of cryptic encipherment.

These seeming disparities between his theory and practice, however, did not deter Trithemius from steadily adhering to the kind of magical rationale outlined in his epistles to Westerburg, Joachim, Capellarius, and Ganay—accompanied, we must add, by a persistingly defensive way of presenting that rationale which gave evidence of residual effects springing from his steganographical operations. Further conveying that rationale was the abbot's polygraphical handbook, which, despite displaying a surface appearance of innocent cryptic notations having little in common with the strange-sounding rituals found in its forerunner, presents a theoretical justification of magic not unlike that explicated to the foregoing correspondents. For by reaffirming, in this least likely vehicle for a full-fledged magical theory, the plea for the cryptographical adept to pursue behind his operations "the discernment of things both physical and metaphysical," Trithemius further underscored his conviction that magic is not an end in itself. It is but a means, he judged, to a higher end grounded in Christian theology.

Not only is the soul blessed with such occult wisdom driven to a more comprehensive knowledge of the world, Trithemius averred in the preface to his *Polygraphia*, but it is also "driven upward by the desire for a more sublime understanding." And how is this "sublime understanding" to be achieved? When a mind "has returned to unity from the ternary," Trithemius explained, "it at last is easily able to rise to the denary." Passages like these found in the apologetical introduction to his polygraphical handbook attest to the Pythagorean way of thinking which continued to inform the magic of Trithemius even after he had decided to replace the earlier steganographical method of cryptic communication with one showing no dependency on angelic mediation. Also carrying over into his polygraphical manual was a Pythagorean interpretation of the esoteric rule, arising out of his supposition that, as therein stated, "in these numbers are hidden profound mysteries, made accessible only to few men."[105] In clarification of this now familiar motif of his magic, whereby, as stated in an appended *pinax polygraphiae*, "one thing lies concealed within the outer shell (*in cortice*) and another is brought to light in the public performance of signs," Trithemius furnished an elucidative parallel from human physiology. "Just as the spirit (*spiritus*) in the blood vivifies the human body," noted Trithemius in this regard, "so does the force (*vigor*) lying hidden in this art commend its operation."[106]

It appears, if we are to lend credence to the abbot's extensive Pythagorean-Hermetic justification of his magical operations, that he construed this physiological parallel to the dynamics of polygraphy as something more than a metaphor. He interpreted it to signify the substantive identification of the energizing "force lying hidden in this art" with the invigorating *spiritus mundi* coursing through and animating all things. It is the identical *spiritus*, as Trithemius indicated in affiliated writings, which drives successive inward transmutations of the alchemist to match his outward material ones—in this way binding the artist and his art in a joint quest for purification.

The *spiritus* occultly binding the polygrapher to nature, Trithemius insisted in this connection, should not be confused with the evil "spirits" which his critics called demons. As for those who might think otherwise, Trithemius confidently assured them that, "upon prudently pealing away the shell until arriving at the hidden nucleus," they would discover the volume at hand to be "a good and natural work, which can be turned to good or to wicked use, depending on how the free will of anyone in its charge is moved." The language of polygraphy as viewed by Trithemius, that is to say, is written into the natural fabric of the cosmos itself, provoking his proclamation that "whatever is visible in the universe, and has been placed in the world, provides a pillar of support (*fulcimentum*) for the prompt ministry of this novel art of mine."[107]

But while basing the enigmas of polygraphy in nature, Trithemius did not mean thereby to suggest that its operant cannot also employ their powers to transcend nature. For the range of possible categories relevant to the polygraphical art, he determined, extends beyond visible reality into the sphere of invisible and even imagined entities. "All of those things which language is able to express or the soul is able to ponder," boldly declared the abbot with this wider potential of his art in mind, "furnish the very secret of polygraphy with data and promise to enlarge this art, so far as it is able to be known by mortals, even to infinity (*in infinitum*)."[108] The bold assertion that the language of polygraphy can conceivably reach beyond the naturally finite to the supernaturally infinite realm of existence was not casually evinced by the abbot. To the finite minds of men, as Trithemius baldly put this claim on behalf of polygraphy, "we show a way to the infinite" (*finitis modum dedimus ad infinita*).[109]

The occult pathway to the infinite promised in passages like these by Trithemius attests not only to a Pythagorean constituent of his magical doctrine, but also to the reconstructed version of the Pythagorean tradition bequeathed by Nicholas Cusanus. "In the same way as a finite and circumscribable number is reducible by progression into infinity," Trithemius observed in testimony to this Cusan influence on his polygraphical theory, "in the same way is the instruction of this art extendible, by a diverse metathesis, into the endless reaches of the world."[110] To assist us in the arduous task of traversing the chasm separating these two realms—the finite from the infinite—Trithemius promised in characteristically Cusan language that "we will employ the circle in great things (*in magnis*), and the line or the point in the least things" (*in minimis*).[111]

Under the sway of a comparable outlook Cusanus himself adopted a quietist doctrine of learned ignorance (*docta ignorantia*) as the epistemological correlate to his mystical theology. Trithemius, on the other hand, similarly steeped in the traditions of mystical theology, rather chose to express his revised Pythagoreanism in the form of a restless magical surge of the soul to the infinite. Calling on Cabala—what he termed "the Cabalistic method of the arcana" (*cabalisticus arcanorum modus*)[112]—to complete the magical journey of the polygrapher, Trithemius thereby underscored, by implication if not by explication, fundamental continuity with the occult theory underlying the earlier steganographical manual. To the extent that Cabala, a cornerstone of the earlier steganographical tract, continued to play an explicit role in polygraphy for Trithemius, it was primarily in its utility as a device for linguistic obfuscation. Implicitly, however, its substantive presence still continued to be felt. For to the extent that the occult theory underlying the *Polygraphia* expanded from a mere justification of operational magic to constitute a kind of theology in itself, that is, *theologia magica*, to that same extent its operator still required the angel-conjuring powers of Cabalism to fill in the gap between finite nature and an infinite God.

It is clear from the theoretical defense of polygraphy as here outlined, then, that it was not Trithemius's intention to descend into mere verbal and numerical trickery. Theoretically at least, his second major cryptological work was guided by the same lofty principles of magic, and was inspired by the same motive of inward spiritual transmutation to accompany outward transmutations of nature, as also informed the earlier tract—minus only the underpinning of assisting spirits. The principal connective theme of the two cryptographic manuals, at least in theory, is a blend of Pythagorean number mysticism, Hermetic alchemical and natural magic, astrology, and Cabala.

If the astrological-angelogical system on which Trithemius's earlier steganographical operations depended appears to have fallen away in his subsequent polygraphical operations, this is not the same as saying that it altogether disappeared. It is not by chance, in this regard, that the same year 1508 which saw the dedication of the *Polygraphia* to Maximilian also saw, addressed to the same exalted personage, the appearance of the *De septem secundeis* presenting that astrological-angelogical system in explicit form. Much as, for Trithemius, the planetary orbits and their governing angels arched over the world, so can it be said that this small but pregnant tract arched over the abbot's magical speculations. To conclude this section, accordingly, we need now to speak directly to the astrologically and angelogically based tract which, while coming into view only in Trithemius's latter years, represented a cosmic backdrop for his occult speculation.

In 1507 Trithemius sent a letter to his half-brother Jacob which, aimed at encouraging an attitude of learning in his sibling, examined, each in its turn, the traditional seven liberal arts. Concerning one among these, the art of astronomy which "teaches the course of the stars, discerns the passing of time, divides the year, and marks out the hours and days," Trithemius pointed out that among its practical benefits is its utility in assisting the computation of the feast days for the ecclesiastical calendar.[113] But a year later Trithemius brought to light another application of astronomy which he did not indicate to Jacob in his epistolary tribute to the seven liberal arts. Dedicated to Maximilian along with the *Polygraphia*, the writing in question, the *De septem secundeis* claimed to coordinate all of human history with the varying positions of the planets and of their celestial rulers, the planetary angels.

The fundamental affiliation of astrology with magic was underscored for Trithemius by his medieval hero Albertus, whom he reported in his Hirsau annals to have authored a *Speculum astronomiae* "in which, with very accurate industry, he distinguishes the books of natural magic from the superstitious and prohibited variety."[114] That, in establishing an astrological framework for his occult studies, Trithemius had not abandoned his earlier attestations to free will is loudly proclaimed in the pages of the *De septem secundeis* itself. "The mind is free," reaffirmed its author therein, "and does not admit the influence of the stars."[115] According to the scheme of planetary history lying behind this pronouncement, borrowed from the thirteenth-century Paduan Pietro d'Abano, each of the seven planetary spheres is governed by an angel, termed a "secondary intelligence" because it is presumed to rule under the supervision of the overseeing "First Intelligence," God the Creator. Each of the planetary angels in turn is held to rule over a given epoch of human history astrologically calculated to last exactly 354 solar years and four lunar months. Identified as the planetary angels, in the order of their successive rules, are Orifiel in the sphere of Saturn, Anael in the sphere of Venus, Zachariel in the sphere of Jupiter, Raphael in the sphere of Mercury, Samael in the sphere of Mars, Gabriel in the sphere of the moon, and Michael in the sphere of the sun.[116]

A possible occult application of this system of planetary history, pointed out by Trithemius within the pages of the *De septem secundeis* itself, is the art of prophecy. The supposition guiding the abbot in this endeavor is that prophecy, being intuitively attuned to the cosmic process governed by the seven secondary intelligences occupying their respective planetary spheres, represents the extension of history into the future. Conversely, history is consummated prophecy. The postulate that history is past prophecy, and prophecy, future history, comes to a head in the last section of the tract, addressed to the third rule of Martial Samael, in which the enigmatically ominous words appear which have been taken by some as a prediction of the impending Protestant Reformation:

A great religious sect will arise, and with it the destruction of the old religions. It is to be dreaded that the fourth beast will lose its one and only head. Through the medium of Samael, Mars first of all governed over the flood, and the second time over the destruction of the Trojans. This time, near the end of the epoch [viz., 1525], it will watch over the great loss of unity. For from preceding events future ones can be inferred which will follow them. This third revolution of Mars will not be completed without a prophecy of some new institution of religion.[117]

Apart from what Trithemius intended by this passage, it represented an attempt on his part to carry his jointly astrological and Cabalistic conception of world history beyond the time in which he was writing.

The angelic-planetary system conditioning the *De septem secundeis*, if we are to believe Trithemius's own account of the matter, also conditioned the steganographical method of cryptic communication triggering the abbot's magical legend. Surely it was as much with the controversy in mind set in motion by this writing as from any implication of fatalism in the tract's astrological overview that Trithemius beseeched its dedicatee, Maximilian, at its close: "I declare by my own hand and profess with my own mouth that, in all those matters, I believe nothing and admit nothing unless the Catholic Church also believes it. All the rest I repudiate and condemn as vain, feigned, and superstitious."[118] While the question of free will may have played a part in this concluding plea to the emperor, the resemblance of its words (signaled by the word *superstitious*) to those with which he overtly engarrisoned his magical writings also places the *De septem secundeis* in their ranks and a suitable introduction into the steganographical and polygraphical investigations of the abbot.

## From Occult Theory to Cryptographical Practice

Contrary to Trithemius's contention to Bostius that the marvels effected by steganography "are completely natural . . . without the invocation or assistance of any spirits whatsoever," the very structure of the extant work (two completed books and part of a third),[119] organized according to three angelic orders presumed to assist the transmission of secret messages, seems to argue against the abbot's claim. The reader of these pages, our analysis will show, is left with three possible options. The first option is to agree with Bovillus that, in his steganographical operations, Trithemius engaged in demonic magic; the second option, to distinguish between the good spirits of Trithemius's cryptic operations from the demonic spirits behind the operations of the sorcerers; and the third option, to adopt the view that the many ritualistic invocations prescribed in the *Steganographia* constitute a cryptic cover to conceal the linguistic enigmas of his art from those for which they are not intended.

The angelic hierarchy described in the *De septem secundeis*, we learn from the partially completed *Steganographia*, represents the highest of three ranks of spirits upon which the steganographer can draw for the ministration of his cryptic operations. The first book delineates thirty-one regional or district spirits ruling over as many domains, or mansions, of the heavens; the second book, twenty-four temporal spirits ruling over each hour of the day and night; and the third book, the seven planetary angels to which the foregoing spirit-rulers of the celestial regions and temporal durations are ultimately subject. All three classes of spirits are declared to be capable of assisting the operations of steganography, together with a multitude of subordinates under their aegis.

From the outset of the tract, whereby the steganographer is instructed to turn in a predetermined direction and voice an incantation appropriate to a spirit-ruler said to reside there, we can see grounds for the criticisms its author was trying to counter. The same directive is applied to the receiver of the secret message, who previously has been apprised of the name of the spirit by a cryptic symbol inserted near the close of an earlier letter. A reply, we are told, can be returned to the sender by the same technique.

The opening sentence of the first book—evidently catching Bovillus's eye at the outset of his brief encounter with the manuscript and making him resistant to a further inspection of its contents—reveals the fine line separating Trithemian magic from the illicit demonic kind. The operation called for by the first chapter, it is cautioned, "is very difficult and full of danger because of the pride and rebellion of its spirits, who do not obey a man unless he is very experienced in this art; for they not only refuse to obey novices and those untested in the art, but also, if they should be too strongly pressed on, they frequently do injury to them and offend them by various delusions." Disobedience by rebellious spirits might take the form of an unwanted disclosure of shared information to a wrong party, or, as another possibility, "no sooner are they dispatched, together with the appropriate letter, than they fly away to him to whom the letter has been sent and burst in upon him unexpectedly and without order." Spirits which have been improperly summoned can also cause great havoc in the vicinity of the transmitter, so that, "being in a frenzied state, they so fill the air with their clamor that they often reveal their arcana to all who are in proximity to the sender."[120] Clearly, if we are to take at their face value passages like these, the steganographical magic that Trithemius set out to distinguish from its demonic look-alike is not natural in the sense indicated to Bostius, and repeatedly restated in response to the Bovillus attack, but supernatural in the manner of Cabalistic spirit-magic.

The text that follows confirms this reading of steganography, with each chapter addressed to a different spirit. Since the pattern of ritual prescribed to the steganographer repeats itself with considerable regularity from chapter to chapter, the procedures outlined in the first chapter, addressed to the regional spirit Pamersyel, can be taken as typical of the work as a whole. First of all, we are told, the sender of a secret message should place before himself, blessed "in the name of the father, the Son, and the Holy Spirit," a blank folio for the inscription of the plaintext, the ostensible message of which can consist of anything the sender chooses. The only proviso is that it should be written simply enough that "all who read it may understand its contents, either in Latin, the tongue of the fatherland, or any other language one may choose."[121] The precise choice of words inscribed on the folio is unimportant, but the same does not hold true when it comes to the direction the sender faces when inscribing his words. To obtain the assistance of Pamersyel, for example, he must look east where the mansion of Pamersyel is located.

In the midst of his letter writing the sender is instructed to articulate the appropriate conjuration, beginning with the spirit's name, and await the summoned spirit's arrival. If the said spirit fails to appear, the rite should be repeated until the conjuration succeeds. Upon the spirit's arrival the sender completes the letter and sends it by courier to its intended recipient. Having earlier been made privy to the appropriate spirit by a secret character affixed to the end of the letter, its recipient must in turn pronounce the necessary incantation. "These words being pronounced," the sender can be assured that their receiver "can know your mind perfectly."[122] With these instructions, however, also comes a crucial caveat. Success in the operation described, Trithemius stressed, occurs only if the receiver conjures the correct spirit. If he should misunderstand the enigmatic sign indicated in the surface text and try to invoke the wrong spirit, he not only will fail in his attempt to elicit the correct encrypted message, but will provoke great hardship and suffering in both himself and those in his vicinity.

"Consider diligently all the things we have declared in this chapter," its concluding sentence advises, "and you will easily be able to understand what we are about to say in the following ones."[123] All that follows in the first book, from the second chapter revolving around the spirit Padiel to the thirty-first chapter revolving around Badiel, can thus be viewed as a chain of variations on the operations described in the first chapter. A concluding chapter summarizes the instruction previously given, and prescribes eight rules, or methodological guidelines, for the successful transmission of secret messages through the agency of the foregoing spirits. We can presume that the same rules apply to the transmission of messages through the office of the spirits of the hours and planets taking up the remaining two books.

The first rule of sound steganographical practice states that both sender and receiver must show great diligence in their pursuit of the fruits promised by its powers, since "the great mysteries of this art can be penetrated only by very studious men," and the second rule enjoins the steganographer to esoteric secrecy, inasmuch as "nothing is more foolish than to inculcate the knowledge of this profound art in those who neither wish nor are fitted to gaze upon its very lofty heights."[124] The third rule in turn instructs the steganographer to familiarize himself with "the differences, locations, names, orders, and offices of the loftiest spirits, together with as many dukes and counts under their governance," in compliance with which the sender is directed to assess accurately "when each spirit is to be invoked, and on behalf of what offices or arcana they are enlisted, in order that he will not err either in the places or in the names of particular spirits which he may wish to call."[125] The fourth rule demands the correct enunciation of the appropriate conjuration, since if there is any error made in the words spoken, "the spirits which have been invoked or are about to be invoked not only do not obey, but outrightly resist the command."[126] A corollary of this stipulation is that a conjuration meant for one spirit should never be used to procure another spirit's aid, the violation of which not only will result in failure in the operation, but also will call great danger upon the head of the operator.

The fifth rule of steganography urges that the gravity of subject matter and loftiness of purpose be preserved in the exchange of a message, and that this method be employed only when the conventional one is unsuitable by reason of the need for absolute confidentiality. Bluntly put, this rule states that the art of steganography should be used exclusively "for the transmission of great and arduous pronouncements which, if they were to be divulged, would inflict injury or cause peril." The sixth rule in turn cautions the practitioner to know as precisely as possible "the characters of the spirits," that is to say, "which spirits are good, which are bad, which are prompt and benevolent in obeying and which are harsh and rebellious, and again which are efficacious in nocturnal operations and which in diurnal ones." For unless the steganographer apprehends the true natures of the spirits at the outset, warned the abbot, "he will advance only with very great difficulty, and at last succumb to stupor." The seventh rule in its turn underscores the solitary circumstances in which steganography should be conducted. If the sender is not in a position to remove himself from society when he makes his conjuration, he should get as far from others as he can, and when a given spirit appears in obedience to a conjuration, the secret to be entrusted to the spirit should be delivered in silence, or at least in a whisper. The reason given for this injunction is that "all the spirits ministering to this art have been endowed with such a nature and condition that they completely detest and flee the throng of men, and hate public gatherings." Finally, the eighth rule calls for the sender always to employ the correct notation or "character" to attract the desired spirit, inasmuch as the spirit must perceive the character before it can act upon the command. If, on the other hand, the spirit "does not see the impression of that character, it utterly refuses to obey the person summoning it to bear a secret message to someone."[127]

These rules of steganographical methodology continue to weave, like warp and woof, through the two remaining extant books, addressed to the spirits of the hours and planets respectively. If the credulity of the reader is still intact by the author's restatement in the preface to the second book that "nothing in this art of mine is meant to be frivolous, nothing is contrary to our evangelical tradition or to the Catholic faith, nothing taught here is the least bit superstitious," the same cannot be said with regard to his further assurance that the art described rests not only on good and honest principles, but also on entirely "natural ones." For the characterization of a technique calling for the conjuration of angel-like spirits as "natural" was obviously as puzzling to an intended reader like Bovillus as to unintended ones like the prior of Bostius's cloister. The lesson Trithemius elicited from the endeavors of his critics to point up this contradition was only to underscore the oft-stated imperative for esoteric secrecy. To wit, he responded, "its mystery, veiled by solitary and exotic instructions, and its language, wrapped up in the names of spirits, requires an erudite reader."[128]

As in the first book, the first chapter of the second book, addressed to the time spirit Samael, can be taken as a model for the chapters to follow. Like his counterparts invoked in the first book, Samael is claimed to have at his disposal numerous subordinate ministers, though this time more systematically detailed in a hierarchy of "dukes, counts, and lesser servants." Again the sender is cautioned against carrying out incorrect procedures, this time with the observation that Samael and the other temporal spirits will appear only in the hours assigned to them. The violation of this rule will produce much the same result as that indicated in the previous book: rebelliousness and injury in place of obedience and service, the reason being that these spirits of the hours "are impudent and very prone to deceive and deride men, and are especially wont to ridicule and mock those whom they judge to be least skilled in the art of steganography, whereas they revere and fear those whom they believe to be bold, constant, and expert in this art, and in their trepidation and reverence speedily obey their commands."[129]

Apropos of these spirits of the hours, Trithemius further enlisted on steganography's behalf an indispensable auxiliary. Any attempt to procure the assistance of Samael or any other temporal spirit, Trithemius admonished, would necessarily be in vain if it were not based on a firm knowledge of astrology. Taking stock "first of the moon, then of the rest of the planets in accordance with their accustomed order," the steganographer is instructed to affix to his text the character correctly identifying the order of the planetary constellations operative at the precise moment when the message is inscribed.[130] This, of course, is also a moment when a given spirit, such as Samael, is dominant. In this way the receiver is occultly apprised of the right hour, on a succeeding day, when he can safely unravel the secret message by appeal to the appropriate spirit. Reasserting many times in the succeeding chapters of the second book the indispensable role of astrology for steganographical operations, Trithemius consistently added the proviso that such astrological expertise is in vain if it is not rigorously harnessed to a virtuous disposition. The last chapter summarizes this dual requirement, and adds several more to it.

Once the condition of a virtuous soul has been established, declared Trithemius, the ground is prepared for the next step in the steganographical process, instruction in the seven liberal arts, "especially in the science of the stars, so that [the steganographer] might know their general movements, passages back and forth, changes, natures, locations, rises and descents, and the effects of the stars, constellations, and planets; for without the competent knowledge of these things no one is able to have access to the profundities of this art."[131] Beyond these requisites Trithemius indicated three more, like the foregoing specifically aimed at gaining access to the spirits of the hours but also more generally applicable to gaining entry into the spirit world in general. The first is instruction by a qualified master; the second, the selection of an appropriate locale and planetary interval for instruction; and the third, the declaration of an oath of secrecy between master and student. Each of these steganographical requisites calls for elaboration.

Concerning the need for a qualified master, Trithemius declared along his usual esoteric lines that "it is impossible, except for a few men skilled in many erudite subjects (especially in magical ones), to lay claim to this knowledge without a preceptor." And for the master to be qualified means that he is no less required to subordinate knowledge to virtue than is his student. Concerning the need of an apt locale for instruction, Trithemius urged that when a student is about to embark on his tutelage, "let his teacher lead him to some secret and purified place for his instruction!"[132] And concerning the need for a propitious time, highlighting the crucial role of astrological conditioning in setting the proper stage:

Let the moment be tranquil and serene, with the moon, having come completely around into opposition with the sun, shining brightly in reflection from the rays of the latter! And let Mercury, if it is possible for it to be accomplished, come into the ascendant, conjoined to either Venus or Jupiter! And let Saturn and Mars remain remote, since if either of these come into conjunction with the ascending planet the instruction will not be perfected.[133]

The ideal locale of instruction having thus been chosen and a time selected when the stars are most propitiously ordered, the student of steganography is then ready to proceed to the third requirement of his initiation, a vow of secrecy.

The vow of esoteric confidentiality binding the steganographical student to his master was formulated by Trithemius as follows:

I swear and promise by the virtue of Almighty God, by the blood of our Lord Jesus Christ, by the resurrection of the dead and by the Last Judgment, and by the salvation of my soul in the holy Catholic faith—I swear and promise this to the omnipotent God, to the blessed Virgin Mary, to all the saints, and to you—that I will faithfully keep this art of steganography concealed all the days of my life. Nor will I teach it to anyone without your will and consent. Above all, I swear and promise by this same virtue that I will not use this science against God and His commandments, nor against the Holy Roman and Universal Church and its ministers, nor against justice and equity. May God thus help me, and may He save me in the Last Judgment.[134]

Upon hearing this oath the master is then instructed to read to his disciple a set "general conjuration in the mystical tongue" (*conjuratio generalis . . . in lingua mystica*), to interpret its meaning, and to impart the remaining conjurations pertinent to the steganographic endeavor. In so doing he is urged to avoid suspicion that there is anything therein "diabolical, superstitious, or contrary to God, or that there is latently hidden, either implicitly or explicitly, a pact with demons."[135]

Repeating a *leitmotif* of the abbot's magical writings, the second book closes on the absolute imperative for secrecy in these procedures—this lest the ~~Copyrighted Material~~ of steganography should end up in the wrong hands. And the rule of esoteric secrecy, the abbot stressed in this reworking of his favored theme, can be safely enforced only if instruction is put in oral form before the student is in a position to grasp its precepts. "After the master of this art has explained the conjurations, order, and succession of all the spirits," Trithemius typically admonished in this connection, he must take great care that "the most secret arcana of this science, which have never been written down and must never be written down," be transmitted to his pupils in the same oral form in which it was transmitted to himself.[136] If the Steinmoel and Bovillus affairs had taught Trithemius a hard lesson in this regard, it was not one of modifying his requirement of private oral instruction, but rather one of being more rigorously selective in his choice of suitable students.

The uncompleted third book of the *Steganographia* is addressed to the third set of spirits of possible use for the transmission of cryptic messages, the superior planetary angels, each of which, we are told, rules for intervals of 354 years and four months.[137] Whereas, in the affiliated *De septem secundeis*, Trithemius credited Pietro d'Abano with devising the cosmic scheme of planetary angels informing this writing, here he reached to an authority of far greater antiquity, a certain Menastor, who taught him that "there are seven planets presided over by seven angels, to which are subjected twenty-one spirits; through these are enunciated the arcana." In addition, claimed the abbot, the "ancient philosopher" Menastor discovered that, with the assistance of these planetary angels, "it is possible for us, by means of a special art, to make known to a friend, however distant he is, an idea in our minds—and this in twenty-four hours, without words, without books, and without a messenger, very perfectly, reconditely, and secretly." What Trithemius failed to tell his readers was that his "discovery" of Menastor was reserved to himself alone. Much like the names of Hunibald and Meginfrid in his historical writings, the name of Menastor in his exposition of steganography appears to be nothing more than a figment of its inventor's imagination.[138]

Before laying aside his controversial work Trithemius was able to treat only the first of the planetary angels, Orifiel, ruling over the sphere of Saturn. As in the prior two books, however, we can assume that the pattern of instruction emerging in the first chapter would have repeated itself in the projected chapters to follow. This also, of course, applies to instruction in the auxiliary art of astrology, which, if it played an especially prominent part in the second book, occupies a still more conspicuous place in the third book revolving around the planetary angels. "When you wish to produce an effect through this very profound speculation," the abbot declared with this requirement in mind, "it is obligatory that you know the ascent, exaltation, and descent of all the stars of the eight spheres through which the operations are carried out, and likewise how distant each star is from the other."[139]

Concerning the services of saturnine Orifiel in particular, Trithemius urged that "if you want to perform in steganography through this angel, especially on the day named for Saturn [viz., Saturday] and in those things, affairs, and causes which pertain to Saturn, you must above all be acquainted with its different movements." Such knowledge should consist not only of the general formulation of planetary laws, but also of the concrete applications of those laws. With this need in mind Trithemius would incorporate in each of the succeeding chapters the appropriate astrological information for the planetary spirit under consideration, "without the observation of which no one can operate in this science."[140]

Trithemius's transference of the planetary angel scheme from his *De septem secundeis* to the *Steganographia*, however, poses a peculiar problem for the latter work which the abbot did not very successfully answer. Given that, with regard to the temporal spirits ruling over the hours of the day, Trithemius required an exchange of a cryptic message to be carried out within the very hour the invoked spirit was dominant, we would logically expect the same requirement to be applied to the planetary angels ruling, not for an hour only, but for lengthy 354-year-plus intervals assigned to them. And indeed, Trithemius suggested as much, declaring that "whoever, therefore, wishes to perform without difficulty in accordance with the known principles of this art is advised to work his effects through the planet whose pre-eminent angel is found, by an easy calculation, to govern the world in that given period."[141] Since, however, the rule of Orifiel, the subject of the present discourse, would not come around again until the year A.D. 2234 (the abbot, as shown in his *De septem secundeis*, believed that he was currently living under the hegemony of Samael in the sphere of Mars), Trithemius could not rigorously push this counsel to wait for the time of the planet's domination without effectively ruling out Orifiel as a possible current steganographic medium. We must assume, if

Trithemius were serious about this demand, that the contemporary reader of his partially completed text was expected to transfer to the reign of Samael, with minimal variation, those operations which the abbot addressed to the reign of Orifiel.

In light of the above observations pertaining to the *Steganographia* it appears that the crux of Trithemius's challenge to his critics should have consisted, not of the reduction of magic from a supernatural to a merely natural science, but of a distinction between two contrasting supernaturalist disciplines: one dependent upon good (or at least morally neutral) spirits and one dependent upon wicked demonic spirits. By the abbot's own testimony he based the theory of steganography on the premise that its operative spirits belong exclusively to the former category rather than, as Bovillus and his cohorts would have it, to the latter category. The effect of Cabala on Trithemius's thought, invoked at least partly with the motive of acquiring angelic help in the operations of magic, was undoubtedly to help reinforce this conviction. Nevertheless, the Cabalist component of Trithemius's steganographical operations, it also needs to be emphasized, stands conceptually apart from his Hermetic one. The two forms of magic, natural and supernatural, can be comfortably reconciled only on the supposition, never systematically developed by the abbot, that natural magic constitutes a preliminary stage to a higher form of angelic magic.

The fact that Trithemius failed to make this case in a rigorous and sustained way probably owes to the defensive posture he was forced to assume when composing his various magical disquisitions, causing him to formulate them in disparate fits and starts rather than in an extended form allowing for systematic connections. To confuse matters further, the abbot offered a written "key"— a *Clavis steganographiae*, later attached to the published text—that permitted a linguistic unraveling of its enigmas altogether independently of either natural or supernatural magic. The effect of this steganographical key is to demystify the work through whose labyrinth it is intended to lead us by unveiling, in direct anticipation of the spirit-free *Polygraphia*, a system of codes and ciphers utterly independent of externally occult powers.

For the most part, at least as compared to modern cryptological practices, the steganographical methods of Trithemius seem to be rather cumbersome. Thus, to cite one example given in the *clavis steganographiae*, it requires a plaintext of 143 Latin words, with the first letter of every word counted, to produce a 30-word encrypted message in German calling for a secret meeting. The two-word greeting alone introducing this secret message, "Lieber Getruwer," highlights the unwieldy character of Trithemius's method, calling for no less than fifteen words to begin the plaintext: "*L*ucidum *i*ubar *e*ternae *b*eatitudinis *e*xcellentiss. *R*ex, *g*ubernator *et t*utor *r*obustissime *u*iversorum *v*irtuose *v*iventium, *e*xulum *r*efugium. . . . " Or to cite another example similarly setting up a covert meeting, a 21-word encrypted message, "hac nocte post duodecim, veniam ad te circa ianuam, quae ducit ad ortum, ubi me expectabis, age ut omnia sint parata," with the first letter of every other word counted, calls for a 174-word plaintext beginning: "*H*umanae salutis *a*mator, qui *c*reavit omnia, *n*obis induxit *o*bedientiam mandatorum, *c*ui omnes *t*enemur obedire *e*t obsequi, . . . ."[142] Opting in the first of two books of the *Clavis* to establish his alphabetical permutations in linear form, in the second book he provided a series of circular permutations (*tabulae rotundae*) resembling a method of mnemonic correspondences worked out by the late medieval polymath Ramon Lull in his *ars combinatoria*.[143]

While the *clavis steganographia*, then, appears to reduce the ostensibly spirit-riddled tract to which it refers to little more than mere wordplays, the Renaissance equivalent of modern anagrams and acrostics, it does not succeed altogether in dissipating the suspicion that there still lingers beneath its seemingly innocent codes and ciphers a presumption of supernatural intervention. For even if we should agree that the first two books consist of nothing more perilous than disguised modes of encipherment, we nonetheless are left with the disconcerting third book addressed to the planetary angels, the completed portion of which, as pointed out by D. P. Walker, lacks any instance of an encoded message. Only very recently has it been established—this by Thomas Ernst—that the enciphered text of the third book is as linguistically solvable as its predecessors, thereby dispensing of the need, as presumed by Walker, to refer its hidden meaning to supernatural mediation.[144]

The waters of the controversy stirred up by the *Steganographia* were further muddied by the addition to its mix of its cryptographic successor, the *Polygraphia*. Especially in response to the negative flak incurred by the Bovillus affair, Trithemius decided to expunge all mention of supernatural spirits from its pages. However, as acknowledged by the author himself in the course of its exposition, by this tactic he escaped one objection to his art only to be met with another. For this time the crux of the argument against him, as distinct from that of demon-conjuration plaguing his prior cryptographic efforts, consisted of the accusation that his methods were ineffectual and unworthy of serious consideration. To those who "ridicule these studies of mine as vain and puerile," Trithemius passionately responded that "the genius of man, when aided by study and art, is capable of the very greatest achievements, and he who spurns the least things will never attain to the greater ones."[145]

The text of the *Polygraphia* consists in the main of columns of charts needed for the cryptographic transposition of sentences, a far cry from the pages of its steganographical antecedent with their explicit references to assisting spirits and sample conjurations for procuring their assistance in the secret transmission of messages. And as in the case of its steganographical forerunner, the text of the *Polygraphia* is provided with an attached key—a *Clavis polygraphiae* (see title page, plate 2)—to aid in the unravelment of its contents. As noted by Shumaker, the polygraphical operations of Trithemius are presented in a straightforward manner, lacking "most of the teasing disguises of the *Steganographia*."[146]

The first book, for example, is made up of 384 vertical rows of letters from A to Z and their various verbal and numerical correspondences; the second, of 304 rows; the third, of 132 rows, and so on through the six books of the work. The first nine verbal offerings of each column, corresponding to the letters A to F, show how the polygraphic technique might function:

| A | Deus | clemens | creans | coelos | impendant | |
| | omnibus | vitam | permansuram | sanctis | | |
| B | Creator | clementissimus | regens | colestia | conferit | |
| | cunctis | amoenitatem | aeternam | electis | | |
| C | Conditor | pius | conservans | supercoelestia | donet | |
| | universis | jocunditatem | sempiternam | praedilectis | | |
| D | Opifex | piussimus | moderans | mundum | largiatur | |
| | credentibus | consolationem | coelestem | sanctissimus | | |
| E | Dominus | magnus | gubernans | mundana | concedit | |
| | nobis | laetitiam | supercoelestem | justus | | |
| F | Dominator | excelsus | ordinans | homines | condonet | |
| | christianis | gloriam | perpetuam | justificatus | | |

Using this partial chart we can, for instance, elicit the encrypted word *faba* from a plaintext reading "Dominator clemens conferat sanctis...," or, alternatively, the word *baca* from the plaintext "Creator creans donet vitam..." or "Creator clemens conservans coelos...."[147] Clearly, as this example illustrates, the shift of Trithemius from a steganographical to a polygraphical mode of communication, while perhaps putting his readers at greater ease on the question of how his cryptic messages were conveyed, did little to simplify the cumbersome method he prescribed for devising those messages.

Again with appeal to the revered antiquity of the art to be expounded, Trithemius in his polygraphical preface called attention to various respectable ancients who lauded its utility. Cryptic inscription as such, Trithemius called upon Plato to testify (*Phaedrus*, 274D–275C), originated in Egypt, where the priest Theuth is said to have invented hieroglyphical and arithmetical symbols and taught them to King Thamus. From Egypt the art of secret writing reputedly spread to Greece and Rome, where, its benefits came to the attention of such figures as Archimedes, Cicero, and Augustus Caesar, and eventually to Christians like the martyr St. Cyprian, who thereby found a technique for concealing their thoughts from the intolerant authorities. Two later beneficiaries of the cryptographic invention, according to Trithemius, were the Goths and Franks, the latter who had succeeded in reunifying Christendom after the collapse of the Roman Empire. Witnessing the first of these developments—and, in the process, proving himself to be highly proficient in the art he described—was the Venerable Bede, who noted that the Goths, "in order that they might take counsel concerning their arcane ideas, invented a novel and excellent mode of writing which they contrived from Greek letters." But it is the eventual conquerors of the Goths, the Franks, who are said to have stood out in this regard, with Charlemagne himself achieving expertise in cryptographical techniques. "It is by the imitation of such men as these," Trithemius announced to Maximilian, "that I have been moved to undertake this work entitled *Polygraphia*."[148] The emperor, a successor to Charlemagne, was now urged to follow in these same venerable footsteps.

In this way, supported by his role as ecclesiastical historian, Trithemius could credibly present the cryptographical art to which he was referring not so much as an invention as a discovery, the methods of which were secretly bequeathed to him by many centuries of usage. His polygraphic system was not a truly novel creation, but rather represented a culling of the best from systems of the past. The aforementioned exemplars testified that Trithemius, far from espousing a novel technique, was perpetuating a time-tested one.

Serving to reinforce this reading of polygraphy—and, at the same time underscoring its essential bonds of continuity with its steganographical predecessor—is the place assigned by Trithemius to its evolution within the cosmic-historical setting described in the *De septem secundeis*. The planetary period in which the art of cryptography entered the world, according to Trithemius, was during the first rule of the angel Raphael, in the sphere of Mercury, when the art of poetry came into being, the foremost practitioners of which "promised to conceal the great arcana of things under the cloak of their fables." As mankind multiplied and became scattered throughout the world under the governance of the successive planetary angels, observed the abbot against this cosmic-historical backdrop, "the unity of letters did not long remain in force, but the division of bodies and minds, separated from one another by great distances, dictated the discovery of divergent and variegated modes of writing."[149] Thanks to this dynamic, one desirous of concealing his true meaning did not need to invent novel alphabets to achieve his purpose. For he already had at hand, if he only had sufficient patience and zeal to gain entry into their preestablished notations, foreign alphabets from which the ordinary person is excluded.

At the same time, however, Trithemius did not wish to restrict the polygrapher to tapping foreign tongues for his cryptic notations. Also at his disposal were disciplines transcribed in his own tongue, such as astronomy. Indeed, as a kind of concluding caveat (*cautela*), Trithemius recommended that the polygrapher disguise his intended message with a language of signs belonging to a known discipline, the object of which is to have the polygrapher mislead the casual reader into thinking that the notations of the secret message refer to a discipline with which they are generally familiar.[150] In this same connection Trithemius acknowledged that he had discovered a valuable source for his polygraphical notations in the language of alchemy. Putting aside any ambivalence he may have previously expressed toward this enigmatic art, Trithemius reported that he only recently had discovered a cryptic alphabet invented by "a certain alchemist, consisting of forty-eight alchemical symbols, which he was accustomed to use for the purpose of concealing his arcana." Inasmuch as elsewhere he had unflatteringly characterized alchemy as a "chaste whore," Trithemius prudently prefaced his list of alchemical ciphers with a statement carefully distinguishing the true art from which they had been extracted, dedicated to a spiritual transmutation of the alchemical lover, from its false look-alike seeking worldly rather than heavenly enrichment.[151]

With the proper esoteric safeguards in place for the protection of his art from unwanted encroachment, promised Trithemius, the polygrapher will not only come into contact with a realm infinitely transcending the present finite one. He will also be permitted, through hidden powers elicited therefrom, to perform marvels at the finite level inexplicable to the uninitiated. His list of the various "utilities" of polygraphy reminds us of similar utilities he earlier had assigned to steganography.

The first and most obvious use of polygraphy offered up by Trithemius is that it will permit arcane thought to be exchanged between two figures separated by a great distance "safely, secretly, and without any suspicion from those who may be witnesses to the transaction." A further utility of polygraphy is that it will allow one hitherto ignorant in the Latin tongue or other language to discourse fluently and eloquently in its vocabulary and, if he so wishes, to conceal profound secrets under its cover. Yet another utility is that it will aid its adept "to augment his memory without labor." In passing through these various practical applications of the polygraphic art Trithemius was careful to repeat the arithmetic basis of its precepts, and further to restate the ironclad rule that not everyone is equally fitted to receive instruction in its procedures, "but only he whom art and nature, aided by the special grace of God, have dignified."[152]

If Trithemius did not thereby succeed in dispelling the cloud of suspicion that had come to gather around his head that what here passes as polygraphy is really steganography under another name, he had himself at least partly to blame. "For in order that the kernels of my steganography (*nuclei Steganographiae nostrae*) may not be made accessible to unworthy babblers," he exclaimed in the concluding words of an introduction to the sixth and last book of his *Polygraphia*, "they have for good reason been buried under a shell."[153] As to how we are to interpret the meaning of this purportedly internal continuity between two cryptological tracts, we are left with three choices, of which the third, in this observer's opinion, best meets the test of evidence furnished in the present chapter.

The first view of the relationship between these successive cryptological phases in the career of Trithemius states that the manifestly demon-free art of polygraphy did not really negate the demon-laden character of steganography preceding it, but only represented a further diabolically inspired attempt to free its author of the magical notoriety ensuing from the earlier cryptological manual. The second view in turn states that, in one cryptographic mode as in the other, Trithemius intended nothing more than to present a harmless systems of codes and ciphers, with the spirits of the celestial regions, hours, and planets of the former functioning as nothing more than obfuscating devices in fulfillment of the requirement of esoterism. Finally, a third view emerges which, being a middle way between these extremes, corresponds best of all to what Trithemius was truly about in his cryptological writings. This is that, in the *Polygraphia* as in the *Steganographia* before it, Trithemius attempted to chart a magical course from earth to Heaven convergent with the course he earlier had charted through the melding of conventional mystical theology with Christian humanism. If the attainment of that theologically conditioned goal also entailed the ability to perform extraordinary feats by a select few, reasoned Trithemius, paradigms were already furnished by the miracle working of Christ and His saintly apostles, who were optimally endowed to give outward material testimony in the finite realm to what at bottom was an inward drive to spiritual purity ultimately attainable only in the infinitely removed realm of God.

The modern scholarly debate over this question has been conditioned nearly as much by assessments of Trithemius's later critics and apologists as by evaluations of his own stated intentions. As the next chapter will show, the viewpoint reading arcane natural *spiritus* into the supernatural spirits of the *Steganographia* was a primary magical motif not only of Trithemius himself, but also of

his magical followers and sympathizers of the next two centuries—
an age simultaneously characterized by widespread calls for religious reform, by the climax of the witch hunts, and by the so-called
age of reason which, at least on its face, was far removed from the
kinds of occult principles motivating Trithemius. Over and against
these exponents of *magia trithemica*, as will also be spelled out,
stood those who continued to perceive the abbot's magic, along the
path laid out by Bovillus, as demonically instigated. An ironic twist
given to this campaign against Trithemius, also to be noted, is that
the abbot himself inadvertently contributed, through his own
demonological writings, to the posthumous campaign against his
magic. Or to put this historical irony another way, contrary to his
own best intentions: Trithemius the demonologist helped to incrimi-
nate Trithemius the magician.

Also taken harshly to task by those of the next two centuries
following in the demonological tradition was anyone suspected to
have fallen under Trithemius's magical spells. The most notable of
these, whose own major theoretical contribution to Renaissance
occult studies was originally dedicated to Trithemius in gratitude
for their earlier exchanges on this subject, was Agrippa of Nettesheim. Henceforth, as will repeatedly be observed in the course of
the next chapter, the names of Trithemius and Agrippa would be
popularly coupled as paladins of the magical arts by backers and
disparagers alike. In closing the present chapter we will indicate
the expression of a parallel loftiness of purpose lying behind the
magical investigations of the two magicians, a meeting of their
minds brought out by an exchange of correspondence marking a
personal encounter between them in 1509. This is not, however, the
last we will see of Agrippa. For in the next chapter his name will
again surface, this time in his role as a posthumous successor to
Trithemius's doctrine of magical theology and as a bridge to the
restatement of that lofty conception of magic in the age of the
Reformation.

## Trithemius and Agrippa

In 1513 Trithemius was visited in his Würzburg cloister by an
Italian traveler bearing a letter of introduction from a mutual friend,

Conrad Mutian (=Rufus, 1471–1526). Having been "delighted by the honest mysteries of the magicians which have been thoroughly examined by you," Mutian wrote, he hoped that the abbot would find the time and opportunity to impart some of his occult secrets to his Italian guest, who in any case had assured him that he would return home only "after he has greeted you and Reuchlin, who are the most erudite among the Germans."[154] We do not know what came of the meeting between Mutian's occult-loving friend and Trithemius, lacking as we do an epistolary testament of gratitude for what transpired. We do have, however, such a testament arising out of a similar meeting between Trithemius and another admirer of his occult knowledge taking place four years earlier, the youthful Agrippa of Nettesheim (1486–1535). In appreciation of the invaluable guidance he received as Trithemius's guest, Agrippa dedicated the first version of his *De occulta philosophia*, appearing in 1510, to his host of the preceding year. Shortly after putting the finishing touches on his manuscript, Agrippa forwarded it to Trithemius "for your correction and censure."[155]

In the dedicatory epistle making this request Agrippa thanked the abbot for his cordial reception, and reflected on how the two men had discussed for hours on end "many things about alchemy, magic, Cabala, and the like." Among the many questions they had entertained in these discussions was why magic, which at one time was unanimously judged by philosophers to occupy the highest pinnacle of wisdom and was held in great veneration by the priests of the church, subsequently became condemned by the Christian theologians and abolished by ecclesiastical law. After further rumination on this regrettable development Agrippa had concluded that its cause "owes to nothing other than to the fact that many false philosophers and counterfeit magicians, by reason of a certain fatal corruption of the times and of men, have insinuated themselves into our circles."[156]

Those guilty of this deceit, continued Agrippa, "through their various schools of error and factions of false religions, have assembled many wholly execrable superstitions and funereal rites and many impieties held to be sacrilegious by orthodox religion, all for the purpose of carrying on their pernicious pursuit of nature and of men and of bringing injury upon God." The books of these superstitious reprobates, "to which, in their stealth and pillage, they have attached the most honest name and title to magic," have had the effect of sweeping into the same demonic net pious and impious investigators of the arcana, the result being that the sacred name of magic was currently rendered "so odious to all good and honest men that it is held to be a capital crime if anyone should dare to profess, either by his teaching or by his works, that he is a magician." The time had come, therefore, to rehabilitate "the very honorable name of magic" which had prevailed in ancient times before it became corrupted by its abuses.[157]

In pointing up to Trithemius this lofty objective of his occult studies, Agrippa acknowledged many of the same forerunners as had also authorized the abbot's efforts to effect the same result. But whereas the bulk of Agrippa's authorities—Albertus Magnus and Pietro d'Abano among them—had failed to stem the tide of maledictions against magic, Agrippa hoped to succeed where they had fallen short. Conceding that "from an early age I have always been an intrepid and curious investigator of marvelous effects and operations full of mysteries," Agrippa beseeched the man who himself had confessed a like curiosity to assist him in this formidable task. Their joint objective was no less than "to restore ancient magic, the discipline of all the sages, rescued and purged from the errors of impiety and embellished by its own doctrines, and to emancipate it from injury by its detractors."[158]

In response to Agrippa's epistolary plea Trithemius expressed his pleasure in receiving both the manuscript of the *De occulta philosophia* and its dedication, and his admiration for one who had learned, so early in his career, to penetrate "such arcane secrets, hidden even from many wise men, not only excellently and truthfully but also appropriately and decorously." But praise, the abbot admonished, should be tempered with caution. With the memory still fresh in his mind of the far less fruitful visit to Sponheim of Bovillus, Trithemius admonished his young protegé, in keeping with the rule of esoteric confidentiality: "Guard this precept: that you communicate vulgar secrets to vulgar friends but higher arcane secrets only to nobler and secret friends, giving hay to the cow but sugar to the parrot! Understand my words, lest you should be stomped upon by the hooves of cows!" With the same contemptuous allusion to Bovillus in mind, Trithemius counseled Agrippa "to imitate, not cattle, but birds," that is, he should not tarry over particulars, "but rather boldly strain your mind to universals" (*sed universalibus confidenter intendito animum*).[159]

Agrippa's receptivity to Trithemius's sage counsel is eloquently captured in a treatise composed by the latter during a journey to Italy in 1516, the year of his preceptor's death. Echoing the noble sentiments of another great magician of his age who had played a part, if indirectly, in Trithemius's occult education, Pico della Mirandola, Agrippa passionately proclaimed in his *De triplici ratione cognoscendi Dei*: "O what a great miracle is man, especially he who is a Christian" (*O magnum miraculum homo, praecipue autem Christianus*). Expanding on this Christianized reworking of a Hermetic theme, Agrippa characterized the said *miraculum Christianum* as "one who has been established in the world, dominates over the world, and effects operations resembling those of the world's Creator." The marvelous operations (*opera*) performed by such Christians, declared Agrippa, "are popularly termed miracles, of which the root and foundation is faith in Jesus Christ.[160] What more succinct statement can be furnished of a theme, worked out in elaborate theoretical form in Agrippa's *De occulta philosophia*, which also lay at the hub of the Trithemian theory of magic?

As will now be established, this joint endeavor by Trithemius and Agrippa to effect an accord between magic and Christian doctrine would find considerable resonance in the two centuries after the abbot's death, coinciding with the Reformation debate, the passage from a still medieval-conditioned Renaissance to the "new philosophy" of the seventeenth century, and the intensification of the witch persecutions. In light of the vigorous Augustinian revival taking place at the same time, however, this Trithemian-Agrippan take on magic could also be expected to meet with vehement opposition—this for two principal reasons. The first reason is that it effaced a sharply drawn distinction between miracle and magic that had been a cornerstone of Christian theology from St. Augustine to St. Thomas, and the second reason, abetted by the subsequent circulation of an apocryphal fourth book of Agrippa's *De occulta philosophia* in alleged mimicry of the *Steganographia*, that it appeared to traffic with demons.[161] Following this view of the matter, magic is no more compatible with true Christian doctrine than Christ is compatible with the Devil.

The equivocal influence of Trithemius on the ensuing debate over the occult studies was portended by a commemorative inscription carved on the pedestal of the statue marking his Würzburg place of entombment. Extolling the abbot in a conventional manner as "a glory of the Germanic world . . . admired as much for his excellence in letters as for his virtue," the inscriber of the epitaph added a supplication that also betrayed a very unconventional aspect of the abbot's life. "May he be far from suspicion concerning the magical art of the Demon," the epitaph pleaded, "against which he began to write a great work." This posthumous commemoration of Trithemius, today no longer verifiable in its replaced stone but not lost to letters,[162] bears witness to the ambivalent influence of the abbot's legacy on posterity. For if one way in which Trithemius would exert significant influence on the subsequent debate over the occult studies was to encourage the identification of the Christian miracle with magic, another way was to discourage that identification with his corresponding demonological output. In this manner, revealing the weakness of his grand strategy of throwing a protective demonological wall around his arcane studies, Trithemius the demonologist would prove to be of assistance in incriminating Trithemius the magician.

# Chapter 5

## The Debate over Trithemian Magic during the Renaissance, Reformation, and Age of Reason

### Agrippa's Later Ambivalence

Two magicians often presented by Renaissance scholars as having received personal instruction in the arcana from Trithemius are Agrippa of Nettesheim and Paracelsus. The case for the indoctrination of Paracelsus by Trithemius, as will shortly to be brought out, has never been satisfactorily documented, and to this day remains largely tentative and conjectural. The case for Agrippa's tutelage by Trithemius, on the other hand, is indubitably established, the visible testimony of which is Agrippa's dedication of the *De occulta philosophia* to his mentor. Further bearing witness to the Trithemius-Agrippa relationship are references in Agrippa's correpondence after his mentor had passed from the scene. In 1520, for example, a correspondent of Agrippa referred in passing to "your Trithemius" (*Trithemius tuus*), and two years later another correspondent reminded Agrippa that during a recent meeting in Lyons "I heard from your own mouth that you were once an auditor and disciple of Trithemius."[1]

The demonstrable association between the two men, also reflected in the text of the *De occulta philosophia,* of course meant that Agrippa would also share many of the unpleasant repercussions of the controversy over Trithemian steganography. For this reason Agrippa warded off attacks upon Trithemius as if they were attacks upon himself, as in his irate reference in a 1524 letter to Bovillus's "diatribe against Trithemius, born from ignorance of his character and of his enigmas."[2] An example of the ground shared by the abbot and Agrippa is furnished by a chapter in an augmented version of the *De occulta philosophia,* published in 1533, treating of the marvelous property of air to behave as an occult transmitter of the "forms of things" (*rerum species*). Explaining that the transference of forms by aerial mediation is made possible only after the forms receive from the heavens "some impression . . . by means of which, depending upon the disposition and fitness of the receiver, they are conveyed to the senses of one man rather than to those of another," Agrippa found validation for his postulate in the steganographical techniques of Trithemius, based as they are upon the supposition that "it is possible, without recourse to any superstition whatsoever or to mediation by any spirit, for a man to report his thought naturally to someone in a very short time, no matter how far removed they are from one another or how unknown their distance and respective stations." Not only Trithemius had personally verified this phenomenon, but also Agrippa himself.[3]

To the puzzlement of Renaissance scholars, however, another side to Agrippa's personality came into prominence about the same time as he made the above observations, evidenced by the appearance of his skeptical *De incertitudine et vanitate omnium scientiarum et artium* (1531), in which he attacked the same magical doctrines he had countenanced in the *De occulta philosophia.* Nor did Agrippa exempt Trithemius from his apparent about-face, revisiting the Trithemian cryptographical art under the heading "panderism" (*lenonia*). Designating cryptography therein, that is, "the manner of writing secretly," as a special branch of grammar, Agrippa traced its evolution from Archimedes and Aulus Gellius to Trithemius, the latter who, Agrippa now sarcastically reported, "related the ways and means of communicating the ideas of one's mind securely and secretly to as great a distance as one might desire, so that neither

the omniscient jealousy of Juno nor the most artful custodianship
of the Danaides can oppose them, nor can the all-watchful hundred
eyes of Argus detect them."[4] While it was not Agrippa's intention in
these words to charge his former mentor with demonic magic, their
effect all the same was to ridicule his cryptological operations for
pretending to transmit through occult means the same kinds of
vain ideas transmitted by grammar and poetry in more conventional ways. From this pandering point of view polygraphy is just
as blameworthy as steganography.

Notwithstanding this derision of an art which he concurrently
extolled in the *De occulta philosophia,* we do not need to assume
that Agrippa changed his mind in moving from one tract to the
other. Consistency between the two different versions of cryptography, as of magic as a whole, can be discovered in the supposition
that the pandering art lampooned by Agrippa in the *De vanitate* is
a bastard form of the perfectly respectful art of cryptic communication through natural means depicted in the *De occulta philosophia.*
After all, it will be remembered, Trithemius, with help from
Cusanus's doctrine of learned ignorance, can be said to have helped
point the way to Agrippa's skepticism as well as to his magic, a
notion aphorized on the title page of the *De vanitate:* "To know
nothing leads to a very happy life!" (*Nihil scire foelicissima vita*).
The Cusan finite-infinite discontinuity which conditioned the mystical theology of both Trithemius and Agrippa, from this larger
perspective, should also be viewed as conditioning their affiliated
magical theology. Any suggestion that Agrippa was thereby led into
a "skeptical" repudiation of his magic by Luther is thus undercut
at its foundation, since, as Agrippa's biographer Nauert has shown,
there is no hard evidence that Agrippa ever broke with Catholicism
in the first place. The relationship between magic and skepticism
thrust into the limelight by Agrippa's literary output is better explained, like that of his abbatial preceptor, by the kinds of late
scholastic tendencies culminating in Cusanus than by any supposed conversion to Protestantism.[5]

Their everyday practical applications aside, steganography and
polygraphy were proclaimed by Trithemius to be capable of furnishing a linguistic bridge to the obscurely shrouded infinite foreclosed to the finitely discursive language of reason. Surely this is
a lesson Trithemius imparted to his young student in their earlier

Sponheim meeting, whose own major contribution on this subject, the *De occulta philosophia*, likewise posited in magic a possible solution to the finite-infinite quandary. And just as surely, with the experience of Steinmoel's abuse of his instruction behind him, Trithemius must have instructed his student in the dangers of abusing the steganographical art for avaricious or other wicked motives. It is not by chance that Trithemius's description of this abuse by Steinmoel closely resembles that directed by Agrippa at the abbot's own art in the *De vanitate*, where it is reduced to mere pandering for money or other worldly rewards. The warning conveyed to Steinmoel by Trithemius, to wit, that opprobrium called down upon the student necessarily redounds upon the teacher, here receives—in the writings of another Trithemian acolyte—striking confirmation.

Unfortunately for Trithemius's future reputation, it was often the defamed version of his cryptic art set forth in the *De vanitate* rather than the complimentary version extolled in the *De occulta philosophia* that governed subsequent discussions of its value. An example is furnished by the "Swiss Pliny," Conrad Gesner (1516-1565), who in his *Bibliotheca universalis*, with Agrippa his authority, declared that the Trithemian art of steganography "is not so necessary to kings as it is a great convenience to procurers and to all their lovers."[6] Sharing similar sentiments, but perceiving more of absurdity than avaricious procuration in the art, was Erasmus (1466-1536). While sharing an enthusiasm for the humanist disciplines with Trithemius, Erasmus did not agree with the abbot's attempts to extend the scope of those disciplines to embrace magic, in particular ridiculing the proposition that Cicero, the paragon of literary decorum and lucidity, was also a forerunner of an obscurantist cryptographical art. With this thought in mind, upon advising a correspondent that the precepts guiding his writing should be "few but of the very best," Erasmus added the wry disclaimer that "if this is not pleasing to someone, I do not see that anything remains for him but to flee into those inept magical and ridiculous polygraphic activities which, so far as I can see, have been of no use to anyone to this day."[7]

To be sure, unflattering characterizations of Trithemius's cryptography like those put forth by Gesner and Erasmus must be distinguished from that of the demonologists. If the matter were to be left here, the magical legend left behind by Trithemius would have been a fairly innocuous one. As has been shown, however, Trithemius himself, through his contributions to the literature of demonology, can be said to have inadvertently contributed to a climate of opinion that would turn his legend to a far more sinister purpose. Assisting in the promotion of this feature of the abbot were witch-baiting publications like the *Theatrum de veneficis* (1586), a demonological anthology that included in its collection of offerings a translated excerpt from the *Octo quaestiones*. Some demonologists carried away by the frenzy of the witch hunts, it is true, like the credulous physician George Pictorius von Villingen (ca. 1500–1569), acknowledged their indebtedness to Trithemius's demonological writings without compromising that authority by further reference to his magical writings.[8] Others, however, with Trithemius's own words to encourage their fanatical views, were far less generously disposed to the abbot's arcane interests. Considerably complicating this question, to be addressed in the following pages, is the impact of the impending Reformation debate, with members of both sides disposed to associate demonic magic with the demonically instigated theological errors of their opponents. But this strategy of the antimagical reformers, whether belonging to the Catholic or Protestant side, rang ever hollower as it was made increasingly clear that the apologists of magic, including the apologists of Trithemian magic in particular, were as likely to be found among their coreligionists as among their religious opponents.

## The Monastic Apologists

The biographer André Thevet (1502–1590), who found much to admire about Trithemius in his *Pourtraits et vies des hommes illustres,* also detected one reprehensible flaw in his subject. Praising Trithemius as "a diligent student in all the good sciences who always accompanied his scholarly zeal with piously virtuous behavior," Thevet regretted to add, on the negative side, that "by being too curious in the black and occult sciences of magic, he wrote in his book called *Steganographia* several things which are superstitious and unworthy of a man of the cloth."[9] Despite Thevet's implication that the divine calling of the clergy stands sharply at odds

with the "superstitions" of magic, some of the abbot's most passion-
ate defenders, as it turned out, proved to be clerics, including
members of his own Benedictine order. True, as illustrated by two
monks in personal contact with the abbot, Wolfgang Trefler (d.
1516) and Johann Butzbach (1477–1526), not all who were sympathetic to Trithemius's occult investigations were themselves practicing magicians. For these disciples of the abbot in the more
conventional fields of monastic theology and ecclesiastical history,
it was enough to exonerate their master of wrongdoing in magic
without becoming directly implicated in its principles.

Shedding direct personal light on Thevet's mixed review of the
Trithemian legacy was the Mainz monk Trefler, who reluctantly
felt compelled, in a 1508 letter to a friend describing an earlier
visit to Sponheim, to acknowledge a controversy surrounding its
harried abbot. Having deservedly earned a place in the ranks of
those rare souls who are "pinnacles of nature and images of God,"
according to Trefler, Trithemius had recently been tarnished by
another kind of reputation that was quite undeserved. Having
undoubtedly heard that Trithemius "has been accused by certain
men of various superstitions and, so they add, necromantic arts
unworthy of a Christian and of one adorned with the habit of
monastic religion," the correspondent should take such malicious
rumors with a grain of salt. While not denying the abbot's extensive interest in occult studies, well publicized as a result of the
Bostius letter, Trefler vehemently rejected the deprecative reading
placed on them by his critics. Citing several passages from the
controversial Bostius letter, Trefler affirmed his belief that, while
exhibiting certain questionable features, the promises made therein
are in basic harmony with Catholic doctrine. Repeating one of
Trithemius's own favored arguments in this regard, Trefler recalled
the parallel example of Albertus Magnus, "to whom was also ascribed something of a superstitious nature," and yet who, despite
this slander, was currently held in higher esteem than ever.[10]

Similarly disposed to an acceptance of Trithemius's arcane
queries without himself entering into them was the Maria Laach
monk Butzbach, who incorporated his defense of his master's arcane studies (which Trefler did not in a similar work) in an
*auctarium,* or augmentation, of Trithemius's catalogue of ecclesiastical writers. Recalling such complimentary sobriquets extended to

him by his admirers as *lux mundi* and *Johannes Magnus,* coined respectively by the scholars Alexander Hegius and Heinrich Bebel, Butzbach did not hesitate to include the abbot's occult speculations among the intellectual conquests earning him such praise. Extolling Trithemius at one point in his catalogue, for example, as one who, among his many other scholarly proficiencies, was "very skillful in medicine and in all the natural secrets," at another point he lauded the abbot for "having many years now very earnestly penetrated the secrets of the Hebrews and the Greeks" (*hebreorum graecorumque secreta . . . enixissime penetrans*)."[11] In recognition of achievements like these Butzbach opted to add to the flattering epithets of Hegius and Bebel two of his own, labeling Trithemius *miraculum aetatis istius* and *mundi stupor.* Concerning the widespread accusation of demonic magic directed against this great man, Butzbach protested that it arose out of "an empty and fictitious invention propagated among the vulgar; for the marvels about which he is said to have written were effected, not by sorcery, but by the hidden powers of nature." Enlarging on this line of defense, Butzbach echoed Trithemius's rationale that "many stupendous events are able to be accomplished naturally, and occult powers, such as the prediction of the future, are disclosed in such a way as to be misjudged by the uninitiated to lie beyond the limits of nature."[12]

The entry on Trithemius in Butzbach's *Auctarium* is almost a verbatim extract from his unpublished *Macrostroma* unfolding the complex justification behind Trithemius's program of monastic erudition. Enlarging on the above points in the latter work, Butzbach heartily endorsed Trithemius's efforts, in the footsteps of Albertus Magnus and Giovanni Pico before him, to extend the boundaries of the traditional liberal arts curriculum to embrace natural magic. Echoing a foremost theme of his master's own rationale for magic, Butzbach recounted the noble connotation given to the word *magus* by the ancients, revalidated by sacred scripture in the account of "men wise in both heavenly and earthly matters" empowered by their occult knowledge to recognize the miraculous significance of the virgin birth of Jesus. So carried away with this line of reasoning was Butzbach that he even stretched it to include an ancient marvel worker whom Trithemius had refused to admit into the ranks of legitimate magicians, Apollonius of Tyana, furnishing

further evidence, he declared, that "true philosophy is identical
with that subject which ordinary men call magic." At the other end
of the spectrum, undoubtedly with an eye to the abbot's hefty
demonological output to complement his occult speculations,
Butzbach insisted that Trithemius "condemns, detests, and refutes
all magic that has been prohibited by the Church."[13]

Thus, while showing no signs of adding magic to their own
scholarly repertories as a result of their lessons from Trithemius,
monks like Trefler and Butzbach nonetheless helped to establish a
more propitious climate in the church—indeed, in their own
Benedictine order—within which future magicians might be able to
operate. But if monkish followers of Trithemius like Trefler and
Butzbach saw no conflict between what they were supposed to be
doing in their cloisters and the study of magic, others among their
coreligionists, chastened by the attacks on their beliefs by the radical reformers, did not prove to be so indulgent. To better appreciate
the concerns of these Catholic critics of Trithemian magic we will
first take note of the challenge thrown down to them by the Protestant demonologists, spearheaded by Luther, who detected a cor-
relation between the monastic way of life adopted by a figure like
Trithemius and the magical studies he championed.

The common bond linking these two purported perversions of
sound Christian doctrine, contended the typical Protestant critic of
Trithemian magic, are the demons. Viewed as being easily drawn
into the melancholy solitude of the cloister, the demons were viewed
by Luther and his followers as also becoming readily accessible to
a solitary monk like Trithemius for the purpose of promoting sorcery. As will be established in the pages to follow, however, the
appeal of magic would not be to Catholics alone. Among those attracted to the occult studies during next two centuries—not infrequently, as it happened, with express reference to the very Catholic
Trithemius—were also a fair number of Protestants.

While it may be granted that Protestant lovers of the occult
rejected the solitary monastic study as an ideal retreat for their
magical flights of imagination, it can equally be said that they
could not dispense with a solitary retreat of their own for the
theorization and practice of the occult arts. Stocked with many
volumes of magical texts, some Protestant libraries must have
resembled in many ways the monastic library of Trithemius with

its comparable plethora of arcane offerings. Seated alone at their desks like the magical abbot before them, they too, particular theological differences aside, were faced with harmonizing their occult with their religious and theological principles. As will shortly be made clear, the accusations of witchcraft and sorcery bandied about during the Reformation did not fly in one direction only. They were mutually exchanged recriminations, with magicians in the manner of Trithemius found on both sides of the Catholic-Protestant divide.

## The Protestant Reaction

Of the advice Martin Luther (1483–1546) is reported to have imparted to his dinner companions in a compilation of his dinnertime counsels, titled *Tischreden*, one word to the wise recorded therein is that "where there is a melancholy head, there Satan has his bath," and another, with his own monastic experience to back him up, that nowhere is a "melancholy head" more likely to be produced than in encloistered solitude.[14] Moreover, if we are to believe a report on his opinion contained in the same work as related by his later editor Johann Aurifaber, Luther discerned a connection between the monastic profession and magic, his logic being that the same demons serving to instill melancholy sorrow in the solitary monk can also conceivably be called into play by the monk to effect sorcery.

The relevant passage pertains to Luther's interpretation of the biblical reference to Samuel's restoration to life (I Samuel 28:11ff.) by a prophetess in the presence of King Saul. It was Luther's opinion, according to Aurifaber's version of his remarks, that the shape appearing before Saul was not really Samuel "but a ghost or evil spirit," the likelihood of which was supported by an episode of far more recent note pertaining to the "magician and necromancer" Trithemius. At the request of Emperor Maximilian, as this story went, Trithemius conjured from the depths of Hell not only a number of dead heroes of the past such as Alexander the Great and Julius Caesar, but also Maximilian's recently deceased bride Mary of Burgundy. This early legend of the magical abbot was intended by its Protestant spokesmen as an admonition as much against the "superstitious" practices of Catholics in general as against Trithemius's magical practices in particular.[15]

The reputation of Trithemius was further damaged within the Lutheran movement by an anecdote circulated, among others, by Philipp Melanchthon (1497–1560) after receiving it from Pirckheimer. While once on a journey, as related by Melanchthon's disciple Johannes Manlius, Trithemius stopped at an inn inadequately supplied with food for dinner. As a joke some guests of the inn who had been apprised of the abbot's magical fame asked him to procure a large tray of fish to satisfy their hunger, in response to which he struck the window, following which a servant entered the inn—in truth, the writer was convinced, a demon in the guise of a servant—bearing a platter of cooked herring.[16] The inference which Manlius, following Melanchthon, drew from as story like this was that Trithemius, together with another ostentatious marvel worker of their day, Faustus, were implicit confederates of the Devil. Serving further to confirm this association in the popular mind between Trithemius and the man dubbed by Manlius earlier in the text as "a sewer of a multitude of demons" (cloaca multorum daemonum) was the conflation of their necromantic legends, with a story circulated about Faust's conjuration of deceased souls distinguishable from that of Trithemius only by the particular names of those said to be materialized and the name of the petitioner Charles V substituted for Maximilian.[17]

At times, it is true, Protestant critics of Trithemius relegated his magic to a lesser status of danger than those kinds of sorcery overtly invoking demonic assistance, characterizing the abbot as more of a sleight-of-hand charlatan than a true demon conjuror. Two such skeptics of Trithemian magic were the English physician Ricardus Argentinus (fl. 1550) and the Silesian physician Johannes Scultetus (fl. 1590). For Argentinus the main problem of the steganographic fad lay in its encouragement of a superstitious climate of opinion. Just as honor once was paid to the superstitious pronouncements of the Roman lawgiver Numa Pompilius, charged Argentinus, "likewise today the astounding and bestial avidity of steganography, the books of which the abbot Trithemius has authored, is producing the same effect."[18] Similarly unconvinced that Trithemius's magic involved demon conjuration was Scultetus, who, like Manlius, saw a resemblance between Trithemian and Faustian marvel working but read an opposite lesson into the comparison. Distinguishing between three classes of wicked magic,

Scultetus noted that some servants of the Devil, such as Trithemius of Sponheim, "only produce their effects so that they might reveal their remarkable sophistries and great art, and on that account will be held in high repute"; others, like Faustus, "amuse their fellow men for their own pleasure or for the sake of profit and avarice"; and still others, the worst of all, "under the influence of Satan, deceptively report incorrect things and cause misfortune as if lacking a will of their own."[19] The image of Trithemius here projected approximates one of magical impostors projected by Trithemius himself, which found prime representatives in Apollonius of Tyana in ancient times and Giovanni Mercurio and Faustus in his own day.

Not surprisingly, however, other Protestant critics of Trithemius took a more ominous view of his magical activities, some of whom, it would appear, could have been assisted by the abbot's own demonological writings. Among these can be singled out the Lutheran Caspar Goltwurm (fl. 1570) and, writing under the pseudonym of Augustine Lercheimer, the Calvinist Hermann Witekind (1522–1603). Referring to the story of Trithemius's necromantic feats in the court of Maximilian and expanding on Luther's list of heroic figures reputedly brought up from the dead by the abbot, Goltwurm in his *Wunderzeichen Buch* labeled the magic behind this necromantic ritual "seductive and idolatrous superstition" (*verfürung und abgöttischen Aberglauben*), making no secret of his belief that it was a practice of a piece with the religious superstitions of Catholic monasticism to which Trithemius also adhered.[20] Spurred by a reference to the same necromantic episode in Maximilian's court as provoked Goltwurm's remonstrations, Witekind, labeling Trithemius "the Devil's abbot" (*der Teufel Abt*), heartily endorsed Bovillus's verdict on the *Steganographia* that Trithemius "has written a widely circulated book full of the horrible Devil's art."[21] Sealing the abbot's guilt in Witekind's eyes was his close association with Agrippa of Nettesheim, "who led the Devil behind him in the form of a black dog."[22]

As to why Witekind assumed his pseudonym, the answer likely relates to the larger issue of the witch persecutions. For while displaying considerable hostility to the kind of learned magic championed by Trithemius, Witekind at the same time sided with those opponents to the witch persecutions who saw more to pity than to fear in the typically illiterate female prey of the inquisitors.[23] Likewise finding the foolish delusions of those persecuted by the witch hunters to be one thing and the intellectually calculated sorcery of the professional magicians to be another was the physician Johann Weyer (=Wier, 1515–1588), who unlike Witekind bravely inscribed his opinions under his true name. Restating the proposition in his *De praestigiis daemonum*, so deftly turned by Luther against the institution of monasticism, that "the Devil . . . very freely insinuates himself into the melancholy humor, as in a material agreeable to his sport," Weyer also insisted, in response to the excessive zeal of the witch hunters, that "though all demoniacs, by reason of their bitter torments and depressed desires, are rendered melancholics, nevertheless, not all melancholics are in the power of the demons." While willing to apply this skeptical proviso to unlettered witches, Weyer, like Witekind, extended no such tolerance to the intellectualized magic of Trithemius.[24]

In one way, however, Weyer's attack on Trithemian magic stands distinctly apart from that of Witekind. For having once studied under Agrippa and even resided for a time in his home, Weyer defended his former teacher against those, like Witekind, who were spreading the rumor of Agrippa's accompaniment by the Devil in the guise of a black dog. He did not, however, do the same for Agrippa's teacher Trithemius. Conceding that he had read a manuscript of the *Steganographia* while a guest in Agrippa's house, even going so far as to make a copy of it in his own hand, Weyer excused this act as a youthful indiscretion, and now sought to correct it by censuring Trithemius for the necromantic feats said to take place in Maximilian's court and endorsing Bovillus's attack on the abbot. Accordingly, striking a very different pose from that which he presented to the witch question, Weyer designated those willfully partaking of the abbot's art, which taught how to counterfeit miracles through diabolically instigated illusions, "monsters of impiety" who are not to be tolerated.[25]

Witekind and Weyer were not alone among the Protestant critics of Trithemius who, while endeavoring to mitigate the torments of accused witches, were equally determined to keep magic of the type attributed to *der Teufel Abt* outside the perimeters of their circle of defense. A further example was the Rostock jurist Johann Godelmann (1559–1611). "Witches err," Godelmann indulgently allowed, "because they succumb to so great an alienation of the mind from the tricks of the Devil that, being vexed by melancholy disease, they do not know what they are doing." Indeed, Godelmann's treatment of the witch question reveals his familiarity with a demonological writing by Trithemius, in response to which he agreed with its author that many of the things attributed to witches more likely happened in the imagination than in the real world.[26] When it came to professional magic like that of which Trithemius was also a spokesman, however, Godelmann was convinced that the sorcerer was as much deceiver as deceived, an outstanding example consisting, in agreement with both Witekind and Weyer, of the abbot's conjuration for Maximilian of demons assuming the forms of deceased personages.[27]

By implication, if not by explication, Godelmann continued a trend by the Protestant opponents of the occult studies, quite apart from their position on the witch question, to view "superstitious" magical practices as a logical outgrowth of "superstitious" monastic practices. Two opposing trends of this age will now be observed, however, which greatly complicated this attempt by the Protestants to forge a link between what they perceived to be two separate but related forms of superstition. The first is a movement among Catholics themselves to purge the church of its magical accretions, and the second, of a penchant by some Protestants for the kinds of magical theories championed by Trithemius. Thus, as we will see, the real struggle in early modern Europe over the kind of magical legacy left by Trithemius would not, in the end, be between Protestants and Catholics. Quite independently of what side they might take in the Reformation theological debate, that fight would rather be between those who aspired to blend magic with the principles of their theology and those who aspired to purge theology of magic.

## The Catholic Reaction

Among the Renaissance opponents to the witch persecutions, the Catholic physician-mathematician Girolamo Cardano (1501–1576) set forth skeptical arguments which in many ways resemble those of the Protestants Witekind, Weyer, and Godelmann. A telling sign of Cardano's skepticism is found in his *De rerum varietate,* where he noted that "there is a certain humor residing within us which we call black bile; when it rages it occupies the highest citadel of the brain and casts the mind down from its position. Many call this a demon." As in the parallel cases of Cardano's Protestant counterparts, we can infer from this physiological diagnosis of "demonic" inspiration that those pursued and arrested as witches are more accurately to be classified as foolish melancholics than true demoniacs deserving, not of burning, but of curing. It is with considerable irony, therefore, that Cardano himself, whose own philosophical speculations were not utterly free of occultist preconceptions, was sharply taken to task by a critic of his own, Giulio Cesare Vanini (1585–1619), for evincing excessive credulity in supernatural causation not far removed from that of Trithemius.[28]

Trithemius, according to Cardano, was a dissembling impostor who provoked not only his spectators and readers into wild phantasizing, but also himself into the bargain. In keeping with this unflattering portrait Cardano declared Trithemius to be "more deceitful than Agrippa and more inane than Raymon Lull," one who, he further specified, "filled an entire book of quite a large size with one single [steganographic] fancy, which, nevertheless, he did not complete." For Cardano the author of the *Steganographia* was more accurately to be characterized as preposterous than sorcerous. "And in order that he might induce belief in his fiction," Cardano continued his cutting invective, Trithemius "imagined that he had been accused of necromancy, when he rather should have been accused of foolishness." To such a person, Cardano maintained, ridicule was a better retort than earnest refutation, since "if ever there were an impudent sycophant among mortals, it was most certainly he."[29]

As events demonstrated, however, Cardano's skeptical attitude to sorcery, whether of the witch's unlearned version or of the Trithemian learned version, was more often the exception than the rule among counterreform Catholics. More typically representative of the climate in which Cardano was working was the strident demonologist Jean Bodin (1530–1596), who, however, found the principal foil for his antimagical tirades, not in Cardano, but in the more moderate Weyer. For apart from the fact that the two men largely agreed on the threat of Trithemian magic, Bodin all the same took Weyer to task for admitting that, while a guest of Agrippa, he had transcribed his host's copy of Trithemius's steganographical manual, "a work filled with prayers and invocations to demons," which Bovillus had so appropriately cast from his sight as unfit for Christian eyes.[30] By so doing, chided Bodin, Weyer in effect had shown himself to be as fully a friend to professional magicians like Trithemius as to witches.

Of course an attack upon Trithemian magic like that of Bodin did not necessarily mean that the writer behind it was unyieldingly opposed to all forms of magic. He might adopt a position theoretically resembling that of Trithemius himself, agreeing to the underlying precepts of natural magic purged of all demonic aids. The attitude of this school of Trithemian critics is illustrated by the Catholic bishop Antonio Zara (d. ca. 1615), who established the basic legitimacy of natural magic in his *Anatomia ingeniorum et scientiarum* while concurrently doing his best to rid it of supernatural encroachments.[31]

Referring to the spirit-riddled *De septem secundeis*, Zara proclaimed on the heels of an unflattering account of its contents that "the opinion stating that intelligences cleave to the heavens must be completely rejected (*explodenda est*)."[32] One concern which lay behind this verdict, as Thorndike has suggested, may have been Zara's perception of astrological fatalism in the planetary governing system of the work in question.[33] However, given that Trithemius himself had answered that potential objection within the pages of the tract with the explanation that the stars do not predetermine but only dispose, the more central issue for Zara likely lay, not in the tract's *astrological* assumptions, but in its *angelogical* assumptions. Intent on freeing the planets of ruling intelligences, Zara was seeking a more thoroughgoing consistency than was displayed by Trithemius with his mingling of supernatural with natural elements. Though his principal target was the *De septem secundeis* rather than the *Steganographia,* the objection applying to one tract also necessarily applies to the other.

Of those adopting a more sternly demonological posture toward the magic of Trithemius among later sixteenth- and early seventeenth-century Catholics, some of the more visible belonged to the clerical order acting as the cutting edge of the Catholic reform movement, the Society of Jesus. Leading the charge against the magic of Trithemius at an early stage of the Jesuit movement was Martin Delrio (1551–1608), whose efforts in this regard bore official fruit in 1609 with the addition of the *Steganographia,* scarcely three years after its completed portions had been published, to the newly revised Index of Prohibited Books.[34] As viewed by Delrio, Trithemius's handbook of steganography was a dangerously superstitious work which so far had escaped official prohibition only "because the book, which has not yet been circulated in printed form, has fallen into the hands of few people." Now, however, with the great proliferation of hand-copied texts, the guardians of religious orthodoxy could no longer afford to sit back and hope that the threat posed to Christian salvation by Trithemian magic would go away by itself. Recommending that the steganographical manual of Trithemius be quickly placed on the Index, along with the equally dangerous work of his disciple Agrippa bearing the title *De occulta philosophia,* Delrio placed both men on a continuum with such earlier sorcerers as Pietro d'Abano, who were reliably reported, he claimed, to call up spirits from the dead among the more disgraceful of their magical activities.[35]

If Delrio saw good reason to proscribe the *Steganographia* while it was still limited to scattered manuscript copies, his Jesuit colleague Antonio Possevino (1534–1611) saw even more reason to do so after the completed portions of the suspect tract came into print in 1606. The sister writing which Trithemius had lauded in the preface to his *Polygraphia* as "a work to be admired," cautioned Possevino, was not the innocent cryptographic manual its author pretended. On the contrary it was "full of superstition and peril, partaking, not of that natural magic under whose name many men conceal its filth, but that kind of magic which has been prohibited by the Holy Catholic Church," for which reason "it must without fail be cast from our presence!"[36]

Making his anti-Trithemian vituperations public a few years after those of Delrio and Possevino, Robert Bellarmine (1542–1621) was gratified to find that the campaign to have the steganographical manual placed on the Index was a fait accompli. The incriminating evidence appears at the close of a list of titles ascribed to Trithemius in Bellarmine's *De scriptoribus ecclesiasticis,* a work for which Trithemius, in his more conventional role as church historian, had furnished its author a suitable model. Thus, on the heels of a generally favorable treatment of the abbot's monastic career, Bellarmine felt compelled at last to give fair warning against two of his writings, the *De septem secundeis* and the *Steganographia,* which he correctly perceived to be related through their sharing of an angelic-planetary overview. Putting both writings down as examples of Trithemius's flirtation with superstition, Bellarmine claimed, with not an iota of evidence to back up his contention, that their author had already started the process for a return into the protective arms of the church by having realized and confessed the error of his ways.[37]

These attacks on Trithemian magic by Bellarmine were prompted by more than what he perceived to be the transgressions of a single man. Rather, they were prompted by what he saw to be a wider movement within the church, exemplified by Trithemian magic, which threatened its divine mission. For Delrio and Possevino the attacks on Trithemius were largely ad hominem, owing to their concession that there theoretically exists a licit form of natural magic behind which magicians like Trithemius might seek to hide their malefic intentions.[38] For Bellarmine, on the other hand, it was not only the kind of spirit magic espoused by Trithemius which contravened the laws of the church, but magic in principle, of which Trithemian magic was but one of the more conspicuous instances. For Bellarmine there was no more room for compromise between magic and the church than between sin and virtue or between the Devil and Christ. Against the claims of those who would confound the marvels of the magicians with the miracles of Christ and the saints, with Trithemius now included in their number, Bellarmine assumed a rigorously antimagical posture resembling one assumed by St. Jerome and St. Augustine over a millennium earlier.

For Bellarmine the valid choice was not between wicked demonic magic and good natural and Cabalistic magic, but between demonic magic and the miraculous sacraments of Christ. At stake in this matter, as Bellarmine was forcefully reminded by the Protestant accusation of superstitious practices against the Romanists, was the continued sanctity and integrity of the church. Following Bellarmine's reasoning, only an inflexibly uncompromising opposition to magic in all its forms, natural magic included, could insure, against Protestant allegations, that the Catholic priesthood was not harboring superstitious magic within its holy sacramental system and subsidiary rituals. As this key point of Bellarmine's theology is made in no uncertain terms in his *Disputationes adversus haereticos:* "For inasmuch as all magic depends upon a covenant with the Devil, and the power of the sacramental words depends upon a covenant with Christ, it clearly follows that either there is no magic in our sacraments, or else Christ is the Devil."[39]

A closer look at the controversy surrounding the name of Trithemius, however, reveals that Bellarmine's was not to be the last word on this subject for Catholics, or, for that matter, for Jesuits. There were those among Bellarmine's own coreligionists who saw in the above antimagical declamation a false syllogism, a form of twisted logic. Some of those favorably disposed to the beleaguered abbot, it is true, among whom his fellow Benedictine Arnold Wion (1554–ca. 1610) can be taken as an example, based their praise of Trithemius, not on his magic, but upon his exemplary life and contributions to the literature of Christian piety.[40] Others, however, beheld in the magic of a demonstrably pious Trithemius, not something to be merely tolerated, but as something to be zealously pursued as an active aid to piety. A "renaissance" of ancient magic was in the making which was part of the larger revival of ancient science, art and letters, with the argument being made, assisted by Trithemius, that magic could just as legitimately be employed as a handmaiden to theology as any other of the liberal arts. Moreover—in this also resembling the larger literary renaissance—this occult renaissance cut across formal ecclesiastical divisions. Indeed, as will now be our object to show, some of its leading exponents argued that it could show the way to how the current ecclesiastical schism could be healed. Much as magic was viewed by its Renaissance advocates as a suitable vehicle for the conciliation of pre-Christian and Christian theology, by the same token it could be credibly presented at its Reformation stage as a suitable vehicle for the *re-conciliation* of Catholics and Protestants.

Already as early as 1525 the Venetian Franciscan Francesco Giorgi (=Zorsi, 1466–1540) had pointed the way to this conciliating potential of magic by calling on a mix of Neoplatonism, Hermeticism, Cabala, and orthodox Catholic doctrine to produce what he termed, in his *De harmonia mundi,* "a man well harmonized with God" (*homo bene chordatus cum Deo*).[41] With the same conciliatory function of magic in mind, but this time under more turbulent circumstances following the congelation of the Protestant break with Rome, Francesco Patrizi da Cherso (1529–1597) declared: "The first and most excellent part of magic is nothing else but theology and religion, and if it is not completely true, as the truth subsequently has been revealed by Christ, it nevertheless approaches more closely to that truth than all the other studies."[42] Patrizi's aspiration in this writing was to enlist the Hermetica, together with other surviving texts of the so-called *prisci theologi,* in support of a universalist-minded Catholic reform movement in constructive reply to the Protestant schismatics and offering a framework for the eventual return of the Protestants to the Catholic fold. In making his appeal to a *reformatio magica* Patrizi recommended to Pope Gregory XIV, in the dedicatory preface to his *Nova de universis philosophia* (1591), that the hierarchical church vest the program of magical renewal in the Society of Jesus as its most suitable vehicle.[43]

On their side of the Reformation split, Protestant occultists similarly expressed a resolve to delve below their formal theological differences with the Catholics to arrive at a common ground of arcana which they presumed to be shared between them. Conveniently coming to their aid for this purpose was the very Catholic abbot Trithemius. While there is some question of whether one of the leaders in this Protestant campaign, Paracelsus, had any personal dealings with Trithemius, there is no question whatever, to be be highlighted in the following pages, that the occult movement fathered by Paracelsus usefully served the abbot after his death as a principal vehicle for the defense of his reputation and magical ideals.

Of the specialized branches of late Renaissance magic to find in Trithemius a cornerstone of their underlying principles, two in particular stand out. The first, referring to Trithemius's own primary interest, is cryptography, and the second, issuing out of the Hermetic mode by which the abbot endeavored to undergird his magical theory, alchemy. Needless to say, as Trithemius also pointed the way, these occult fields will be observed to overlap and interconnect in various of their leading expositors, with alchemy serving as a theoretical underpinning for the art of cryptography and furnishing some of its symbols, and the enigmas of cryptography, in turn, serving as a linguistic agent for putting the alchemist into touch with the occult wellspring out of which his art has emanated. Formal theological differences aside, these two fields of arcane endeavor, sometimes practiced in association and sometimes apart, were just as likely to attract Protestants as Catholics. First taking note of this occurrence in its sixteenth-century setting, in upheaval over the witch question, we will then do the same for the seventeenth century to follow, when the witch persecutions, instead of becoming extinguished by the effects of rationalism as we might expect, became even more greatly aggravated and expanded.[44]

### The Cryptographical and Alchemical Revivals

Natural magic, wrote Giovanni Battista della Porta (1535–1615) in a monograph on this subject, "excels all the sciences (I except only divine philosophy), so that in relation to it, the queen, it appears that all the other arts and sciences are no more than mere servants."[45] One of the prominent forms of magic into which Della Porta delved with this noble conceit to guide him, as illustrated by his *De furtivis literarum notis* (1563), is the art of cryptography. While indicating awareness of Trithemius's pioneering efforts in this regard, Della Porta did not make clear to what extent, if at all, his cryptological methods were dependent on those of the abbot. The same cannot be said, however, for other Renaissance cryptographers more patently indebted to the abbot, among whom Count Friedrich von Öttingen-Wallerstein (1556–1615), the author of a still unpublished *Steganographia nova* (1601) "ad imitationem Trithemii," stands out as one of the age's more conspicuous cases in point.[46]

This is not to say, however, that every extoller of Trithemian cryptographical methods understood them in the same way. Illustrating a school of Trithemius-beholden cryptographers preferring to remain within the strict confines of language and number was Johannes Aventinus (=Turmair, 1477–1534). What for his contemporary Erasmus were "inept magical and ridiculous polygraphic activities" were, for Aventinus, legitimate and useful attempts to devise a language of codes and ciphers for the covert transmission of information, the legacy of which was traceable not only to Trithemius, but behind Trithemius to the much earlier Venerable

Bede. If this view appears to suggest more the polygraphical than steganographical approach to cryptic communication, supported by Trithemius's own reference to Bede's cryptic methods in the *Polygraphia*, Aventinus disclosed in his preface to a reedition of the relevant Bede tract that he was not among those who made a distinction between them. "That which the Venerable Bede calls the calculation and language of digits," Aventinus wrote in his preface to Bede's *Abacus*, "the Sponheim priest Johannes Trithemius terms steganography."[47] If, however, the judicious Aventinus saw in the steganographic techniques of Trithemius nothing more mysterious than a reworking of ancient cryptographic practices, others of a more mystical bent, such as the Englishman John Dee (1527–1608) detected something in them transcending the mere manipulation of signs.

By his own acknowledgment Dee began the composition of his Cabalistically inspired *Monas hieroglyphica* in 1564 (see title page, plate 3) after a chance discovery of a manuscript copy of Trithemius's steganographical handbook the year before. The circumstance occasioning this discovery was Dee's diplomatic assignment to Antwerp on behalf of his patron and secretary to Queen Elizabeth, William Cecil, where, writing to his protector to request more time than official business required, he gave as the reason that he had stumbled upon a manuscript which would prove to be important to his studies "for which a thousand crownes have been by others offred, and yet could not be obteyned; a boke for which many a lerned man hath long sought and dayly yet doth seeke; whose use is greater than the fame thereof is spred; the name thereof to you is not unknown." The writing to which Dee referred, "a boke for your Honor, or a Prince, so meet, so nedefull and commodious, as in humayne knowledg none can be meeter or more behovefull," was identified by the writer as the partially completed *Steganographia* of Trithemius, "whereof in both the editions of his *Polygraphia* mention is made, and in his epistles, and in sundry other mens bokes." The cause for a request of delay, Dee explained to Cecil, was that during his allotted time he had managed to copy only about half the text. If Cecil mercifully indulged Dee, he would shortly be presented with what he would surely agree to be "the most precious juell that I have yet of other mens travailes recovered," and, into the bargain, hear his name praised far and wide for his "wisdome and honorable zeal toward the avauncement of good letters and wonderfull divine and secret sciences."[48]

Evidently Dee got his way with Cecil, the result being that the magical legend of the abbot Trithemius was infused with new life and reached a wider public than ever. Dee's was another in the proliferation of manuscripts of the *Steganographia* which, coupled with the widespread impact of the *Polygraphia,* finding its way into printers' molds in two editions by 1550 (Basel, 1518, and Frankfurt, 1550) and two more in the following decades (Cologne, 1564 and 1571), turned the art of cryptography into a popular European vogue. With the appearance of further printed editions of the polygraphical tract after the turn of the century (1600 and 1613 at Strassburg), coupled with the eventual publication of its steganographical forerunner in 1606, that vogue can be said to have made a smooth passage from the Renaissance revival of magic to its congelation in the seventeenth century.

Of the possible relevance of steganography to the secular realm, as Trithemius pointed the way to Dee, the practice of statecraft stands out as one of the more obvious beneficiaries.[49] Much as Trithemius had appealed to princes like Philip, Joachim, and Maximilian to increase the prospects of success, so did Dee appeal to Queen Elizabeth's adviser Cecil—and, by extension, to Elizabeth herself—to produce the same result. Yet Dee, in this also following the example of his admired monastic precursor, did not mean thereby to reduce magic to a mere worldly phenomenon. While acknowledging that magic is capable of being turned to worldly use, Dee accepted Trithemius's premise that the essential powers of magic are located in a higher spiritual drive of the soul to achieve proximity to God. In this capacity cryptography is tied into other branches of magic—astrology, alchemy, Cabala, and the like—which not only furnish it with notations from their alphabets, but also have the capacity to point it away from worldly transience and vicissitude to heavenly permanence and constancy.

In keeping with this higher purpose Dee adopted not only the system of angelic intelligences claimed by Trithemius, in conjunction with the planets, to be capable of mediating the ciphers of steganography even as they carried on their more majestic role as governors of world history. He also adopted Trithemius's blend of Hermetic alchemical and Pythagorean numerological principles in the formulation of his magical theory, together with the abbot's defensive way of responding to those who were not like-minded. Thus, included with Socrates, Apuleius, and Pico della Mirandola among his persecuted role models, as Dee made clear in his preface to Euclid (1570), was Trithemius, whose apology on behalf of his magic "will specify how he had occasion to make public Protestations, as well by reason of the rude, simple folk, as also in respect of such as were counted to be the wisest sort of men."[50]

Writing, however, under circumstances of religious upheaval not faced by Trithemius, Dee apprehended a potential residing within magic, including the specialized magic of cryptography, which had not been so pressing to the pre-Reformation abbot. This was the need to find a common ground of communication between orthodox and heterodox versions of Christianity. Such a meeting point, Dee determined from a Protestant perspective formally distinguishable from the Catholic one overseeing Trithemius's occult speculations, lay in a concordance of magic, Platonism, and the rudimentary basics of Christian doctrine. Implicit in a harmonizing program like this is a view of Trithemian cryptography which, transcending mere wordplay, presents it as an occult agent for reconciling the opposing sides to the debate over what it means to be a Christian.[51]

As might be expected in light of the heightened campaign against witches during Dee's time, by placing his imprimatur upon the more suspect of Trithemius's two cryptographic endeavors Dee laid himself open to the charge that he was engaging in the same kind of demonic magic Trithemius was widely believed to have employed. As Dee could not have failed to understand in this regard, it is one thing to profess powers of secret communication through the use of cryptic ciphers, as in the *Polygraphia,* and quite another thing to claim the assistance of disembodied spirits in the transmission of messages, as in the *Steganographia.* Dee's bold refusal to buckle under this prospect, however, causing his name to be popularly added by the demonologists to those of Agrippa and Paracelsus among the abbot's later disciples, was the exception rather than the rule for those favorably disposed to Trithemian magic. More typical was the French author of a *Traicté de chiffres,* Blaise de Vigenère (1523–1596), one who, like Dee, praised Trithemius for pioneering the art he described,[52] but unlike Dee made no reference to angelic agents for the mediation of its ciphers. Rather, Vigenère limited his explication to those marvel-working occult powers which, as Trithemius had also maintained in his theoretical writings, lay embedded in nature itself.

The art of writing, Vigenère asserted, is divisible into two basic forms: common everyday script and a secret enciphered script intelligible only to the sender and receiver. Concerning the latter form of writing Vigenère recognized an elevated origin, noting that the ancient Hebrews, Chaldeans, Egyptians, Ethiopians, and Indians employed ciphers "for the purpose of veiling their sacred secrets of theology and philosophy." With the passage of time, however, the art of encipherment also demonstrated more practical, everyday applications—this "for the affairs of the world and for negotiations and practices which are as much the business of individuals as of princes."[53] One expressly cited by Vigenère with assisting in both of these uses of cryptography, veiling divine truths and concealing practical intentions in the work-a-day world, was the abbot Trithemius.

Vehemently taking Trithemius's side in his famous dispute with Bovillus, Vigenère found no cause to doubt the abbot's pious protestation, with God as witness, that all he had incorporated into the pages of the *Steganographia* "accords only with natural behavior and with the dexterity of the human wit." If the marvels of steganography appeared to some to exceed the limits of human ability, the same could be said for other natural sciences in which "we see the truth only in its effects."[54] Once the occult cause behind the manifest effect is understood, insisted Vigenère, all wonder dissipates, and what before appeared to be naturally impossible is now judged to be easy and predictable. The abbot's readers, accordingly, needed to express no more amazement at the marvel-working powers locked up in the art of steganography than they needed to marvel at corresponding powers locked up in other arts dependent upon hidden natural forces.

A prime factor conditioning Vigenère's reading of Trithemian cryptography lay in his concurrent interest in a discipline also playing a key part in Trithemius's theory of magic, the art of alchemy. His dual cryptological-alchemical investigations parallel those of his countryman Jacques Gohory (d. 1576), writing under the name of Leo Suavius in his Latin writings, who penned a contribution to cryptographic literature of his own under the title *De usu et mysteriis notarum.*[55] If Trithemius can be said to have discovered a useful reservoir of cryptographical symbols in alchemy, more openly alchemical admirers like Vigenère and Gohory can be said to have reappropriated Trithemian cryptography for their alchemical investigations. While Vigenère's approach to cryptography superficially appears to be more practically than spiritually oriented, thereby reversing the emphasis the abbot himself gave to it, a further consultation of his related alchemical interests, together with those of like-minded contemporaries like Gohory and Gerard Dorn, reveals the emergence of a motive restoring the Trithemian subordination of material to spiritual concerns. Taking the lead of the abbot, these more mystically inclined admirers of Trithemius deemed the essential goal of the alchemist to be the effectuation, not of material gold, but of pure souls for which metallic gold represents but a metaphor.

The "spagyrical" movement of the late Renaisance represented by the above figures (from the Greek words *spao*=divide and *ageiro*=unite, corresponding to the Latin *solve et coagula*, a characteristic rallying cry of the alchemists) found its primary inspiration, not in Trithemius, but in Paracelsus. Nevertheless, apart from whether Paracelsus and Trithemius ever personally met, the Paracelsians, as will now be established, joined forces with the cryptographers in furnishing Trithemius a propitious medium for a defense of his magic. In this connection the Paracelsians also endowed the abbot with a constructive posthumous role in promoting an objective also prominently urged by the Cabalistically inspired cryptographer Dee: the reconciliation, through magic, of Protestant and Catholic theology. Trithemius himself, as earlier indicated, seemed to have some presentiment, recorded in his *De septem secundeis,* of an imminent religious schism. Concerning the Catholic-Protestant schism which actually came into being shortly after the abbot's 1516 death, the Paracelsians, motivated by the Cusan mystical principle of the *coincidentia oppositorum* also informing the magical vision of Trithemius, enlisted the abbot's help in their campaign to present magic as a viable way of rehealing the breach between opposing interpretations of Christ's life and meaning.

A perplexing question raised in Renaissance studies is whether Theophrastus Paracelsus von Hohenheim (ca. 1493–1541), whose

youth coincided with Trithemius's latter years, was personally instructed in the art of magic by the abbot. For many years it was
virtually an uncontested axiom of Renaissance scholarship, on the
basis of a passing reference by Paracelsus to an "abbot of Sponheim"
(*ept von Spanheim*) among his early teachers, that at some point in
his early career Paracelsus made his way to Trithemius at Würzburg,
attracted by the abbot's already blossomed magical reputation. This
assumption, first surfacing in the sixteenth century, is no longer so
securely held. Apart from the question of whether the paths of
Trithemius and Paracelsus ever actually crossed, we can establish
with considerable evidence that, by sharing a belief that magic and
religion are reciprocal means for coming into a state of intimacy
with God, the two men met in their minds if not in person.[56]

"Magic," wrote Paracelsus, "has power to experience and fathom
things which are inaccessible to human reason." With words like
these Paracelsus revealed that, even if he were not a personal
disciple of Trithemius, he was still in essential agreement with the
abbot's way of thinking. As viewed by Paracelsus, the Christian
magus is a kind of saintly marvel worker who elicits his wonder-
working virtues, not from a place above nature, but from the hidden recesses of nature itself. "As God awakens the dead to new
life," exclaimed Paracelsus, "so the 'natural saints,' who are called
*magi,* are given power over the energies and faculties of nature."
And again: "God shows His miracles through His holy men, both
through those of the beatific life and through those of nature."[57] For
Paracelsus as for Trithemius before him, the art best suited to cer-
tify this "saintly" character of magic was alchemy, the goal of which,
he insisted, is to produce, in conjunction with a pure substance
through the alchemical operation, a pure soul in the operator. If one
sentence can be extracted from the alchemical literature of the later
Renaissance to summarize this joint Trithemian-Paracelsian axiom
of Christian magic, it can be found in Vigenère's declaration, with
reference to the initial, putrefactive stage of alchemical catharsis,
that lead signifies "the vexations and sufferings through which God
visits us and by which He brings us back to our right minds."[58]

If for Paracelsus the alchemical magus was a kind of saint, for
Cesare della Riviera (d. ca. 1615) he was a kind of hero endowed
with a rare ability to tap into occult powers of nature. What makes
Della Riviera especially suitable to our purposes is that, in pressing

# IOÁNNIS TRITEMII

Abbatis sancti Iacobi apud Herbipolim; quondam vero Span‐
hemensis: Liber Octo questionū ad Maximilianum Cesarem.

¶ Cum priuilegio Cesaree maiestatis de nō imprimēdo in regno,
imperio, & terris suis nec alubi impressis isthic vēdēdis intra de‐
cenniū subpenis in priuilegio expressis dece marcarū auri puri et
amissione librorū eorundem omnium, zē.

Plate 1: Trithemius presenting *Octo quaestiones* to Emperor Maximilian.
Title page, Oppenheim, 1515. Reprinted by permission of Rare Books
Division, New York Public Library (Astor, Lenox and Tilden Foundations).

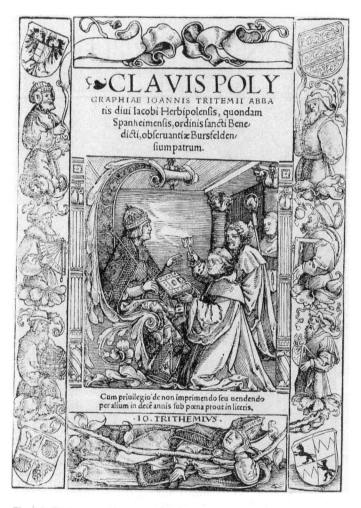

**CLAVIS POLY**
GRAPHIAE IOANNIS TRITEMII ABBA
tis diui Iacobi Herbipolensis, quondam
Spanheimensis, ordinis sancti Benedicti, obseruantiæ Bursfelden-
sium patrum.

Cum priuilegio de non imprimendo seu uendendo
per alium in decé annis sub pœna prout in literis.

·IO. TRITHEMIVS·

Plate 2: Trithemius presenting *Polygraphia* to Emperor Maximilian.
Title page, *Clavis polygraphiae*, Basel, 1518.

Plate 3: Title page, John Dee, *Monas hieroglyphica*, Antwerp, 1564.
Reprinted by permission of The Huntington Library, San Marino,
California.

Plate 4: Title page, Robert Fludd, *De macrocosmi historia*, Vol. II, Oppenheim, 1619. Reprinted by permission of The Huntington Library, San Marino, California.

Plate 5: Title page, Gustavus Selenus (Augustus II), *Cryptomenytices et cryptographiae*, Lüneburg, 1624. Reprinted by permission of The Huntington Library, San Marino, California.

Plate 6: Title page, Gaspar Schott, *Schola steganographica*, Nuremberg, 1665. Reprinted by permission of The Huntington Library, San Marino, California.

**PHYSICA**
**CURIOSA**

*Ad Sereniss. ac Potentiss. Principem*
**CAROLUM LUDOVICUM**
*Comitem Palatinum Rheni, S. R. J.*
*Archithes, Principem Electorem,*
*Ducem Bavariæ*

**AUCTORE**
P. GASPARE SCHOTTO
*Societatis Jesu.*

**MDCLXVII**

Plate 7: Title page, Gaspar Schott, *Physica curiosa*, Würzburg, 1667.
Reprinted by permission of The Huntington Library, San Marino,
California.

Plate 8: Engraving, Albrecht Dürer, *Melencolia I*, 1514. Photo: Warburg Institute, University of London.

this point home, he found valuable backing in the writings of Trithemius. Lauding magic, in the typical language of the alchemists, as "the stone of the heroes and our tree of life," Della Riviera referred his readers for testimony to Trithemius's 1505 letter to Ganay characterizing natural magic as "wisdom in physical things and understanding in metaphysical things, which consists of the knowledge of the virtue of things both divine and human." Inasmuch as such arcane knowledge is accessible only to those surpassing the ordinary limits of human ability, reasoned Della Riviera, it can justly be termed *una heroica scienza*—a "heroic knowledge," for which reason magic "is called by God the fountain of every good, just as light proceeds directly from light."[59]

Della Riviera's amalgamation of Paracelsian with Trithemian themes is implied rather than expressed. Not so, however, is a similar amalgamation by Gerard Dorn (fl. 1570), whose credentials included the translation of Paracelsus's works into Latin for their dissemination to the wider scholarly community. Thus, in the midst of a tract purporting to explicate the Genesis account of creation in accordance with the Paracelsian philosophy, *De naturale luce physica,* Dorn ingrafted a special section, under the heading "Concerning the Spagyrical Art of Johannes Trithemius" (*De Spagirico Artificio Io. Trithemii*), consisting of a nearly verbatim composite of passages from the four expository letters from Trithemius to selected acquaintances in the period 1503–1505. "This philosophy of ours is heavenly, not earthly," declared Dorn in keeping with the elevated view of magic indicated therein, "for it is that highest principle which we call God." Another distinctively Trithemian theme was caught by Dorn in his plea for strict esoteric secrecy, indicated in the caveat that "this ascent is not vulgar, nor does its imitation suffice for those who are carried aloft by one wing only, but is possible only to those very few who neither rashly nor improperly attempt to reduce themselves to unity." Specifying seven stages of magical-mystical ascent along the same lines as the Pythagorean-Hermetic-Cabalistic sequences laid out by Trithemius, Dorn maintained that upon the completion of this upward spiritual journey "we at last will be enabled to grasp the knowledge of all the arcana, both natural and supernatural."[60] A scarcely more pointed restatement of the abbot's doctrine of magical theology can be found among his later disciples.

While Dorn did not appear to be particularly disturbed by the negative campaign being waged in his day against Trithemian magic, others in the Paracelsian school were, and did their best to ward it off. The accusations of those, like Conrad Gesner, that Paracelsus was "an impious man and a magician who communicated with demons" reminded them of comparable accusations against Trithemius. As depicted by Gesner, Paracelsus belonged to a school of superstitious wonder workers "popularly known as wandering scholars (*quos vulgo scholasticos vagantes nominabant*), among whom a certain Faustus, who died not so very long ago, is wisely celebrated."[61] Trithemius, who spent only the better part of two years (1505–1506) wandering between stable monastic posts at Sponheim and Würzburg, scarcely fits the label of *scholasticus vagans* applied by Gesner to Paracelsus and Faustus. Nevertheless, given the widespread belief among the Paracelsians, virtually uncontested until modern scholarship brought it into question, that Paracelsus received personal tutelage in magic from Trithemius, any doubts about the legitimacy of Paracelsus's magic also readily redounded upon the reputation of the magical abbot.

It was under the assumption of such personal intercourse between the two magicians that the alchemically engaged Paracelsian Jacques Gohory, previously cited for his contribution to cryptographical literature, took upon his shoulders the defense of Trithemius along with that of his Hohenheim hero. The main culprit behind the vicious campaign against Trithemian magic, Gohory complained in scholia on Paracelsus's *De vita longa*, was Bovillus. Railing, in deprecatory language carried over from the abbot himself, "against that cur Bovillus, or rather, against the cow" (*adversus Bovillum istum seu potius bovem*), Gohory ridiculed several of Bovillus's slanders, finding especially absurd the charge that the abbot's steganographical notations "are in Arabic, or Hebraic, or Aramaic, or Greek, but few, or almost none, are in Latin."[62] Far from proving the abbot's engagement in demon conjuration, countered Gohory, this line of argument only betrayed Bovillus's ignorance of the foreign languages in question. But while serving Gohory as a principal target for his indignation, Bovillus was not alone in drawing the fire of the Paracelsian commentator. Also provoking Gohory's ire were two later critics of the abbot's magic, Weyer and Cardano, "who followed the cow as your leader." By casting their undeserved aspersions on Trithemius, charged Gohory, they had also effectively besmirched earlier students of the arcana, such as Roger Bacon, Albertus Magnus, Pietro d'Abano, and Arnaldus of Villanova, whose motives were no less noble than those of their Benedictine successor.[63] Backed by this venerable tradition, Gohory held not only the cryptological speculations of Trithemius to be vindicated, but also his alchemical speculations.

While revealing himself to be an ardent defender of Trithemian magic, then, Gohory saw that defense as but a component of a larger and more comprehensive defense of Paracelsian magic. The primary importance to him of *magia trithemica* lay in its position as a principal link, forged by a purported personal interaction between the abbot and Paracelsus, in the linear chain of esoteric teachings connecting the occult traditions of the earlier centuries and *magia paracelsica* coming to fruition in the present century. Gohory made this incentive for his Trithemian apologetic explicit. "And so with these calumnies refuted and turned aside by the writings of the loftiest philosophers against the exceedingly ignorant and impudent enemies of letters," Gohory concluded his Trithemian excursus in the preface to his Paracelsian scholia, "the foundations of the discipline laid down by Paracelsus seem solid to me, confirming the teachings of Trithemius, whom he acknowledged as his preceptor."[64]

Nevertheless, while detecting a common goal of spiritual purification and enlightenment in the magical speculations of Trithemius and Paracelsus, Gohory also acknowledged differing ways in how the two men went about their labors. In his role as magus-physician, noted Gohory, Paracelsus "concealed the miracles of things under the cloak of human life" (*rerum miracula . . . sub humane vitae praetextu . . . obumbravit*), whereas Trithemius, in his role as a magus-theologian, concealed miracles "under the cloak of the conjuration of spirits" (*sub spirituum evocatione*).[65] For this unabashed Paracelsian, however, the substantive agreement between the two magicians was more significant than any technical methodological differences between them.

Likewise seeing no contradiction between his religious beliefs and a favorable opinion of Trithemian magic was Gohory's compatriot Jean-Jacques Boissard (1528–1602). In his *De divinatione et magicis praestigiis,* published posthumously (1615), Boissard enthusiastically backed Trithemius and opposed Bovillus in the famous dispute between the two men over the meaning of steganography. For Boissard as for Gohory, the Bovillus affair only reconfirmed the critical importance of the rule of esoterism, whereby, as the abbot had cautioned the count-elector Philip, he must carefully guard the secrets imparted to him from those "who might be tempted to abuse these arcane mysteries of nature and thereby accomplish many profane, impious, and impudent things."[66] The significance of Boissard's tract for the present study lies partly in its role as a vehicle for Trithemian apologetics into the seventeenth century. But just as importantly, having been composed by a scholar with Calvinist leanings, it represents a conscious campaign by its Calvinist publisher Johann Theodore de Bry to propagate the notion of a magical means for rehealing the breach dividing Protestants and Catholics.[67] Boissard's was but one of a number of tracts flowing from the De Bry press during the seventeenth century, including writings by Robert Fludd to be treated below, signifying the resolve of the publisher to achieve two separate but related aims. The first aim was to keep alive the concept of magical theology in the sense bequeathed to it by the abbot Trithemius, and the second aim, to highlight in such a concept a theoretical point of juncture between Protestants and Catholics.

As publicized by Patrizi's call for a Jesuit-run *reformatio magica*, however, Protestants were not the only side to the Reformation debate to make this kind of conciliatory appeal on behalf of the occult studies. It was also manifestly present on the Catholic side. Indeed, as we will now bring to the forefront of this study, it was to become an issue within the Society of Jesus itself. Much as the demonological campaign against magic could as readily be observed among Catholics as Protestants, serving, so to speak, as an additional polemical weapon to be employed against the theologically heterodox opposition, so could the campaign on behalf of magic, with emphasis now upon what occultly united rather than divided the two religious camps.

### The "Jesuit Labyrinth" and Demonological Response

In a 1608 pamphlet, under the telling title *De studiis Jesuitarum abstrusioribus,* the converted Lutheran Johann Cambilhon (= Cambilhom, fl. 1610) accused the Society of Jesus of fostering illicit magical studies, the effect of which, he charged, was to represent Jesus and His apostles as sorcerers. What lent Cambilhon's broadside great weight is that its author had been a Jesuit before his conversion, giving him, he claimed, first-hand knowledge of what he was attacking. Happily, he exulted, he had taken leave of the "Jesuit Temple" (*de Templo Jesuitico*) before taking leave of his senses, an architectural monstrosity, he contended, marked by "subterranean hiding places and Circean caves" (*subterraneas illas latebras, & Circaea antra*) running beneath its innocent-looking foundations. Having himself escaped from the dark passages of this underground labyrinth, Cambilhon was in a unique position to warn others away from its enticements.[68]

It's possible that this 1608 indictment of his former order by Cambilhon helped to push members similarly disposed against magic, such as Possevino and Bellarmine, further to the right than they otherwise would have been inclined to go. In any event, a foremost anathema to this group, the *Steganographia* of Trithemius, appeared on the Catholic Index the very next year. Among those in basic agreement with this reactionary trend within the Society of Jesus was Jacob Gretser (1562–1625), who immediately penned a retort to Cambilhon "concerning the abstruse studies of the Jesuits," the substance of which was that it was not the Catholic Jesuits, but the Protestants to whom Cambilhon had switched allegiances, who were serving as mainline religious propagators of the black arts. Far from promoting illicit kinds of magic like these, rebutted Gretser, the Jesuits had consistently observed the sage judgment of Athanasius when he deemed it seemly to amputate the hand of the heretic Arsenius "lest it should be misused in the performance of magical operations."[69] In contrast, the Lutherans had shown themselves to be guilty of the very offense their spokesman Cambilhon had charged against the Jesuits.

For evidence to back up this contention Gretser took note of the circumstances surrounding the recent Frankfurt publication (1606) of the *Steganographia*. Before the ill-conceived decision to print that demon-riddled tract, Cambilhon was reminded, only the few people who chanced upon its rare manuscript copies were exposed to its nefarious contents. The decision to greatly enlarge that number by printing the dangerous manual was made, not by Catholics, but by Protestants. In Gretser's own damning words: "After all, who are those who have published the *Steganographia,* and moreover have adorned it with an elegant title page so that it might be made more easily vendible? Are these not the Lutherans, and did not this event take place in a Lutheran city?" In the same indignant tone Gretser inquired of Cambilhon "by whom this art has been greatly desired," with the answer again being self-evident. "In no manner could they be Catholics, much less Jesuits," inasmuch as both the church as a whole and the Society in devotion to the church had taken a firm stand against the kinds of magical operations advocated in the suspect tract. If the impious tract in question had not yet been added to the Roman Index (an occurrence still a year away), this was only because its comparatively few circulating manuscript copies had made that drastic step unnecessary. As a consequence of its 1606 printing, however, Gretser was confident that this oversight would soon be rectified.[70]

Using the example of Trithemian steganography as a test case, then, Gretser adopted the stratagem in his 1608 polemic with Cambilhon of bringing to the surface what he conceived to be an underlying connection between two contemporary movements which, in his eyes, were destructive of Christian solidarity. The first was magic, and the second, evangelical Protestantism. Concerning the first of these corosive factors Gretser assured his readers that the Jesuits "dispute both privately and publicly against superstitions, whether magical or otherwise, and overthrow and trample them by whatever means they have at hand," and concerning the second factor, that the Jesuits understood that the same demonic powers invoked by magicians like Trithemius also promoted the schismatic heresies of Luther and Calvin. The stringent warnings against demonic magic earlier expressed by St. Thomas Aquinas, insisted Gretser, were again being expressed with great vigor by his fellow Jesuits. It is not by chance that the same Jesuits had taken up a position in the vanguard of the counterreform movement to oppose the schismatic forces of Protestantism, for these aberrations of sound theological thinking were two sides to the same coin. For this reason, he pleaded, "do not the works, statements, and deeds of the Society stand up with equal force against magic, with all its superstitions, and against the heresy of Luther and Calvin?"[71]

Similarly detecting a common denominator beneath the magical and Protestant movements, with Trithemius a key component, was Christopher Brouwer (1559–1617), who perceived of Lutheranism and magic as variant but related kinds of superstition working under the auspices of the same demonic ruler. Thus, under the years 1503 and 1504 of his Trier annals Brouwer charged that Trithemius, by succumbing to the Devil's magic, had also unwittingly expedited the Devil's scheme to rupture Catholic unity. In presenting this criticism Brouwer stressed that he did not wish to slight Trithemius's many pious writings, such as his ecclesiastical histories (influential on the present work) or his many exhortations on behalf of monastic reform. Regrettably, however, Trithemius's many positive contributions to the Catholic reform movement had been seriously compromised by his misguided magical speculations. "That he might vindicate himself from the defamatory accusation that he practiced superstition and goetic magic," conceded Brouwer, Trithemius "protested that he was a virtuous man, and that he knew that he had committed no injury to God and to the Christian faith, and again that he had never employed his leisure and solitude in any other way than in the service of God."[72] In Brouwer's judgment, however, the self-exculpatory attempts of Trithemius proved to be an abysmal failure. Indeed, going still further, Brouwer charged that the abbot's protestations of innocence themselves comprised a part of his diabolical apparatus, inasmuch as it was a favorite trick of the Devil to hide his machinations behind the mask of holiness.

That Trithemius "above all filled the minds of many princes with the desire for his art" did not exonerate him in the least, charged Brouwer, since, as was well known, princes had also played a critical role in the spread of heretical and schismatic Protestantism. "There is a fine line of error which separates magicians from heretics," Brouwer noted in confirmation of a principal axiom of the Catholic Inquisition, explaining that "magic is either the parent of heretical opinions or, as Tertullian testifies, its authoress."[73] For Brouwer it was no coincidence that the Protestant reform movement was sprouted on German soil, for its seeds had already been planted by German magicians such as Trithemius, Agrippa, and Faustus. The blurring of the "fine line of error" between heretical schismatics and magicians (*breve inter magos, & haereticos confinium falsi*) found in the lands of Germany a fertile ground, with a widespread climate of magical credulity easily evolving into a widespread climate of religious credulity. Brouwer was not surprised, therefore, that the German principalities, "already teeming with curiosity and in contempt of our ancient demands for abstinence and discipline, gave birth to the monster of Lutheranism."[74]

Brouwer's invocation of the name of Faustus along with that of Trithemius in this connection is especially intriguing, since his principal information in this area was supplied by Trithemius himself. However, with hindsight lacking to Trithemius, Brouwer was able to detect a feature of the Faustian legend that had the effect of highlighting and reinforcing his thesis of a connection between the magical and Lutheran departures from orthodoxy. The additional evidence, claimed Brouwer, consisted of Faustus's personal association with a key player in the Lutheran revolt, the subversive knight Franz von Sickingen, "a vigorous defender of heresy," wrote Brouwer, "whom Trithemius remembers as being a man very desirous of mystical things, that is, of magic."[75] It did not seem to matter to Brouwer that the witness for the prosecution in this case, Trithemius, was also a chief defendant of the trial. For it was Brouwer's conviction that Trithemius and Faustus had jointly played significant roles in preparing the ground for the "Lutheran monster."

Given the sustained effort by Jesuits such as Gretser and Brouwer to establish underlying linkage between the occult and Protestant evangelical revivals, coupled with the stridently anti-magical vociferations of colleagues like Delrio, Possevino, and Bellarmine, Cambilhon's charge that his former Jesuit colleagues were themselves acting as a foremost medium for the spread of magic would appear, without further evidence at our disposal, to have nothing to go on. But in truth the Jesuit-turned-Lutheran was not simply inventing empty accusations against his former colleagues. There indeed was a movement afoot within the Society of Jesus, in polar opposition to that represented by Delrio, Possevino, Bellarmine, Gretser, and Brouwer, to legitimize magic for pious Christians. Moreover, at the hub of this promagical campaign within the Jesuit order, as of the antimagical campaign heretofore described, lay the doctrine of magical theology as laid out by the abbot Trithemius.

Already Delrio and Possevino, by distinguishing what they regarded to be the demonic magic of Trithemius from permissible natural magic under which it was deceptively cloaked, had established some kind of foothold within the Jesuit order for a possible revindication of the abbot at a later time. Interestingly, another example of this moderate position on magic was provided by a Jesuit specifically cited by Gretser in evidence against Trithemius, Benito Pereira (1535–1610). For while Pereira's express object in a treatise on this subject was to eradicate "the deceitful and superstitious arts," he also acknowledged that not all magic is bad. In agreement with a fundamental theme of Trithemius, Pereira distinguished malefic demonic from salutary natural magic, the latter conceded to be "a certain more secret and abstruse part of wisdom." Admittedly, Pereira allowed, "there is scarcely any mortal, or at the most, very few, endowed with sufficiently penetrating genius and patient enough to carry out diligent observation over a long time adequate to meeting the demands of such natural magic."[76] But while stopping short of specifying who might belong to that privileged group, Pereira nevertheless left the door open for others after himself, including his fellow Jesuits, to locate Trithemius in their number.

One who boldly stepped through that open door was Adam Tanner, furnishing evidence that the Italian Patrizi's plea for a Jesuit-led *reformatio magica* did not fall on deaf ears. Significantly, the first printing of Pereira's tract took place in the Society's Bavarian stronghold of Ingolstadt. It would soon be publicly demonstrated, beginning with a pivotal oration delivered in 1614 by Tanner on the same site (published the following year, also in Ingolstadt, as the opening discourse of the author's *Astrologia sacra*) that the Jesuits, far from being of one mind when it came to the subject of Trithemian magic, were in disagreement among themselves. To help dispel the popular prejudice that had come to surround the name of Trithemius—a stream of which, regrettably, had seeped into the speaker's own religious order—Tanner declared his intention to furnish the beleaguered abbot with a Jesuit forum for the defense of his posthumous reputation. The choice of the Ingolstadt location for both the delivery and printing of Tanner's oration, as also the further issuance from the same city of a vindication of Trithemian magic by the Benedictine abbot Sigismund of Seeon, greatly weakens a central plank of Gretser's case against Protestantism. For while it is true that Protestant towns like Frankfurt and Darmstadt produced the first printed editions of the *Steganographia,* it is equally true that the safely Catholic Bavarian town of Ingolstadt, the German bastion of Counterreformation Jesuits,[77] served as a base for two of the most vigorous defenses of Trithemian magic after 1600.

Adam Tanner (1572–1632) approached the question of the relationship between the current religious and magical revivals from a vantage point precisely opposite to that of his fellow Jesuit Bellarmine. Instances of demonic magic, Tanner held in his Ingolstadt oration of 1614, no more entail the rejection of magic in principle than instances of heresy entail the rejection of theology in principle. The same rule applies to magic as to religion with which it is fundamentally bound up: the winnow must be separated from the chaff. Taking up the question of Trithemian magic in particular to illustrate his point, Tanner presented three possible interpretations of its meaning. The first is that, being indicators of true religion, the abbot's magic is divinely instigated in the same sense as the miracles of Moses, of Christ, and of the saints; the second, that it is "superstitious and demonic"; and the third that it wholly natural. The first of these options, Tanner maintained, which would identify the magic of Trithemius, "as the theologians say, with the potency of the miracles, with the gift of prophecy, or with any other bestowal of divine grace," can be excluded from the outset, inasmuch as a divinely inspired virtue does not depend upon the kinds of ritualistic formulas and caveats prescribed by Trithemius.[78] The second option, however, charging the abbot with illicit dealings with the demons, was not so easily dispensed with, and therefore called for a fuller treatment by Tanner.

Who, Tanner pleaded, could conceivably charge such a man with the crime of sorcery, "one whose entire course and condition of life made him exceedingly adverse to such magic?" As evidenced by large tomes of his historical and spiritual writings recently coming to light, exhorted Tanner, Trithemius proved himself to be not only a piously faithful Christian and reform-minded monk but also an illustrious paradigm of Christian erudition sought out for counsel by the foremost princes and ecclesiastical dignitaries of his age. Moreover, as also testified by several recently published writings "against sorcerers and all the arts and superstitions prohibited by the Church," Trithemius both abstained from utilizing the black arts in his own arcane operations and discouraged them in the operations of others. This of course left only the third-named option for further consideration, namely, that Trithemius's occult operations were entirely natural. Inasmuch as the required natural virtue (*vis naturale*) is hidden away and made inaccessible to those ill equipped to penetrate to its source, Tanner pointed out, it is commonly mistaken for either a miraculous supernatural virtue (*vis supernaturalis*) issuing from a heavenly place or a wonder-working diabolical virtue (*vis diabolica*) issuing from an infernal place.[79]

Admittedly, Tanner allowed, there is much in the Trithemian art which appears uncanny to the ordinary person—this in the same way that modern inventions like the telescope and *camera obscura* also appear uncanny to those excluded from the knowledge of nature's inner workings. Nevertheless, he insisted, the *vis naturale* by which Trithemius accomplished his magical marvels is the same occult power of nature that sometimes produces seemingly uncanny effects of its own accord. Following this logic, "if the lodestone possesses the occult power of attracting iron, and amber of drawing chaff to itself, and the moon of moving the sea, and the oars of stopping a boat, and the electric ray of paralyzing the hand of one who grasps it, why might not a fixed observation of the stars, and an appropriate operation conforming to this observation, possess the power of announcing to friends the secrets which we wish to transmit to them?"[80]

The foregoing line of reasoning, together with the title of the volume—*Astrologia sacra*—in which it appeared in print, points up a basic assumption of Tanner's apologetic of Trithemian steganography that distinguished it from some others. For Tanner the art of steganography was comprised of more than a mere linguistic system of codes and ciphers. While dispensing with the apparatus of the angelic hierarchy ostensibly sustaining the steganographic operations, Tanner kept in place the planetary system which Trithemius had conjoined to the angelic hierarchy. Now, however, astrology was to be construed, not as an illicit adjunct to supernatural angelic magic, but as a quite licit adjunct to *magia naturalis*. While acknowledging the identity of the angelic scheme employed in the third book with the governing scheme described in the *De septem secundeis,* Tanner took the author at his own word, in keeping with the esoteric rule, that "this has been done by Trithemius for no other reason than to conceal his craft from ill-adept and vulgar men." One properly initiated in the secrets of steganography will have no cause for alarm, he insisted, discerning for himself the truth of its inventor's vow that all its its operations are performed "by a natural power and method." Moreover, by conjoining to this understanding a further appreciation for the abbot's exceptional contributions to the literature of Christian piety—including several learned exhortations against sorcery, he will allay his suspicions even further, seeing him for what he really is, "a man very learned and orthodox in his Catholicism, in which capacity he served not only as a monk but as a high priest of monks."[81]

As we will subsequently observe, Tanner's Ingolstadt appeal was to find significant resonance not only among his fellow Catholics, including other Jesuits, but also among similarly disposed Protestants. Unfortunately for its future prospects, however, likewise reverberating on both sides of the Catholic-Protestant divide, there continued to be waged a stridently demonological campaign against it, the participants of which were not convinced by Tanner's disclaimer that an occult *vis naturale* working in the Trithemian art was mistakenly construed by the unenlightened to be a *vis diabolica*. A sinister turn to the Trithemian magical legend is humorously illustrated by a comment written into a play by William Cartwright (1611–1643). So foul is the breath of a certain acquaintance, one party to this interchange exclaimed, that it "would rout an Army, sooner than / That of a Cannon," to which his respondent replied that it "would lay a Devill / Sooner than all *Trithemius'* charmes."[82] Events surrounding the witch persecutions, however, put the abbot's magical reputation in a far more serious light than is implied by this whimsical dramatic line, throwing up a formidable demonological obstacle to the pursuit of Trithemian magic which needs to be addressed before we pursue further instances of those persuaded to follow up on Tanner's appeal.

Poignant testimony of Trithemius's role as a flashpoint for seventeenth-century Catholic opponents to magic is provided by a Spanish Franciscan, Francisco de Quevedo (1580–1645), who sought to rectify and bring up to date what he considered to be a glaring omission in Dante's vision of Hell. Dante, Quevedo regretted to report, had neglected to include in his infernal circles of sin one which contained the gicians. Specifying, in his reconstructed "dream" (*sueño*) of the Inferno, various of the magical disciplines whose devotees were deserving of eternal punishment—alchemy, astrology, chiromancy, and the like, Quevedo then passed to some of the more notable representatives of these outlawed disciplines whose shades were distinctly recognizable. In the front ranks of these, in the company of D'Abano, Agrippa, and Paracelsus, loomed Trithemius, displaying as his identifying signature his two cryptographical manuals. As depicted by Quevedo in this unholy setting, Trithemius was "glutted with demons, of which, so it seemed, he could never have enough during his lifetime."[83]

Catholic demonologists were not alone, however, in visualizing Trithemian magic in this fashion. A nearly mirror image of Quevedo's infernal apparition, for example, was furnished by the Lutheran Conrad Dieterich (1575–1639), who added the visage of Faustus to that of Trithemius and Agrippa in his imaginative depiction of the sorcerers of the ages consigned to the pit of Hell. "Behold," railed Dieterich under the force of this Protestant version of Quevedo's vision, "they long ago received their due reward, and were conveyed, together with their black arts, into the black hole—into the black, dark crater of fire—presided over by their black master the Devil, where they might henceforth perpetrate their deceptions for all of eternity."[84] Similarly invoking a fiery image in the same regard, but this time less extremely calling for the burning of the offending writing rather than the malfeasant author, Dieterich's coreligionist Sigismund Scherertz (=Scherertzius, 1584–1639) declared that the dangerous steganographical handbook "would have been better committed to flames than published and read."[85]

The case of Tanner lent credibility to the charge of a Protestant like Cambilhon's that a major share of the blame for a failure to carry out the above recommendation on a broad scale was borne by the Society of Jesus. Further charging the Jesuits with providing fertile ground for the cultivation of demonic magic, for example, was the Utrecht theologian Guisbert Voet (1593–1680), who cited their indulgence toward sorcerers like Agrippa and Trithemius as encouraging the current craze for occult studies. Striking all three targets with one volley—Trithemius, Agrippa, and the Jesuits—Voet declared in the same breath that "so long as the books under the title of *De occulta philosophia* of Agrippa, even among papists, are held in disrepute, likewise Trithemius cannot possibly be absolved, even if the Jesuits, including Tanner who published an apologetic oration on behalf of Trithemius, should deliver a hundred orations in his support." Nor did Voet's antimagical invective stop with the Jesuits, extending, so to speak, to the entire Catholic Church. Further to be added to his list of prominent malefactors, not by chance all practicing Catholics, were the previously encountered Jacques Gohory and, still to come to our attention, Abbot Sigismund and Gabriel Naudé.[86] Like many other Protestants of his stripe, Voet considered superstitious adherence to magic, Trithemian or otherwise, to be of a piece with superstitious adherence to the Catholic faith.

The Calvinist Voet's conflation of an anti-Jesuit with an antimagical outlook was also shared by certain Lutherans, among whom the Wittenberg theologian Balthasar Meisner (d. 1684) can be taken as representative. The papacy, charged Meisner, actively encouraged the Jesuits in their campaign to effect a resurgence of ancient pagan magic, as corruptive then as now of proper religious sanctity. If it is true, as prior supporters of the occult studies have held, that the ancient word *magus* pertained to the priestly function, Meisner read an opposite meaning into that contention than was usually intended by its spokesmen. For what the advocates of magic characterized as a continuous stream of divinely sanctioned arcane teachings stretching from ancient times to the present was characterized by Meisner as a demonically polluted subterranean stream, so that, God willing, "all the magical superstitions of the pagans have flowed into the papal realm as if it were a cesspool of all evils" (*omnes Ethnicorum superstitiones magicas in regnum Papisticum, veluti communem omnium malorum sentinam, ... confluxisse*)."[87] Assisting the Jesuits in contributing to this papal "cesspool of all evils," Meisner maintained, was the monk Trithemius.

Admittedly, acknowledged Meisner, "there are some who would excuse Trithemius, interpreting his spirits to be, not demons and spiritual substances, but something other than they appear to be," even going so far as to identify his steganographic invocations with "the invocations and prayers of the Trinity." However, Meisner let it be known that he took a far more sinister view of what the abbot was about, as also of the Jesuit campaign to justify the occult activities of one who furnished their diabolically driven conspiracy with a secret language for transmitting "their numerous clandestine and bloodstained counsels" (*multa clandestina & sanguinolenta consilia*). Being unimpressed by Trithemius's self-portrayal as "a most accomplished master of natural magic," Meisner rather assigned Trithemian magic to the category "divinatory"—this by reason of calling upon the same kinds of "familiar spirits" (*spiritus familiares*) as were also invoked by demonically inspired prophets. For this reason, judged Meisner, Bovillus was completely on target when he condemned the abbot for demon conjuring.[88]

Given his linkage of anti-Trithemian with anti-Jesuit sentiments, it is not by chance that Meisner followed up his castigations of Trithemian magic with a retelling of a story concerning the uncanny disappearance of the corpse of Loyola, the Jesuit order's founder, while it was waiting to be transferred to its crypt. The claim made by Loyola's followers was that their master had been miraculously carried away by holy angels. On the heels of his censure of Trithemius for demon conjuring, however, Meisner read into this legend a message quite different from that encouraged by Loyola's disciples. If Loyola's cadaver were truly transported by angels, Meisner retorted, "these are understood to be evil angels (*angelis malis*)," identical, as it were, to the evil spirits conjured by Trithemius for use in his steganographical operations.[89]

Mirroring the jointly anti-Jesuit and antimagical sentiments of Voet and Meisner, with explicit reference to their opinions, was the Saxe-Coburg physician Johann Christian Frommann (b. 1640). Declaring Trithemius to have greatly augmented the number of magicians in his day, Frommann inveighed against the Society of Jesus for its predominant role in effecting this regrettable result. With express help from Meisner, Frommann charged the Jesuits with an ulterior motive in promoting the Trithemian art of steganography, perceiving in it, so he claimed, a suitable means for clandestinely conveying their conspiratorial designs between one another. And in express help from Voet, he cited Tanner's pro-Trithemian Ingolstadt oration as a foremost testament to this same diabolically driven conspiracy.[90]

In his professional role as physician Frommann might be expected, in a diagnosis of an accused witch or sorcerer, to consider natural causes in preference to supernaturally demonic ones. However, much like his Lutheran predecessor Weyer, he demonstrated that, in matters like this, higher theological concerns could easily come to prevail over mere physiological ones. In the final analysis this characterization also fits a Lutheran physician of an earlier generation often presented by modern scholarship to be of a more judicious, less "superstitious" disposition, Daniel Sennert (1572–1637). If Frommann accepted Voet's and Meisner's view of Trithemius as an explicit conjuror of demons, Sennert rather saw the abbot's magic as incited more by implicit than explicit demonic means.

As an outspoken critic of the Paracelsians, it is true, Sennert included Trithemius in a group of excessively enthusiastic magicians, also numbering Agrippa and Paracelsus in their number, who had allowed their high-flying imaginations to dominate over the kind of sober reason praised by Hippocrates and Galen as the proper standard of good mental health. Singled out by Sennert as a prime example of such unrestrained flights of phantasy was Trithemius's Cabalistically based art of stegangraphy, through the operations of which, so it was claimed, "voices can be naturally heard from a distance of a hundred miles." Following the formulas concocted for receiving such a voice, scoffed Sennert, Trithemius presumed that he could even have his dinner delivered to him from France or Italy by uttering but one word, "Affer," which, translated, means "Bring it to me!"[91] By allowing themselves to be carried away by such unbridled phantasies, charged Sennert, magical enthusiasts following Trithemius's lead, far from accomplishing the feats to which they pretended, were more likely to fall into fits of melancholy by failing to effect their imagined objectives. But this did not mean, Sennert insisted, that melancholy magicians were necessarily free of demonic inspiration. After all, as the Protestant physician cautioned in a manner not far removed from that of his theological mentor Luther, such unhinged magical enthusiasm "belongs to that melancholy which, popularly and rightly, is said to be the bath of the Devil."[92]

These fear-mongering representations of the abbot in the thralls of the witch hunts give a good sense of the kind of obstacles that still lay in the path of those who sought to follow Trithemius's example into the decades of the seventeenth century. They put the magical disciples of Trithemius on notice that, at the conclusion of their terrestrial careers, they could expect a similar fate of eternal punishment in the infernal depths. While some of those favorably disposed to Trithemian magic were undoubtedly intimidated by such a menacing picture of what the abbot was about in his occult studies, others are on record as bravely standing up against the persisting demonological tide to which that picture belonged.

Of the ways in which Trithemius placed his distinctive stamp on occult theory in the unstable aftermath of the Reformation and shift to a more blatantly secular configuration of nation-states, one lay in the area of astrological prediction. Illustrating this aspect of Trithemius's posthumous influence is a tract of William Lilly (1602–1661), a namesake of the more famous contemporary of the abbot, who invoked the scheme of cyclic governances of the world depicted in the *De septem secundeis* to explain a series of calamitous events taking place during his lifetime and to predict some more soon after his death.[93] Two other ways by which Trithemius made his mark on that same period, however, can be said to be geared more to improving the present status of mankind than predicting its future status. The first of these ways was through cryptography, and the second way, through alchemy. In corresponding fashion, these two disciplines, sometimes independently of one another and sometimes in conjunction under the auspices of a new secret movement known as Rosicrucianism, continued to serve as foremost cutting edges of the movement to rehabilitate the name and magic of Trithemius.

To be sure, a foremost motive for the increasing popularity of cryptography, the first of these vogues to be considered, lay in the practical needs of statecraft and private intercourse, especially in view of the seventeenth-century exacerbation of a climate of intolerance making a technique for hiding one's private thoughts increasingly attractive. The title page for a plagiarized French translation of the *Polygraphia*, attributed to a certain Dominique de Hottinga, puts this pragmatic appeal of Trithemian cryptography in bald terms. The work at hand, the author promised, offers a method of arcane communication "useful, suitable, and necessary primarily to kings, princes, counts, republics, and all devotees of subtlety, of ingenuity, and of rarity."[94] Nevertheless, a more spiritually oriented incentive for the cryptographical vogue was also evident during this period, conditioned, we will also now observe, not by crass worldly desires, but by a drive to transcend the material world.

## The Cryptographical Vogue

In his *Thresor de langues* Claude Duret (d. 1611) maintained that the Cabalists, who employed their enigmatic ciphers and characters "to express secretly the most hidden mysteries of their divine law," found their supreme exemplar in Moses, who received from God, not a direct statement of the Law, but rather, lest it be contaminated, "the Law inscribed in confused and perplexing letters." This, added the writer, "is the true steganography, which the abbot Trithemius has sought to imitate."[95] Duret, that is to say, conceived of the Trithemian art on the model of Moses' need to receive and transmit the divine law to his priesthood through esoteric means.

A technique perceived by Duret as capable of bridging the mundane and supermundane realms was also recognized by his compatriot Jean Belot (fl. 1625), a parish priest, this time in conjunction with one of the traditional liberal arts. Expressing dissatisfaction with the limitations of conventional Ciceronian rhetoric, Belot in his *L'oeuvre de oeuvres* (1622) advocated the contrivance of a "new rhetoric" (*rhetorique nouvelle*) capable of going beyond an attempt to achieve a more pleasing style to probe the deeper levels of the disciplines being expressed. The dual goal of this renovated rhetoric, announced Belot, is "to acquire the gift of discoursing purely and elegantly and of disputing and arguing in a learned manner, together with arriving at the perfect knowledge of all the arts and sciences." Replacing the parts of conventional Ciceronian rhetoric with five new parts of arcane origin better suited to the ambitious goal called for, Belot identified the Trithemian art of steganography with his fifth part, termed by him "the art of revelations, which Trithemius declares to come from Orphiel, that is, from the mercurial spirit, for the disposition."[96]

Declaring steganography to reveal "lofty and difficult things to us which are very worthy of our admiration," Belot maintained that the powers unlocked by this noble art are so great that "they seemingly surpass the forces and order of nature as revealed in the Cabal, Gematrie, Germantie, Sephirotz, and Notariacon of the Hebrews." Steganography, contended Belot, is one of the subtlest of the human sciences, with its enigmatic notations possessing in some ineffable way "a signification and correspondence with the names of the good angels unknown to us, whom we honor without being acquainted with them."[97] As judged by Belot, accordingly, a crucial distinction is to be made between a true conjuration of evil spirits and the *signification* of holy spirits, or angels, exercised under the guise of conjurations. Instead of being proscribed by the church as Trithemius's critics would have it, this method of cryptic communication should be actively encouraged, stimulating as it does a veneration of the holy angels "so that our devotion and service will not be in vain, and so that we may be rewarded for it by their society."[98]

Accolades to Trithemius like those of Duret and Belot represent passing tributes to the cryptological achievements of the abbot in which their subject played a meaningful but still relatively minor role in the overall theory of human language being expounded. A number of others appearing on the scene during the same period, however, reveal far greater dependency on Trithemius and involvement with his cryptological methods, in conjunction with which they provide him with extensive vindicatory discourses. Notable representatives of this group of Trithemius defenders are the Benedictines Sigismund of Seeon and Jean d'Espières; the Worms scholar Wolfgang Ernst Heidel who, while not identifying himself as a Benedictine, reveals close affiliations with that order; the Cistercian Juan Caramuel y Lobkowitz; the Jesuits Athanasius Kircher and Gaspar Schott; and a Protestant prince, Duke August II of Braunschweig-Lüneburg, writing under the pseudonym Gustavus Selenus. Through the likes of these, now to be attested by a chronological assessment of their writings, not only Trithemius' cryptological methods reached a wider audience than ever, but also the magical rationale upon which he based those methods.

"The great Trithemius stands readied with illustrious weapons, And by their use will vindicate his own reputation."[99] In this way a Benedictine abbot following the example of Trithemius in more than the conventionally monastic manner, Sigismund of Seeon (=Dullinger, d. 1634), signaled his intent, in an introductory ode of his *Trithemius sui-ipsius vindex* (1616), not so much to defend his subject's cryptographical brand of magic as to have him articulate his own defense. Expressing puzzlement as to how the esteem for "so great a man, one who has been so aptly commended by the Catholic Church for his letters and learnedness," had fallen to its present nadir, Sigismund typically faulted Bovillus as the main culprit. Noting that Trithemius himself had provided a key for unlocking the mysteries of this art, missed by Bovillus, Sigismund expressed confidence that one gaining entrance into its inner workings will be apprised that "there is no need for an art which is diabolically magical, but only for one which is physical and natural."[100]

Posing the question of whether, by his choice of the suspicious language in which the writing was cast, Trithemius played at least some part in bringing his troubles upon himself, Sigismund replied that this decision was made for good reason. "Trithemius was warranted in employing numbers, signs, and strange names belonging to spirits and other entities," the writer explained following the usual esoterist guideline, "so that he might so fully envelop his art in mysteries that it would not be easily penetrated by anyone who was not first, in honesty and piety, initiated into its precepts."[101] In adopting this esoterist expedient, continued Sigismund, Trithemius was but following the example of the ancient sages, who likewise, "if they discovered any arcana, either of nature or of art, lest they came to the notice of depraved men, concealed them by various modes and figures." And if that were not enough to prove the legitimacy of this practice, we have the testimony of holy scripture itself, with examples like that of Moses, who found it necessary to explain "the arcane and ineffable mysteries of the creation of heaven and earth" in the language of riddle and enigma, and of St. John, who, according to St. Jerome, phrased his apocalyptic writings in the figurative idiom of allegory. In like manner "the Greeks and Egyptians always used figures and obscurities for the concealment of sacred and divine things."[102] In parallel fashion the jurists, mathematicians, musicians, rhetoricians, poets, alchemists, and even strategists of the military art have long recognized the need to hide their ideas under the mask of cryptic enigmas—this to make them inaccessible to those for whom they were unintended.

One could of course, like the Jesuit Delrio, agree to a theoretical justification of natural magic while still placing Trithemius's particular brand of steganographic magic outside its pale. Sigismund, however, rejected this easy way out, specifically answering Delrio that "if forbidden magic can be defined as a faculty or art by means of which, by the power of a pact initiated with demons, certain marvels and the conquest over the common sense of men are brought about, the very religious man and most perfect master of natural magic, Johannes Trithemius, most certainly never entered in his work into a pact with the demons." On the contrary, he insisted, presently to be reinforced by an arsenal of quotations from his own writings, Trithemius was "a lover of a more secret philosophy" (*secretioris philosophiae amator*) who, far from enlisting demons in his steganographical operations, was always careful to employ only "licit and natural means."[103] In further fullfillment of his promise to have Trithemius act as his own vindicator, Sigismund appended the expressly demonological fifth, sixth, and seventh books of the *Octo quaestiones,* the effect of which, Sigismund agreed with their author, was to establish a clear-cut boundary between Trithemian magic and that of the wicked sorcerers.[104]

Following up on Sigismund's 1616 apologetic of Trithemian magic was another appearing in 1624, albeit this time at the behest of a Protestant. He was the Lutheran prince August II of Braunschweig-Lüneburg (1579–1666), whose *Cryptomenytices et Cryptographiae,* appearing under the anagrammatic pseudonym Gustavus Selenus, expressly acknowledged on its title page (see plate 5) its indebtedness to Trithemian methods. The effect of the pseudo-Selenus tract was to underscore not only the appeal of the abbot's cryptological methods to the secular world beyond the cloister, but also their facility in cutting across formal religious boundaries. For it was August's stated desire, reflected in his forthright support for the Catholic Habsburgs at the helm of the Holy Roman Empire, to heal the rift between Protestants and Catholics. Testifying to this desire is the dedication of his pertinent cryptological work, set forth as a plausible linguistic aid in the reconciliation of the opposing sides, to the sitting emperor Ferdinand II.

Declaring that the the ingenious abbot only "played" (*ludit*) under the cover of spirits to conceal his true purpose from the vulgar, August-Selenus maintained that, despite its angelic subterfuge, steganography is really no more supernatural than its sister art, polygraphy. Or for that matter, he added, it is no more supernatural than other spirit-free cryptographic competitors devised through the centuries to conceal ideas such as cryptology, steganology, the notary art, and encipherment. A fitting ancient simile for its God-given role, he observed, is presented by the myth of Ariadne's thread by which Theseus was led out of the labyrinth of King

Minos.[105] Needless to say, the labyrinthine character of Trithemian cryptography here expressed is far removed from that depicted by Cambilhon in his hostile allusion to the dark underground caverns of the "Jesuit Temple."

Another admirer of Trithemius to go beyond mere lip service to actively taking up his cryptographical methods was the Spanish Cistercian Juan Caramuel y Lobkowitz (1606–1682), whose defensive approach to the subject at hand was indicated on the title page of his 1635 reedition of the *Steganographia* by his assurance that any effects resulting from the techniques prescribed were accomplished "without dependency upon any pact or superstition, but rather issued, through a necessary sequence, from natural principles and causes."[106] In its introductory prologue Caramuel expressly entered into the debate over Trithemian magic on the side of those, like Sigismund, who looked on the *Steganographia* in the same way, in the process of which he called attention to the recent publication of the abbot's *Octo quaestiones* confirming the author's demonological credentials.[107] In response to the controversy stirred up by the steganographical manual, Caramuel inveighed against various of the abbot's detractors, most notably Delrio and, recently joining the fray, Quevedo. Taking irate exception to Quevedo's expansion of the Dantean vision of Hell to embrace a magician like Trithemius, Caramuel chided the author of the *Sueños* that "if God were no more merciful than Quevedo, not only you, my Trithemius, would have been damned, but also other good Catholics into the bargain."[108] The Inquisition, urged Caramuel, rather than attempting to staunch the efforts of those following Trithemius's example, would be better advised to put a stop to self-appointed censors of the abbot like Quevedo.

Further illustrating monastic receptivity to Trithemius's cryptological achievements is a 1638 tract by the Benedictine Bernard von Mallinckrott (1591–1644), titled *De natura et usu literarum disceptatio philologica . . . .,* in which a chapter "concerning furtive or occult writing" credits the abbot, with Sigismund and pseudo-Selenus to back him up, with pioneering the subject at hand.[109] Three years later (1641) appeared a more substantial Benedictine homage to the abbot, this time by the Hennegau prior Jean d'Espières (d. 1664), in the form of a "specimen of steganography" accompanied by a vigorous defense of its inventor. Prefacing his work with excerpts from prior tributes to the abbot, including those recently published by Caramuel, Malinckrott, and, still to be considered for our purposes, Gabriel Naudé, Espières further set the stage for the follow-up *vindiciae trithemianae* with the usual caveat against the necromantic brand of magic widely but unjustly charged to Trithemius, "the object of which is to thunder conjurations, to evoke subterranean spirits, to prescribe the vain transformations of bodies," and the like. Far from being diabolically inspired as the abbot's critics charge, Espières exclaimed, "this steganography of ours" (*nostra haec Steganographia*), now stripped bare, uncovered, transparent, and pure, does not know dissimulations, does not conjure evil spirits, and does not dawn a magical garment."[110] Steganography in this form, insisted Espières, is purged not only of all evil, but of all appearance of evil.

Trithemius observers, as determined by Espières in the *vindiciae* proper, belonged to one or another of three basic categories, with some outrightly accusing the abbot of demonic magic, others condemning the work but not the man, and still others cherishing and defending the work together with the man. Locating himself within the last-named group, Espières compared the critics of Trithemian magic to a foolish blind man who, failing to understand that the darkness lies within rather than without himself, changes his position with the hope of seeing better. In the same way, he reasoned, it was not obscurities lying ensconced within the steganographical handbook that truly obstructed the vision of its critics, but their own blindness. Those approaching the subject with the necessary clarity of understanding will perceive a suitable antecedent in a practice of the ancient Jewish priesthood, whereby, heeding their need to exchange precious information privy only to their own members, its members devised methods of cryptic writing to be penetrated only by those properly initiated in its principles and alphabet. Beginning with a rudimentary art of *abbreviatura,* which did little more than substitute a few letters for complete words, they purportedly progressed to the much more complex cryptic methods of Cabala. Trithemian steganography, contended Espières, represented a further stage in this development, now happily put to the disposal of Christ.[111]

In typical fashion Espières fastened on Bovillus for doing the greatest damage to Trithemius's posthumous reputation, responding point by point to the objections raised in the mean-spirited letter to Ganay. For Espières the testimony of sacred scripture, relating the attendance upon the Christ child of those "who are honorably called *Magi*," was greatly to be preferred to Bovillus's wild ravings. Reproaching Bovillus for failing to follow "the philosophical subtleties of Trithemius," he declared that the ungrateful Sponheim guest had arrived at his judgment all too hastily. The writing in question, Espières scolded, "should not be randomly perused, but deliberately and leisurely inspected; for it requires, not a skirmisher and deserter, but an explorer, and ought not to be cursorily and perfunctorily tasted, but gradually and earnestly imbibed." Fortunately others followed Bovillus, such as Agrippa, Paracelsus, and Della Porta, "men celebrated for their learning and genius, if not for their religion," who better met the demands of this requirement.[112]

Regrettably, Espières lamented, Bovillus's anti-Trithemian cavils also found receptivity in others just as blind, among whom could be singled out "Johann Weyer, an ape of Bovillus," and Girolamo Cardano.[113] That the likes of these were deceived by Trithemius's enigmatic art did not especially trouble Espières, who counted them among the rude types Trithemius had intended to exclude from access to his precious secrets. But the same could not be said for certain other opponents to Trithemian magic for whom he held far greater respect, among whom he counted Delrio and Bellarmine. Fortunately these opponents of Trithemian magic did not speak for the entire church, nor for that matter, as illustrated by Tanner, even for the Jesuits. That the suspect steganographical handbook had been placed on the Catholic Index did not of itself condemn it as superstitious, Espières pointed out, inasmuch as its prohibition was required only so long as it remained unemended. Like the proverbially moral-free sword, it is usable for evil or for good, depending on the motives of its user. Granting to the guardians of orthodoxy that the work, "though good and virtuous," was rightfully prohibited in times past "by reason of the considerable scandal it has generated," Espières now dedicated himself to dispelling that scandal and restoring the Trithemian art to the divinely commended uses for which it was intended.[114]

What was interpreted by the Protestant critics of Trithemian cryptography, then, as an occult aid in the cohesion and advancement of a diabolically manipulated Catholic conspiracy was interpreted by its Catholic defenders as an aid in the unification and advancement of a reformed hierarchical church under the sponsorship of the papacy. This was especially true in the order of Delrio and Bellarmine, where Jesuits specializing in the art of cryptography, taking their lead from Trithemius, further cultivated the seed planted by Tanner in his 1614 Ingolstadt oration. A significant shift in methodological emphasis, however, illustrated by Hermann Hugo (1588–1629), is evident among the earliest of these Jesuit cryptographers. Indicating a desire to utilize Trithemian cryptological techniques without being drawn into the heated controversy over the conjurational apparatus described in the *Steganographia,* Hugo put himself on notice as preferring the patently spirit-free polygraphical over the ostensibly spirit-riddled steganographical method. For Hugo Trithemian polygraphy was nothing more than an updated version of ancient cryptological operations like that adopted by Cicero and augmented by St. Cyprian.[115] Following Hugo in professing a preference of the polygraphical over the steganographical version of cryptic communication, as revealed in the title of his *Polygraphia nova et universalis* (1663), was Athanasius Kircher (1599–1680).

The task envisaged by Kircher was one of separating out what is good in Trithemian cryptological methods from what is bad—that is, of sifting out the polygraphical winnow from the steganographical chaff. Being mindful of certain suspect elements that had seeped into the art of polygraphy as a result of confusion with its steganographical counterpart, Kircher was eager to establish that he was no uncritical beneficiary of the Trithemian art, to which end he prudently attached to his text an appendix declaring that "the arcane paradoxes proposed by Trithemius . . . are partly approved and partly refuted as superstitious."[116] As gauged by Kircher, the Trithemius problem came down to a question, not of whether the abbot associated with demons, but whether he presented his demon-free cryptographic principles in their very best light.

In his qualifying appendix to the *Polygraphia nova,* as also in his *Oedipus Aegyptiacus* published the same year, Kircher was unequivocal about what he believed to be the crux of the abbot's "superstitious" proclivities. In the *Oedipus* Kircher conceded that Trithemius, by making use of a complex system of spirits whose name he "recites from the tradition of the Hebrews," had led not only his detractors into confusion about what he was trying to do, but his own followers into the bargain. But while allowing that Trithemius's system of spirit mediators "is so muddled that I do not see by what manner anything of certainty can be concluded from their invocation," Kircher did not thereby find cause, as did the abbot's extreme traducers, to condemn its author to eternal perdition. Rather, he took it only as a reminder to correct the shortcomings of Trithemius's methodology so that it could more effectively produce its desired fruits.[117] Kircher had reluctantly concluded that the reputed obfuscating device of spirit magic employed by Trithemius in the *Steganographia* was a counterproductive mistake, trading off any possible advantage of esoteric concealment for the much greater disadvantage of misinterpretation. To rectify this fault Kircher addressed his energies to devising a "new polygraphy," purged of the suspect traits characterizing the old version.

Quoting verbatim Trithemius's explanatory letter to Bostius and taking note of Duke August's previous attempt to put a good face on his steganography, Kircher contended that the abbot could have prevented much unnecessary misunderstanding about his motives if he had held more faithfully to the various ancient models which he had put forth as worthy of emulation. An example is Archimedes, who, as illustrated by his discovery of the principle of the lever, always kept his imagination rigorously in check by a rational understanding of what is actually possible. Regrettably, rather than holding firm to the rational standard for cryptic communication bequeathed to posterity by Archimedes, Trithemius all too easily succumbed to phantasies like those of the alchemists in their vain quest for the "unique universal stone" (*lapidem illum suum unicum*). As many of the alchemists had permitted their inherently noble principles to be popularly misconstrued by burdening them with obscure enigmas, imagined miracles, and empty promises, the same thing can be said about Trithemius, who, encouraged by many of his own injudicious pronouncements, had become widely looked upon as a man "entangled by so many spirits, both hostile and amiable, by so many ghostly specters and owls (*bacuceis bubonibusque*), and by so many unseen and unheard promises, that he has exceeded all the possible inventions of the human intellect."[118] As a result, Kircher regretted to say, the noble art of cryptography had acquired undeserved notoriety, being viewed, at worst, as trafficking in demons, and, at best, as constituting a trival game for childre

Modestly acknowledging that neither he nor Trithemius had proffered the last word on this subject, Kircher expressed the hope that "there will perhaps come another later of a more fertile genius who, by grasping hold of Ariadne's thread, will penetrate into the innermost shrines of the steganographic labyrinth."[119] One directly responding to this challenge was Kircher's fellow Jesuit Gaspar Schott (1608–1666), who, with venerable forerunners like Tanner and Sigismund to support his case, declared in his *Physica curiosa* (see title page, plate 7) that the Trithemian art of polygraphy was no more deserving of suspicion than the secret Laconian script utilized by the ancient Spartans to conceal their intentions from their enemies.[120] However, in a *Schola steganographica* (see title page, plate 6) appearing shortly after Kircher's *Polygraphia nova,* Schott also reveals that the Trithemian polygraphical method had not altogether superseded the steganographical one in the eyes of the abbot's Jesuit admirers. Indeed, in the dedication to this writing Schott named Kircher as the latest in the line of very learned men comprising the "steganographic" tradition, headed up by Trithemius.[121]

In his *Magia universalis,* under the heading "Concerning Cryptographic and Cryptologic Magic," Schott reiterated this noble legacy, beginning with Trithemius and concluding with "Father Athanasius Kircher, who has devised not a few very ingenious modes of speaking or writing to those who are absent."[122] Whereas, however, Kircher's tribute to the abbot was less than a whole-hearted one, being blunted by a mingling of praise with criticism, Schott's was more uniformly approbatory. Taking his point of departure from the Bostius letter announcing the invention of steganography, Schott declared that the so-called utilities of polygraphy spoken of by Trithemius, and restated by his mentor Kircher, were identical to the utilities of steganography specified by the abbot to Bostius. Polygraphy, Schott averred, is nothing other than steganography "with its title or inscription changed" (*titulo seu inscriptione mutata*). Taking note both of Bovillus's earlier cavils against the abbot's magic and Cardano's later ones, Schott facetiously responded with regard to the latter that "if not by reason of anything else, then by reason of this, Cardano merits the vexation of Scaliger."[123] However, Schott saw a more formidable obstacle than Cardano standing in the way of his campaign to revitalize the "steganographic school." He was Cardinal Bellarmine, who, by mounting his attack on Trithemian magic from a Jesuit platform, made his assignment all the more pressing.

Boldly facing up to Bellarmine's anti-Trithemian bluster, Schott fully accepted the abbot's explanation that he had cloaked his doctrine in mysteries and exotic language "so that the great secret of this new steganography would not fall into the possession of vulgar, ignorant, or depraved men, and so that no one, unless he be very studious in the Cabala after its transmission and reception through a master, can penetrate by his exertions into the arcanum." In response to Bellarmine's claim that Trithemius had consorted with demons, Schott protested, in language close to the abbot's own, that everything set forth in his steganographical manual, both as a whole and in its particular parts, "are in harmony with God—this performed in good conscience, and with the integrity of the ecclesiastical tradition in mind, without injury to the Christian faith; without superstition; without idolatry; without any pact whatever, either explicit or implicit, with malignant spirits; without suffumigation, adoration, veneration, worship, sacrifice or oblation with respect to demons; and without any culpability or sin either venal or mortal."[124] Accordingly, despite the high regard in which he held his colleague, Schott felt compelled to conclude that "the verdict of Bellarmine, who . . . has held the *Steganographia* of Trithemius to be filled with pernicious teachings pertaining to magic and has alleged that Trithemius realized this and confessed to it, is excessively severe."[125]

Closing out this seventeenth-century cryptological legacy of Trithemius was the Worms scholar Wolfgang Ernst Heidel (d. 1721), who republished the *Steganographia* in 1676 together with a derivative "new steganographic artifice." Significantly, in an introductory biography of Trithemius, Heidel broached on the controversy over Trithemian magic late (chapter 17) in its sequence of nineteen chapters, concentrating for the most part on presenting a protracted tribute to the abbot's illustrious career as monastic reformer and paragon of Christian erudition. When he arrived at the subject of Trithemian magic, however, Heidel fell into perfect accord with an underlying axiom of the abbot's magical theory by holding that the deep and hidden roots of his cryptography are engrafted with those of other arcane arts and exchange with them its life-giving juices. Two among these singled out by Heidel are astrology and alchemy, referrable, he concurred with Trithemius, not to extranatural demonic powers, but to natural powers occultly residing in nature.

Concerning the art of astrology, Heidel fully conceded to Trithemius's involvement in the subject but, as amply spelled out in the explanatory letter to Ganay, held it to be of the permissible, predisposing kind compatible with free will. And concerning the art of alchemy in astrology's association, Heidel favorably recounted the precepts outlined by Trithemius to Westerburg, commenting that "only in this way is the secret of nature made accessible to the alchemists, without which neither the understanding of the art is acquired nor the effect of the operation discovered." Indeed, as Heidel recapitulated the abbot's occult theory, alchemy represents but one within a wide spectrum of arcane operations dependent on these precepts for their efficacy, so that "without knowledge of this middle, end, and beginning through numbers, grades, and orders, the magician cannot give virtue to his images without committing a crime or sin, nor can an alchemist imitate nature, nor can a man compel spirits, nor can a prophet predict the future, nor can any curious man whatever grasp the laws of his experiments."[126]

To sum up, Heidel invoked Trithemius's epistolary exposition to Joachim to bear witness that the magic of which he spoke was not, as many feared, "superstitious and diabolical," but rather "natural magic, through which Trithemius was wont to understand nothing other than wisdom." Such wisdom, Heidel elaborated, pertains to knowledge "of things both physical and metaphysical," with the latter kind of knowledge corresponding "to both divine and natural virtues." Thus, while confessing "that indeed Trithemius was a magician," Heidel found it encumbant to add that he was a wholly natural magician "who knew and performed all the things which he ever professed to know in obedience to God and without injury to our Christian faith."[127]

Sharing Heidel's favorable verdict on Trithemian magic was a Jesuit who, while lacking specialized cryptological skills, was no less amiably disposed to the abbot's magic. It will be recalled that, while at work on the Trier annals earlier in the century, Christopher Brouwer had fallen into line with a dominant Jesuit bias by taking Trithemius's occult investigations to task. Of a very different mindset, however, was the man commissioned to continue the

Trier annals after Brouwer's death, Jacob Masen (1606–1681). In Masen's view Brouwer had uncritically swallowed the calumnies of Bovillus without making a thoroughly independent investigation of his own. While not questioning the good intentions of his predecessor, Masen still considered his judgment of Trithemius to be erroneous and stated his resolve, "by just reasons," to restore the respectability of the abbot's name.[128]

As usual in Trithemian apologetics, Masen adopted a two-pronged strategy, the first emphasizing Trithemius's personal piety and renown as a monastic reformer, and the second arguing for the legitimacy of his occasional excursions into the arcana. Significantly, Masen found testimonial support for both of these positions in fellow Jesuits, the first offered up by Johannes Busaeus in his recent publication of two collections of theological writings by Trithemius, and the second in the arguments of Kircher and Schott, "each a perspicacious investigator of natural things and of the mathematical disciplines." With witnesses like these to guide us, pleaded Masen, "who will be so rash as to declare this man to be guilty of magical superstition and impiety?" On the contrary, all who have known him "have held him to be very praiseworthy in such matters and blameless in his faith, and held that he never engaged in anything more dangerous than natural philosophy (*nullam nisi naturalem . . . pertractari*)."[129] Masen's revised judgment of Trithemius in the work at hand, while coming too late to influence his well-meaning but misguided predecessor, hopefully was not too late to influence the opinions of subsequent readers.

Representing a corresponding movement within the Benedictine order to rehabilitate the reputation of its former member, picking up where Abbot Sigismund left off, was the Weingarten monk Gabriel Bucelin (1599–1681), whose 1679 call for a "revived Benedict"—*Benedictus redivivus*—embraced, as a key component, a call for a "revived Trithemius"—*Trithemius redivivus*. While largely subordinating Trithemius's magic in this tract to his larger monastic and theological program, Bucelin at the same time did nothing to discourage the supposition that one seeking to effect his renovative ideal might also, like Trithemius, legitimately add occult studies to his slate of interests. Calling on his demonological writings for evidence, Bucelin, in his entry for 1503, contended that Trithemius "detested magic and familiarity both open and clandestine with infernal spirits, and labored as best as any man could to extirpate the wicked superstitions of mortals and all the sorceries which were spreading without restriction throughout all the provinces."[130]

Elaborating on this position in the entry for 1516, Bucelin took issue with the claims of those who, carried away by their zeal for religious reform, had errantly concluded that Trithemius's magical studies had played a part in preparing the ground for the heresies of Luther. As illustrated by the Jesuit Schott among others, insisted Bucelin, Trithemius was far more instrumental in resisting than assisting the heretical and schismatic tendencies that had culminated in the Protestant revolt. The misinformed slanderers of the abbot, failing to grasp this truth, "have dared, because of the publication of his very subtle work called *Steganographia,* not only to cast the suspicion of magic upon this man, who is famed for his extraordinary religious piety and merits, but to damn him publicly." Far from deserving of being burned as these critics of the abbot's magical writings suggest, Trithemius's books "rather are worthy to endure for all eternity, admired and venerated by all men, for they have been composed by a very holy priest."[131] By turning an injurious hand to Trithemius, Bucelin charged, those falling into this error had likewise turned their hand against St. Benedict, whom Trithemius had earnestly sought to emulate. Or even more to the point, they had also turned their hand against Christ, the prototypal inspiration of Benedict and Trithemius alike. In short, there is nothing in Bucelin's program of religious revitalization that precluded a "second Trithemius"—a *Trithemius secundus* patterned after the controversial abbot—from appearing in the midst of a Catholic cloister.

Conveyed by the likes of the above-named emulators and admirers of Trithemian cryptological practices, the occult theory on which the abbot's methods rested can be said to have gained a crucial foothold in the post-Renaissance world. If the cryptographers themselves represent one main avenue by which this was brought about, two other avenues, thrown into relief by Heidel in conjunction with cryptography, will also now be shown to serve as further footholds for Trithemian magic. The first was astrology, and the second, alchemy. Serving as an important further medium for these disciplines, as will now be the focus of our concern, was the movement triggered by a series of Rosicrucian manifestos published on German soil in the early seventeenth century,[132] the effect of which was to trigger a vigorous debate over the occult studies in which the name of Trithemius prominently figured. The overall effect of this "Rosicrucian" reading on Trithemian magic, setting it apart from that maintaining its author to be a mere encipherer of letters, was to construe Trithemius as a leader of those upholding not only the inner affiliation of magic with theology, but also magic's ability to reunite the externally opposing Catholic and Protestant expressions of theology.

## The Rosicrucian Debate

Putting in capsule form the basic epistemological premise of the age now commonly referred to as the Enlightenment was René Descartes (1596–1650), who defined philosophical intuition as "an illumination of the soul, whereby it beholds in the light of God those things which it pleases Him to reveal to us by a direct impression of divine clearness on our understanding, which in this is not considered as an agent, but only as receiving the rays of divinity."[133] According to an alternative rendition of this concept, however, for which the anonymous German publication of the Rosicrucian manifestos in 1614–1615 can be said to have sounded the trumpet call, enlightenment is attained, not through reason, but through a transrational, magical vision akin to that acquired by the Christian mystics through their ecstasies. Those following Descartes's view of rational enlightenment, exoterist rather than esoterist in outlook and methodology, assumed that the minds of ordinary human beings, if furnished with the necessary intellectual tools and an environment optimally conducive to the performance of their experiments, are capable of arriving at the same basic truths as the most gifted of mind. The proponents of a Rosicrucian-style enlightenment, on the other hand, esoterist rather than exoterist in their approach, assumed that only the minds of a few secretly initiated souls are capable of penetrating the dark cloud of unknowing to the realm of divine truth.[134] As we will now see, a leading voice invoked on behalf of this form of enlightenment was that of the abbot Trithemius.

The suggestion that Trithemius had engaged in alchemical experiments, we have at least as far back as the notorious Bovillus letter, implying as it did that Trithemius had sought to generate through alchemical means, with the Devil's help, extra funds for the financing of his exceptional library and other precious furnishings of his cloister. More often than not, the Paracelsians themselves, by insinuating that Trithemius had engaged in the very kinds of collusion with the "chaste whore" he had frequently warned against, had the effect of reinforcing this suspicion. An example is found in a letter appearing in an anonymously authored 1604 alchemical tract, attributed to Paracelsus but really the product of a later disciple, declaring Trithemius to be a foremost exponent of "these secrets of our art" (*diese Geheimnis unser Kunst*). However, rationalized this Paracelsian enthusiast, not for his own enrichment but for the benefit of others and to God's greater glory did "the great and clandestine philosopher of the German nation, our father Trithemius, the abbot of Sponheim, acquire many millions of gold pieces displaying the highest tincture."[135]

Spurred by much the same mentality, a number of alchemical treatises appeared during this period, bearing such titles as *Chemicus nobilis, De lapide philosophorum,* and *Libri experimentorum,* spuriously ascribed to the abbot. Helping to propagate the belief that Trithemius's own pen lay behind such writings was the inclusion by Lazarus Zetzner of the first two of these, together with an amalgam of his genuine thoughts on the subject under the misleading, Paracelsian-inspired heading *De spagirico artificio,* in his multivolumed *Theatrum chemicum* (1613–1661).[136] The essential message conveyed by such discourses, we have shown, is that the prime objective of the alchemist is not the pursuance of material gold, but a goldlike purity of soul.

Underscoring the principles at issue in this matter was a polemic between the magically inebriated Robert Fludd (1574–1637), the author of an occultly conceived *Macrocosmi et microcosmi historia* (see title page of vol. II, plate 4), and the magic-hating Minim friar Marin Mersenne (1588–1648), a friend and admirer of Descartes who, in a series of writings beginning with his *Questiones in Genesim* (1623), campaigned to purge religion and science alike of the occult pollutions he viewed as having insidiously seeped into them during the previous centuries. The main brunt of Mersenne's attack, it is true, was directed at the occult-loving sixteenth-century Franciscan Francesco Giorgi, whom he accused of having been illicitly engaged in "filthy and dreadful magic." Needless to say, however, Mersenne did not stop there, widening the scope of his anti-Giorgi attack to include co-conspiritors such as Trithemius and Agrippa in earlier days and Robert Fludd in his own time. Labeling themselves either Catholic or Protestant, Mersenne maintained, was beside the point, for, no matter what their particular religious affiliation, at bottom all three abettors of the occult arts had the same effect of undermining the Christian faith. Not only is magic justly to be accused of fomenting heresy, he charged, but also, conversely, "heresy is deservedly called the way... to atheism, idolatry, and magic."[137]

One conceit in particular directed Mersenne's attention to Trithemius. A ridiculous claim was once made by a certain heretic, Mersenne recalled, that he could conjure any one of eight angels at a moment's notice by an invocation of its name and the performance of the required ritual. Given, however, as agreed upon by some of the most revered fathers of the church, that the names of only three angels are known, to wit, Michael, Gabriel, and Raphael, Mersenne did not doubt that if the said heretic had summoned spirits with other names as claimed, these "were not angels but demons." Among those further fostering such nonsense, Mersenne added, was Trithemius, who in two separate writings had espoused the absurd doctrine that there exists, for possible manipulation by the magician, a distinct angel in charge of each of the seven planetary spheres.[138]

Caught up with Trithemius in Mersenne's antimagical offensive was the abbot's protegé Sigismund of Seeon. Although in truth, gibed Mersenne in his *Quaestiones in Genesim*, Trithemius "propagated demonic magic by means of conjuration through various characters, numbers, and modes," Sigismund would have us believe, on the analogy of the ancient Egyptians, that he was really "no more than hiding natural arcana under those names." The steganographic techniques construed by Sigismund as no more violating the articles of Christian faith than do "the artrology and dactyology of Bede" received a far more sinister reading from Mersenne. Citing the explanatory letter of Trithemius to Bostius, Mersenne turned the strategy back upon Sigismund of having the accused speak on his own behalf—this by showing that the effect of Trithemius's own words was rather to convict than acquit their spokesman of the charge of demonic magic.[139] This observation should caution us against taking Mersenne's Cartesianism too far, one who in some ways appeared to agree more with the unscientific demonologists of his day than with the scientific rationalism today generally associated with the name of Descartes.[140]

While many of the personal targets of Mersenne, including Trithemius, had long passed from the scene and thus were unable to answer his attacks, their intellectual heir Fludd, whose efforts to uphold the legitimacy of magic for Christians had earned him the epithet *haereticomagus* from the hostile friar,[141] was under no such constraint. And just as the name of Trithemius prominently played into Mersenne's attacks on magic, so did it just as prominently play into Fludd's corresponding defense of magic, especially in conjunction with the secret society of magicians whose cause Fludd had taken upon himself to champion, the Rosicrucians. Henceforth Trithemius could be perceived, Mersenne's objections aside, as a forerunner of the brotherhood whose magic Fludd lauded in a 1617 apologetic of the Rosicrucians as "the true scourge of ignorance and illumination of its shadows; the rectification of the human soul, which has been immersed in the mists of ignorance and worldly exigency; and the restoration of the heavenly mind, following its brief sojourn in earthly form, to its original condition."[142]

Caustically reacting to Mersenne's antimagical aspersions in his *Sophiae cum moria certamen,* Fludd responded that Mersenne "does not hesitate in many passages of his work to accuse the abbot Trithemius, Ficino, Bacon, Agrippa, and myself, together with many others, of being black magicians, and to pronounce as false and injurious what on the contrary is true and pure."[143] On the heels of this polemical offering by Fludd came another, titled *Summum bonum,* in which, this time under the pseudonym Joachim Frizius, he expressed his intention to rescue from Mersenne's invective, together with other coreligionists of his antagonist, "a man held in the highest regard in the Roman Church, the abbot Trithemius, one who was known to all learned men and was greatly celebrated for his profound knowledge, who not only speaks for himself, but also has other religious men speaking on his behalf."[144]

Resuming his polemic with Mersenne in a somewhat later *Clavis philosophiae et alchymiae,* Fludd berated the friar as "a man more inclined to strife and to cavils than engaged in the deeper arcana either of God or of nature."[145] Taking issue with Mersenne's assertion that magic was proscribed by the church, Fludd offered as evidence against his position two of the most eruditely devout interpreters of religious doctrine who had ever lived. The first was Trithemius, who, in the certainty of his orthodoxy, dedicated several arcane writings to the emperor Maximilian, and the second, Johannes Reuchlin, who under the same assumption addressed arcane tracts to Pope Leo X. Concerning the Maximilian dedications in particular, Fludd queried Mersenne why, if he harbored any doubts about their author, the emperor accepted them without a hint of protest.[146]

As to why maligners of magic like Mersenne had enjoyed such success in turning the general populace against occult studies, Fludd presented in his *Clavis* what is now a familiar esoterist explanation. Given, he noted, that far more in this world is hidden than revealed to us, and that the truth, therefore, "lurks in the shadows," it is scarcely surprising that vulgar men lacking access to the abstruse mysteries of the world condemn those who have such access and endeavor to outlaw their speculations and practices. Because the profound secrets of magic are frequently misunderstood does not mean that they should be disallowed, but only that they should be entrusted to a rare few minds capable of penetrating to their noble depths. Along analogous lines, "because the Church which is external and political does not understand, though they are the most excellent and precious of all, the mysteries of the internal and mystical Church, since these are centered in the arcana of the Kingdom of God and of His mystical Wisdom, are these nonetheless to be repudiated and damned by Christians?"[147]

For Fludd as for Trithemius before him, this parallel between the mystical truths of the church and the occult truths of magic was based on more than a superficial comparison. It was based on the bedrock belief that the arcana of Christian mystical doctrine and the arcana of angelic, natural and Cabalist magic issue out of a common spiritual wellspring, hidden from the ordinary eye but accessible to the inner eye of a few priest-magicians secretly initiated in its dark enigmas. Echoing the title of a related tract in which, under his Frizius pseudonym, he had made many of these same points, Fludd reminded Mersenne that "the highest good" (*summum bonum*), like the summit of a mountain, is approachable from different directions. More particularly, "it is called by the theologians the Divine Light, by the Cabalists, the angelic virtue;

by the magicians and philosophers, the essential wisdom; and by the pious alchemists it is termed gold purified by Christ."[148]

The universalist outlook characterizing this magical revision of the traditional scholastic notion of the *summum bonum* explains why the nominally Protestant Fludd had no problem taking the side of Catholic monks like Trithemius and Sigismund against their demonological opponents, no matter on which side of the ecclesiastical divide they might be located. The arcane principles of Rosicrucianism, Fludd believed, were radically independent of particular theological dogmas, so that the "true investigators of the divine mysteries" who covertly belonged to the Rosicrucian brotherhood "can be found in all religions—Papist, Lutheran, Calvinist, and all the rest."[149] Fludd was persuaded that, no matter what the outward religious profession of a Rosicrucian might be, the real driving force of his life is the aspiration for occult gnosis. Though divided in their outward ecclesiastical allegiances, Protestants and Catholics are inwardly unified in their pursuit of magical enlightenment.

Whereas Fludd's doctrine of magical theology, then, shares essential ground with that of Trithemius, it represents a crucial further stage in its evolution that could not possibly have been contemplated by the pre-Reformation abbot. Magic for Trithemius had constituted a divinely sanctioned branch of mystical theology expressible wholly within the preestablished structures of papal orthodoxy. For the abbot's post-Reformation heir Fludd, on the other hand, magic had burst the bounds of all preestablished ecclesiastical bounds, Catholic and Protestant alike, to take on a life of its own independent of formal religious dogma.

This is not to say that Fludd advised his fellow Rosicrucians to take leave of their chosen ecclesiastical affiliations to attend to higher occult matters. On the contrary, he expressly counseled that "each and every Brother of the Rosy Cross diligently observe the rites attaching to the religion which he embraces." The motive for this advice, however, issued from a quite different consideration than had inspired Trithemius's coalescence of religion and magic, issuing, as it were, more out of political than of substantive theological grounds. The Rosicrucian identified with a given religion, Fludd acknowledged, "not because anything of the revelation of the divine mystery is elicited from these rites, but, lest he should offend his brothers, so that he may live, dwell, and exult in the external and political laws and ceremonies of the Church."[150]

For Fludd, that is to say, magic was no longer, as it had been for Trithemius, an adjunct to Christian theology, at least so far as theology expressed itself through a given set of religious rites and ceremonies. On the contrary, Christian theology now had become an adjunct to magic. In promoting this essentially independent mission of magical theology Fludd was ably assisted by others caught up in the excitement fomented by the Rosicrucian manifestos, several of whom joined him in holding Trithemius to be a suitable precursor. As we will now see, the English seat from which Fludd carried out his campaign to justify Christian magic also ably served these to the same end. In spite of Mersenne's best efforts to forestall this course of events, it exhibited an inner dynamic which was to be stilled neither by a widespread fear of witches nor by the sobering restraints of Cartesian "reason."

Joining Fludd in singing praises to the newly emerged brotherhood of the Rosy Cross, under the pseudonym Eugenius Philalethes, was Thomas Vaughan (1622–1666), who envisioned, in keeping with the principles spelled out in the Rosicrucian manifestos, a revamping of the Aristotelian-based European university system of studies with his own Oxford as its springboard. Also in agreement with Fludd, Vaughan beheld in Trithemius a forerunner of the Rosicrucian remedy to the corrupt Aristotelian status quo, declaring in his *Anthroposophia Theomagica* (1650), for example, that the Stagyrite "is as short of Nature as the grammarians are of steganography."[151] Along the same lines, in his *Anima Magica Abscondita* of the same year, Vaughan credited "the dark disciple of the more dark Libanius Gallus," together with Trithemius's own "dark disciple" Agrippa, with prefiguring his proposal for the reform of education.[152]

In yet a third writing published at mid-century, his *Magia Adamica,* Vaughan traced the precepts of the Rosicrucian reform movement behind Trithemius and Agrippa to ancient kings, priests, and prophets "acquainted with the substantial spiritual mysteries of religion." Unhappily, according to Vaughan, these arcane precepts were subsequently tarnished through two main causes. The first was the uninformed judgments of the ignorant, "lawyers and common divines who knew not these secrets," and the second, the actions of various impostors, so that the appointed legal authorities, "perusing the ceremonial, superstitious trash of some scribblers who pretended to magic, prescribed against the art itself as impious and antichristian, so that it was a capital sin to profess it and the punishment no less than death." Instead of having its intended effect of discouraging investigation into the arcana, however, according to Vaughan, the conventional bias against magic rather had the opposite effect of strengthening the resolve of its investigators to bury their dark truths all the more deeply away from the eyes of vulgar intruders. But now, Vaughan exulted, the time was at hand to retrieve these truths from their murky depths and place them at the disposal of the larger public. In preparation for this great event, "God, having suffered His truth to be obscured for a great time, did at last stir up some resolute and active spirits who—putting pen to paper—expelled this cloud and in some measure discovered the light." Placing Trithemius, with his teacher Libanius Gallus and student Agrippa, in the ranks of these "resolute and active spirits," Vaughan called on his own pseudonymous alter ego, Eugenius Philalethes, to serve as an "usher to the train."[153]

Also advocating a reform of the educational curriculum during this period, but with a view, at the opposite pole from Vaughan, of replacing the prevailing Aristotelian philosophy with a magic-free Platonic one compatible with the new philosophy of Descartes, was the Cambridge scholar Henry More (1614–1697). It might be inferred from the title of a treatise by More appearing soon after the foregoing writings by Vaughan, the *Conjectura Cabbalistica* (1653), that its author was not all that far removed from the arcane ideas of his Oxford contemporary.[154] The mystical speculations conditioning More's Cabalistic venture, however, were formulated on entirely different foundations than those on which rested Vaughan's call for a Rosicrucian reform of education. More's Cabala was a purely symbolical system of notations having little in common with Vaughan's Rosicrucian-based presupposition, prefigured in Trithemius's steganographical operations, that animating occult powers course through the world waiting to be tapped by those properly instructed in the correct techniques. Under the pseudonym of Alazonomastix Philalethes [alazon=quack, mastix=whip], in a burlesque of Vaughan's Eugenius Philalethes, More made the difference between their educational outlooks clear in "observations" on Vaughan's recommendations.

The allowance of philosophy into the service of religion by the church fathers, More instructed Vaughan, was done, not with the intent of scuttling reason with unbridled flights of magical phantasy, but of lending faith the support of reason. Having been seduced and misled by "your ador'd Magus with the black Spaniell [viz., Agrippa], and that dark Disciple of Libanius Gallus [viz., Trithemius]," according to More, Vaughan had corrupted the good name of philosophy the church fathers had wisely put to the use of theology.[155] From More's broader perspective on this subject the choice to be made was not simply between reason and magic. A more basic choice at issue here, he determined, was between faith rationally supported and faith irrationally subverted, the second option of which, as emphasized in his *Antidote against Atheism,* leads as readily to atheistic materialism as to unchecked "enthusiasm." The underlying premise of this tract, restated in his later *Enthusiasmus Triumphatus* (1656), is that untrammeled eruptions of the imagination, whether expressed through conventional religious or through magical means, is but the reverse side of the coin from materialistic atheism of the kind given contemporary currency by Thomas Hobbes (1588–1679), the reasoning being that widespread disenchantment with religion triggered by excessively fanciful claims on its behalf induces a swing to the opposite pole. Accordingly, exclaimed More in the *Antidote,* "Atheism and Enthusiasm, though they seem so extremely opposite one to another, yet in many things they do very nearly agree."[156] The same of course goes for specifically magical enthusiasm of the kind exercised by Vaughan. Implied in this way of thinking, of course, is that Trithemius, an "enthusiastic" by More's standards, was an inadvertent contributor to the Godless materialism for which More proffered his "antidote."

Sharing More's repugnance to "enthusiasm" was Meric Casaubon (1599–1671), a son of the scholarly emigré Isaac (1559–1614), whose *Treatise Concerning Enthusiasme* appeared almost simultaneously (1655, revised 1656) with More's better known tract on that subject. Already Meric's father Isaac, a first-rate classical scholar, had taken considerable wind out of the sails of the magical reform movement by demonstrating that the extant writings of one of its foremost ancient inspirations, the "Egyptian" Hermes Trismegistus, were written in post-Christian times. While not at home with the dry scholarly methods utilized by his father in undercutting what he viewed as the inflated claims of the magical enthusiasts, Meric adopted the more polemical approach of his contemporary More to the same end. Having been carried away by their "enthusiastick divinatory fits," fulminated Casaubon, the false religionists and magicians had confused with divine inspiration from above what was in truth "extraordinary, transcendent, but natural fervency, or pregnancy of the soul, spirits, or brain, producing strange effects, apt to be mistaken for supernatural."[157]

Whereas a prime target of More in his campaign to stem the tide of enthusiastic irrationalism was the contemporary Rosicrucian apologist Vaughan, a prime target of Casaubon was a touted forerunner of the Rosicrucian movement, John Dee. Composing an entire tract to the end of discrediting Dee (1659), Casaubon discovered in the process, also like More, that he could not ignore the part of the magical abbot of Sponheim, upon whom Dee had expressly drawn for inspiration, in encouraging the "phantasticall" folly he detested. Restating in the preface the core idea of his earlier *Treatise Concerning Enthusiasme* by decrying "supposed Inspiration and imaginary Revelations," Casaubon scoffed that the heads of those under the sway of this trait "are full of mysteries; they see nothing, they read nothing but their brain is on work to pick somewhat out of it that is not ordinary; and out of the very ABC that children are taught, rather than fail, they will fetch all the Secrets of Gods Wisdom, tell you how the world was created, how governed; and what will be the end of all things."[158] Among those faulted by Casaubon for leading Dee down the wrong path was Trithemius, "a man that was supposed by most to have dealt with Spirits a long time, and to have been instructed by them in some of those secrets that he pretends unto by his Books."[159]

But while singling out Dee for special mention among those who, carried way by the magical fancies of Trithemius, "have thought him innocent, or at least, have attempted to justify him," Casaubon did not ignore others succumbing to the same temptation. Another figure specifically named in this regard was Dee's French contemporary Vigenère, "who in his old age was grown himself very Cabalistical." Having immersed himself long and deeply in Trithemius's cryptographical method and at last confessed that "he could make nothing of it," admonished Casaubon, Vigenère gave notice to us all that our own result will be the same. That so many have found themselves in this bind, Casaubon speculated, was the main reason that the *Steganographia*, "mentioned and promised in this first work, was so long after his death before it was Printed." While its eventual publication had given hope to some that it would help to unravel the enigmatic knots of the earlier published polygraphical one, "neither of that, nor of this latter, could ever any thing, that ever I could hear, be made by any man."[160]

Given that the criticism of Trithemius's cryptographical magic here presented seems to be geared more to debunking it as a phantastical creation of the abbot's mind than to pointing up its demonic origin, we may be surprised to hear Casaubon labeled a "sworn witchmonger" by one of his opponents, John Webster (1610–1682).[161] In truth, however, as Trithemius himself had made clear in his own contributions to the demonological tradition, these two perspectives on magic do not necessarily cancel each other out, since lying behind the absurd professions of the boastful charlatan can conceivably lurk more sinister demonically inspired motives. Webster's willingness to take on Casaubon in these matters sprang out of a vested interest. For like Vaughan, Webster was intent on effecting a program of educational reform in the universities to embrace the study of magic, the principal fruit of which, his *Academiarum Examen* (1653), urged the introduction into the English universities of various occult arts and sciences, including, as a branch of grammar, cryptography in the Trithemian manner. Noting that the ancients, with their "Emblems and Hieroglyphicks," uncovered and preserved great mysteries, Webster beheld comparable powers as residing in the cryptographical operations of Trithemius. That such speculations not only are permissible but highly valuable contributions to the welfare of mankind, vaunted Webster, "let that monopoly of all learning, the Abbot of Spanheim speak, let Porta, let Cornelius Agrippa, let Claramuel, let Gustavus Silenus, Frier Bacon, and many others speak, who have written so learnedly and accurately therein, even to wonder and amazement!"[162]

Taking note of what he saw as a distinct demonological shift in Casaubon's thinking from earlier times before he had allowed his emotions to run away with his reason, Webster declared Casaubon's main motive to be, owing to earlier having placed excessive weight on the natural causes of enthusiasm, of saving himself from condemnation for consorting with the atheistic materialists. While the main victim of this misguided attempt to clear himself of "the censure of being a Sadducee or Atheist," Webster noted, was John Dee, other "dauntless Spirits" who had similarly demonstrated their courage in going against the current of popular opinion were likewise tainted by Casaubon's vitriolic pen. Not surprisingly, heading up this train of brave souls was the "Honour and Ornament of Germany" Trithemius, one, Webster was happy to report, who "wanted not a Bovillus to calumniate and condemn him of unlawful Magick, from which all the Learned in Europe know he is absolved." Far from deserving censure for black magic, urged Webster, Trithemius should be warmly commended, together with Agrippa, Paracelsus, and Fludd in his company, "for striving to purge and purifie the ancient, natural, laudable, and lawful Magick from the filth and dregs of Imposture, Deceit, Ceremonies, and Superstitions."[163]

That, in rebuking Casaubon for "witchmongering," Webster was not entirely off the mark is evidenced by two subsequent volumes from Casaubon's pen further dedicated to the eradication of the superstitious arts in which the demonological theme was more prominently displayed. Beginning each volume with the words *Of Credulity and Incredulity,* their author therein illustrated the contradictory influence of the abbot in the debate over occult studies by finding corroboration for his antimagical crusade in the very figure whom he elsewhere held to be a major contributor to the problem. This time taking particular aim at Agrippan magic, which he presumed to depend on help from the demons, Casaubon noted in the first of the pertinent volumes that "Trithemius, in his answers to the questions, proposed unto him, as the man then in Europe, best able to resolve him, by Maximilian, the Emperor, concerning the power of Witches, &c., doth much inveigh against the malice, wickedness, and fraudulency of those Spirits."[164] In this way, at a time when the witch hunts were reaching their strident climax, Casaubon lent further witness to the contradictory ways in which Trithemius entered into the debate over magic, with Trithemius the demonologist employable in helping to combat Trithemius the magician.

As future events were to show, however, the positioning of Trithemius in the seventeenth-century debate over the occult studies also sometimes diverged from this one construing him to be a credulous believer in magic, with emphasis placed more on the practical benefits of his cryptographical operations than on the theoretical language in which they were embedded. Trithemius himself had pointed the way to this alternative view of what his magic was about by acknowledging, first of all, that the elaborate apparatus of conjurational rituals presented in his steganographical manual was really an obfuscatory device to protect its secrets from undesirable intruders, and secondly, by replacing the suspect steganographical tract with a less dubious polygraphical one dependent on an ability to manipulate, not angels, but human language. If, from one point of view, Trithemius could be located by his posthumous defenders at a crossroad between two kinds of credulity, magical and demonological, from another point of view he could be located at a crossroad between gullible credulity and skeptical incredulity. Following one line of thought Trithemius was perceived as a prominent spokesman of magical theology in anticipation of the ideals laid down by the Rosicrucian manifestos, whereas, following another line of thought, he could be perceived as a free thinker at basic odds with such forces of intolerance as led to the witch hysteria.

To close out this chapter we will now indicate some Trithemian apologists belonging to this latter group, the basic inclination of which was to rescue Trithemius from his critics without necessarily rescuing the magical theory to which he adhered. Their effect is to instruct us that the posthumous friends of Trithemius could as easily belong to the novel forces of change signified by the Cartesian and Newtonian intellectual revolutions as to the time-worn forces of the medieval past, with its demonological trappings, to which the authentic Trithemius actually belonged. A foremost incentive for this continuing appeal of Trithemian cryptological methods, quite apart from the claim of the magical theorists to offer a way of healing the Protestant-Catholic breach, was the need to forge secret methods of communication impermeable to opposing sides in the hostile religious, political and social climate climaxing in the English civil wars and continental Thirty Years' War. For those driven by this blatantly pragmatic motive for defending the abbot, there was no assumption made, as in the case of their more occult-minded counterparts, that cryptic communication is driven by anything more mysterious than the power of language itself to say one thing and mean another.

## The Skeptical Shift and the Scientific Revolution

The plea of Jean Belot for a magically conditioned *rhetorique nouvelle,* earlier cited for the incorporation of Trithemian steganography into its five-part composition, was dubiously received by his fellow countryman Gabriel Naudé (1600–1653), who mocked it in a chapter of his *Apologie pour les grands hommes soupçonnez de magie.* The fame of the man behind this absurd rhetorical theory was growing so quickly, Naudé chided, that in time tales would be spreading about him "as are now circulating about Doctor Faustus, De Maugis, Merlin, Nostradamus, and others who have been marked with red on the Magician's Calendar."[165] But while showing scorn for Belot's attempt to reformulate the art of rhetoric as a magical discipline, Naudé displayed a far kinder face to the abbot who had figured so integrally in Belot's innovative program. Admittedly, Naudé gave little credence to the kinds of spectacular claims made by magicians like Trithemius. However, he gave even less credence to the claims of the "demonographers" (*demonographes*) in their zealous pursuit of the magicians, whom he believed to exploit the fear of demons for the real purpose of suppressing the free flow of ideas. It was, therefore, not technically the magic of Trithemius that Naudé set out to exonerate in the chapter of his *Apologie* given over to the abbot, but Trithemius's purported role as a fighter for the freedom to express unpopular ideas.

Naudé offered three main causes for the stigma attaching to the name of Trithemius. The first cause, he held, was the attribution to Trithemius's authorship of a suspect tract recently appearing under his name concerning magical seals; the second cause, that "he so persistently speaks of magic, and calls himself a magician in some of his epistles"; and the third cause, his authorship of a cryptographic manual "said to be crammed with the names of devils and filled with invocations, and for this reason condemned as very pernicious." Naming Bovillus, Delrio, and Godelmann among the abbot's more prominent critics, Naudé pledged to save from their maledictions "the memory of a man—and, at that, an ecclesiastical man—upon such paltry grounds as these frivolous conjectures, which are absolutely vain, false, and contumacious."[166]

The easiest charge to counter, Naudé pointed out, was the first one, since the pertinent work, "telling of engraving images and characters upon stones under the influence of certain constellations, is a complete imposture and deception of booksellers who have seen fit to print it as though it were recently issued from the study of Trithemius."[167] Less readily disposed of is the second charge that Trithemius incriminated himself in certain of his letters. Far from inculpating Trithemius, contended Naudé, these letters rather exculpate him, "as can be seen by the reading thereof by Gerard Dorn and Jacques Gohory, who clearly demonstrate, by an explication of their enigmatic sense, that they cannot be interpreted as anything else but chemistry (*que de la Chymie*)."[168] The third charge, too, that the abbot's steganographic operations are dependent on evil spirits, though more difficult than the previous two to counter, could similarly be answered with the help of subsequent writers who had demonstrated their ability to penetrate beneath the superficially "demonic" cover of steganography to its hidden layers of meaning.

Starting with the same Gohory as also served him in good stead in his "chemical" defense, "who directed a brief defense of the *Steganographia* against the calumnies of Weyer, Bovillus, and Cardano," Naudé added the further names of Vigenère, Boissard, Duret, Tanner, Sigismund, and Duke August in testimony that "the sole aim of Trithemius in this book was nothing other than to teach a novel and much more secure method than that of the *Polygraphia* for writing and communicating freely, between one man and another, all the most secret and hidden things." Of these Naudé credited Duke August with being especially effective in undercutting the demonological presuppositions of the abbot's critics, lending backing thereby to the popular saying that "the most learned men are not always the most sensible." Pointing out that these "blame things which they do not understand," Duke August, according to Naudé's, gives us pause to appreciate why Trithemius had made his steganographic method so difficult to grasp, "and why he makes use of the mask of these spirits and invocations (*du voile de ces esprits & de ces invocations*) instead of some other disguise."[169]

By outward appearances a person unlikely to find himself in Naudé's company in Capuchin friar Jacques

Chevanes (=d'Autun, ca. 1608–1678), who, following a 1669 republication of Naudé's *Apologie,* sought to offset its author's skeptical
influence by attaching to the text of his *L'Incredulité sçavante et la
credulité ignorante* (1671) a separate response. Nevertheless, while
in many matters finding little to agree with in Naudé's volume, in
one respect Chevanes fell into perfect accord with the French skeptic. Recalling the main stimulus behind the controversy which had
come to surround the name of Trithemius, a book from his hand
"about a way of writing so peculiar that those who do not possess
its key are unable to possess its understanding," Chevanes concurred with Naudé not only that the writing in question was something other than it seemed, but also that this "something" was not
of the sinister demonic sort indicated by some of its critics. Rejecting the contention that, by employing "names so extravagant, which
might be taken for the terms of sorcery," Trithemius truly engaged
in sorcerous rites, Chevanes rather accepted Naudé's more benevolent contention that the dangerous-sounding language of
steganography was contrived "to conceal his artifice so that it would
not be made accessible to the common sort." If the reputation of
Trithemius were genuinely deserving of the stigma of demon conjuration and manipulation often attached to it, Chevanes pointed
out, equally deserving of that reputation would have been his
princely patrons who encouraged him in his cryptographical activities. Fortunately for the survival of the abbot's art, however,
his royal patrons were no more frightened off by the accusations
of the demonological extremists than was Trithemius himself. To
condemn Trithemius's steganography on the basis of its abuse by
a few false disciples, Chevanes held, made no more sense than
condemning the things which God had created "because some men
abuse them."[170]

   In his search for a middle way between superstitious credulity
and skeptical incredulity of the sort promoted by Naudé, then,
Chevanes walked a fine line between opposing Naudé's skeptical
outlook in general and accepting Naudé's imputation that overly
zealous demonologists had overstepped their just boundaries in a
particular case like that of Trithemius. However, in marking out
his position on the abbot, Chevanes was solicitous of distinguishing
his motives not only from those of an out-and-out skeptic of magic
like Naudé, but also from those of true believers of magic like
Fludd and Vaughan, whose efforts to extricate Trithemius from his

posthumous notoriety were integrally linked to their own personal campaigns to justify the occult studies. The Capuchin author of the *Incredulité* was very definite that his defense of Trithemian cryptography should not be misconstrued as a defense of magic in principle.

Properly speaking, Chevanes insisted, the art of steganography bringing the name of its inventor into such ill repute was not magic at all, but only a system of linguistic artifices not far removed from the artifices of sleight-of-hand jugglers, entertaining and possibly even useful for certain hidden purposes but not really harmful to the soul. What, then, did Chevanes make of the elaborately constructed magical principles also cropping up in various writings by Trithemius ostensibly designed to furnish theoretical buttressing to his cryptographical operations? These, Chevanes decided, were also to be taken with a grain of salt, having less to do with truly establishing a justifying rationale for cryptography and more to do with the practical problem of disguising the cryptographer's true intentions. The main appeal of the Trithemian art to the prince, held Chevanes, lies, not in its theoretical buttressing, but in its practical applications. Most notable among these is the practice of statecraft and diplomacy, so that rulers acquiring command over its principles "conceal the secrets of their counsel, and manifest them by writing to their ministers, without anyone being able to understand them except those in possession of its key, inasmuch as it encloses as many enigmas as it contains characters."[171]

For Chevanes, then, the exoneration of Trithemius's cryptological methodology was not to be mistaken for an exoneration of the magical theory upon which it was formally based. A still staunchly antimagical posturing of Chevanes in a time when witches and sorcerers were actively being pursued and executed is highlighted by his stated refusal, after acquitting Trithemius of consorting with demons, to extend the same open-mindedness to the three Magi "who came to adore Jesus Christ." Taking St. Chrysostom as his authority, though he could just as easily have called on St. Augustine or St. Jerome, Chevanes maintained that the Magi were led to the Christ child, not by virtue of their magic, but in spite of it, and that their arcane speculations were no more acceptable after than before their homage to Jesus. The primary lesson elicited by Chevanes from the biblical account of the Magi was not that the occult arts are theologically justified, but rather that a policy seeking the redemption and regeneration of sorcerers is preferred to one advocating their execution. Declaring with reference to the Magi that "their conversion does not give less of glory to the Saviour of the world than if they had not been idolaters and been given to superstition and magic," Chevanes extended the same principle to lovers of the occult in general, namely, that "their conversion is all the more glorious as the art of magic to which they devoted themselves is more detestable."[172]

The unmistakable approach to Trithemian cryptography reflected in the versions of Naudé and Chevanes is to extract it from the occult matrix in which it was steeped by the abbot and treat it as a purely linguistic system of encipherment requiring no external natural or supernatural aids. The view of Trithemian cryptography they upheld is in basic accord with that articulated by the Dutch philologist Gerhard Voss (=Vossius, 1577–1649), who in his *De arte grammatica* (1635) contended that the "spirits" invoked by the abbot for the transmission of steganographical messages are really nothing more than obfuscatory grammatical devices intended to obscure the true method of his art. Pretending "to deliver demonic conjurations to scare off vulgar souls," according to Voss, Trithemius in fact "is actually relating ways of writing secretly to princes and philosophers, the knowledge of which, though dangerous to the wicked, is exceedingly beneficial to those who, whether in a public or private capacity, are upright in the loftiest matters." Their misinterpretation by the uninitiated, therefore, is to be expected, since they are doing only what they are supposed do: conceal the true meaning of a message by a grammatical veil. "By conjuration or the intonation of enchantments," Voss explained his position, "is meant an artifice for the reading of hidden words, an expedient of the art, I allow, which well may be mistaken by the ignorant for an incantation."[173]

This is the same "Learned and Judicious Vossius," it so happened, who was lampooned by Casaubon together with others, such as Dee and Vigenère, for taking the part of Trithemius in the controversy over his steganographical magic. According to Casaubon, Voss "hath shewed himself very willing to think the best of him and his Books, yet . . . gives it over at last, and rather concludes on the contrary."[174] However, as the above rendering of Trithemian cryptography suggests, the pragmatic Voss belongs to a different category of Trithemius apologist than true believers of magic like Dee and Vigenère. Accordingly the man dubbed a "sworn witch-monger" by his opponent Webster in effect found himself in opposition not only to the outright exponents of magical theory in his day, but also to those, like Voss, who chose to work through the intricacies of Trithemian cryptography with a view to the practical benefits obtainable therefrom. These further included, as it happened, rigorously scientific-minded members of the English Royal Society, some members of which, like John Wilkins and Robert Hooke, joined Voss in rehabilitating the Trithemian art of cryptography without concurrently rehabilitating the occult principles upon which that art was founded.

The more immediate repercussion of Webster's call for a magical reform of English education, accordingly, was not Casaubon's response, which came decades later, but a derisive rejoinder to Webster's revolutionary vision from two Oxford defenders of the educational status quo. Collaborating under the title *Vindiciae Academiarum* (1654), in rebuff of Webster's revolutionary occultist vision, were John Wilkins (1614–1672) and Seth Ward (1617–1689). Scoffing at Webster's campaign to admit the occult arts into the university curriculum, Wilkins, in his introduction to the *Vindiciae,* singled out as "a loose and wild kind of vapouring" the art of cryptography as it was currently being advocated and practiced by the secret-loving occultists. In the text to follow, Ward went on to give Wilkins's unflattering characterization of that accusation specificity, furnishing a point-by-point refutation of Webster's *Examen* in which he reminded his readers that there is a great difference between the "concealment of things," which is the property of cryptography, and the "explication of our kinds and notions," which is the property of grammar.[175] A closer reading of what was at issue in the debate between, on one hand, the magically minded Webster and, on the other hand, the antimagical authors of the *Vindiciae* reveals, however, that the basic choice to be made was not necessarily between cryptographical magic and grammar. The choice could also lie between a view of cryptography as magic and a view of cryptography as a specialized branch of grammar.

Evidence to this effect is furnished by Wilkins himself, who, several decades before entering into affairs of the newly founded

Royal Society, composed a cryptological tract admitting to a Trithemian input. He who has gained expertise in this art, Wilkins had declared therein with Trithemius one of his sources, can rightfully be termed a "second Mercury," instructing us in the art, as the subtitle to his tract puts it, of "how a man may with privacy and speed communicate his thoughts to a friend at any distance."[176] As the later Webster controversy helped Wilkins clarify, however, the rationale on which he based his cryptography was a very different one from that guiding the magicians. His view of the art popularized by Trithemius better accorded with one who would prove himself to be a guiding light of the Royal Society to come, Francis Bacon (1561–1626), than with the occult-minded Webster. If, as acknowledged by Wilkins, Bacon refers cryptography "to the art of *Grammar,* noting it as a deficient part," Wilkins let be known his intention to help fill out the deficiency indicated by Bacon.[177]

It is possible, of course, that, in his later association with Ward in opposition to Webster, Wilkins changed his mind about the value of cryptography, or at least wished to temper his younger indiscretions regarding the subject. Inasmuch, however, as Wilkins never disavowed the earlier writing, it is more likely that the "loose and wild kind of vapouring" he ridiculed in the introduction to the *Vindiciae* referred, not to the magic-free cryptographical techniques he earlier extolled, but to the kinds of magically conditioned cryptographical operations espoused by the Rosicrucians. Corroboration for the latter reading of Wilkins's motives is furnished by one of his young associates of the Royal Society, Robert Hooke (1635–1703), who similarly established that the stated mandate of the newly chartered association (1662) "for the promoting of Physico-Mathematicall-Experimentall Learning" was not altogether incompatible with the magical operations of cryptography as presented by Trithemius. The form of this evidence is a lecture given by Hooke before the society, posthumously published, which, while principally addressed to redeeming the reputation of the speaker's countryman John Dee, in the same sweep caught up the Sponheim abbot upon whom Dee had expressly drawn for assistance.[178]

The crux of the Trithemius-Dee pairing for Hooke is highlighted in his characterization of Dee's supposed conversations with "demonic" spirits, from the point of view of those looking at it from the outside, as "a Rapsody of incoherent and unintelligible Whimsies of

Prayers and Praises, Invocations and Apparitions of Spirits, strange Characters, uncouth and unintelligible Names, Words and Sentences, and Relations of incredible Occurrences."[179] It is just such a characterization which was also a keynote of many of the anti-Trithemian obloquies concurrently appearing, the resemblance of which was not lost to Hooke. Taking particular issue with Casaubon, who in his anti-Dee diatribe had noted the same resemblance, Hooke in response determined that an exoneration of Dee also necessarily entailed a corresponding exoneration of Trithemius.

Thus, to counter the charge that Dee's *Monas* was "a Book of Conjuration, . . . dealing with the Devil and his Imps," Hooke invoked the parallel case of Trithemius's *Steganographia* as testimony "that divers Books have been condemned for supposed Crimes, of which yet, upon further Inquiry, they have been found innocent, and to have quite a differing Design from what they seemed at first sight to intend." Singled out by Hooke for special mention among the impetuous critics of the Trithemian art were Bovillus, Weyer, Bellarmine, and Possevino. Of the more judicious types who "have vindicated and cleared him from those Calumnies," on the other hand, Hooke hailed Duke August for detecting beneath the outward cover of spirits distinguishing the writing in question "the whole Artifice of the whole Book, which had nothing of the Design for which the illiterate and unskilful Readers did generally condemn it."[180]

Significantly, however, by his decision to pursue a defense of Trithemius in conjunction with that of Dee before his Royal Society colleagues, Hooke can be said, in effect, to have rescued the messenger only to gut the inner essence of his message. For if we are to accept Hooke's view of an intrinsic affinity between Dee's *Monas* and Trithemius's *Steganographia,* we are also compelled, by extension, to accept the applicability of Hooke's assessment of the *Monas* to its steganographical counterpart: "I think it may be as properly referred to the Improvement of Natural Knowledge to understand it, as of any other Book that has plainly and expresly treated of the History of Nature and Art."[181] The upshot of this way of thinking, by ignoring the Pythagorean, Hermetic, and Cabalistic principles which can conceivably lift magic from its natural substratum to a realm transcending nature, is effectively to turn the occult principles of Trithemius on their head. Whereas Trithemius was always

careful to subordinate natural magic, its cryptological branch included, to a higher spiritual purpose, Hooke, by subordinating magic
to the thoroughly nature-based goals of the Royal Society, effectively divested it of its theological essence.

Along the same line, if we are to accept Hooke's opinion concerning the *Monas* "that the greatest part of the said Book, especially all that which relates to the Spirits and Apparitions, . . . are
all *Cryptography,*" and further "that some Parts also of that which
seems to be a Journal of his Voyage and Travels into several Parts
of *Germany,* are also *Cryptographical,*" we are equally bound to
extend the same kind of reading to Trithemius's steganographical
handbook with which it bears affiliation. To do so, however, is to
reduce Trithemius's motives to the same worldly ones Hooke assigned to Dee in the Englishman's role as a wandering secret agent
on behalf of his queen, made clear in his contention that the author
of the *Monas* utilized his cryptographical techniques so that "he
might the more securely escape discovery, if he should fall under
suspition as to the true Designs of his travels, or that the same
should fall into the hands of any Spies, or such as might be imployed
to betray him or his Intentions; conceiving the Inquisition that
should be made, or Prosecution, if discovered, would be more gentle
for a Pretended Enthusiast, than for a real Spy."[182] By this kind of
cynical reasoning, in truth closer in tenor to the baldly secular
calculations of a Machiavelli than to the exalted mystical speculations of a Trithemius, Hooke can be said to have drained Trithemian
magic of its spiritual meaning.

If it is granted, as has recently been argued, that Hooke shared
a number of underlying presuppositions with the magicians of his
day,[183] his treatment of Trithemian cryptography nevertheless appears to have more in common with the new philosophy of Galileo,
Descartes, and Hooke's Royal Society colleague Newton than with
the old philosophy of the medieval mystics and scholastics still
largely conditioning the speculations of those caught up in the
Rosicrucian movement. To be sure, Newton even more decisively
than Hooke retained internal affiliations with the occultist traditions, judiciously opting in this connection, however, to retain his
arcane findings in unpublished confidentiality.[184] His attitude closely
corresponds to that of Bacon before him, whose celebrated induc-
tive method went hand in hand with an announced resolve to "revive

and reintegrate the misapplied and abused name of natural magic; which in the true sense is but natural wisdom, or natural prudence; taken according to the ancient acception, purged from vanity and superstition."[185] But to admit to a historical continuum between magic and experimental science in the form promoted by the Royal Society of Wilkins, Hooke, and Newton is by no means tantamount to identifying the status of one with the status of the other. For whereas the magicians conceived of scientific experiments largely as illustrative cases of their occult theories, the scientific spokesmen of the new philosophy conceived of their theories as flowing out of their mathematically measurable experiments.

It is in this same light that we should also understand the difference between the attraction of the Rosicrucians to Trithemian cryptological methods and the attraction of Royal Society mainstays like Wilkins and Hooke. Conditioned by the exoteric standards of the Royal Society rather than by the esoteric standards of the Rosicrucians, Wilkins's interest in Trithemian cryptography was prompted by his search for a universal language accessible, not to just a privileged few, but to all who were knowledgeable in the required experimental methods for ferreting out the truth of things. The crowning result of this endeavor of Wilkins, coinciding with a contemporary endeavor of his compatriot George Dalgarno (ca. 1627–1687), was his *Essay towards a Real Character and a Philosophical Language* (1668). The primary inspiration of this drive for universal communication did not come from those, like Trithemius and Paracelsus, who sought to integrate magic with theology, but rather from those, like Francis Bacon, who sought to chart a way out of magical esoterism through the application of modern scientific method.[186]

The prismatic angle from which magicians viewed Trithemian cryptography, on the other hand, was a very different one, with their epistemological guideline consisting of the principle, not of exoteric openness, but of esoteric confidentiality. The main thrust of this outlook, as reformulated, for example, by the German Protestant mystic Jacob Böhme (1575–1624), was to highlight the intersection of magic, not with the quantifiable sciences, but with unquantifiable religion. While acknowledging no direct lineage of ideas from Trithemius, Böhme revealed an indirect lineage through the Paracelsians, and in turn helped to convey that lineage to the

modern theosophical movement. "Magic," declared Böhme in a
moment of psychic exultation, "is the best theology, for in it true
faith is both grounded and discovered."[187] In this pregnant statement the Lutheran Böhme brought to flower a seed planted, among
sundry Christian forerunners, by the very Catholic abbot Trithemius.
In so doing he gave further testimony to the observation that magic
in the early modern period, like experimental science with which
it competed, had a broad popular appeal traversing formal religious divisions.

# Chapter 6

## Conclusion: Trithemian Magic in Later Perspective

### The Persisting Scholarly Conumdrum

I f Trithemius had been permitted to live into the period of the Reformation, there is little question as to which side of the ensuing religious debate he would have chosen to affiliate himself. From the day he first declared his monastic vows at Sponheim to the last day of his controversy-riddled life in an obscure Würzburg cloister, Trithemius consistently espoused the cause of orthodox Catholicism against all forms of heterodoxy. As Johann Hermes pointed out at the beginning of the present century: "The thesis that Trithemius was a forerunner of the Reformation can be sustained only in the sense that he, like many others, recognized and condemned the great abuses which in the course of time had crept into the discipline of the monastic and secular clergy."[1] The present study adds an important addendum to Hermes's caveat.

Just as, in his more conventional religious writings, Trithemius should not be considered a forerunner of Luther, the same can be said for the contention made by his Catholic critics that, by his magic, Trithemius inadvertently helped to prepare the ground for Luther. Believing magic to be just as deserving of study as any other "handmaiden" to theology included in the traditional *artes liberales*, Trithemius considered it to be an adjunct to sound Catholic doctrine rather than an alternative to that doctrine. Despite the argument of Catholic demonologists, especially Jesuit ones, that magicians like Trithemius, Agrippa, and Faustus had helped to prepare the way to religious schism, it has been shown that the defenders of magic were as likely to be found in the Catholic as in the Protestant camp, indeed, within the "Jesuit Temple" itself.

In addressing the debate over Trithemian magic in the foregoing chapters, we have encountered a wide spectrum of positions attesting to the protean nature of its legacy. One of these, we have noted, especially evident in the Trithemius's own Benedictine order, was to downplay a purportedly minor digression of the abbot in light of the larger picture of his eminently pious way of life and unrelenting commitment to his monastic vows; another, to distinguish Trithemius's good natural and Cabalistic magic from the wicked magic of the demonically inspired sorcerers; and still another, to extricate Trithemius's cryptological magic from reliance upon objective occult causes altogether, turning it into a purely linguistic system of codes and ciphers masked by an apparatus of spirits to deceive the uninitiated. Following this last-named line of thought in particular, we are led to believe that Trithemius more properly anticipated such mundane modern practices as devising and solving acrostics and anagrams than the deeply spiritual speculations of the theosophists and their occultist kin. In association with these variant readings on Trithemian magic, two opposing portraits of the abbot have emerged to inform modern Trithemian scholarship.

One of these portraits, emphasizing his demonological output, casts Trithemius as an exemplar of intolerance, unwilling to grant to others the same benefit of doubt that he granted to his own occult speculations and practices. This side of Trithemius's personality was highlighted by his apparent willingness, in agreement with the notorious authors of the *Malleus maleficarum*, even to put accused sorcerers to death. However, another portrait of Trithemius has also emerged from the maelstrom of controversy surrounding his magic that places him in a far more favorable light. This is the view of the abbot, shared as fully by his Rosicrucian admirers as by skeptics of magic like Naudé and Hooke, that he represented a progressive step in the struggle for a free flow of ideas. Modern scholarship about the abbot appears to be as ill prepared to resolve the paradox behind these two opposing pictures of the abbot as its earlier expressions, with the cause largely attributable to Trithemius himself. For by failing to establish a consistently coherent picture of how linguistic ciphers, natural magic, spirit magic, and demonology fit together in their role as constituents of his magical theology, Trithemius has left his modern observers in an imbroglio of conjectures about his true intentions little advanced from that of his contemporaries and immediate disciples.

Of the later admirers of Trithemius, it has been established that some were accepting of the abbot's excursions into magic without themselves being practicing magicians, practicing cryptographers, or a combination of the two. This was especially the case in Trithemius's own Benedictine order where, with precedence furnished by such Trithemius admirers as Butzbach and Bucelin, the trend was to treat the abbot's magical investigations as a relatively minor rivelet within the larger stream of his spiritual output. A further example of this apologetical mode is found in a "life and apology of Trithemius" contributed by Oliver Legipont, in collaboration with Magnoald Ziegelbauer, to the mid-eighteenth century *Historia rei literariae ordinis S. Benedicti*.[2] Others favorably disposed toward the general career of Trithemius, however, have looked upon the abbot's magic as something more to be embarrassingly explained away than proudly extolled, a temporary relapse in what was otherwise a stainless monastic career. Thus, redolent of Thevet's mixed sixteenth-century review, a mid-nineteenth-century contributor to the *Encyclopédie Théologique* lamented, in the midst of a generally approbatory account of Trithemius's contributions to Catholic thought and piety, that in his occult speculations he had foolishly succumbed to consorting with "fallen angels" (*anges déchus*).[3]

For the most part, however, as common sense as well as familiarity with the subject tells us, the great bulk of Trithemius defenders were most likely to be found in the ranks of those most directly served by the abbot's magical speculations, the Hermeticists. Adding fuel to this flame were further magical writings fallaciously appearing under the name of Trithemius, such as the alchemically conceived *Güldenes Kleinod oder Schatzkästlein* (1782);[4] a tract included by Francis Barrett in his *Magus, or Celestial Intelligencer* (1801) purporting to present "the magic and philosophy of Trithemius of Spanheim; containing his book of secret things and doctrine of spirits . . . translated from a valuable Latin manuscript";[5] and a *Wunder-Buch von der gottlichen Magie* (not to be confused with the sixteenth-century *Wunder Büchlein*, a translation of the *De septem secundeis*), purportedly first published at Passau in 1506.[6] Later editions of Trithemius's genuine writings in the same genre have further placed the abbot at the center of this development. A French translation of the *De septem secundeis* appeared in two separate printings at the end of the nineteenth century (1897, 1898), and an English translation of portions of the *Steganographia* has recently come to light as part of the current Hermetic movement.[7]

A characteristic representative of this kind of medium for the conveyance of the Sponheim abbot's influence to the modern age is the Hermetic Brotherhood of Luxor, an esoteric movement founded in the nineteeth-century for the teaching of "practical occultism," which discovered in the astrological-angelogical system as set forth in the *De septem secundeis* a starting point for its own projection of a series of prophecies extending to the year 3114. In an important sense, however, showing shades of Naudé and of the acadamicians of the English Royal Society, the thrust of this school of thought was to perceive in Trithemius, in utter contrast to his true historical role as an abettor of the witch hunts, a champion of a free exchange of ideas. In keeping with this view of the abbot's long-term significance it has been revealed to the Brothers of Luxor, in the prophecy pertaining to our own period in the cycle of ages reputedly ruled by the archangel Michael: "Empires will shine full of glory, the Human intellect will have full play and all Churches, Religious Creeds and Ecclesiastical dogmas will fall to the ground and become things of the past."[8]

Other admirers of Trithemius, continuing a trend represented by, among others, Abbot Sigismund, Duke August and Heidel, have been drawn more to the abbot's ingenious cryptological devices than to the occult theory on which he based them. In his role as the inventor of steganography, according to the cryptographical specialist Ernst Dröscher, Trithemius "served as the prototype and stimulus for many later investigations."[9] Going even further in this regard is Arnold in his Trithemius biography, crediting the Sponheim abbot with fathering the field of modern cryptography.[10] As pointed out by another scholar of this subject, however, Fletcher Pratt, Trithemius's influence on future generations of cryptographers might easily be exaggerated. Taking note of the great effort needed both to devise and unravel the codes devised by the abbot, Pratt has wryly observed: "It is fairly safe to say that no Trithemius cipher has ever been used where the transmission of secret information in a hurry was a consideration; and time is nearly always a consideration."[11]

Apart from the question of the extent to which Trithemius actually impacted on the history of cryptography, the question still remains for modern scholars of what he intended by cloaking his codifying operations in the language of spirit conjuration. Contemporary scholarly speculation about Trithemian cryptography by and large reveals the same kinds of impasses that plagued its Renaissance and seventeenth-century expressions. At one extreme are those who, taking the spirit conjurations of the *Steganographia* at their face value, see at least some serious endeavor on its author's part to employ supernatural spirits for the mediation of his cryptographic messages. At the opposite pole are those who, with the help of published keys and the contributions of later disciples such as Sigismund, pseudo-Selenus, and Heidel, rather construe the cryptographic magic of Trithemius as consisting of nothing more than an enigmatic system of codes and ciphers in the guise of angel magic. Occupying a middle ground between these extremes are those who, taking note of Trithemius's sustained effort to synthesize Pythagorean, Hermetic, and Neoplatonic principles in his various theoretical expositions of magic, identify as the true conveyors of Trithemian cryptic communications, not supernatural angels, but occult natural powers.

Representative of the first camp of scholars are Frances Yates, who has termed the *Steganographia* "a main Renaissance manual of practical Cabala or angel-conjuring," and her Warburg Institute colleague D. P. Walker, who, at once more guardedly and more damning, has characterized the work as "partly a treatise on cryptography in which the methods of encipherment are disguised as demonic magic, and partly a treatise on demonic magic."[12] Representative of the second camp, on the other hand, are Klaus Arnold, Wayne Shumaker, and Thomas Ernst, who would persuade us, with help from the steganographical key furnished by Trithemius, that the art of steganography, just as its sister art of polygraphy, can be reduced to word games—*ludibria vocis*, with its complex system of magical rites and conjurations but a cryptic cover to disguise its true intentions.

While concurring with Yates that Trithemius found in the Jewish Cabala a suitable ancient paradigm for his modus operandi, Arnold cautions us that it was not an "angel-conjuring" Cabalistic art Trithemius had in mind in this connection, but rather "the symbolical Cabala, holding that, in accordance with fixed rules, the individual letters of words can become transposed and a new meaning yielded." In support of this contention Arnold furnishes some illustrative steganographical decipherments, followed by polygraphical ones obeying similar rules for alphabetical permutation.[13] Shumaker's view of Trithemian cryptography, in basic agreement with Arnold's, is elaborated through the further assessment of a number of later cryptographers, most notably Della Porta, Vigenère, and pseudo-Selenus, showing apparent or avowed dependency on the abbot's example. With these further cryptographic aids to reinforce his case, Shumaker has concluded that "the portions of the *Steganographia* which appear to rely on daemonic help consist of obscure explanations and enciphered messages, the plaintext of which the reader must puzzle out with the help of directions that are themselves enciphered."[14] Like Arnold, to whom he has chiefly deferred as an authority on Trithemius's life, Shumaker sees no need to posit the effectuation of occult forces in the cryptographic operations of the abbot, including the operations of steganography, beyond the ability to play games with human language. Ernst's further contribution to this debate, for whom Heidel above all led the way, has been to establish a homogenously cryptographical analysis of the *Steganographia* through a linguistic solution of its previously undeciphered third book.

As noted above, however, there is still a third position on Trithemian cryptography to be considered which occupies a place midway between its relegation to spirit conjuring and its reduction to mere wordplay. This is the presumption that Trithemius believed in the existence of hidden forces of nature capable of being tapped for the transmission of secret messages by those esoterically furnished with the necessary knowledge. Trithemius's earlier biographer Schneegans pointed up this position when, with reference to the indirect influence of Giovanni Pico on his subject through the mediation of Pelagius and Libanius Gallus, he underscored the distinction between natural magic, "which teaches how to produce marvelous effects through the mediation of powers residing in nature," and another kind of magic "which, by virtue of calling on evil spirits for assistance, is condemned by the Church."[15] This is also the kind of magic which constitutes the crux of Peuckert's treatment of Trithemius in his Paracelsian-inspired *Pansophie*.[16]

The three variant positions on Trithemian cryptography here indicated contain inherent difficulties which, after due consideration, might well have the effect of reinforcing rather than resolving our quandary. If, as Yates and Walker have maintained, Trithemius truly believed that spirits could be conjured and manipulated to facilitate cryptic communication, why did the abbot feel the need to resort to simple coding techniques in conjunction with his conjurations explainable without reference to either supernatural or natural occult powers? But if, as Arnold, Shumaker, and Ernst have maintained, Trithemius employed his spirit scheme as a mere cryptic device, how do we meet the objection, entertained by Walker when considering the same possibility, that Trithemius chose an unnecessarily dangerous disguise which could easily be misconstrued by his critics as demonic magic?[17] Finally, if we are to make the assumption, following Schneegans and Peuckert, that Trithemius enlisted natural rather than supernatural demonic or angelic magic for the transmission of his secret messages, we are hard put to explain why his cryptic enigmas can be resolved by linguistic keys radically free of externally occult forces of nature. As these examples show, Trithemius has left the modern students of his "magic" with a kind of intellectual puzzle, the separate pieces of which are as difficult to assemble now as in the abbot's own time.

Further compounding the Trithemius problem for us is the demonological underbelly to his magic. A striking paradox brought out in the foregoing chapters is why so outspoken a demonologist as Trithemius should have occasioned a stream of accusations by contemporary and later demonologists that he himself was a wicked demon conjuror. The piously reform-minded Benedictine monk who had denounced Faustus as the "fountain of necromancers," as it turned out, ended in accruing his own Faustlike magical legend. As has also been brought out, Trithemius himself can be charged with at least some responsibility in this regard. For by authoring demonological tracts of his own, motivated at least partly by the desire to sanitize his magic, Trithemius inadvertently placed a valuable weapon in the hands of those intent on demolishing his magical rationale.

Downplaying Trithemius's role in promoting the witch persecutions is Arnold, who, while acknowledging that "without question Trithemius was a witch-believer and uncritically adopted the outlook of the notorious *Malleus maleficarum*," has also concluded that Trithemius was far more interested in repelling demons than in putting witches to death. "He had never occupied himself with the worldly witch-hunt," Arnold has attested; rather "his remedies are the ancient exorcisms of the Church, and that which he met with in the medical literature of his library."[18] Uncritically seconding Arnold's verdict on this subject is Paola Zambelli, who has declared on the subject of Trithemius, with Arnold her authority, that "one cannot read anywhere in his writings about instigations to the burning of witches—apart from the quote of Exodus 22:18: 'Maleficos non patieris vivere,' which he repeats as a topos."[19] It may well be true, as maintained by Zambelli, that it was not a main objective of Trithemius in his demonological writings to promote the penalty of death for those convicted of sorcery, but rather, as she puts it, only to apply to those deemed to be under the spell of demons "ecclesiastic means . . . such as exorcisms and purifications." Nevertheless, even if we are to extend to Trithemius the benefit of our doubt in this regard, we are still justified in holding him accountable for encouraging a way of thinking which made the severer solution to the witch problem possible. Given a strain of demonological bigotry in his theological outlook which allowed even innocent children, virtuous non-Christians, and heterodox Christians to incur harsh punishment for their "infidelity," it is scarcely surprising that he did not exempt eccentric Christian women accused of sorcery from the same unsparing judgment.

Closer to the truth of this matter than either Arnold or Zambelli is Couliano, who, while expressly beholden to Arnold for his brief treatment of the abbot's magical career in his *Eros and Magic*, departed from him on this point. Opening his Trithemian excursus on the stridently demonological note by calling attention to the abbot's advocacy of the extreme penalty for witchcraft, Couliano unfortunately carried this aspect of Trithemius's occult career too far, signified by his decision to consider the abbot under the heading "demonomagic." In making that decision Couliano reveals that he did not fully come to terms with Trithemius's significant role in promoting that other kind of magic which formed a basis of his study, "erotic" natural magic, the concept of which he himself traced to the identification of love and magic made by Ficino.[20]

Taking all of these ill-fitting components of Trithemius's magical theory into account, we are compelled to take more seriously the abbot's appeal to transcendental assistance than a strictly linguistic interpretation allows. Trithemius's Benedictine-trained theology, in time coming to comprise unconventional magical together with conventional mystical and demonological elements, embraced the genuine belief that good and evil forces exist in the universe, intermediate between God and man, which are capable of being tapped by human beings for either good or ill. If the occult virtues of nature are morally neutral, the occult virtues of angels and demons are not. Therefore, as the reasoning of a piously monkish investigator of the arcana like Trithemius goes, even natural magic needs support in the celestial angelic spheres if it is not to become subject to diabolical machinations.

Guarding his occult operations with many caveats to keep them free of possible diabolical intrusion and contamination, Trithemius joined Cabalistic to Pythagorean and Hermetic principles in such fashion as to furnish himself—and those deemed to be worthy of instruction in his art—with a continuous magical road from the finite constraints of the material world to the infinite expanses of the supermundane spirit. Indeed, it was to facilitate the passage from the finite to the infinite, so Trithemius expressly testified in his various theoretical justifications of his magic, that he had invented his cryptographical languages in the first place. The practical applications inherent in the arts of steganography and polygraphy, he maintained, were but secondary rewards of a primary impulse to the infinitely divine. It is, accordingly, on this theme of a Trithemian will to the infinite that we will now conclude, which, amidst its variant expressions, can be said to constitute a durable constant of his magical theology.

## The Trithemian Will

Of the great artworks transmitted to our modern world by the Renaissance, one of the most mystifying for the historians of art is Albrecht Dürer's engraving *Melencolia I* (see plate 8). It is now generally accepted, thanks to a 1923 ground-breaking investigation into the intellectual derivations of that engraving by the Dürer scholars Erwin Panofsky and Fritz Saxl, that the principal source of Dürer's aesthetic insight were certain chapters devoted to the subject of melancholy genius contained in Agrippa of Nettesheim's *De occulta philosophia*. As speculated by Panofsky and Saxl, Agrippa's text was made available to the Nuremberg humanist circle of Willibald Pirckheimer, which included Dürer among its members, through the mediation of Trithemius.[21] Yet if we are to believe an earlier Dürer scholar, Franz Leitschuh, Trithemius was not so much a mediator for Dürer's angel-like personification of melancholy genius as its direct inspiration.

In his *melancholia* engraving, wrote Leitschuh at the turn of the present century, "Dürer portrays a [feminine] personification of the restless drive for the acquisition of knowledge who, while seeing that she is surrounded by utterly unsolvable mysteries, has been drained of all means for arriving at her goal of understanding." This image of Dürer's melancholy figure conjured up for Leitschuh the image of the abbot Trithemius in his study, "surrounded by implements and instruments of all kinds, which were said to signify the versatility of his aspirations and accomplishments." For Leitschuh the resemblance between these two scholarly portraits, both rife with emblems of magical paraphernalia in their proximity, was no coincidence, since, as he put it, "Dürer intended in his 'melancholia,' just as he had observed in Trithemius, to personify the inordinate desire to fathom the mysteries of all things—this even to the point of profound dejection (*Schwermut*)."[22]

The moot point of whether Trithemius impacted directly upon Dürer's famous representation of melancholy genius, or only indirectly through his association with Agrippa, does not here have to be answered. What does concern us is the parallel drawn by Leitschuh between Trithemius and the crest-fallen winged figure in Dürer's engraving, temporarily cast into a state of melancholy abjection as the result of the great strain placed upon her by her arduous mental labors. This parallel also points up the opposite connotations that could be placed upon Trithemius's magical endeavors.

Following one connotation, encouraged by the popular adage that "melancholy is the bath of the Devil," it could be argued that Trithemius summoned demons into his presence to assist his magical operations. As Thorndike has observed, "melancholy and magic had long been associated in the history of ideas. Those who sought a natural explanation for what others regarded as possession by demons found it in an excess of melancholic humor."[23] The connotation placed on Trithemian magic a half-century earlier by Leitschuh, on the other hand, was a very different one, suggesting, with assistance from the Dürer engraving, that the melancholy often found to afflict the magician signifies but a temporary setback in his strenuous effort to gain access to the hidden mysteries of nature and of God.

It was a working assumption of the Renaissance Platonists, mirrored in Agrippa's *De occulta philosophia* dedicated to Trithemius, that melancholy is the natural counterpart of the divine frenzy— of the *furor divinus*.[24] Inasmuch as Plato had assigned the philosophers—termed such because they are "lovers of wisdom"—to the erotic species of divine frenzy, it took only a short step for one in the magical mold of a Trithemius or of an Agrippa to extend the benefits of frenzied love to lovers of occult philosophy in particular. Perceived against this backdrop, the notion of the "Faustian will" is also eminently translatable into a "Trithemian will." For just as Faustus has become a popular metaphor for the heroic human desire to break through finite limitations to the unlimited beyond, so is Trithemius suitable for the same purpose, one who boldly maintained that an insatiable quest for knowledge, when faithfully expressed within the guidelines of Christian orthodoxy and conditioned by an elevated spiritual and moral bearing, is not a vice but a virtue.

Frank Baron has noted, with a comparison of Trithemius and Faustus in mind, that "the portrait of the Renaissance magician is by no means a uniform one." Not only did Trithemius and Faustus display variant magical practices, according to Baron, but they also differed in the "forms of their magical thought."[25] While this is undoubtedly true, reflected in Trithemius's unsympathetic portrayal of Faustus following a chance encounter, it is difficult to elicit a theoretical "form" from the Faustian legacy whatsoever. For the portrait of Faustus bequeathed to posterity depended entirely on secondary accounts of marvelous feats, beginning with the *Faustbuch* of 1587. By contrast, Trithemius left to posterity a sizable corpus of occult writings with the express purpose of justifying his magical practices.

If we have revealed one reservoir of Trithemius's magical theory to consist of medieval mysticism, we have revealed another reservoir to consist of Renaissance humanism. In this regard Trithemius can be credibly presented as a full-fledged participant in what a recent scholar of Renaissance arcana has termed "the renaissance of occultism."[26] Baron, with an eye to this humanist context of the abbot's magic, maintains that "Trithemius was, in the things of magic, a true student of the great theorist of magic during Renaissance times, Pico della Mirandola."[27] The basic thrust of the present study, however, while fully conceding to an unmistakable humanist input into Trithemian arcane theory, has pushed us into a modification of this postulate. While certainly touched by the ideas of the Florentine Platonists, we have shown, Trithemius consciously adopted as his ideal prototype, not Ficino or Giovanni Pico in the thick of the Italian occult movement, but the thirteenth-century German scholastic Albertus Magnus. In his correlative role as ecclesiastical historian, Trithemius saw himself as participating not so much in a "renaissance of occultism" as in an unbroken continuum of occult teachings stretching from the ancient world to his own day.

So far as the Italian revival of ancient magical theory came into play in German thought during the Renaissance, Trithemius's Italian mediator Reuchlin and his youthful admirer Agrippa of Nettesheim better than Trithemius himself mirrors the philosophical depth and range of its principal participants.[28] But though we must concede to Trithemius a modestly peripheral role in the conveyance of the magical "renaissance" into the recesses of modern thought, this is not to say that his example is not of great value to the study of the history of ideas in another way. For if Trithemius must be counted as a minor player in the Renaissance revival of ancient occult theory, he was also a player who accurately and eloquently reverberated the main issues that lay behind the Renaissance campaign to justify magic.

The occult theory of Trithemius, combining precepts of Hermetic natural magic with Cabalistic angel magic, evolved out of his need to rationalize the practice of sending secret messages through supernatural means. While the abbot's second major cryptographic achievement, the *Polygraphia*, was conceived along less controversial lines, expressly exchanging the premise of angelic mediation for a system of codes and ciphers independent of supernatural transmission, Trithemius did not therein abandon the occult theory buttressing the earlier tract. In its polygraphic as in its prior steganographic expressions, the cryptography of Trithemius hypothetically rests on occult foundations located simultaneously *above* nature and deeply *within* nature's bowels. His magic is explicitly based on the assumption that a Christian instructed in the requisite language is granted access not only into the obscure caverns of nature, but also into the planetary-angelic spheres enveloping nature.

As Trithemius gleaned from his clerical training, Catholic doctrine presented an ambiguous authority that could work both for and against his magical goals. From the latter point of view, as evidenced by the Augustinian and Hieronymite strains of church history, the guardians of orthodoxy could often be found to uphold a clearcut theoretical distinction between religion and magic even as they defended the sanctity of rites within their ecclesiastical system bearing uncomfortably close resemblance to forbidden magical practices. As Walker has put the reason for this discomfiture in trenchant form: "The Church has her own magic; there is no room for any other."[29] Alternatively however, there were also proponents of Catholic orthodoxy, among whom is to be counted Trithemius, who upheld, not an unyielding incompatibility between the miracles of the church and magic, but their theoretical concordance and even coalescence. Trithemius's occult outlook represents a conscious attempt on his part both to minimize the distinction between miracle and magic and to justify magic by affiliating it with the occult mystical underpinnings of his Catholic religion. His restatement of the Hermetic *magnum miraculum* in Christian terms resulted in his formulation of a doctrine of magical theology—of *theologia magica*—corresponding to his more conventional religious doctrine of mystical theology—*theologia mystica*. It directly pointed the way, as it were, to Agrippa's likewise Hermetically inspired notion of a *magnum miraculum Christianum.*

As we have seen, those holding to a strict Augustinian position on this question have been quick to cast suspicion on Trithemius's occult speculations. Taking their cue from Bovillus, some of these viewed Trithemius's magic in a demonological light, whereas others, as Erasmus can be taken as an example, saw in the abbot's cryptographic operations something more to ridicule as vain and useless than to fear as a threat to the soul's salvation. The stridency of these criticisms, as we might expect, became more distinctly pronounced as the witch persecutions became more intense and widespread.

A further source for this rabidly anti-Trithemian tone lay in the antagonism between the Protestant and Catholic reform movements. Under the sway of this theological conflict, some Protestant demonologists charged magic with being at one with the superstitious practices of his Catholic religion, whereas their counterparts among the Catholics rather declared magic to be a contaminating, diabolically inspired incursion into the church's sacred rites that helped prepare the ground for Protestantism. On both sides of the reformation divide, accordingly, demonological extremists were to be found who demanded that true ecclesiastical reform must include the expurgation of magic as a primary component, with Trithemian magic being no exception to the rule. Fortunately for the legacy of Trithemius, however, also to be found on both sides of the Protestant-Catholic divide were others accepting of the abbot's thesis that religious reform, rather than excluding magic, should embrace it as one of its primary constituents. Despite their formal theological differences, Catholics and Protestants were jointly turning over the intellectual soil which permitted magic to flourish on Christian ground. For these, with Trithemius an illuminating beacon, the Hermetic concept of the *magnum miraculum* coincided at bottom with such miracles as were performed by Moses, Christ, and the saints.

It was, of course, not mathematical and scientific enlightenment that Trithemius heralded for sundry lovers of the occult in the centuries after his death, but magical enlightenment. The cultural evolution from the Middle Ages and Reformation to "Enlightenment," as Yates has emphasized, could just as readily signify a belief in esoterically intuited magical as in exoterically demonstrated and mathematically quantifiable causation. As such it was a direct forerunner of what the scholar of nineteenth-century occult developments, Joscelyn Godwin, has termed "the theosophical enlightenment."[30] As we have observed, a foremost medium for the exculpation of Trithemius in the centuries following his death was the school located by Yates at the center of her concept "Hermetic enlightenment," the Rosicrucians. This is not to say, as we have also shown, that Trithemius failed to find defenders among the anti-occultist spokesmen of the "new philosophy" of Descartes, Galileo, and Newton. Skeptics of magic like Naudé and Hooke could find good things to say about Trithemius as well as occult-loving admirers like Robert Fludd. The fundamental difference between them, however, lay in the way they framed their Trithemian defense. Whereas the scientific skeptics of magic might well save the reputation of the cryptological abbot but eviscerate his occult philosophy of its theological core, their Rosicrucian contemporaries, beholden to his theory as much as to his cryptological practice, addressed themselves to saving not only the reputation of the man, but also the theological underpinnings of his occult philosophy.

If mathematical precision of the kind called for by Descartes, Galileo, and Newton can be said to constitute the warp of the seventeenth-century intellectual matrix, the opaquely abstruse principles of magicians like Trithemius's Rosicrucian admirer Fludd can be said to constitute its woof. Or, as an alternative metaphor can be invoked to make the same point: in the culminating Rosicrucian and theosophical stages of the Christian magical movement, what heretofore were relatively minor subterranean streamlets of Christian thought—astrology, Pythagorean numerology, and Hermetic and Cabalistic magic—became expanded into major streams and rivers. As pointed out by Antoine Faivre in the introduction to his *Modern Esoteric Spirituality*, with recourse to the identical metaphor, it is a legacy which continues to bathe our hearts and minds. According to Faivre:

One could be forgiven for thinking that these rivers and streams disappeared with the Renaissance. But when the great epistemological rupture of the seventeenth century was completed, they survived, and nineteenth-century scientism did not force them to dry up. Esotericism is present today more than ever."[31]

To the extent that we can agree with this appraisal, to the same extent can we also locate the abbot Trithemius within the mainstream of the enduring esoterist-theosophical currents.

# Notes

## Chapter 1. Introduction

1. Lynn Thorndike, *A History of Magic and Experimental Science*, 8 vols. (New York: Columbia University Press, 1929–1958), I, 2.

2. See Frances Yates, *Giordano Bruno and the Hermetic Tradition* (London: Routledge and Kegan Paul, 1964), and a summary of her thesis in "The Hermetic tradition in Renaissance Science," in *Art, Science, and History in the Renaissance*, ed., Charles S. Singleton (Baltimore: Johns Hopkins Press, 1967), pp. 255–74. For challenges to the Yates thesis see Robert S. Westman and J. E. McGuire, *Hermeticism and the Scientific Revolution: Papers Read at a Clark Library Seminar, March 9, 1974*, (Los Angeles: University of California Press, 1977); Paolo Rossi, "Hermeticism and the Scientific Revolution," in M. L. Righini Bonelli and William R. Shea, eds., *Reason, Experiment and Mysticism in the Scientific Revolution* (New York: Science History Publications, 1975), pp. 245–73; and, still more severely, Brian Vickers, "Frances Yates and the Writing of History," *Journal of Modern History*, 51 (1979): 287–316. Cf. the various offerings of Vickers in his edited *Occult and Scientific Mentalities in the Renaissance* (Cambridge: Cambridge University Press, 1984). Pleading for a middle ground in this debate is Wayne Shumaker, *Natural Magic and Modern Science: Four Treatises, 1590–1657* (Binghamton, N.Y.: Medieval & Renaissance Texts and Studies, 1989), pp. 15–17. Placing this question within the wider framework of Renaissance intellectual history are essays in Allen G. Debus, ed., *Science, Medicine and Society in the Renaissance: Essays to Honor Walter Pagel*, 2 vols. (New York: Neale Watson, 1972); Ingrid Merkel and

Debus, eds., *Hermeticism and the Renaissance: Intellectual History and the Occult in Early Modern Europe* (Washington D.C.: Folger Shakespeare Library/London-Toronto: Associated University Presses, 1988); August Buck, ed., *Die okkulten Wissenschaften in der Renaissance*, Wolfenbüttler Wissenchaften in der Renaissance, no. 12 (Wiesbaden: Harrassowitz, 1992); and Debus and Michael T. Walton, eds., *Reading the Book of Nature: The Other Side of the Scientific Revolution*, Sixteenth Essays and Studies, vol. 41 (Kirksville, Mo.: Sixteenth Century Journal Publications, 1998).

3. Bronislaw Malinowski, *Magic, Science, and Religion* (New York: Doubleday-Anchor, 1954), p. 90.

4. For a summary of this subject see my paper "The Shift from Mystical to Magical Theology in the Abbot Trithemius (1462–1516)," *Studies in Medieval Culture*, XI, eds. John R. Sommerfeldt and Thomas H. Seiler (Medieval Institute, Western Michigan University, 1977): 147–59. Similarly approaching the issue of Trithemian magic from this mystical perspective are two essays, the first by Jean Dupebe, "Curiosité et Magie chez Johannes Trithemius," in Jean Céard, ed., *La Curiosité a la Renaissance* (Paris: Société d'Edition d'Enseignement Supérieur, 1986), pp. 71–97, and the second by Frank L. Borchardt, "The *Magus* as Renaissance Man," *Sixteenth Century Journal*, 21 (1990): 57–76, esp. pp. 67–68.

5. Not atypical in this regard is Geoffrey Scarre's *Witchcraft and Magic in 16th and 17th Century Europe* (Atlantic Highlands, N.J.: Humanities Press International, 1987), which, while making references to the influence of Ficino, Giovanni Pico, and Agrippa on the history of magic, ignores that of Trithemius.

6. Christoph Zeisseler, *Neu-eröffneter Historischer Schauplatz* (1595), excerpted in Alexander Tille, ed., *Die Faustsplitter in der Literature des sechzehnten bis achtzehnten Jahrhunderts nach den ältesten Quellen* (Berlin: Emil Felber, 1900), no. 146, p. 149. For further references in this anthology illustrating the popular mingling of the Faustian and Trithemian magical legends see no. 12, pp. 14–15; no. 31, pp. 62–68; no. 51, pp. 99–101; no. 59, pp. 111–14; no. 62, pp. 118–22; no. 89, pp. 173–78; etc. Cf. Josef Fritz, ed., *Das Volksbuch vom Doktor Faust: Nach der um die Erfurter Geschichten vermehrten Fassung* (Halle a/S: Max Niemeyer, 1914, based on 1596 ed.), part III, pp. 69–70. In this study the Latin name Faustus is preferred to the Germanic Faust because of its greater frequency of use in the primary sources employed. Focusing on the conflation of the Faustian and Trithemian legends, with special attention to the resemblance between the two necromantic episodes in the imperial court, is Frank Baron, "Trithemius und Faustus: Begegnungen in Geschichte und Sage," in Richard Auernheimer and Baron, eds., *Johannes Trithemius: Humanismus und Magie im vorreformatorischen Deutschland,* Bad Kreuznacher Symposien

I., 1985 (Munich: Profil, 1991), pp. 38–57, and "The Precarious Legacy of Renaissance Humanism in the Faust Legend," in Manfred P. Fleischer, ed., *The Harvest of Humanism in Central Europe: Essays in Honor of Lewis W. Spitz* (St. Louis: Concordia, 1992), pp. 303–15. For further treatments of the Faust legend see Philip Mason Palmer and Robert Pattison More, eds., *The Sources of the Faust Tradition from Simon Magus to Lessing* (Oxford: Oxford University Press, 1936); E. M. Butler, *The Fortunes of Faust* (Cambridge: Cambridge University Press, 1952); Karl Kiesewetter, *Faust in der Geschichte und Tradition.* . . . (Hildesheim: Georg Olms, 1963); John W. Smeed, *Faust in Literature* (Oxford: Oxford University Press, 1975); Baron, *Doctor Faustus from History to Legend* (Munich: Wilhelm Fink, 1978), and *Faustus. Geschichte, Sage, Dichtung* (Munich: Winkler, 1982); and Peter Boerner and Sidney Johnson, eds., *Faust through Four Centuries: Retrospect and Analysis / Rückblick und Analyse* (Tübingen: Max Niemeyer, 1989).

7. For older full-scale biographies of Trithemius see Isidore Silbernagel, *Trithemius: Eine Monographie* (Landshut: F. G. Wölfle, 1868; 2d ed., Regensburg: 1885) and Wilhelm Schneegans, *Abt Johannes Trithemius und Kloster Sponheim* (Kreuznach: Reinhard Schmithals, 1882). More recent biographies are furnished by Paul Chacornac, *Grandeur et Adversité de Jean Trithème, Bénédictin Abbé de Spanheim et de Wurtzbourg (1462–1516)* (Paris: Editions Traditionelles, 1963); Klaus Arnold, *Johannes Trithemius (1462–1516)*, Quellen und Forschungen zur Geschichte des Bistums und Hochstifts Würzburg, vol 23 (Würzburg: Kommissionsverlag Ferdinand Schöningh Würzburg, 1971; 2d ed., 1991); and my own *The Abbot Trithemius (1462–1516): The Renaissance of Monastic Humanism*, Studies in the History of Christian Thought, vol. 24 (Leiden: E. J. Brill, 1981), from which this biographical account is summarized. For briefer accounts of the abbot's more conventional monastic career see the collection of lectures gathered in H. Gerwalin, ed., *500-Jahrfeier Johannes Trithemius 1462–1962 am 11. August 1962 in Trittenheim / Mosel* (Trittenheim: Gemeinde Trittenheim: 1962), and of Trithemius's magical career, heavily dependent on Arnold for factual data but differing on substantive points, Ioan P. Couliano, *Eros and Magic in the Renaissance*, trans. Margaret Cook, with forward by Mircea Eliade (Chicago: University of Chicago Press, 1987), pp. 162ff.

8. Brann, *Trithemius*, pp. 3–4. Cf. Arnold, *Trithemius*, pp. 1–3.

9. Brann, *Trithemius*, pp. 5–6. Cf. Arnold, *Trithemius*, pp. 8–10. On Celtis's key role in organizing this and other literary sodalities in the Germanic north see Lewis Spitz, *The Religious Renaissance of the German Humanists* (Cambridge, Mass.: Harvard University Press, 1963), pp. 86–87. For a summary of the intellectual developments surrounding this trend see my essay "Humanism in Germany," in Albert J. Rabil, Jr., ed.,

*Renaissance Humanism: Foundations, Forms, and Legacy*, 3 vols. (Philadelphia: University of Pennsylvania Press, 1988, 1991), II, ch. 21, pp. 123–55. On the essentially conservative character of the German humanist movement see also my article "Pre-Reformation Humanism in Germany and the Papal Monarchy: A Study in Ambivalence," *The Journal of Medieval and Renaissance Studies*, 14 (1984): 159–85.

10. Brann, *Trithemius*, pp. 6–8. Cf. Arnold, *Trithemius*, pp. 11–16.

11. Brann, *Trithemius*, pp. 9–14, and 156ff. Cf. Arnold, *Trithemius*, pp. 56ff. See also my article, "A Monastic Dilemma Posed by the Invention of Printing: The Context of *De laude scriptorum manualium* by Abbot Johann Trithemius," *Visible Language*, 13 (1979): 150–67.

12. Brann, *Trithemius*, pp. 14–20. Cf. Arnold, *Trithemius*, pp. 22ff. and 36ff.

13. Brann, *Trithemius*, pp. 20–31. Cf. Arnold, *Trithemius*, pp. 180ff.

14. Brann, *Trithemius*, p. 25. Cf. Arnold, *Trithemius*, p. 79. The words are those of Johannes Vigilius, in a 1496 letter to Conrad Celtis.

15. Brann, *Trithemius*, pp. 18–20. Cf. Arnold, *Trithemius*, pp. 182–83. This aspect of Trithemius's literary career is subordinated in my own intellectual biography to the abbot's more conventional humanist interests. But Arnold, with a wider range, has assigned a separate chapter (10) to this subject, pp. 180ff.

16. Brann, *Trithemius*, pp. 29–31. Cf. Arnold, *Trithemius*, pp. 183–84.

17. Brann, *Trithemius*, pp. 33ff. Cf. Arnold, *Trithemius*, pp. 201ff. Trithemius was originally buried in the Schottenkirche of Würzburg, which site was marked by a headstone bearing his features from the workshop of Tilmann Riemenschneider. In 1720 the grave and headstone were moved to their present location in the Neumünsterkirche.

18. Brann, *Trithemius*, pp. 81ff.

19. Brann, *Trithemius*, pp. 92–95, 100–101. Cf. Arnold, *Trithemius*, pp. 190ff., and append., "deperdita," pp. 255, 257.


## Chapter 2. The Magical Inheritance

1. Lactantius, *The Divine Institutes: Books I–VIII*, trans. Sister Mary Francis McDonald. Fathers of the Church, vol. 49 (Washington, D.C.: Catholic University Press, 1964), p. 155. Latin text in Jacques-Paul Migne, ed.,

*Patrologiae . . . latina*, 222 vols. (Paris: Garnier Fratres, 1844–1905), 6:337. On ancient and early Christian demonology see Thorndike, *Magic*, I; Penethorne Hughes, *Witchcraft* (London: Longman, Greens, 1952; Penguin, 1965), pp. 11–55; E. R. Dodds, *Pagan and Christian in an Age of Anxiety: Some Aspects of Religious Experience from Marcus Aurelius to Constantine* (New York: Norton, 1965, 1970); Jeffrey Burton Russell, *Witchcraft in the Middle Ages* (Ithaca, N.Y.: Cornell University Press, 1972), pp. 45–63, and *The Devil: Perceptions of Evil from Antiquity to Primitive Christianity* (Ithaca, N.Y.: Cornell University Press, 1977); Norman Cohn, *Europe's Inner Demons* (Sussex: Sussex University Press, 1975; London, Paladin, 1976), pp. 1–15; Henry Ansgar Kelly, *The Devil, Demonology, and Witchcraft: The Development of Christian Beliefs in Evil Spirits* (New York: Doubleday, 1968), pp. 3–42.; Richard Kieckhefer, *Magic in the Middle Ages* (Cambridge: Cambridge University Press, 1989, pp. 19–42; and Valerie I. J. Flint, *The Rise of Magic in Early Medieval Europe* (Princeton, N.J.: Princeton University Press, 1991).

2. Origen, *Against Celsus*, trans. F. Crombie and W. H. Cairns, in *The Ante-Nicene Fathers*, IV, ed. Alexander Roberts and James Donaldson (New York: Charles Scribner's Sons, 1899), bk. I, ch. 38, p. 412–13. Greek text and Latin trans. in Migne, *Patrologiae . . . graeca*, 161 vols. (Paris: Garnier Fratres, 1857–1912), 11:33–34. Cf. ch. 6, pp. 398–99; ch. 71, p. 428; bk. VIII, ch. 9, p. 642 (Migne, PG 11:665–66, 791–92, 1531–32).

3. Ibid., bk. I, ch. 28, p. 407 (Migne, PG 11:713–14). Celsus had interpreted Moses' victory over the magicians of Pharoah (Ex. 7:11–12) as a conquest of superior over inferior magic.

4. Tertullian, *The Apology*, trans. S. Thelwall, in *Ante-Nicene Fathers*, III, ed., A. Cleveland Doxe, ch. 21, p. 35 (Migne, PL 1:458). On Tertullian's uncompromising hostility to magic see Thorndike, *Magic*, I, 463–65.

5. St. Chrysostom (ca. 345–407), *Homiliae in Matthaeum*, 6 (3), in Migne, PG 57:61ff., esp. 66; St. Jerome, *Commentarii in Isaiam*, lib. VII, cap. 19, in Migne, PL 24:250. Unless otherwise indicated, translations are my own. For good accounts of persisting pagan magical traditions in Christian antiquity see A. A. Barb, "The Survival of the Magical Arts," in Arnaldo Momigliano, ed., *The Conflict between Paganism and Christianity* (Oxford: Clarendon Press, 1963), ch. 5, pp. 100–25, and Peter Brown, "Sorcery, Demons, and the Rise of Christianity," in *Religion and Society in the Age of Saint Augustine* (London: Faber & Faber, 1972), pp. 119–46.

6. St. Augustine, *The City of God*, trans. Gerald G. Walsh and Grace Monahan, bk. VIII, ch. 19, in *Writings of St. Augustine*, VII (New York: Fathers of the Church, 1952), bk. X, ch. 9, pp. 129–30 (Migne, PL 41:285–86).

7. Ibid., p. 131 (Migne, PL 41:291).

8. Ibid., p. 132 (Migne, PL 41:291); bk. VIII, ch. 23, p. 63 (Migne, PL 41:248–49). On the theurgical practices of certain third-century pagan Neoplatonists see Thorndike, *Magic*, I, ch. 11, pp. 298ff., with special attention given to Porphyry, pp. 307ff. For the Lactantius references see *The Wrath of God*, ch. 11, in *The Minor Works*, and *Divine Institutes*, bk. I, ch. 6, trans. McDonald, in *Fathers of the Church*, vol. 50, p. 87 (Migne, PL 7:112), and vol. 49, pp. 31–32 (Migne, PL 6:137–38). On the Greek-inscribed Hermetica see Thorndike, *Magic*, I, ch. 10, pp. 287ff., and on the key role of Lactantius, together with St. Augustine, in furthering the legend of the extreme antiquity of Trismegistus, Yates, *Bruno*, pp. 6ff.

9. Ibid., bk. X, ch. 12, p. 139 (Migne, PL 41:248–49).

10. Isidore of Seville, St., *Etymologies* (*Etymologiarum libri XX*), lib. 8, cap. 9 (9), cited in Thorndike, *Magic*, I, 629 (Migne, PL 82:310).

11. Hincmar of Rheims, *De divortio Lotharii et Tetbergae*, inter. xv and resp., in Migne, PL 125:716,718.

12. Rabanus Maurus, *De magicis artibus*, in Migne, PL 110:1095ff. On Isidore's influence see Thorndike, *Magic*, I, 630.

13. For the later medieval preparation of the witch persecutions see Joseph Hansen, *Zauberwahn, Inquisition und Hexenprozess im Mittelalter und die Entstehung der Grossen Hexenverfolgung* (Munich: R. Oldenbourg, 1900); Thorndike, *Magic*, vols. II–IV; Hughes, *Witchcraft*, pp. 56–195; Julio Caro Baroja, *The World of Witches*, trans. Nigel Glendinning (London: Weidenfeld and Nicolson, 1961, 1964); Kelly, *The Devil*, pp. 50ff; Russell, *Witchcraft*, pp. 63ff; Cohn, *Europe's Inner Demons*, pp. 16ff; Edward Peters, *The Magician, the Witch, and the Law* (Philadelphia: University of Pennsylvania Press, 1978); Kieckhefer, *European Witch Trials: Their Foundations in Popular Culture, 1300–1500* (Berkeley: University of California Press, 1976), and *Magic*, pp. 56ff.; and Joseph Klaits, *Servants of Satan: The Age of the Witch Hunts* (Bloomington: Indiana University Press, 1985), pp. 19–47. For alphabetical accessibility to the subject see Rossell Hope Robbins, *The Encyclopedia of Witchcraft and Demonology* (London: Peter Nevill Ltd., 1959). Anthologies of primary source material are furnished by Hansen, *Quellen und Untersuchungen zur Geschichte des Hexenwahns und der Hexenverfolgung im Mittelalter* (Bonn: 1901; Hildesheim: Georg Olms, 1963); Henry Charles Lea, *Materials Toward a History of Witchcraft*, ed., Arthur C. Howland, 3 vols. (Philadelphia: University of Pennsylvania Press, 1938); and Alan C. Kors and Edward Peters, eds., *Witchcraft in Europe, 1300–1700: A Documentary History* (Philadelphia: University of Pennsylvania Press, 1972, 1978).

14. Kors and Peters, eds., *Witchcraft*, no. 11, p. 79 (Hansen, *Quellen*, I:1, p. 1). See also Peters, *Magician*, p. 99.

15. Gratian, *Decretum* (=*Concordia discordantium canonum*), pars II, cau. 26, qu. 7, c. 15, in Kors and Peters, eds., *Witchcraft*, no. 1, p. 29 (Migne, PL 187:1369). Gratian pioneered the systematic study of canonistic jurisprudence at Bologna. On the *Canon episcopi* see Russell, *Witchcraft*, pp. 75ff.; Cohn, *Demons*, pp. 210ff.; and Peters, *Magician*, pp. 72ff. The text of the *Canon episcopi* is found in Hansen, *Quellen*, II:1, pp. 38–39, with an English trans. in Lea, *Materials*, I, 178–80. Anticipating Gratian's erroneous assumption of the conciliar origin of this document are Burchard of Worms, *Decretorum libri XX*, lib. X, cap. 40, in Migne, PL 140:839, and Ivo of Chartres, *Decretum*, par. XI, cap. 67, in Migne, PL 161:745ff.

16. John of Salisbury, *Policraticus*, bk. II, ch. 17, in Kors and Peters, eds., *Witchcraft*, no. 3, pp. 36–37 (Migne, PL 199:436). On the influence of Isidore of Seville on John's demonology see Thorndike, *Magic*, I, 63 and II, 158, and on the influence of the *Canon episcopi*, through the mediation of Burchard of Worms, II, 163 and note. See also Peters, *Magician*, pp. 47ff. But concerning John's greater hostility to learned sorcery see *Polic.*, lib. I, cap. 9, in Migne, PL 199:406.

17. Kors and Peters, eds., *Witchcraft*, no. 13, p. 82, and no. 16, p. 98 (Hansen, *Quellen*, I:5, pp. 5–6, and I:26, p. 17). See also Russell, *Witchcraft*, ch. 7 and 8, pp. 167ff; Cohn, *Demons*, pp. 180ff.; and Peters, *Magician*, pp. 129ff.

18. The *Malleus* has been trans. into English by Montague Suumers (London: John Rodker, 1928, repr. 1948; repub. New York: Dover, 1971), with a preface to the 1948 reprint establishing Summers as a modern-day defender of the witch persecutions. For excerpts, together with critical commentary, see Hansen, *Quellen*, Pt. III, pp. 360ff., and for summaries of these excerpts, Lea, *Materials*, I, 306ff., with special reference to Hansen's treatment, pp. 336ff. For an excerpt in English, prefaced by Pope Innocent VIII's papal bull *Summis desiderantes* of 1484, see Kors and Peters, eds., *Witchcraft*, part IV, nos. 18 and 19, pp. 105ff.

19. Richalmus, *Liber revelationum de insidiis et versutiis daemonum adversus homines*, cap. 12, in Bernhard Pez, ed., *Thesaurus anecdotorum novissimus*, 6 vols. (Augsburg: Sumptibus Philippi Martini, & Joannis Veith Fratrum, 1721), I, col. 396. On Richalmus's demonology see Cohn, *Demons*, pp. 71ff., and Peters, *Magician*, pp. 92ff.

20. See esp. Caesarius's *Dialogues of Miracles* (*Dialogus miraculorum*), trans. H. Scott and C. C. Swinton Bland, 2 vols. (London: G. Routledge,

1929). On Caesarius's demonology, treated in conjunction with that of Richalmus, see Cohn, *Demons*, pp. 69–71, and Peters, *Magician*, pp. 92ff.

21. Hildegarde of Bingen, *Liber divinorum operum*, pars III, vis. 28, in Migne, PL 197:1028. On Hildegarde see Thorndike, *Magic*, II, ch. 40, pp. 124ff., with particular reference to this vision, pp. 138–39.

22. Hugh of St. Victor, *Didascalicon*, lib. VI, cap. 15, in Migne, PL 176:810. On Hugh's enmity to magic see Thorndike, *Magic*, II, 13ff.

23. Peter Lombard, *Collectanea in omnes d. Pauli apostoli epistolas*, in Migne, PL 191:1625. Maintaining that scholasticism played a key role in the promotion of the witch hunts are Hansen, *Zauberwahn*, p. 4. and H. R. Trevor-Roper, *The European Witch-Craze of the Sixteenth and Seventeenth Centuries and Other Essays* (New York: Harper & Row, 1969), reprint of chaps. 1–4, *The Crisis of the Seventeenth Century: Religion, the Reformation and Social Change* (New York: Harper & Row, 1956, 1968), ch. 3, pp. 90ff. Downplaying the influence of scholasticism on the witch hunts, however, is Russell, *Witchcraft*, p. 142.

24. Alexander of Hales, *Summa theologica*, ed. Bernardin Klumper, 4 vols. (Florence: S. Bonaventurae, 1930), III, lib. II, par. 2, inqu. 3, tract. 8, sect. 1, qu. 2, memb. 6, cap. 9, art. 6, p. 778.

25. Peter Abelard, *Ethica seu scito te ipsum*, cap. 4, in Migne, PL 178:647. On this demonological excursus by Abelard see Thorndike, *Magic*, II, 7–8.

26. Thorndike, *Magic*, II, 607, perceives the influence of Thomas's teacher Albertus in this writing. Noting the influence of this tract on Ficino is Brian P. Copenhaver: "Astrology and Magic," in Charles B. Schmitt, Quentin Skinner, Eckhard Kesler, and Jill Kraye, eds., *The Cambridge History of Renaissance Philosophy* (Cambridge: Cambridge University Press, 1988), ch. 10, p. 283.

27. St. Thomas Aquinas, *Summa contra gentiles*, bk. III, ch. 101, in Anton C. Pegis, ed., *Basic Writings*, 2 vols. (New York: Random House, 1945), II, 198 (trans. L. Shapcote, O.P.). On Thomas's demonology see Thorndike, *Magic*, II, ch. 60, pp. 593ff.; Charles E. Hopkin, *The Share of Thomas Aquinas in the Growth of the Witchcraft Delusion* (Philadelphia: University of Pennsylvania Press, 1940); and Peters, *Magician*, pp. 96ff.

28. Pseudo-Aquinas, *Aurora consurgans*, trans. R. F. C. Hull and A. S. B. Glover, ed. Marie-Louise von Franz (New York: Pantheon, 1966).

29. William of Auvergne (=William of Paris), *De legibus*, cap. 1, in *Opera omnia*, ed. B. Le Feron, 2 vols. (Orléans: Apud Michaelem du-Neuf-Germain, 1674), I, 70. On William's demonology see Thorndike, *Magic*, II, ch. 52, pp. 338ff., and Peters, *Magician*, 89ff.

30. *De universo*, pars II, iii, cap. 22, in *Opera omnia*, I, 1060. For the background of William's magical beliefs see Antoine Faivre, "Ancient and Medieval Sources of Modern Esoteric Movements," in Faivre, Jacob Needleman, and Karen Voss, eds., *Modern Esoteric Spirituality* (New York: Crossroad, 1992), pp. 1ff. On the blending of ancient magical with messianic motifs see Howard Clark Kee, "Magic and Messiah," in Jacob Neusner, Ernest S. Frerichs and Paul Virgil McCracken Flesher, eds., *Religion, Science, and Magic in Concert and in Conflict* (Oxford: Oxford University Press, 1989), pp. 121–41.

31. Albertus Magnus, *Super Dionysium de divinis nominibus*, ch. 2 (74), in *Opera omnia*, ed. Bernhard Geyer, vol. 37 (Monasterium Westfalorum: In Aedibus Aschendorff, 1972), solut. (reply to obj. 1), p. 90.

32. Albertus, *Summa theologica*, pars II, tr. 8, qu. 30, memb. 1, art. 1, in *Opera omnia*, ed. P. Jammy, 21 vols. (Leiden: Sumptibus Claudii Prost, 1651), XVIII, 178.

33. Albertus, *Commentarius in Evangelium secundum Matthaeum*, cap. 2, in *Opera omnia*, ed. Jammy, IX, 24. On Albertus's magical ideas see Thorndike, *Magic*, II, ch. 59, pp. 517ff. Concluding vol. 21 of the Jammy ed. is a tract titled *Libellus de alchimia,* apparently, however, a spurious attribution which Thorndike omits from his Albertus sources. Cf. Peters, *Magician*, p. 95: "Far more than Aquinas, Albertus appears to have approached magic from the direction of the natural sciences, and he draws a clear distinction between natural magic and demonological magic."

34. Albertus, *Summa theologica*, pars II, tr. 8, qu. 21, memb. 2, in *Opera omnia*, ed. Jammy, XVIII, 181. Cf. *De somno et vigilia*, tract. II, cap. 4, in *Op. omn.*, V, 105. On the scholastic role in furthering this notion of the close relationship between magic and melancholy see Raymond Klibansky, Erwin Panofsky, and Fritz Saxl, *Saturn and Melancholy: Studies in the History of Natural Philosophy, Religion, and Art* (New York: Basic Books, 1964), ch. 2, pp. 67ff., with special attention given to Albertus, pp. 69ff.

35. Roger Bacon, *Opus majus*, trans. Robert Belle Burke, 2 vols. (Philadelphia: University of Pennsylvania Press, 1928), I, pt. IV, p. 411. For original Latin see ed. of John Henry Bridges, 2 vols. (Oxford: Clarendon Press, 1897), I, 395–96.

36. Ibid., pp. 410–11 (Bridges, I, 394–95). While declining to apply the term *magia naturalis* to these disciplines, preferring instead the term *scientia experimentalis*, Bacon unquestionably retained the meaning of natural magic in his notion of experimental science. On Bacon as, simultaneously, occultist and "experimental scientist," see Thorndike, *Magic*, II,

ch. 61 (with two appendices), pp. 616ff., and on Bacon as demonologist, Peters, *Magician*, p. 88.

37. Ibid., p. 411 (Bridges, I, 395).

38. Ibid., II, pt. VI, pp. 630–32 (Bridges, II, 218–21).

39. Ibid., p. 633 (Bridges, II, 221).

40. On the magical and astrological speculations of D'Abano, with focus on his *Conciliator controversiarum* (1303), see Thorndike, *Magic*, II, 874ff., esp. pp. 888ff., and Peters, *Magician*, p. 105. Concerning the Joachimite climate helping to condition this way of thinking see Henry Bett, *Joachim of Flora* (London: Methuen, 1931), and Marjorie Reeves, *The Influence of Prophecy in the Later Middle Ages: A Study in Joachimism* (Oxford: Clarendon Press, 1969).

41. Robert Holkot, *Phoenix rediviva....* (Köln: Apud Arnoldum Metternich, 1689), cap. 17, lect. 190, p. 329.

42. Pierre d'Ailly, *De falsis prophetis*, tract. II, append. in Jean de Gerson, *Opera omnia*, ed. M. Lud. Ellies Du Pin, 5 vols. (Antwerp: Sumptibus Societatis, 1706), I, cols. 513, 517.

43. See Thorndike, *Magic*, IV,, ch. 42, pp. 101ff. For the background of this subject see Eugenio Garin, *Astrology in the Renaissance: The Zodiac of Life,* trans. Carolyn Jackson, June Allen, and Clare Robertson (London: Routledge & Kegan Paul, 1983).

44. *Chartularium Universitatis Parisiensis*, ed. Henricus Denifle, O.P., and Aemilio Chatelain, 4 vols. (Paris: Ex Typis Fratrum Delalain, 1887), IV, 32ff. (no. 1749): "Conclusio facultatis theologie super materia fidei nunc agitata novissime determinata de superstitionibus." Gerson's *De erroribus circa artem magicam et articulis reprobatis* is printed in Du Pin, ed., *Opera omnia* (see above, note 42), I, cols. 210ff. On Gerson's attitude to the arcane studies see Thorndike, *Magic*, IV, ch. 43, and with reference to the *De erroribus*, pp. 125ff., and Peters, *Magician*, p. 143. For the transfer of Gerson's antimagical views to Germany prior to Trithemius, through the mediation of his disciple Johann Nider's *Formicarius* (ca. 1435), see Brian P. Levack, *The Witch-Hunt in Early Modern Europe* (London: Longman, 1995; first ed., 1987), p. 34.

45. Gerson, *De erroribus*, in Du Pin, ed., *Opera omnia*, I, cols. 210–12. Cf. *Tractatus de probatione spirituum.* cols. 37ff.; *Tractatus de distinctione verarum visionum a falsis*, cols. 43ff.; *Tractatus adversus profanas superstitiones*, cols. 185ff.; and *An liceat Christiano initia rerum observare ex coelestium syderum respectu,* cols. 220ff.

46. On this theme see D. P. Walker, *The Ancient Theology: Studies in Christian Platonism from the Fifteenth to the Eighteenth Century* (London: Duckworth, 1972), and Stephen A. McKnight, *The Modern Age and the Recovery of Ancient Wisdom: A Reconsideration of Historical Consciousness, 1450–1650* (Columbia: University of Missouri Press, 1991), esp. ch. 3. For a summary of this development see Kieckhefer, *Magic,* pp. 144–50. On Ficino's scholastic methodology see Paul Oskar Kristeller, "The Scholastic Background of Marsilio Ficino," in *Studies in Renaissance Thought and Letters* (Rome: Edizioni di Storia e Letteratura, 1969), pp. 34ff., and on Ficino's integration of magic into his scholastic system, Brian Copenhaver, "Scholastic Philosophy and Renaissance Magic in the *De vita* of Marsilio Ficino," *Renaissance Quarterly*, 37 (1984): 523–54.

47. Marsilio Ficino, *Apologia, in qua medicina, astrologia vita mundi . . . agitur*, in *Opera omnia*, 2 vols. (Basel: Ex officina Henricpetrina, 1576; facsimile, Torino: Bottega d'Erasmo, 1959), I, 573. On Ficino's magic see Thorndike, *Magic*, IV, ch. 63, pp. 562ff.; D. P. Walker, *Spiritual and Demonic Magic from Ficino to Campanella*, Studies of the Warburg Institute, Vol. 22 (London: Warburg Institute, 1958; reprint, Nendeln/Liechtenstein, 1969); Yates, *Bruno*, pp. 62ff., and *The Occult Philosophy in the Elizabethan Age* (London: Routledge & Kegan Paul, 1979), pp. 17ff.; and Klibansky et al., *Saturn*, pp. 254–74. Concerning the astrological component of Ficino's magic see Garin, *Astrology in the Renaissance*, pp. 61ff.; Shumaker, *The Occult Sciences in the Renaissance: A Study in Intellectual Patterns* (Berkeley: University of California Press, 1972), pp. 120–33; and Copenhaver, "Astrology and Magic," in Schmitt et al., eds., *Cambridge History of Renaissance Philosophy*, pp. 274ff., and "Platonism," in Copenhaver and Schmitt, eds., *Renaissance Philosophy*, pp. 127–95, esp. pp. 143ff.

48. See, e.g., Copenhaver, "Astrology and Magic," in Schmitt and Skinner, *Renaissance Philosophy*, p. 287: "It was clear to Ficino and his Renaissance readers . . . that Plato's *eros* was a powerful magical force." Expanding this theme into an entire book is Couliano, *Eros and Magic*, with Ficino treated pp. 28ff. Maintaining that, in the particulars of this concept, Ficino was more dependent on the Neoplatonist Plotinus than on Plato himself, is Al Wolters, "Ficino and Plotinus' Treatise 'On Eros,' " in Konrad Eisenbichler and Olga Zorzi Pugliese, eds., *Ficino and Renaissance Neoplatonism*, University of Toronto Italian Studies, 1 (Ottawa: Dovehouse Editions, 1986), pp. 189–97.

49. See Yates, *Bruno*, pp. 12ff. However, Copenhaver (see note above), p. 280, takes issue with Yates on this question, emphasizing Neoplatonic over Hermetic elements in Ficino's theory. Cf. Copenhaver, "Hermes

Trismegistus, Proclus, and the Question of the Philosophy of Magic in the Renaissance," in Merkel and Debus, eds., *Hermeticism and the Renaissance*, ch. 4, pp. 79–110. According to Zambelli in this same volume, however, p. 128, the trend to downplay Hermeticism in Ficino and his Platonic circle "is valid primarily in the field of the history of science." The controversy over the principal ingredients of Ficino's magical doctrines can now be checked against an English ed. of his *De vita libri III*, trans. as *Three Books on Life: A critical Edition and Translation with Introduction and Notes*, ed. and trans. Carol V. Kaske and John R. Clark, Medieval and Renaissance Texts and Studies, vol. 57 (Binghamton, N.Y.: State University of New York, 1989).

50. Ficino, *Apologia*, in *Opera omnia*, I, 573.

51. Giovanni Pico della Mirandola, *Conclusiones*, nos. 2, 3, and 13, in *Opera omnia*, 2 vols. [vol. I: Giovanni Pico; vol. II: Gianfrancesco Pico] (Basel: Ex officina Henricpetrina; facsimile, Hildesheim: Georg Olms, 1969), I, 104–105. Still forthcoming is Stephen A. Farmer's eagerly anticipated edition and translation of the Nine Hundred theses under the title *Pico's 900 Theses: Syncretism in the West* (Binghamton: State University of New York Press, due in 1998), based on the *editio princeps* of 1486. On Pico's ties with Scholasticism see Avery Dulles, *Princeps Concordiae: Pico della Mirandola and the Scholastic Tradition* (Cambridge, Mass.: Harvard University Press, 1941), and on his magic, Thorndike, *Magic*, IV, pp. 485–89; Garin, *Giovanni Pico della Mirandola: Vita e Dottrina* (Florence: Felice Le Monnier, 1937), esp. pp. 155ff.; and Yates, *Bruno*, pp. 84ff. Cf. Yates, *Occult Philosophy*, pp. 17ff. Concerning Pico's difficulties with astrology in conjunction with magic, centering on the problem of free will, see Garin, *Astrology in the Renaissance,* esp. pp. 78ff., and Shumaker, *Occult Sciences* pp. 16–27, and on his further difficulty of distinguishing magic from miracles, Louis Valcke, "Magie et Miracle chez Jean Pic de la Mirandole," in Eisenbichler and Pugliese, eds., *Ficino and Renaissance Neoplatonism*, pp. 155–73.

52. Pico, *Conclusiones,* no. 15, in *Opera omnia*, I, 105. For this feature of the Renaissance esoterist traditions see Joseph Leon Blau, *The Christian Interpretation of the Cabala in the Renaissance* (New York: Columbia University Press, 1944); François Secret, *Les Kabbalistes Chrétiens de la Renaissance* (Paris: Dunod, 1964); and Philip Beitchman, *Alchemy of the Word: Cabala of the Renaissance* (Albany: State University of New York Press, 1998). Presenting this theme in briefer form are Moshel Idel, "The Magical and Neoplatonic Interpretations of the Kabbalah in the Renaissance," in Bernard Dov Cooperman, ed., *Jewish Thought in the Sixteenth Century* (Cambridge, Mass.: Harvard University Press, 1983), pp. 186–

242, and G. Mallary Masters, "Renaissance Kabbalah," in Faivre et al., eds., *Modern Esoteric Spirituality,* pp. 132ff.

53. Pico, *Oration on the Dignity of Man,* trans. Elizabeth Livermore Forbes, in Ernst Cassirer, P. O. Kristeller, and John Herman Randall, Jr., eds., *The Renaissance Philosophy of Man* (Chicago: University of Chicago Press [Phoenix], 1948), pp. 246–7. This section of Pico's *Oratio* is excerpted almost verbatim from his more comprehensive apologetic of the *Conclusiones,* entitled *Apologia adversus eos qui aliquot propositiones theologicas carpebant,* in *Opera omnia,* I, 120–21.

54. Ibid., p. 249.

55. See Spitz, *Religious Renaissance,* pp. 61–62. These Italian journeys took place in 1482 and 1490.

56. Johann Reuchlin, *De verbo mirifico* (printed and bound with *De arte cabalistica,* 1517; facsimile, Stuttgart-Bad Cannstatt: Friedrich Frommann Verlag, 1964), lib. II, sig. c 8ᵛ. On Reuchlin's Cabalism see Spitz, *Religious Renaissance,* pp. 61–80, and Secret, *Kabbalistes Chrétiens,* pp. 44–70. Denying Reuchlin's belief in the operative power of magic is Ludwig Geiger, *Johann Reuchlin: Sein Leben und Seine Werke* (Leipzig: Dunker & Humblot, 1871), pp. 176ff., as also Spitz, p. 74, following Geiger's lead. But this view has been contested by Charles Zika, "Reuchlin's *De Verbo Mirifico* and the Magic Debate of the Late Fifteenth Century," *Journal of Warburg and Courtauld Institutes,* 39 (1976): 104–38, and again by Yates, *Occult Philosophy,* pp. 23–27. Cf. Zika, "Reuchlin and Erasmus: Humanism and Occult Philosophy," *Journal of Religious History,* 9 (1976–77): 223–46.

## Chapter 3. The Demonological Vision

1. Willibald Pirckheimer to Trithemius, 13 June 1515, in Pirckheimer, *Briefwechsel,* ed., Emil Reicke, 2 vols. (Munich: C. H. Beck, 1966), II, no. 362, pp. 555–56. On Pirckheimer see Spitz, *Religious Renaissance,* pp. 155ff.

2. Johannes Trithemius, *Sermones vel exhortationes ad monachos libri II,* I:13, in Johannes Busaeus, ed., *Opera pia et spiritualia* (Mainz: Ex typographeo Ioan. Albini, 1604, 1605), p. 462.

3. Trithemius *De tentationibus monachorum libri II,* lib. I, cap. 4, in Busaeus, *Opera pia,* p. 668.

4. Trithemius, *Annales Hirsaugienses,* 2 vols. (St. Gall: J. G. Schlegel), I, 27.  *Copyrighted Material*

5. Ibid., I, 395–97.

6. Trithemius, *Catalogus illustrium virorum Germaniae,* in Marquard Freher, ed., *Opera historica, quotquot hactenus reperiri potuerunt omnia,* 2 parts (Frankfurt: Typis Wechelianis apud Claudium Marnium & haeredes Ioannis Aubrij, 1601; facsimile, Frankfurt a/m, 1966), I, 177. For corresponding Latin excerpts from Trithemius's demonological writings see Hansen, *Quellen,* Pt. II, pp. 291ff., with summaries found in Lea, *Materials,* I, 369–70. For studies of the patristic, medieval and early Renaissance background to Trithemius's demonology see above, ch. 2, notes 1 and 13.

7. Trithemius to Nicholas Gerbel, Würzburg, 16 July 1507, *Epistolae familiares,* II:32, in Freher, ed., *Opera historica,* II, 545.

8. Trithemius to Rutger Sicamber, Würzburg, 31 August 1507, *Epist. fam.,* II:51, in Freher, *Opera historica,* II, 565.

9. Trithemius, *De demonibus,* lib. I, in Arnold, "Additamenta Trithemiana: Nachträge zu Leben und Werk des Johannes Trithemius, insbesondere zur Schrift *De demonibus,*" *Würzburger Diözesan-Geschichtsblätter,* 37–38 (1975), 259. On this work see Arnold, *Trithemius,* p. 199, and Brann, *Trithemius,* p. 93.

10. Ibid., lib. II, p. 259.

11. Ibid., lib. II, p. 260.

12. Trithemius, *Antipalus maleficiorum libri IV,* in Busaeus, ed., *Paralipomena opusculorum Petri Blenensis et Ioannis Trithemii* (Cologne: Apud Ioannem Wulffraht, 1624), lib. II, cap. 1, p. 317.

13. *De demonibus,* pref., pp. 257–58. For the history of the capital vice scheme see Morton W. Bloomfield, *The Seven Deadly Sins: An Introduction to the History of A Religious Concept, with Special Reference to Medieval Literature* (East Lansing: Michigan State College Press, 1952), and for the history of "acedia" in particular, Siegfried Wenzel, *The Sin of Sloth: Acedia in Medieval Thought and Literature* (Chapel Hill: University of North Carolina Press, 1967). Concerning the latter vice see also my article, "Is Acedia Melancholy? A Re-examination of this Question in the Light of Fra Battista da Crema's *Della cognitione et vittoria di se stesso* (1531)," *Journal of the History of Medicine and Allied Sciences,* 34 (1979): 180–99. For the specifically sexual motif in witchcraft see Lyndal Roper, *Oedipus and the Devil: Witchcraft, Sexuality and Religion, 1500–1700* (London: Routledge, 1994).

14. *Antipalus,* lib. II, cap. 1, 318.

15. Ibid., lib. IV, qu. I, p. 401.

16. Ibid., lib. II, cap. 2, pp. 319–20.

17. Ibid., lib. II, cap. 3, pp. 320–21.

18. *Liber octo quaestionum,* qu. 2, in Busaeus, *Paralipomena,* 1. p. 449. Hereafter, cited as *Octo quaestiones.*

19. *Antipalus,* lib. IV, qu. 1, p. 401.

20. *Octo quaestiones,* qu. 3, p. 459.

21. See, e.g., Cohn, *Europe's Inner Demons,* pp. 16ff., and Levack, *Witch-Hunt,* p. 50: "Magicians were, after all, considered to be heretics and were vulnerable therefore to the same charges that were traditionally made against other heretics."

22. *Octo quaestiones,* qu. 7, p. 520.

23. Ibid., qu. 6, p. 497.

24. Ibid., qu. 7, p. 507.

25. Ibid., pp. 511–12.

26. Ibid., p. 513.

27. Ibid.

28. Ibid., p. 514.

29. Ibid., pp. 514–20.

30. *De demonibus,* lib. VII, p. 264.

31. Ibid., pref., p. 258.

32. *Octo quaestiones,* qu. 3, p. 466. On the theme of excessive curiosity cf. *De demonibus,* pref., p. 258.

33. *De demonibus,* pref., p. 258.

34. Ibid., lib. VIII, p. 264.

35. Ibid., lib. IX, p. 265.

36. Ibid.

37. *Octo quaestiones,* qu. 3, p. 455.

38. Ibid., p. 458.

39. Ibid., p. 456.

40. Ibid., pp. 463–64.

41. See above, p. 39.

42. Ibid., pp. 460–61.

43. Ibid., p. 462.

44. Ibid.

45. Ibid., pp. 465–66.

46. Ibid., p. 468.

47. Ibid., p. 465.

48. Ibid., p. 467.

49. Ibid., p. 465.

50. Ibid., p. 468.

51. Ibid., p. 471.

52. Ibid.

53. Ibid., p. 473.

54. Ibid., qu. 5, pp. 486ff. See also above, p. 47.

55. *De demonibus,* lib. X, pp. 265–66.

56. Trithemius to Elector Joachim of Brandenburg, Würzburg, 16 October 1508, prefacing *Antipalus,* p. 275. For excerpts see Hansen, *Quellen,* pp. 294–96, and for an epitome dependent on these excerpts, Lea, *Materials,* I, 369–70.

57. *Octo quaestiones,* qu. 6, p. 506.

58. *Antipalus,* lib. I, cap. 1, p. 278; cap. 2, pp. 280, 288.

59. *De demonibus,* lib. 11, p. 266; *Antipalus,* lib. I, cap. 4, pp. 311–13. One item listed above in particular, the association of demons with epilepsy, appears to have attracted special attention from Trithemius, provoking him to compose an entire tract on the subject, the now no longer extant *De morbo caduco et maleficiis.* On this writing see *Annales Hirsaugienses,* II, 692, and Arnold, *Trithemius,* append., "deperdita," p. 257.

60. *Antipalus,* lib. I, cap. 4, pp. 312–13.

61. Ibid., lib. IV, qu. 1, p. 402.

62. Ibid., lib. IV, qu. 3, pp. 405–406.

63. *Chronicon Hirsaugiensis,* in Freher, ed., *Opera historica,* II, 46.

64. *Antipalus,* lib. I, cap. 2, p. 289.

65. Ibid., lib. IV, qu. 3, p. 406.

66. Ibid., qu. 6, p. 500.

67. Ibid., qu. 5, p. 490.

68. Ibid.

69. Ibid., lib. I, cap. 4, p. 313.

70. *Annales Hirsaugienses,* II, 204.

71. Ibid., II, 159–60.

72. Trithemius, *Compendium . . . de origine regum et gentis Francorum,* XVIII, in Freher, ed., *Opera historica,* I, 15.

73. On this motif in Trithemius's historical writings see Arnold, *Trithemius,* pp. 164ff., and Brann, *Trithemius,* pp. 236ff. and 325ff.

74. *Annales Hirsaugienses,* I, 399.

75. *De demonibus,* pref., p. 258.

76. *Annales Hirsaugienses,* II, 519.

77. *De demonibus,* pref., p. 258.

78. Trithemius to Rutger Sicamber (see above, note 8), p. 565.

79. *De demonibus,* lib. IV, pp. 261–62.

80. *Octo quaestiones,* qu. 3, p. 466.

81. Trithemius to Dietrich von Lebus (=von Bülow), Würzburg, 16 April 1507, *Epistolae familiares,* II:22, in Freher, *Opera historica,* II, 535. For Trithemius's earlier promise to evaluate the Apollonius biography for Dietrich, the bishop of Lebus, dated 31 October 1505, see I:49, in Freher, *Opera historica,* II, 483.

82. Ibid., p. 536.

83. *Annales Hirsaugienses,* I, 596.

84. Ibid., I, 608.

85. Trithemius to Johannes Virdung de Hasfurt, Würzburg, 20 August 1507, *Epistolae familiares,* II:48, in Freher, ed., *Opera historica,* II, 559. This letter is reprinted in Trithemius, *De septem secundeis, id est,*

*intelligentiis sive spiritibus orbes post Deum moventibus.* . . . Cologne: Apud Johannem Birckmannum, 1567), pp. 140–41; in Tille, *Faustsplitter,* no. 1, pp. 1–3; and in Hans Rupprich, *Humanismus und Renaissance in den deutschen Städten und an den Universitäten* (Leipzig: P. Reclam jun., 1935; repr., Darmstadt: Wissenschaftliche Buchgesellschaft, 1964, 1965), pp. 184ff. For translations of this letter into German, French, and English respectively see Kiesewetter, *Faust,* pp. 4–6; Chacornac, *Jean Trithème,* pp. 59–61; and Palmer and Pattison, *Sources,* pp. 83–86. On this documented Trithemius-Faust encounter see Dieter Harmening, "Faust und die Renaissance-Magie: zum ältesten Faustzeugnis (Johannes Trithemius an Johannes Virdung, 1507)," *Archiv für Kulturgeschichte,* 55 (1973): 56–79; Hansjörg Maus, *Faust: Eine Deutsche Legende* (Vienna/Munich: Meyster, 1980), pp. 109ff.; Arnold, *Trithemius,* p. 185; Brann, *Trithemius,* p. 48; and Baron, *Doctor Faustus,* pp. 23ff. For general accounts of the historical Faustus see E. M. Butler, *The Myth of the Magus* (Cambridge: Cambridge University Press; New York: Macmillan, 1948), pp. 121ff., and Mahal Günther, ed., *Der historische Faust: Ein wissenschaftliches Symposium (26/27 September 1980)* (Knittlingen: Publikationen des Faust-Archivs (PFA), 1982). For corresponding references to the Faust legend, see above, ch. 1, note 6.

86. Ibid., p. 560.

87. *Annales Hirsaugienses,* II, 584–85. On the identity of Mercurio see Kristeller, *Studies,* pp. 228ff., pp. 249ff.

88. Ibid., p. 585.

89. Trithemius, *Catalogus de viris illustribus ordinis s. Benedicti,* lib. IV, cap. 9, in Busaeus, ed., *Opera pia,* p. 119. The source of Gerbert's magical legend is William of Malmesbury, *De gestis regum anglorum libri V,* lib. II, in Migne, PL 179:1137ff. Concerning the allegation of the further magical corruption of the papacy following the precedent laid down by Gerbert, see Hansen, *Zauberwahn,* p. 96, and Peters, *Magician,* p. 28.

90. *Antipalus,* lib. I, cap. 3, p. 298.

91. Ibid., p. 292.

92. Ibid., p. 293. On the Hermetic background of this writing see Yates, *Bruno,* pp. 49ff.

93. Ibid., pp. 310–11.

94. Trithemius, *De scriptoribus ecclesiasticis,* in Freher, ed., *Opera historica,* I, 311. On D'Abano's occult interests see above, p. 25.

95. *Antipalus,* lib. I, cap. 3, p. 298.

96. Ibid., lib. I, cap. 2, p. 281. On this mnemonic technique and its inventor, Ramon Lull, see Thorndike, *Magic,* II, ch. 69, pp. 862ff., and Frances Yates, *The Art of Memory* (London: Routledge & Kegan Paul, 1966; Harmondsworth, Middlesex, Eng.: Penguin, 1969), ch. 8, pp. 175ff.

97. *Antipalus,* lib. I, cap. 2, p. 280.

98. *Annales Hirsaugienses,* II, 225 reported under year 1354. For further cases reflecting this hostile attitude to alchemy see pp. 286–88, reported under the year 1388.

99. Trithemius, *Polygraphiae libri VI* (Cologne: Apud Johannem Birckmannum & Theodorum Baumium, 1571), lib. VI,, pp. 597–98. First ed., Basel: M. Furter, 1518.

100. *Annales Hirsaugienses,* II, 123, reported under year 1310. Cf. *De scriptoribus ecclesiasticis,* in Freher, ed., *Opera historica,* I, 320–21. On Arnaldus's arcane interests see Thorndike, *Magic,* II, ch. 68, pp. 841ff., and III, ch. 4, pp. 52ff., and Peters, *Magician,* p. 106. On Rupescissa see Thorndike, *Magic,* III, 347ff.

101. *De demonibus,* lib. V, p. 262.

102. Ibid.

103. Ibid., lib. VI, pp. 262–63.

104. Ibid., pp. 258–59.

105. Ibid., p. 259.

106. Ibid., pref., p. 258.

107. See above, p. 51.

108. *Antipalus,* lib. II, cap. 3, pp. 326–27. For a further reference to the Pelagian powder see lib. III, p. 390.

109. Ibid., p. 327.

110. Ibid., lib. III, p. 333.

111. *De demonibus,,* lib. XII, p. 267.

112. *Octo quaestiones,* qu. 4, p. 426.

113. *Antipalus,* lib. 2, pref., p. 314.

114. Ibid., pp. 315–16.

115. Ibid., p. 315.

116. Ibid., lib. III, p. 332.

117. Ibid.

118. *Annales Hirsaugienses,* I, 577–79.

119. *Octo quaestiones,* qu. 5, p. 489.

120. *Antipalus,* lib. III, pref., p. 393.

121. Ibid., p. 390.

122. Ibid., lib. IV, qu. 3, p. 406.

123. Ibid., lib. III, pref., p. 329.

124. Ibid., pp. 329–30. Cf. lib. IV, qu. 4, p. 426.

125. Ibid., lib. IV, qu. 2, p. 405. On the body-soul duality in Trithemius and the dilemma it poses for natural medicine see my article "George Ripley and the Abbot Trithemius: An Inquiry into Contrasting Medical Attitudes," *Ambix,* 26 (1979): 212–20.

126. *De demonibus,* lib. 12, p. 266.

127. *Octo quaestiones,* qu. 7, pp. 514–15.

128. *Antipalus,* qu. 2, pp. 402–405.

129. Ibid., lib. IV, qu. 4, p. 409.

130. Ibid., p. 493.

131. Ibid., p. 495.

132. Ibid., lib. III, p. 332.

133. Ibid.


## Chapter 4. The Occult Vision


1. Trithemius to Arnold Bostius, Sponheim, 26 March 1499, in *Polygraphia,* p. 100. Also pub. in Johann Weyer, *De praestigiis daemonum, incantationibus ac veneficiis libri VI* (Basel: Per Joannem Oporinum, 1566), pp. 150ff., and Athanasius Kircher, *Polygraphia nova et universalis* (Rome: Ex Typographia Varesii, 1663), "Appendix Apologetica," pp. 1–2. Though originally choosing the Palatinate prince Philip for the dedication of the *Steganographia,* Trithemius later changed his mind and addressed it to Joachim of Brandenburg, as disclosed in the *Annales Hirsaugienses,* II, 693.

2. See above, p. 7.

3. Trithemius to Bostius, in *Polygraphia,* pp. 100–103.

4. Cornelius Aurelius to Trithemius, Paris, ca. 1499, in P. C. Molhuysen, *Cornelius Aurelius: Korte Schets van Zijn Leven en Werken* (Leiden: S. C.

Van Doesburgh, 1902), pp. 28–32, esp. p. 31. Cf. Brann, *Trithemius*, pp. 30–31.

5. Trithemius to Aurelius, in ibid., pp. 32–34, esp. p. 33. On this exchange of correspondence see Arnold, *Trithemius*, p. 87, and Brann, *Trithemius*, pp. 228–29.

6. Bovillus to Germanus de Ganay, 8 March 1509 (?), in Bovillus, *Liber de intellectu* . . . (Paris: In aedibus Francisci de Hallewin, 1510; facsimile, Stuttgart-Bad Cannstatt: Friedrich Frommann Verlag [Günther Holzboog], 1970), sig. 172ʳ. Republished in Michel Mattaire, *Annales typographici ab artis inventae origine ad annum MDCLXIV*, 5 vols. (Vols. I–II: Den Haag: Apud Fratres Vaillart et Nicolaum Prevost, 1719–22; reprint, Graz, 1965), II, pp. 210–11. On the circumstances of the Bovillus visit see above, p. 7. The precise time of Bovillus's Sponheim visit has never been pinned down. Augustine Renaudet, *Préréforme et Humanisme à Paris Pendant les Premieres Gueres d'Italie (1494–1517)* (2d ed., Paris: Librairie d'Argences, 1953), pp. 417–18, places it in 1503, a dating confirmed by Joseph M. Victor, *Charles de Bouelles, 1479–1533: An Intellectual Biography* (Geneva: Droz, 1978), pp. 14, 31ff. But Arnold, *Trithemius*, p. 183, assigns the meeting to 1504.

7. Ibid.

8. Ibid.

9. Ibid., sigs. 172ʳ⁻ᵛ.

10. Ibid., sig. 172ᵛ–173ʳ.

11. On Lefèvre's interest in the arcana see Renaudet, *Prèrèforme et Humanisme,* p. 150; Thorndike, *Magic,* pp. 513ff.; and Walker, *Spiritual and Demonic Magic,* pp. 169–70. Cf. Eugene F. Rice, Jr., "The *De Magia Naturali* of Jacques Lefèvre d'Etaples," in Edward P. Mahoney, ed., *Philosophy and Humanism: Renaissance Essays in Honor of Paul Oskar Kristeller* (New York: Columbia University Press, 1976), pp. 19–29. On Bovillus's own occult interests, esp. in relation to the Druids, see Walker, *Ancient Theology,* pp. 77–78, and Victor, *Bouelles,* ch. 2, pp. 27ff. Cf. the posthumously added entry on Bovillus in Trithemius's *De scriptoribus ecclesiasticis,* in Freher, ed., *Opera historica,* I, 406. For an account of the arcane climate of thought within which the Frenchman Bovillus was working, see Copenhaver, *Symphorien Champier and the Reception of the Occultist Tradition in Renaissance France* (The Hague: Mouton, 1978).

12. It is puzzling as to why Bovillus took so long after his Sponheim visit, some five years if the 1509 date of this letter is correct, to register his indignation toward Trithemius's magic. Another puzzle, curiously ignored

by Arnold, p. 184 et passim, is how reference to this "1509" letter and its ensuing dispute was able to show up in the dedicatory preface of the *Polygraphia* to Emperor Maximilian, dated 26 April 1508. Both of these puzzles can be simultaneously solved by the hypothesis, verifiable only by reference to the missing original ms., that the "9" in Bovillus's date is a transposed "6," and therefore that the true date of the Bovillus letter to Ganay is 8 March 1506. Confirming this hypothesis is Will-Erich Peuckert, *Pansophie: Ein Versuch zur Geschichte der weissen und schwarzen Magie* (Stuttgart: W. Kohlhammer, 1936), p. 93.

13. Trithemius to Carolus Bovillus, Speyer, 22 August 1505, *Epistolae familiares*, I: 39, in Freher, ed., *Opera historica*, II, 476.

14. Germanus de Ganay to Trithemius, Paris, 30 July 1505, *Epistolae familiares*, I:33, in Freher, ed., *Opera historica*, II, 471.

15. Trithemius, *De triplici regione claustralium et spirituali exercitio monachorum,* pars I, tract. iii, in Busaeus, ed., *Opera pia,* p. 618. Also quoted in Brann, *Trithemius,* p. 194.

16. Trithemius, *Nepiachus,* in Johann Georg Eccard, ed., *Corpus historicum medii aevi,* 2 vols. (Leipzig: Apud Jo. Frid. Gleditschii B. Fil., 1723), II, col. 1829.

17. Ibid., col. 1831.

18. Trithemius to Bostius, in *Polygraphia,* pp. 102–103.

19. Trithemius, *Catalogus illustrium virorum Germaniae,* in Freher, ed., *Opera historica*, I, 141. Cf. *De scriptoribus ecclesiasticis,* in *Opera historica*, I, 292.

20. *Annales Hirsaugienses*, II, 40.

21. See above, p. 67. For an anecdote highlighting the purported magical powers of Albertus, credited by Trithemius to the fourteenth-century Netherlandish chronicler Johannes de Beka, see *Chronicon Sponheimense,* in Freher, ed., *Opera historica*, II, 280–81, and reiterated in *Annales Hirsaugienses*, I, 592. The specific marvel in question, pertaining to a visit of King Wilhelm of Holland to Albertus's convent in Cologne during the January feast of the Epiphany, consisted of temporarily transforming the conditions of winter into those of spring so that the king's party could be hosted in the convent's garden. Trithemius did not indicate whether he placed credence in this story.

22. *Annales Hirsaugienses,* II, 41.

23. *Nepiachus*, in Eccard, ed., *Corpus historicum* . . . , II, col. 1829. On this striking admission see also Arnold, *Trithemius*, p. 7, and Brann, *Trithemius*, p. 113.

24. Ibid., cols. 1829–31.

25. Trithemius to Count Johannes of Westerburg, Sponheim, 10 May 1503, *Epistolae*, in *De septem secundeis*, pp. 88–89.

26. Ibid., pp. 90–91.

27. Ibid., pp. 91–92.

28. Trithemius, *Steganographia, hoc est, ars per occultam scripturam animi sui voluntatem absentibus aperiendi certa* (Frankfurt: Ex officina typographica Mathiae Beckeri, sumptibus Joannis Berneri, 1606), pref., sig. ) : (4ʳ. A slightly modified version of this preface opens the *Clavis steganographiae*, bound with the main text in the 1606 edition, after appearing in the various post-1518 editions of the *Polygraphia* (e.g., Cologne, 1571, pp. 82ff.), with the title: "Apologia Joannis Trithemii praeposita Steganographiae." An English translation of books I and III of the *Steganographia*, the first by Fiona Tait and Christopher Upton and the second by J. W. H. Walden, has been made available in a limited edition by Adam McLean (Edinburgh: Magnum Opus Hermetic Sourceworks, 1982).

29. Trithemius to Johannes Capellarius, Würzburg, 16 August 1507, *Epistolae familiares*, II:43, in Freher, *Opera historica*, II, 555. This letter indicates that the first choice of Trithemius for receiving the dedication of the *Polygraphia* was Joachim of Brandenburg, not the emperor Maximilian, to whom it was eventually addressed and personally presented. Cf. *Nepiachus*, in Eccard, *Corpus historicum*, II, col. 1843. Trithemius's change of mind is recorded in the *Annales Hirsaugienses*, II, 693.

30. Ibid., pp. 555–56.

31. Trithemius to Emperor Maximilian, Würzburg, 25 April 1508, dedicatory epistle to *Polygraphia*, p. 24.

32. Ibid., pp. 24–25. On the chronological problem posed by the 1509 dating of Bovillus's letter to Ganay, see above, note 12.

33. Ibid., pp. 25–26.

34. Ibid., p. 26.

35. Ibid., p. 27.

36. *Annales Hirsaugienses*, II, 288. Excerpt in Ignatius P. Gropp, ed., *Collectio novissima scriptorum et rerum Wirceburgensium. . . . ,* Vol. I (Frankfurt: Ex officina Wolfgangianus, 1741), pp. 250–51.

37. Ibid. Though expressing regret when he came to this subject in his chronicles that he did not presently have the time to refute more fully Bovillus's vituperations, Trithemius apparently found such an opportunity later. For the final entry of the Hirsau annals, II, 692–93, dated 1513, refers to a work, now lost, beginning with the words *Contra Bovillum, qui me falsò magum & necromanticum . . . calumniatus est . . .* On this tract see Arnold, *Trithemius,* append., I, "deperdita," p. 255.

38. *Steganographia,* pref., sig. ) : (4$^r$.

39. Trithemius to Bostius, in *Polygraphia,* p. 103. Comparison here cannot help but be made between another dream reported by Trithemius to have also exerted a formative influence on his life, prompting him, still a teenager, to map out a career of letters. Concerning this "dream of the two tablets" see Arnold, *Trithemius,* pp. 6–7, and Brann, *Trithemius,* pp. 4–5.

40. *Steganographia,* pref., sig. ) : (2$^r$.

41. *Polygraphia,* pref., p. 17.

42. Ibid., lib. 6, pp. 610–11.

43. Ibid., pref., p. 27.

44. Trithemius to Johann Steinmoel, Cologne, 20 July 1505, *Epistolae familiares,* I:24, in Freher, *Opera historica,* II, 459.

45. Libanius Gallus to Trithemius, St. Quentin, 6 June 1505, *Epistolae familiares,* I:37, in Freher, *Opera historica,* II, 475. Also found in *De septem secundeis,* pp. 76–79. On Libanius's identity see François Secret, "Qui était Libanius Gallus, le maître de Jean Trithème?" *Estudios Lulianos,* 6 (1962), 127–37; Arnold, *Trithemius,* pp. 80–81; and Brann, *Trithemius,* pp. 201–202. The play upon Trithemius's name by Libanius (Tri=three) has the effect of linking the esoteric teachings mastered by the abbot with both the Christian Trinity and "thrice-great" Hermes Trimegistus, an epithet depending on a similar play on a name. However, the suggestion by Chacornac, *Jean Trithème,* p. 21, that Trithemius chose his name with the deliberate aim of fostering this triadic idea is nonsense. He received his name, as earlier indicated, for no better reason than that he hailed from the village of Trittenheim.

46. Ibid.

47. Trithemius to Libanius Gallus, Speyer, 20 August 1505, in ibid., p. 475. Letter also found in *De septem secundeis . . . ,* pp. 133–37.

48. Trithemius to Bostius, in *Polygraphia,* p. 103. On the role of the Heidelberg court in the patronage of letters at the time of Trithemius,

including magical literature, see Martina Backes, *Das literarische Leben am kurpfälzischen Hof zu Heidelberg im 15. Jahrhundert: Ein Beitrug zur Gönnerforschung des Spätmittelalters* (Tübingen: Max Niemeyer, 1992). Giving special attention to patronage of the occult arts in this milieu is Debra L. Stoudt, "'Probatum est per me': The Heidelberg Electors as Practitioners and Patrons of the Medical and Magical Arts," in *Cauda Pavonis,* 14 (1995): 12–18, with dedic. of *Steganographia* to Philip indicated at p. 13.

49. Ibid.

50. *Steganographia*, sig. ) : (3ᵛ.

51. Trithemius to Joachim of Brandenburg, Sponheim, 26 June 1503, *Epistolae,* in *De septem secundeis,* pp. 102, 104–105. On the abbot's special relationship to Joachim see Brann, *Trithemius,* pp. 85ff.

52. Trithemius to Emperor Maximilian, Würzburg, 26 April 1508, dedicatory epistle to *Polygraphia,* pp. 5–6. On the relationship between the abbot and Maximilan see Brann, *Trithemius,* pp. 91ff.

53. Ibid., pref., pp. 21–22. Reference here is to Matthias Corvinus (1440–90), best known for his attempts to import Renaisance humanism to Hungary. For an indication, however, that this preoccupation, coupled with a desire of his own to acquire the imperial crown, may have led Matthias into a policy more of temporizing with the Turks than with boldly confronting them as suggested by Trithemius, see Mirianna D. Birnbaum, "Humanism in Hungary," in Rabil, ed., *Renaissance Humanism,* II, 298.

54. Trithemius to Joachim (see above, note 51), p. 105.

55. *Polygraphia,* pref., p. 22.

56. Trithemius to Bostius, in *Polygraphia,* p. 103.

57. On Libanius see also above, pp. 103–104.

58. *Annales Hirsaugienses,* II, 587 (under year 1501). On Fernando, a.k.a. Pelagius, see Thorndike, *Magic,* IV, 486–87.

59. Ibid.

60. Ibid., pp. 585–86.

61. See above, p. 76.

62. *Nepiachus,* in Eccard, *Corpus historicum,* II, col. 1830.

63. Ibid.

64. Ibid., col. 1830–3. *Copyrighted Material*

65. Ibid., cols. 1820–31.

66. Trithemius to Bostius (see above, note 1), pp. 101–103.

67. *Steganographia*, pref., sig. ) : (2ᵛ On Trithemius's participation in the Cabalist tradition see Blau, *Christian Interpretation of the Cabala*, p. 80, and Secret, *Kabbalistes Chrétiens*, pp. 157–59. But according to Secret, p. 159: "La Kabbale chez Trithème semble jouer un petit rôle." Discovering in Cabala a key to Trithemius's cryptological operations, on the other hand, is Thomas Ernst, "Schwarzweisse Magie: Der Schlüssel zum dritten Buch der *Steganographia* des Trithemius," in *Daphnis: Zeitschrift für Mittlere Deutsche Literatur*, 25 (1996): 1–205, esp. pp. 6ff.

68. Ibid., sig. ) : (4ʳ.

69. *Nepiachus,* in Eccard, *Corpus historicum,* col. 1831.

70. Ibid.

71. Trithemius to Libanius (see above, note 47).

72. *Steganographia*, pref., sig. ) : (2ᵛ

73. *Polygraphia,* pref., p. 20.

74. Trithemius to Westerburg (see above, note 25), pp. 81ff., at pp. 93–94. A Paraphrase of this and the following letters, under the heading "De spagirico Artificio Io. Trithemii sententia," is found in Lazarus Zetzner, *Theatrum chemicum,* 6 vols. (Strassburg: Lazari Zetzneri, 1613–61), I, 425ff. On Pythagoreanism in its ancient setting see J. A. Philip, *Pythagoras and Early Pythagoreanism* (Toronto: University of Toronto Press, 1968), and Walter Burkert, *Lore and Science in Ancient Pythagoreanism,* trans. E. Minar (Cambridge, Mass.: Harvard University Press, 1972), and on characteristic Renaissance reapplications, S. K. Heninger, *Touches of Sweet Harmony: Pythagorean Cosmology and Renaissance Poetics* (San Marino, Calif.: Huntington Library, 1974), and Gary Tomlinson, *Music in Renaissance Magic: Toward a Historiography of Others* (Chicago: University of Chicago Press, 1993).

75. Ibid., pp. 95–96. On Cusanus see esp. Ernst Cassirer, *The Individual and the Cosmos in Renaissance Philosophy,* trans. Mario Domandi (New York: Harper, 1963), ch. 1, pp. 7ff. For the influence of Cusanus on Trithemius see Arnold, *Trithemius,* p. 196, the subject of which also features prominently in responses to a lead-off lecture by Arnold in a Bad Kreuznach symposium on Trithemius, pub. as *Johannes Trithemius: Humanismus und Magie im vorreformatorischen Deutschland,* ed. Richard Auernheimer and Frank Baron (Munich: Profil, 1991), "diskussion," esp. pp. 62–66. Cf. Brann, *Trithemius,* esp. pp. 196–201 and 296–97.

76. Ibid., pp. 82–83.

77. Ibid., p. 84.

78. Ibid., p. 99.

79. Ibid., pp. 87–88.

80. Ibid., pp. 97–98.

81. Ibid., p. 97.

82. Ibid., pp. 92–94.

83. Ibid., pp. 85–86.

84. Ibid., p. 97.

85. Trithemius to Joachim (see above, note 51), pp. 102, 105.

86. Ibid., pp. 106–107.

87. Ibid., pp. 107–108.

88. Ibid., pp. 108–109.

89. Ibid., pp. 110–11.

90. Ibid., pp. 112–13.

91. Ibid., pp. 114–15.

92. Trithemius to Johannes Capellarius (=Jean Chapellier), Cologne, 18 July 1505, *Epistolae familiares*, I:23, in Freher, *Opera historica*, II, 456–57. Also found in *De septem secundeis*, pp. 116–33.

93. Ibid., p. 457. For Trithemius's restatement of this doctrine in the context of monastic humanism, see Brann, *Trithemius*, pp. 128–30.

94. Ganay to Trithemius (see above, note 14), p. 471. As earlier indicated, p. 89–90, Ganay referred in the same letter, with no hint of the altercation to follow, to Bovillus's earlier Sponheim visit.

95. Trithemius to Ganay, Speyer, 24 August 1505, *Epistolae familiares*, I:34, in Freher, ed., *Opera historica*, II, 471. Letter also found in *De septem secundeis*, pp. 65–75. Concerning Libanius's identical play on the name of Trithemius, simultaneously linking him to the Christian trinity and to Trismegistus, see above, note 45. Legend has it that the thirteen alchemical precepts of the Emerald Table were found buried with Hermes Trismegistus in his Egyptian Tomb. For a complete list of these precepts in Latin (purportedly translated from Phoenician) see Julius Ruska, *Tabula Smaragdina: Ein Beitrag zur Geschichte der Hermetischen Literatur* (Heidelberg: Carl Winter, 1926), p. 2, and for an English translation, John Read,

*Prelude to Chemistry: An Outline of Alchemy* (London: G. Bell and Sons, 1936; 2d ed., 1939, repr. Cambridge: Massachussetts Institute of Technology, 1966), p. 54. While acknowledging Trithemius's part in propagating these precepts, Ruska apparently did not have access to the abbot's own writings, citing as evidence for his alchemical interests, pp. 206–207, the later paraphrased collection of his ideas, under the heading *De spagirico artificio,* included by Zetzner in his *Theatrum chemicum* (see above, note 74).

96. Ibid., pp. 471–72.

97. Ibid., p. 472.

98. Ibid. On this passage see Thorndike, *Magic*, VI, 438–39.

99. Ibid.

100. Ibid.

101. Ibid.

102. Trithemius to Nicholas von Merneck, Sponheim, 1487, *Epistolae ad familiares,* no. 15, in Busaeus, *Opera pia,* pp. 954–55.

103. Trithemius to Ganay (see note 95), p. 473.

104. Ibid.

105. *Polygraphia,* pref., p. 22.

106. Ibid., "pinax sive index," p. 36.

107. Ibid., p. 37. On the distinction between the two kinds of magic, natural and demonic, see esp. Walker, *Spiritual and Demonic Magic.* However, with his focus on Trithemius's effort to square his steganographical operations with a concept of spiritual magic (pp. 86–90), Walker left out of consideration altogether the much better case Trithemius made for this concept in his polygraphical handbook. Likewise did Couliano, *Eros and Magic,* whose consignment of Trithemius to the category "demonomagic," pp. 162ff., precluded any serious treatment of the abbot as a theorist of natural magic. For Couliano's merely passing consideration of the *Polygraphia,* see p. 171.

108. Ibid., lib. II, pp. 301–302.

109 Ibid., lib. III, p. 462.

110. Ibid., pp. 302–303. On the Cusan influence on Trithemius see also above, p. 117–18.

111. Ibid., "pinax sive index," pp. 39–34.

112. Ibid., lib. IV, pp. 509.

113. Trithemius to Jacob, 24 June 1507, *Epistolae familiares*, II:1, in Freher, ed., *Opera historica*, II, 506. On the importance of this letter for Trithemius's humanist program see Brann, *Trithemius,* pp. 284–91.

114. *Annales Hirsaugienses*, II, 40. This tract has also been ascribed by some scholars to Roger Bacon. For the controversy surrounding its author-ship see Thorndike, *Magic,* II, pp. 692ff.

115. Trithemius, *De septem secundeis, id est, intelligentiis sive spiritibus orbes post Deum moventibus libellus sive Chronologia mystica . . . ,* xvi, in Freher, *Opera historica,* I, sig. \*\*6ᵛ. First pub. at Nuremberg (H. Höltzel) in 1522.

116. Ibid., dedic. epist., in Freher, *Opera historica,* I, sig. \*\*4ʳ. On D'Abano's formulation of this scheme see above, p. 25, and on its adoption by Trithemius, Arnold, *Trithemius,* p. 163, and Brann, *Trithemius,* p. 94.

117. Ibid., sig. \*\*\*2ʳ. See also Brann, *Trithemius,* pref., p. xiii. Silber-nagel, *Trithemius,* p. 124, contests the view that in this passage Trithemius "habe die Reformation durch Luther vorher gesagt," maintaining rather that the abbot by these words only intended to articulate a general Caba-list pronouncement in accordance with the known martial characteristics of Samael's rule. But Schneegans, *Trithemius,* p. 183, takes issue with Silbernagel on this question, holding that Trithemius indicated, beyond general Cabalistic theorizing about the future, his apprehension of an impending religious crisis. Arnold, *Trithemius,* referring to this passage, p. 163, sidesteps this dispute.

118. Ibid., sig. \*\*\*2ʳ.

119. Trithemius indicated to Bostius that the *Steganographia* was origi-nally conceived in four books. Inexplicably, he expanded its projected scope to eight books before stopping in the middle of the third.

120. *Steganographia,* lib. I, cap. 1, p. 1.

121. Ibid., pp. 1–2.

122. Ibid., p. 2.

123. Ibid.

124. Ibid., lib. I, cap. 32, pp. 90–91.

125. Ibid., pp. 91–92.

126. Ibid., p. 92.

127. Ibid., pp. 92–93.

128. Ibid., lib. II, pref., pp. 94–95.

129. Ibid., lib. II, cap. 1, p. 96. Samael, as indicated in the *De septem secundeis,* is also a planetary angel, located in the sphere of Mars. In this dual capacity, as a temporal spirit of the hours and planetary angel, Samael would be expected to reappear in the third book if the tract were completed.

130. Ibid., pp. 96–97.

131. Ibid., lib. II, cap. 25, p. 157.

132. Ibid.

133. Ibid., pp. 157–58.

134. Ibid., p. 158.

135. Ibid.

136. Ibid., pp. 158–59. Scattered throughout this second book of the *Steganographia* are a number of exemplary texts, these in the form of epistles to acquaintances of Trithemius—Arnold Bostius, Roger Sicamber, Wilhelm Veldicus, and so on. All are dated 1500, though whether they were actually sent to their addressees is unclear. Arnold, *Trithemius,* p. 188, makes no mention of these letters in his cursory treatment of the second book. That he also omits them from his "Briefregister," appendix II, pp. 261ff., indicates that Arnold does not consider them a genuine part of Trithemius's epistolary collection. The inclusion among these of letters addressed to the already deceased Bostius would appear to support this contention.

137. Ibid, lib. III, pref., p. 163.

138. Ibid, p. 160. On Trithemius's historical fabrications see Paul Joachimsen, *Geschichtsauffasung und Geschichtschreibung in Deutschland unter dem Einfluss des Humanismus* (Leipzig/Berlin: B. G. Teubner, 1910), pp. 50ff., Frank L. Borchardt, *German Antiquity in Renaissance Myth* (Baltimore: Johns Hopkins Press, 1971), pp. 127ff., and "Wie falsch war der Fälscher Trithemius," in Auernheimer and Baron, ed., *Trithemius,* pp. 17–28; Arnold, *Trithemius,* pp. 167ff.; and Brann, *Trithemius,* pp. 96–97, 312–13.

139. Ibid., cap. 1, p. 174.

140. Ibid., p. 164.

141. Ibid., p. 174. *Copyrighted Material*

142. Trithemius, *Clavis steganographiae* (Frankfurt: Apud Joannem Bernerum, 1621), pp. 7, 10. The ponderous approach of Trithemius to cryptic communication is further illustrated by the "Hebraic" example furnished by Arnold, *Trithemius*, p. 188, in which forty-five words addressed to the spirit Parmesiel, counting every other letter of every other word, yields a mere thirteen-word Latin message. For further examples of Trithemius's cryptographical methods see Schneegans, *Trithemius*, pp. 196ff.; Chacornac, *Trithème*, pp. 137–39; Shumaker, *Renaissance Curiosa* (Binghamton, N.Y.: State University of New York Press, 1982), pp. 100ff.; Couliano, *Eros and Magic*, p. 170; and Ernst, "Schwarzweisse Magie," esp. pp. 20ff. For a bibliographical summary of Trithemius's contribution to the field of cryptography see Joseph S. Galland, *An Historical and Analytical Bibliography of the Literature of Cryptology* (New York: AMS Press, 1945), pp. 181–85.

143. Ibid., cap. 2, pp. 49ff.

144. Concerning the apparent methodological disparity between the first two and third books of Trithemius's steganographic manual see Walker, *Spiritual and Demonic Magic*, p. 87. However, demonstrating that the third book lends itself as readily to a cryptological analysis as the previous two is Ernst, "Schwarzweisse Magie." I thank Dr. Jim Reeds, a cryptographical specialist of AT&T Labs, for directing me to Professor Ernst's book-length article, also available as an independent volume by its Amsterdam publisher Rodopi. Reeds's independent solution of Trithemius's third book is scheduled to appear in a forthcoming issue of *Cryptologia*.

145. Ibid., lib. V, p. 551.

146. Shumaker, *Renaissance Curiosa*, p. 109, also furnishing a solution to a polygraphically construed message. Cf. David Kahn, *The Codebreakers: The Story of Secret Writing* (New York: Macmillan, 1967), pp. 130ff., esp. pp. 133–37, and Arnold, *Trithemius*, pp. 191–92. The text of this key is bound with the first ed. of the *Polygraphia* (Basel: M. Furter, 1518).

147. *Polygraphia*, lib. I, p. 104.

148. Ibid., lib. VI, pp. 580–82. Cf. pref., pp. 17–20.

149. Ibid., p. 580.

150. Ibid., p. 610.

151. Ibid., pp. 597–98.

152. Ibid., "pinax sive index," pp. 38–40.

153. Ibid., lib. VI, p. 601. Copyrighted Material

154. Conrad Mutian to Trithemius, 9 August 1513, in Mutian, *Der Briefwechsel*, ed. Carl Krause (Kassel: A. Freyschmidt, 1885), no. 285, p. 348. On Mutian's relationship with Trithemius see Arnold, *Trithemius*, pp. 98–99, and Brann, *Trithemius*, p. 26.

155. Agrippa of Nettesheim to Trithemius, prior to 8 April 1510, adjoined to Trithemius, *Epistolae familiares*, II, in Freher, ed., *Opera historica*, II, 572–73. This letter and its reply preface the 1533 printed edition of Agrippa's *De occulta philosophia libri III* (Cologne: 1533; facsimile, ed. Karl Anton Nowotny, Graz: Akademische Druck u. Verlagsanstalt, 1967), sigs. aa iii^r–iiii^r, and is found in English translation in *Three Books of Occult Philosophy or Magic: Book I—Natural Magic*, ed. Willis F. Whitehead (London, 1897; repr., London: Aquarian Press, 1971), pp. 28ff, and *Three Books of Philosophy*, ed. Donald Tyson, trans. James Freake (St. Paul: Llewellyn, 1995), pp. liii–lvii. A new ed. of the *De occulta philosophia* has been prepared by Vittore Perrone Compagni (Leiden: E. J. Brill, 1992). On the Trithemius-Agrippa meeting and subsequent relationship see Charles G. Nauert, Jr., *Agrippa and the Crisis of Renaissance Thought* (Urbana: University of Illinois Press, 1965), pp. 30–33; Arnold, *Trithemius*, pp. 185–86; Brann, *Trithemius*, pp. 116–17; and Tyson's intro. to *Three Books*, pp. xviiiff., and passim. For excerpts from Agrippa's tract see Eugenio Garin et al., eds., *Testi Umanistici su l'Ermetismo: Testi di Ludovico Lazzarelli, F. Giorgio Veneto, Cornelio Agrippa di Nettesheim* (Rome: Fratelli Bocca, 1955), pp. 137ff.

156. Ibid.

157. Ibid.

158. Ibid.

159. Trithemius to Agrippa, Würzburg, 8 April 1510, *Epistolae familiares*, II, in Freher, ed., *Opera historica*, II, 573–74 (*De occulta,* Cologne: 1533), sig. a iiii^r.

160. Agrippa, *Liber de triplici ratione cognoscendi Dei*, cap. 5, in *Opera,* II, 482. This passage also found in Agrippa, *Testi scelti*, ed. Paola Zambelli, in Eugenio Garin et al., eds. *Testi Umanistici*, p. 156.

161. Concerning this spurious attribution see Thorndike, *Magic*, V, 136. For an English trans. and affiililated writings see *Henry Cornelius Agrippa, his Fourth book of occult philosophy....*, trans. Robert Turner (London: Printed by J. C. for J. Harrison, 1655), and for a German one, *Heinrich Cornelius Agrippa's von Nettesheim Magische Werke....*, 5 vols. (Berlin: H. Barsdorf, 1921), the latter, V, 300ff., including Trithemius's pref. to the *Steganographia* and an excerpt from his *Octo quaestiones*.

162. On this inscription see Chacornac, *Trithème,* p. 85, and Brann, *Trithemius,* pp. 101–102. When, in 1720, the remains of Trithemius were removed to their present locale in the church of Neumünster, this inscription was removed and the simpler one showing today was put in its place.

## Chapter 5.  The Debate over Trithemian Magic

1. Johannes Rogerius Brennonius to Agrippa, Messin, prior to 15 June 1520, *Epistolae,* in Agrippa, *Opera,* 2 vols. (Lyons: Per Beringos fratres, n.d. [ca. 1620]; facsimile, Hildesheim: Georg Olms, 1970), II, 771; anonymous friend to *Agrippa,* Lyons, 7 October 1522, *Epistolae,* III:33, in *Opera,* II, 800. On the identity of Brennonius see Nauert, *Agrippa,* p. 62.

2. Agrippa to a friend (=Dionysius), Freiburg, 20 January 1524, *Epistolae,* III:54, in Agrippa, *Opera,* II, 812. On this letter see Nauert, *Agrippa,* p. 88. The "widely circulated writing" referred to in this passage was undoubtedly the now lost *Defensorium mei contra Caroli Bovilli mendacia,* listed by Arnold, *Trithemius,* append. I:f, p. 255, among the abbot's missing works. For an independent listing of some of the more notable contributors to the debate over Trithemian magic spearheaded by Bovillus, the subject of this chapter, see Ernst, "Schwarzweisse Magie," pp. 70ff.

3. Agrippa, *De occulta philosophia*, lib. I, cap. 6, pp. vi–ix (facsimile, pp. 18–21). On this reference see Walker, *Spiritual and Demonic Magic,* pp. 88–89, with a translated excerpt.

4. Agrippa, *De incertitudine et vanitate omnium scientiarum et artium liber,* cap. 64: "De lenonia," in *Opera,* II, 127–28. Hereafter, cited as *De vanitate.* On Agrippa's seeming self-contradiction see Walker, *Spiritual and Demonic Magic,* p. 90; Nauert, *Agrippa;* p. 106; and Copenhaver, "Astrology and Magic," in Schmitt et al., eds., *Renaissance Philosophy,* pp. 264–65. The *De vanitate* was published at Antwerp in 1530; lib. I of the *De occulta philosophia,* together with further editions of the *De vanitate,* at Antwerp, Paris, and Cologne in 1531; and the first complete edition of the *De occulta philosophia* at Cologne in 1533.

5. For Agrippa's very tentative relationship to Protestantism see Nauert, *Agrippa,* esp. pp. 172–73, and for the underlying compatibility between Agrippa's skepticism and his magic, p. 237, with the key part of Cusanus in this development indicated at p. 333. Maintaining that Trithemius had an influence on Agrippa's skepticism as well as on his magic is an article by Paola Zambelli, "A proposito del *De vanitate scientiarum et artium* di Cornelio Agrippa," *Rivista Critica di Storia della Filosofia,* 2 (1960): 167–81, esp. 177–78.

6. Conrad Gesner, *Bibliotheca universalis, sive catalogus omnium scriptorum locupletissimus, in tribus linguis, Latina, Graeca, & Hebraica* (Zürich: Apud Christophorum, 1545), fol. 459$^r$.

7. Erasmus to George Halewin, Louvain, 21 June 1520, in Erasmus, *Opus epistolarum,* ed. P. S. Allen, 12 vols. (Oxford: Oxford University Press, 1910), IV, no. 1115, p. 290. On the humanist philological methods shared by Trithemius and Erasmus see Arnold, *Trithemius,* p. 49, and Brann, *Trithemius,* pp. 228ff. But emphasizing a basic split within the humanist movement regarding occult studies is Zika, "Reuchlin and Erasmus . . . ." (see above, ch. 2, note 56). On Trithemius's view of Cicero as a cryptological precursor see above, p. 148.

8. See, e.g., Pictorius's *De illorum daemonum qui sub lunari collimatio versantur . . . isagoge. . . .* (Basel: Per Henricum Petri, 1563), with the authority of Trithemius invoked at pp. 24, 33, and 44. For English and German translations, annexed to editions of Agrippa's apocryphal fourth book of *De occulta philosophia,* see above, ch. 4, note 161. On Pictorius see Thorndike, *Magic,* VI, pp. 399ff., with this tract treated pp. 404–406. Trithemius's contribution to the *Theatrum de veneficis* (Frankfurt: Nicolaus Basseus, 1586) is found on pp. 355–66. For studies of the later witch hunts see Hughes, *Witchcraft,* pp. 163ff.; Trevor-Roper, *European Witch-Craze,* pp. 90ff.; Klaits, *Servants of Satan,* pp. 48ff.; Scarre, *Witchcraft and Magic;* and Brian Levack, *The Witch-Hunt in Early Modern Europe* (2d ed., London: Longman, 1995; first ed., 1987). Focusing on misogyny in this development is Anne Llewellyn Barstow, *Witchcraze: A New History of the European Witch Hunts* (San Francisco: HarperCollins [Pandora], 1994). Geared to the theoretical principles of demonology during this period are Shumaker, *Occult Sciences,* ch. 2, pp. 60ff. and Sydney Anglo, ed., *The Damned Art: Essays in the Literature of Witchcraft* (London: Routledge & Kegan Paul, 1977). For regional studies of the witch hunts see Alan Macfarlane, *Witchcraft in Tudor and Stuart England* (London: Routledge & Kegan Paul, 1970); Keith Thomas, *Religion and the Decline of Magic: Studies in Popular Beliefs in Sixteenth and Seventeenth Century England* (London: Weidenfeld and Nicolson, 1971); H. C. Midelfort, *Witch Hunting in Southwestern Germany, 1562–1684: The Social and Intellectual Foundations* (Stanford: Stanford University Press, 1972); E. William Monter, *Witchcraft in France and Switzerland: The Borderlands during the Reformation* (Ithaca, N.Y.: Cornell University Press, 1976); Ruth Martin, *Witchcraft and the Inquisition in Venice, 1550–1650* (Oxford: Basel Blackwell, 1989); and Gerhild Scholz Williams, *Defining Dominion: The Discourses of Magic and Witchcraft in Early Modern France and Germany* (Ann Arbor: University of Michigan Press, 1995).

9. André Thevet, *Pourtraits et vies des hommes illustres....* (Paris: I. Keruert et Guillaume Chaudiere, 1584), I, liv. I, ch. 80, fols. 164$^{r-v}$. Excerpt repr. in Trithemius, *Opera historica*, ed. Freher, I, sigs. 883$^{r-v}$.

10. Wolfgang Trefler to Wolfgang de Solms, Mainz, 12 August 1508, in Magnoald Ziegelbauer and Oliver Legipont, *Historia rei literariae ordinis sancti Benedicti*, 4 parts (Augsburg/Würzburg: Sumptibus M. Veith, 1754; facsimile, Westmead, 1967), I, 493. On Trefler's relationship to Trithemius see Arnold, *Trithemius*, pp. 140–41, and Brann, *Trithemius*, pp. 330–31, 365–68.

11. Johann Butzbach, *Auctarium de scriptoribus eclesiasticis*, excerpted in Eduard Böcking, ed., *Ulrichi Hutteni equitis operum supplementum: Epistolae obscurorum virorum cum illustrantibus scriptis*, 2 vols. (Leipzig: B. G. Teubner, 1869–70; repr. Osnabrück, 1966), II, 487–88. On Butzbach's relationship to Trithemius see Arnold, *Trithemius*, pp. 137ff. and passim, and Brann, *Trithemius*, pp. 368–77, and on his ardent defense of Trithemius's magic, Zambelli, "Scholastic and Humanistic Views of Hermeticism and Witchcraft," in Merkel and Debus, *Hermeticism and the Renaissance*, pp. 131–32.

12. Ibid., pp. 488–89.

13. Butzbach, *Macrostroma de laudibus tritemianis...*, Bonn, Universitätsbibliothek, MS no. 357, lib. VI, fols. 186$^{r-v}$.

14. Martin Luther, *Werke: Tischreden*, 6 vols. (Weimar: Hermann Böhlaus, 1912–21), II, no. 1349, and III, no. 2951. Cf. IV, no. 4857. These recollections of Luther's mealtime pronouncements were first inscribed by Anton Lauterbach (1538–1540), and augmented several decades later (1566) by Johann Aurifaber. For the impact of the Reformation on the debate over magic see Levack, *Witch-Hunt*, ch. 4, pp. 100ff.

15. *Tischreden*, IV, no. 4450. Two versions of these remarks appear in the Weimar ed., the first, in Latin, from Lauterbach's *Tagebuch* for 29 March 1539, and the second, in the vernacular, in Aurifaber's 1566 ed. of the *Tischreden*. Whereas Lauterbach's earlier version does not expressly identify Trithemius as Maximilian's necromancer, mentioning only "a certain magician" (quidam magus), Aurifaber assigns the name of Trithemius to the hitherto anonymous magician. On Aurifaber's augmented rendition of the relevant passage see Baron, "Precarious Legacy," in Fleischer, ed., *Harvest of Humanism*, p. 310.

16. Johannes Manlius, *Locorum communium collectanea...per annos, pleraque tum ex lectionibus D. Philippi Melanchthonis....* (Basel: Per Joannem Oporinum, 1563), par. I, pp. 42–43. As noted by Baron, "Precarious

Legacy," in Fleischer, ed., *Harvest of Humanism,* pp. 307–308, Melanchthon also related conjurational activities of an unnamed necromancer in the court of Maximilian resembling Luther's remarks in the Lauterbach version.

17. Tille, *Faustsplitter,* no. 12, pp. 14–16. Cf. Samuel Meier, *De panurgia lamiarum . . . libri III* (Hamburg, 1587), ch. 4, sigs. K ii^v–iii^r, excerpted in Tille, pp. 71–73. For a list of sources relating to the mingling of the two legends see above, ch. 1, note 6. Thus Baron, "Precarious Legacy," in Fleischer, ed., *Harvest of Humanism,* p. 306, points up the irony that "the enemy of Faustus (viz., Trithemius) became transformed into himself."

18. Ricardus Argentinus, *De praestigiis et incantationibus daemonum et necromanticorum liber* (Basel: 1568), ch. 12, p. 78. On this tract see Thorndike, *Magic,* VI, 520–21.

19. Johannes Scultetus, *Gründlicher Bericht von Zauberey und Zauberern* (1598), in Tille, ed., *Faustsplitter,* no. 51, p. 100. Scultetus apparently did not count Paracelsus among these diabolically driven sorcerers. According to Thorndike, *Magic,* VI, 224 note, Scultetus was a teacher of Huser, editor of the first edition of Paracelsus's writings in 1589, and was principally responsible for the preservation of Paracelsus's works in ms.

20. Caspar Goltwurm, *Wunderzeichen Buch . . . zu warnung des menschlichen geschlecht geoffenbaret* (Frankfurt: 1567), fol. 130^r–v. On Goltwurm's invocation of this Trithemian anecdote see Bernward Deneke, "Kaspar Goltwurm: Ein Lutherischer Kompilator zwischen Überlieferung und Glaube," in Wolfgang Brückner, ed., *Volkserzählung und Reformation: Ein Handbuch zur Tradierung und Funktion von Erzählliteratur im Protestantismus* (Berlin: Erich Schmidt Verlag/Druck: A. W. Hayn's Erben, 1974), pp. 125ff. (at p. 158), and Baron, "Trithemius and Faustus," in Auernheimer and Baron, ed., *Trithemius,* pp. 46–48, and "Precarious Legacy," in Fleischer, ed., *Harvest of Humanism,* pp. 309–10. According to Baron, p. 310, it was Goltwurm who identified Trithemius as Maximilian's unnamed necromancer for Luther's editor Aurifaber.

21. Hermann Witekind (=Augustin Lercheimer), *Christlich bedencken und erinnerung von Zauberey. . . .* (Speyer: Bernhart Albin, 1597; repr., ed., Carl Binz, 1885, 2d ed., 1888), pp. 36–37. First ed., 1585. This section of Witekind's tract is also included in the *Theatrum de veneficis,* pp. 261–98. According to Thorndike, *Magic,* VI, 41, Witekind was a professor of mathematics at Neustadt.

22. Ibid., p. 40.

23. On Witekind's lenient approach to witches, as contrasted to his harsh approach to professional magicians like Trithemius, see Midelfort,

*Witch Hunting in Southwestern Germany,* p. 57. Cf. Baron, "Trithemius and Faustus," in Auernheimer and Baron, *Trithemius,* pp. 49ff.

24. Johann Weyer (=Wier), *De praestigiis daemonum, et incantationibus ac veneficiis libri VI* (1583), in *Opera omnia* (Amsterdam: Apud Petrum Vanden Berge, 1660), lib. IV, cap. 25, p. 339. First ed., Basel: Per Joannem Oporinum, 1563; repr. 1564, 1566. A recent English trans. has been rendered as *Witches, Devils, and Doctors in the Renaissance,* eds., George Mora and Benjamin Kohl, trans., John Shea, Medieval and Renaissance Texts and Studies, vol. 73 (Binghamton: State University of New York Press, 1991). On Weyer's principled resistance to the witch persecutions see Thorndike, *Magic,* VI, ch. 46, pp. 515ff.; Gregory Zilboorg and George W. Henry, *A History of Medical Psychology* (New York: W. W. Norton, 1941), pp. 206ff; Walker, *Spiritual and Demonic Magic,* pp. 152–56; and, most recently, the intro. to the English trans. of *De praestigiis daemonum,* cited above, pp. xxviiff. But downplaying Weyer's importance in this regard are two contributions to Sydney Anglo, ed., *Damned Art:* Christopher Baxter, "Johann Weyer's *De praestigiis daemonum:* Unsystematic Psychostherapy," pp. 53–75, and Anglo, "Reginald Scot's *Discoverie of Witchcraft:* Scepticism and Sadduceeism," pp. 106–39. The inclusion of an excerpt from Weyer's *De praestigiis* in the witch-abhorring *Theatrum de veneficis,* pp. 393–96, lends confirmation to this revised view of Weyer.

25. Weyer, *De praestigiis daemonum,* lib. II, cap. 6, in *Opera omnia,* pp. 112–14. The reference to the Maximilian conjurations is found in lib. I, cap. 16, pp. 46–47. On the personal association of Weyer and Agrippa see Thorndike, *Magic,* V, 129, 137, and Nauert, *Agrippa,* pp. 113–14.

26. Johann Georg Godelmann, *De magis, veneficis et lamiis recta cognoscendis et puniendis libri III* (Frankfurt: Ex Off. Typ. Nicolai Bassaei, 1591, lib. II, cap. 2, pp. 9–10. On Godelmann's part in opposing the witch persecutions see Thorndike, *Magic,* VI, 535–37, and Shumaker, *Occult Sciences,* p. 67. On Trithemius's contribution to this argument see lib. II, cap. 3, p. 42: "Joannes Tritemius in tractatu de Maleficis. . . ." This tract is likely the lost *De morbo caduco et maleficiis libri III,* listed in Arnold, *Trithemius,* append. f: "Deperdita," p. 257.

27. Ibid., lib. I, cap. 4, p. 36.

28. Girolamo Cardano, *De rerum varietate libri XVII* (Basel: Per Henrichum Petri, 1557), lib. VIII, cap. 40, p. 509. Cf. lib. XV, cap. 80, p. 573. On Cardano's naturalistic skepticism see Thorndike, *Magic,* V, ch. 26, pp. 563ff. Yet on a credulous streak in Cardano, prompting him to the casting of a horoscope for Christ, see Shumaker, *Occult Sciences,* pp. 36–37, and *Renaissance Curiosa,* ch. 2, pp. 53ff. For Vanini's joint criticism of

Cardano and Trithemius in this regard, charging the former with having even subjected the birth of the "heretic" Luther to the astrological influences envisaged in the *De septem secundeis* by the latter—see his *Amphitheatrum aeternae providentiae*. . . . (Lyons: Apud Viduam Antonii de Harsy, 1615), exerc. 8, p. 67. But for testimony that Vanini's skepticism also extended to the *Steganographia*, the incantations of which he held to effect, not changes in the real world as popularly maintained, but only changes in the hearing of their auditor, see exerc. 6, p. 40. For evidence that Cardano likewise dabbled in the cryptographical art popularly associated with the abbot's name see Kahn, *Codebreakers*, pp. 143–45.

29. Ibid., lib. XII, cap. 61, p. 457.

30. Jean Bodin, *De magorum daemonomania*. . . . (Frankfurt: Typis Wolffgangi Richteri, impensis . . . Nicolai Bassaei, 1603), p. 483. On the Weyer-Bodin debate see Thorndike, *Magic*, VI, 525–27; Walker, *Spiritual and Demonic Magic*, pp. 171–77; and Baxter, "Jean Bodin's *De la Demonomanie des Sorciers: The Logic of Persecution*," in Anglo, ed., *Damned Art*, pp. 76–105.

31. Antonio Zara, *Anatomia ingeniorum et scientiarum* (Venice: Ambrosii Dei & Fratrum, 1615), esp. sect. II, memb. 2: "De magicis artibus," pp. 154ff. Zara was the bishop of Biben in Istria.

32. Ibid., sect. II, memb. 13, p. 270.

33. Thorndike, *Magic*, VII, 282.

34. See Franz Heinrich Reusch, *Der Index der Verbotenen Bücher: Ein Beitrag zur Kirchen -und Literaturgeschichte*, 2 vols. (Bonn: Max Cohen & Sohn, 1885), II, 182–83.

35. Martin Delrio (=Del Rio), *Disquisitionum magicarum libri VI* (Venice: Apud Vincentium Florinum, 1616), lib. II, qu. 3, p. 87. First ed., Louvain: 1599. Walker, *Spiritual and Demonic Magic*, pp. 178–85, largely on the basis of his acceptance of certain forms of natural magic, perceives Delrio as a moderate among the demonologists. For insight into Delrio's occult beliefs see Shumaker, *Natural Magic and Modern Science*, ch. 3, pp. 71ff.

36. Antonio Possevino, *Apparatus sacer*, 2 vols. (Cologne: Apud Joannem Gimnicum sub Monocerote, 1608), II, 945–46.

37. Robert Bellarmine, *De scriptoribus ecclesiasticis liber I* (Lyons: Sumptibus Horatii Boissat & Georgii Remeus, 1663), 400–401. Made a cardinal in 1599, Bellarmine was canonized in 1930.

38. See, e.g., Walker's treatment of Delrio, *Spiritual and Demonic Magic*, pp. 178ff.

39. Bellarmine, *Disputationes . . . de controversiis Christianae fidei adversus huius temporis haereticos*, 3 vols. [in six bindings] (Ingolstadt: Ex Typographia Adami Sartorii, 1605), III, lib. I, cap. 20, p. 112.

40. Arnold Wion, *Lignum vitae, ornamentum, et decus ecclesiae. . . .* (Venice: Apud G. Angelerium, 1595). German trans.: *Lignum vitae. Baum des Lebens. . . .* (Augsburg: In Verlegung Domini Custodis, 1606).

41. Francesco Giorgi, *De harmonia mundi totius cantica tria* (Venice: In aedibus Bernardini de Vitalibus Chalcographi, 1525), cant. III, ton. 4, cap. 12: "Solus homo bene chordatus cum Deo vivit laetus." Cf. Garin et al., *Testi scelti*, pp. 94–95. On Giorgi's philosophical-magical program of concordances see Thorndike, *Magic*, VI, 450–52; Walker, *Spiritual and Demonic Magic*, pp. 112ff.; and Yates, *Occult Philosophy*, pp. 29ff. For Giorgi's influence on art history, springing from the application of his harmonizing principles to the Franciscan convent of San Francesco della Vigna in Venice, see Rudolf Wittkower, *Architectural Principles in the Age of Humanism*, first pub. as vol. 19, *Studies of the Warburg Institute*, 1949, rev. ed. (London: Alec Tiranti, 1962, 1971), pp. 102ff.

42. Francesco Patrizi (=Patrizzi) da Cherso, *Magia philosophica. . . .* (Hamburg: Ex Biblioteca Ranzoviana, 1593), fol. 20v.

43. Patrizi, *Nova de universis philosophia. . . .* (Ferrara: Apud Benedictum Mammarellum, 1591), pref., fol. 1ʳ. Also cited in Walter Scott, ed., trans. *Hermetica*, 4 vols. (Oxford: Clarendon Press, 1924), I, intro., pp. 36–40, esp. p. 39. On this appeal to the papacy see Yates, *Bruno*, pp. 182–83, and Walker, *Ancient Theology*, pp. 11–12.

44. As pointed out by Trevor-Roper, *European Witch-Craze*, p. 91: ". . . there can be no doubt that the witch-craze grew, and grew terribly, after the Renaissance. . . . The years 1550–1600 were worse than the years 1500–1550, and the years 1600–1650 were worse still." Cf. Irving Kirsch, "Demonology and the Rise of Science: An Example of the Misperception of Historical Data," *Journal of the History of the Behavioral Sciences*, 14 (1978), 149–157 (at p. 152): "The longest wave of trials occurred in Europe in the 1660s coinciding with the establishment of the Royal Society of London." Reinforcing this thesis in the same journal is Kirsch's "Demonology and Science during the Scientific Revolution," 16 (1989), 359–68. For further scholarly verifications see above, note 8.

45. Giovanni Battista della Porta, *Magiae naturalis libri viginti* (Rouen: Sumptibus Joannis Berthelin, 1650), sig. A 2ᵛ First ed., 1558.

46. On Della Porta's cryptographical experiments see Kahn, *Codebreakers*, pp. 137–43, and Shumaker, *Renaissance Curiosa*, pp. 114ff. For evidence of Della Porta's awareness of Trithemius see his *De furtivis*

*literarum notis vulgo, de ziferis libri IV* (London: Apud Johannem Wolphium, 1591), pp. 110–11. An earlier ed. appeared at Naples in 1563, and later was repub. as *De occultis literarum notis . . . expiscandi enodandique. . . .* (Strassburg: Impensis Lazari Zetzneri, 1606). On Count Friedrich's *Steganographia nova* see Ernst, "Schwarzweiss Magie," pp. 115–17. According to Ernst, pp. 115–16, note 565, three variant versions of this work (Kassel, 4° Ms. philol. 10, and Wolfenbüttel, Cod. Guelf. 54 Aug. 4° and 56 Aug. 4°), were errantly located by Arnold, *Trithemius*, append. I, p. 260, among writings spuriously ascribed to Trithemius himself.

47. Johannes Aventinus, pref. to Bede, *Abacus atque vetustissima veterum Latinorum per digitos manusque numerandi (quin etiam loquendi) consuetudo. . . .* , in *Sämmtliche Werke*, 6 vols. (Munich: Christian Kaiser, 1881–1908), I, 608. First ed., Regensburg: 1532. For a biography of Aventinus see Gerald Strauss, *Historian in an Age of Crisis: The Life and Work of Johannes Aventinus, 1477–1534* (Cambridge, Mass.: Harvard University Press, 1963).

48. John Dee to Sir William Cecil, Antwerp, 16 February 1563, repr. *Philobiblon Society: Bibliographical and Historical Miscellanies* (London: Charles Whittingham, 1854), I, 9–11. For this letter see also Gerald Suster, ed., *John Dee: Essential Readings* (London: Aquarius, 1986), pp. 22–29, which also furnishes excerpts from the *Monas*, pp. 30ff., derived from C. H. Josten, "A Translation of John Dee's Monas Hieroglyphical (Antwerp, 1564), with an Introduction and Annotations," *Ambix*, 12 (1964): 84–220. For a thumbnail sketch of Dee's life see Suster's introduction to *Essential Readings*, pp. 9–13, and for full-scale biographies, Charlotte Fell Smith, *John Dee (1527–1608)* (London: Constable & Co., 1909), Richard Deacon, *John Dee: Scientist, Geographer, Astrologer and Secret Agent to Elizabeth I* (London: Frederick Muller, 1968) and Peter J. French, *John Dee: the World of an Elizabethan Magus* (London: Routledge & Kegan Paul, 1972). Focusing on Dee's arcane interests are Yates, *Theatre of the World* (Chicago: University of Chicago, 1969), ch. 1, pp. 1ff., *Rosicrucian Enlightenment*, pp. 30ff., and *Occult Philosophy* pp. 79ff.; Josten, introduction to "Translation," pp. 84–111; and Nicholas H. Clulee, *John Dee's Natural Philosophy: Between Science and Religion* (London: Routledge, 1988). Cf. Clulee, "At the Crossroads of Magic and Science: John Dee's Archemastrie," in Vickers, ed., *Occult and Scientific Mentalities*, pp. 57–71 and "John Dee and the Paracelsians," in Debus and Walton, eds., *Reading the Book of Nature*, pp. 111–31. For Dee's cryptographical experiments see Shumaker, *Renaissance Curiosa*, pp. 15ff. Focusing on a single ms. (Sloan MS 3188) to illustrate Dee's magical methods is Christopher Whitby, *John Dee's Actions with Spirits. . . .* , 2 vols. (New York: Garland, 1988). Taking exception to what he considte Yates, too much emphasis

on Dee's magical reputation, however, is his most recent biographer, William H. Sherman, in *John Dee: The Politics and Reading and Writing in the English Renaissance* (Amherst: University of Massachussetts Press, 1995), esp. pp. 12ff.

49. On this cryptographical vogue, especially with attention to its value in communicating secrets of state, see Aloys Meister, *Die Anfänge der Modernen Diplomatischen Geheimschrift* (Paderborn: F. Schöningh, 1902); Ernst Dröscher, *Die Methoden der Geheimschriften* (Leipzig: K. F. Koehler, 1921); James Westfall Thompson and Saul K. Padover, *Secret Diplomacy, Espionage and Cryptography (1500–1815)* (New York: F. Ungar, 1963); Kahn, *Codebreakers*; and James Raymond Wolfe, *Secret Writing: The Craft of the Cryptographer* (New York: 1970). For a bibliographical listing of contributors to this tradition, carried to modern times, see Galland, *Historical and Analytical Bibliography*.

50. Dee, *Preface to Euclid* (1570), in Suster, ed., *Dee: Essential Readings*, p. 45. On this theoretical contribution of Trithemius to Dee see Josten, "Translation" (see above, note 48), pp. 108–110, and Clulee, *Dee's Natural Philosophy*, with extensive references to the abbot at pp. 103–105, 110–114, 136–139, and 218–220.

51. According to French, *Dee*, pp. 120–21, the author of the *Monas* went so far in his personal commitment to a credo of universal religion as to seek spiritual counsel from a Capuchin monk and to take Catholic communion.

52. Blaise de Vigenère, *Traicté des chiffres, ou secretes manieres descrire* (Paris: Chez Abel L'Angelier, 1586), fol. 12$^v$. Chapters are unnumbered. Widening the influence of Trithemius on Vigenère's home soil was the French trans. of the *Polygraphia* by Gabriel de Collange (Paris: J. Kerver, 1561, repr. 1625).

53. Ibid., fol. 3$^r$.

54. Ibid., fols. 12$^v$, 13$^v$.

55. Jacques Gohory (=Leo Suavius), *De usu et mysteriis notarum liber* (Paris: Apud V. Sertenas, 1550). For Trithemius's influence on this tract see James Riddick Partington, *A History of Chemistry*, 4 vols. (London: Macmillan, 1961), II, 162. For a more recent inquiry into the chemical-alchemical connection during this time see Piyo Rattansi and Antonio Clericuzio, eds., *Alchemy and Chemistry in the Sixteenth and Seventeenth Centuries* (Boston: Kluwer, 1994).

56. For the literature pertinent to this question see my article "Was Paracelsus a Disciple of Trithemius?" *Sixteenth Century Journal*, 10 (1979):

70–82. For a modern scholar's view of Trithemius's part in preparing the ground for the Paracelsian movement see Peuckert, *Pansophie* pp. 78–98, and for another scholar's more direct linkage of the two magicians through a Cabalistic analysis of their outlooks, which he distinguishes from the Hermetic one informing the above article, see Ernst, "Schwarzweisse Magie," pp. 109–10 and note 546.

57. Theophrastus Paracelsus, *Selected Writings*, ed., Jolande Jacobi, trans. Norbert Guterman (London: Routledge & Kegan Paul, 1951), p. 213–14. For brief presentations of the Paracelsian movement see Thorndike, *Magic*, V, ch. 29, pp. 617ff., and, more up to date, Heinrich Schipperges, "Paracelsus and his Followers," in Faivre, *Modern Esoteric Spirituality*, pp. 154ff. For fuller treatments see P. Raymund Netzhammer, *Theophrastus Paracelsus: Das Wissenswerteste über dessen Leben, Lehre und Schriften* (Einsiedeln-Waldshut-Köln: Benziger, 1901; Karl Sudhoff, *Paracelsus: Ein deutsches Lebensbild aus den Tagen der Renaissance* (Leipzig: Bibliographisches Institut, 1936); Henry M. Pachter, *Paracelsus: Magic into Science* (New York: Henry Schuman, 1951); Heinz Pächter, *Paracelsus: Das Urbild des Doktor Faustus* (Zürich: Büchergilde Gutenberg, 1955); Walter Pagel, *Paracelsus: An Introduction to Philosophical Medicine in the Era of the Renaissance* (Basel/New York: S. Karger, 1958), *Das Medizinische Weltbild des Paracelsus: Seine Zusammenhänge mit Neuplatonismus und Gnosis* (Wiesbaden: Franz Steiner, 1962), and *The Smiling Spleen: Paracelsianism in Storm and Stress* (Basel: S. Karger, 1984); and Allen G. Debus, *The Chemical Philosophy: Paracelsian science and Medicine in the Sixteenth and Seventeenth Centuries*, 2 vols. (New York: Science History Publications, div. of Neale Watson Academic Publications, 1977). Most recently see Joachim Telle, ed., *Parega Paracelsica: Paracelsus in Vergangenheit und Gegenwart* (Stuttgart: Steiner, 1992) and Andrew Weeks, *Paracelsus: Speculative Theory and the Crisis of the Early Reformation* (Albany, N.Y.: State University of New York Press, 1997).

58. Vigenère, *Tractatus de igne et sale*, in Zetzner, ed., *Theatrum Chemicum*, VI, 76–77.

59. Cesare della Riviera, *Il magico mondo degli heroi* (Mantua: Per Francesco Osanna, 1603), lib. II, p. 108. For further evidence of Trithemius's influence on Della Riviera, see p. 209. On this tract see Thorndike, *Magic*, VI, 275–76.

60. Gerard Dorn, *Tractatus de naturale luce physica, ex Genesi desumta, iuxta sententiam Theophrasti Paracelsi*, in Zetzner, ed., *Theatrum Chemicum*, I (1613), 420ff. esp. pp. 427–28. French trans. in Chacornac, *Trithème*, pp. 125–31. As related by Thorndike, *Magic*, V, 630ff., Dorn translated a number of Paracelsus's German writings into Latin, thus promoting their wider dissemination throughout Europe. For a discussion

of this particular tract see Debus, *Chemical Philosophy*, I, 77–78. Cf. Dorn's *De medio spagirico dispositionis ad adeptae philosophiae veram cognitionem, & lucis naturae purum conspectum*, in Zetzner, I, 428–32.

61. Conrad Gesner to Johannes Cratonus à Crafftheim, Zürich, 16 August 1561, *Epistolae medicinaliae libri III* (Zürich: Excudebat Christoph Frosch, 1577), lib. I, fol. 1ᵛ. On Gesner's criticism of Trithemius's steganography see above, p. 160.

62. Gohory, *Scholia in libros IV Ph. Theoph. Paracelsi de vita longa*, pref., in Paracelsus, *Libri V de vita longa, brevi, et sana* (Frankfurt: Christoph Rab, 1583), pp. 161, 165. On Gohory's Paracelsus commentary see Walker, *Spiritual and Demonic Magic*, pp. 96–106, and Debus, *Chemical Philosophy*, I, 146–48. Cf. Debus, *The French Paracelsians: The Chemical Challenge to Medical and Scientific Tradition in Early Modern France* (Cambridge: Cambridge University Press, 1991), pp. 26–28.

63. Ibid., pp. 168–69.

64. Gohory, *Scholia*, pref., in Paracelsus, *De vita longa*, p. 169.

65. Ibid.

66. Jean-Jacques Boissard, *Tractatus posthumus . . . de divinatione et magicis praestigiis, quarum veritas ac vanitas solida exponitur* (Strassburg-Oppenheim: Johannes Theodorus de Bry, [1615]), cap. 5, p. 49. Thorndike, *Magic*, VI, 504, characterizes this tract as "in the main a stale farrago of bits from various past authors such as Trithemius . . . with no relation to science." However, apart from the fact that our focus here is the relationship of magic to religion rather than to science, the value of this writing for our purposes lies more in its role as a propagandizer of Trithemian magical ideals than in its intrinsic scholarly merits.

67. On this strategy of the De Bry press see Yates, *Rosicrucian Enlightenment*, ch. 6, pp. 70ff.

68. Johann Cambilhon (=Cambilhom), *De studiis Jesuitarum abstrusioribus et consiliis eorum sanguinariis* (1608), in Petrus de Wangen, *Physiognomonia Jesuitica. . . .* (Lyons: 1610), pp. 152–69 (at pp. 161–62).

69. Jacob Gretser, *Relatio de studiis Jesuitarum abstrusioribus*, vii, in *Opera omnia*, 17 vols. (Regensburg: Sumptibus Joannis Conradi Peez, et Felicis Bader, Sociorum; ad Pedem Pontis Typis Mariae Apolloniae Hanckin, 1738), XI, 804–805.

70. Ibid., pp. 805–806. For evidence giving credence to Gretser's accusation of Lutheran attraction to the occult studies see Arlene Miller Guinsburg, "Late German Humanism/Materialism: A Reassessment of the Continuity Thesis," in Fleischer, ed., *Harvest of Humanism*, pp. 197–211.

71. Ibid., p. 806.

72. Christopher Brouwer and Jacob Masen, *Antiquatatum et annalium Trevirensium libri XXX*, 2 vols. (Liège: Ex officina typographica Jo. Mathiae Hovii, 1670), II, lib. 19, p. 315, and lib. 20, p. 321. Brouwer was a rector of the Jesuit college at Trier. Masen's continuation of the project originally assigned to Brouwer, reflecting a reversal of attitude toward magic from that previously indicated in the Trier annals, will be treated below.

73. Ibid., pp. 321–22. For this Tertullian reference see *Liber de praescriptionibus*, cap. 43, in Migne, PL 2:70–71.

74. Ibid., p. 322. Examples Brouwer might have called up for evidence are early sixteenth-century translations into German of the *De septem secundeis*, the first appearing under the title *Von den syben Geysten oder Engeln*. . . . (Nuremberg: durch hieronymum Höltzel, 1522), and the second, *Das Wunder Büchlein* (Speyer: Jakob Schmidt, 1529). A corresponding German trans. of the *Octo quaestiones*, however, appearing as *Antwort Herrn Johann Abts zu Spanhaim, auft act fragstuck*. . . . (Ingolstadt: durch Alexander unnd Samuel Weyssenhorn gebrüder, 1555), attests to a corresponding German campaign to combat these magical tendencies.

75. Ibid.

76. Benito Pereira, *Adversus fallaces et superstitionas artes*. . . . (Ingolstadt: Ex officina typographica Davidiis Sartorii, 1591), lib. I, cap. 3, pp. 21, 23. For Gretser's reference to Pereira, alongside that of Delrio, see *Relatio* . . . , in *Opera omnia*, XI, 806. Regarding this tract, bringing out both its positive and negative views of magic, see Thorndike, *Magic*, VI, 409–13, with the last-named admonitory sentence, closing out the chapter, indicated at p. 411.

77. It was from the seat of Ingolstadt that the Jesuit Peter Canisius (=Peter Kanis de Hondt, 1521–97) initiated his campaign to win the Germans back to Catholicism. Assigned as a professor to the town university, Canisius went on to become the head of the first German Jesuit college, founded at Vienna in 1547.

78. Adam Tanner, *Astrologia sacra: hoc est, orationes et quaestiones quinque*. . . . (Ingolstadt: Ex typographeo Ederiano, apud Elisabetham Angermariam, 1615), orat. I, p. 5. On this oration see Anton Dürrwächter, "Adam Tanner und die *Steganographie* des Trithemius," in *Hermann Grauert zur Vollendung des 60. Lebensjahres: Festgabe zur 7. September 1910* (Freiburg im Breisgau: Herdesche Verlagshandlung, 1910), pp. 354–76.

79. Ibid., pp. 5–6. Under the editorship, respectively, of Marquard Freher and Johannes Busaeus, Trithemius's *Opera historica* appeared in 1601 and

his *Opera pia et spiritualia* in 1604. The *Antipalus maleficiorum*, also edited by Busaeus, appeared in 1605, in conjunction with writings of Peter of Blois, under the title *Paralipomena*.

80. Ibid., p. 6.

81. Ibid., pp. 18, 20.

82. William Cartwright, *The Ordinary*, I, 2, in *Comedies, Tragi-Comedies with other Poems* (London: Printed for Humphrey Moseley, 1651), p. 7.

83. Francisco de Quevedo-Villegas, *Sueños y discursos de verdades descubridoras de abusos, vicios, y engaños en todos los oficios y estados del mundo* (Valencia: Por Juan Bautista Marçal, junto a San Martin, 1628), "Sueño del Infierno," fols. 20$^{r}$ff., esp. fols. 46$^{v}$–47$^{r}$.

84. Conrad Dieterich, *Das buch der weissheit Salomons* (Nuremberg: Wolfgang Endters, 1657), cap. 17, p. 957. Invoking the anecdote of Trithemius's conjuration of deceased personages before the emperor Maximilian, Dieterich cited Luther as a source. This excerpt also found in Tille, *Faustsplitter*, no. 89, pp. 173–78.

85. Sigismund Scherertz (=Scherertzius), *Libellus consolatorius de spectris. . . .* (Wittenberg: Typis Augusti Boreck, sumptibus Pauli Hellwigy, 1621), pars III, admon. 10, sig. I 1$^{r}$. On Scherertz see Thorndike, *Magic*, VI, 534.

86. Guisbert Voet, *Selectarum disputationum theologicarum partes III*, 5 vols. (Utrecht: Apud Joannem à Waesberge, 1648–69), pars III, append. I, pp. 613–14.

87. Balthasar Meisner, *Philosophia sobria*, 3 parts (Jena: Literis Joannis Nisii, 1655), pars II, sec. 2, cap. 2, qu. 1, p. 412. The subject of magic in this section appears as an excursus under the question: "Whether words possess a practical power" (An verba habeant vim practicam), pp. 410ff.

88. Ibid., pp. 421–22.

89. Ibid., p. 422.

90. Johannes Christian Frommann, *Tractatus de fascinatione novus et singularis* (Nuremberg: Sumptibus Wolfggangi Mauritii Endteri, & Johannis Andreae Endteri Haeredum, 1675), lib. III, pars 3, sect. 2, cap. 55 (3), p. 523. On this tract see Thorndike, *Magic*, 572–75.

91. Daniel Sennert, *De chymicorum cum Aristotelicis et Galenicis consensu ac dissensu liber I* (Wittenberg: Apud Zachariam Schurerum, 1619), cap. 13, p. 374: "Hoc modo Trithemium coenam ex Italia vel gallia petisse prolato verbo: Affer, afferunt." Cf. Vickers, "Analogy versus Identity:

the Rejection of Occult Symbolism, 1580–1680," in Vickers, ed., *Occult and Scientific Mentalities*, ch. 3, pp. 95–163 (at p. 138).

92. Ibid., cap. 14, p. 418. This passage cautions us that Sennert's medical rationalism, as emphasized by Vickers (see note above), p. 137, was not entirely free of superrational considerations. For a reference to this passage, though in a different context, see Winfried Schleiner, *Melancholy, Genius, and Utopia in the Renaissance* (Wiesbaden: Harrassowitz, 1991), p. 96. On Sennert's anti-Paracelsian campaign see Debus, *Science, Medicine, and Society* I, 157–62, and *Chemical Philosophy*, I, 191ff. Pagel, however, as indicated by his posthumously published *Smiling Spleen*, places Sennert in the ranks of moderate critics, terming him, p. 86, "an eclectic, one of the conciliators, the peacemakers, who saw the need to make concessions in admitting the strong Paracelsian remedies."

93. William Lilly, *The Worlds catastrophe, or Europes many Mutations untill 1666. . . .* (London: J. Partridge and H. Blunden, 1647). It is not by chance that Lilly came forth the same year with a trans. of Trithemius's *De septem secundeis*. On Lilly's occult outlook see Ann Geneva, *Astrology and the Seventeenth Century Mind: William Lilly and the Language of the Stars* (Manchester: Manchester University Press, 1995), esp. ch. 2, centering on Lilly's melding of cryptological with astrological principles.

94. Dominique de Hottinga (?), *Polygraphie et universelle escriture caballistique . . . utile, convenable & necessaire principalement aux roys, princes, comtes, republiques, & tous amateurs de la subtilitè, industrié, & rarité* (Emden: Chez Halwich Kallenbach, 1620), title page. Showing up this plagiarization was a reissue five years later, by the original Kerver press, of Gabriel de Collange's 1561 trans. (see above, note 52).

95. Claude Duret, *Thresor de langues de cest univers* (Cologne: Par Matth. Berjon, 1613), p. 152.

96. Jean Belot, *L'oeuvre de oeuvres. . . .* (Rouen: Chez Jean Berthelin, 1669), p. 365. First ed., Paris: N. Bourdin, 1622. Earlier Belot had authored an attack on the magic of Agrippa and Pietro d'Abano in his *Les fleurs de la philosophie chrestienne et morale. . . .* (Paris: Pour Anthoine du Brueil, 1603). However, as pointed out by Thorndike, *Magic*, VI, 360–62, Belot directed his attacks on Agrippa and D'Abano from within rather than from without the occultist framework in which they worked.

97. Ibid., pp. 405–406.

98. Ibid., p. 406.

99. Sigismund of Seeon, *Trithemius sui-ipsius vindex. . . .* (Ingolstadt: Ex typographeo Ederiano apud Elisabetham Angermeriam, viduam, 1616), "In Trithemium sui post mortem vindicem," sig. A 1ᵛ.

100. Ibid., p. 17.

101. Ibid., pp. 17, 21–22.

102. Ibid., p. 22.

103. Ibid., p. 28. The quotations begin at pp. 47ff.

104. Ibid., pp. 69ff.

105. Gustavus Selenus (=Duke August II of Braunschweig-Lüneburg), *Cryptomenytices et cryptographiae libri IX*. . . . (Lüneburg: Excriptum typis & impensis Johannis & Henrici fratrum, 1624), lib. III, cap. 1, p. 37. An English extract of this writing, translated by J. W. H. Walden, is appended to Adam McLean's *Steganographia of Johannes Trithemius*, pp. 111ff. On Duke August's cryptology see Gerhard H. Strasser, "Geheimschrift," in *Sammler Fürst Gelehrter Herzog August*. . . . (Wölfenbüttel: Herzog August Bibliothek, 1979), pp. 181–82, and on his Lutheran-based piety, Wolf-Dieter Otte, "Religiöse Schriften," pp. 193–97, and Jörg Jochen Berns, "Einleitung," pp. 343–51, with his pro-Habsburg sentiments indicated at p. 344. For "Selenus's" help in deciphering Trithemius's cryptic enigmas see *Shumaker, Renaissance Curiosa*, pp. 99ff. Cf. Strasser, "The Noblest Cryptologist: Duke August the Younger of Brunswick-Luneburg (Gustavus Selenus) and his Cryptological Activities," *Cryptologia*, 9 (1983), 193–217, with Trithemius's influence indicated at pp. 200–201.

106. Juan Caramuel y Lobkowitz, *Steganographiae . . . Trithemii . . . genuina facilis, dilucidaque declaratio* (Cologne: Typis Egmondanis, sumpt. Auctoris, 1635), title page.

107. Ibid., prologue, sig. B 3$^r$. Reference is to a 1621 edition of the *Octo quaestiones* from the Douai press of Balthazar Beller.

108. Ibid., sig. F 4$^v$.

109. Bernard von Mallinckrott, *De natura et usu literarum disceptatio philologica*. . . . (Monasterii Westphaliae: Excudebat Bernardus Raesfelt, 1638), cap. 25: "De literis furtivis sive occulta scriptura."

110. Jean d'Espières, *Specimen steganographiae Joannis trithemii*. . . . (Douai: Apud P. Bellerum, 1641), sig. a 4$^v$. The list of excerpts begins at sig. c 3$^r$. On Espières' *Specimen* see Arnold, *Trithemius*, p. 190.

111. Ibid., pp. 55–58.

112. Ibid., pp. 62–63.

113. Ibid., pp. 67, 70 Copyrighted Material

114. Ibid., pp. 75–79.

115. Hermann Hugo, *De prima scribendi origine et universa rei literariae antiquitate* (Antwerp: Ex officina Plantiniana, apud Balthasarem & Joannem Moretos, 1617), cap. 18, pp. 138–39.

116. Athanasius Kircher, *Polygraphia nova* (see ch. 4, note 1), "Appendix apologetica," pp. 1ff. (new pagination). On Kircher's occultism see Thorndike, *Magic*, VII, ch. 20, pp. 567ff., and Joscelyn Godwin, *Athanasius Kircher: A Renaissance Man and the Quest for Lost Knowledge* (London: Thames and Hudson, 1979).

117. Kircher, *Oedipus Aegyptiacus*, 2 vols. (Rome: Ex typographia Vitalis Mascardi, 1663), II, pars II, class. 7, sect 4, cap. 11, p. 22.

118. Ibid., pp. 21–23.

119. Ibid.

120. Gaspar Schott, *Physica curiosa aucta & correcta sive mirabilia naturae et artis* (Würzburg: Johannis Andreae Endteri & Wolfgangi, Jun. Haeredum, Excudebat Jobus Hertz, 1667), lib. XII, cap. 4, p. 1287.

121. Gaspar Schott, *Schola steganographica, in classes octo distributa* (Nuremberg: Sumptibus Johannis Andreae Endteri, & Wolfgangi Junioris Haered., excudebat Jobus Hertz, 1680), dedicatory pref., no sigs. First ed., Nuremberg: 1665. On Schott's magic see Shumaker, *Natural Magic and Modern Science*, ch. 5, pp. 137ff.

122. Schott, *Magia universalis naturae et artis*, 4 parts (Würzburg: Sumpt. Haeredum Joannis Godefridi Schonwetteri, 1657–1659), pars. IV, lib. I, pref., pp. 1–2. According to Thorndike, *Magic*, VII, 591, Schott's *Schola* developed out of an earlier work with wider dimensions, his *Magia universalis,* apparently composed under the close watch of Kircher and with access to Kircher's notes. See also Shumaker, *Natural Magic and Modern Science*, pp. 137ff.

123. Ibid., lib. I, cap. 2, pp. 27–28, 30, 36. On the Cardano-Scaliger controversy see Thorndike, *Magic*, VI, 283–84, and Ian Maclean, "The Interpretation of Natural Signs: Cardano's *De subtilitate* versus Scaliger's *Exercitationes*," in Vickers, ed., *Occult and Scientific Mentalities*, ch. 6, pp. 231–52.

124. Ibid., lib. I, cap. 3, pp. 36–37.

125. Ibid., "annotatio," p. 38.

126. W. E. (=Wolfgang Ernst) Heidel, *Vita Joannis Trithemii....*, pref. in *Johannis Trithemii. Steganographia... nunc tandem vindicata, reserata, et illustrata...* (2d ed., Nuremberg: Apud Joh. Fridericum Rudigerum, 1721), cap. 14, p. 36. Also found in Gropp,

*Collectio novissima scriptorum*, I, pp. 218ff. For the Westerburg and Ganay letters see above, pp. 117ff. Heidel omits mention of a clerical affiliation. Deducing his position from internal evidence of the text, Chacornac, *Trithème*, p. 145, identifies Heidel as "un moine bénédiction, de Worms;" Arnold, *Trithemius*, pp. 1 and 190, leaves the question moot; and Ernst, in "Schwarzweisse Magie," p. 157, identifies Heidel as a jurist in the employ of the archbishop of Mainz, Damian Hartard von Leyen, to whom he dedicated his treatise. Heidel, according to Ernst, pp. 157ff., while claiming to have deciphered the third book himself, left posterity in much the same quandary as before by obscuring his result in a new set of ciphers.

127. Ibid., pp. 37–39.

128. Jacob Masen, "Notae et Additamenta ad Tomum II," in Brouwer and Masen, *Antiquitatum . . . Trevirensium*, II, cap. 22: "Annotatio et Additimentum ad Annum Christi 1504: Admirabile Trithemii Abbatis ingenium," in "Cryptographica potissimum magia exhibitum, adversum famam obtrectantium vendicatum," pp. 554ff. On Brouwer, see above, p. 188–90.

129. Ibid., pp. 555–56. On the Busaeus-edited texts referred to here see above, note 79.

130. Gabriel Bucelin, *Benedictus redivivus . . . ab anno Christi M.D. ad praesentem usque aetatem et annos nostros* (Feldkirch: Sumptibus & Typis Joannis Hübschlin, 1679), year 1503, p. 19. On Bucelin's incorporation of Trithemius into his overall plea for a Benedictine revival see Brann, *Trithemius*, pp. 376–77.

131. Ibid., pp. 38–39.

132. On the Rosicrucian movement see Yates, *Rosicrucian Enlightenment*, pp. 41ff.; Hugh Ormsby-Lennon, "Rosicrucian Linguistics: Twilight of a Renaissance Tradition," in Merkel and Debus, eds., *Hermeticism and the Renaissance*, pp. 311–41; and Roland Edighoffer, "Rosicrucianism: From the Seventeenth to the Twentieth Century," in Faivre et al., eds., *Modern Esoteric Spirituality*, pp. 186ff.

133. René Descartes, letter to unnamed acquaintance, 1 April 1648 (?), cited in John Herman Randall, Jr., *The Career of Philosophy: Vol. I, From the Middle Ages to the Enlightenment* (New York: Columbia University Press, 1962), p. 388. Original found in Victor Cousin, ed., *Oeuvres de Descartes*, 11 vols. (Paris: Chez F. G. Levrault, 1824–1826), X (1825), p. 130.

134. For the role of the imperial court at Prague in collecting key play-ers in this movement and promoting its dissemination see R. J. W. Evans, *Rudolf II and his World: A Study in Intellectual History, 1576–1612*

(Oxford: Clarendon Press, 1973), ch. 6, pp. 196ff. For its principles see, in addition to Yates's *Rosicrucian Enlightenment*, Hugh Ormsby-Lennon, "Rosicrucian Linguistics: Twilight of a Renaissance Tradition," in Merkel and Debus, eds., *Hermeticism and the Renaissance*, ch. 16, pp. 311–41. Clarifying the differences in assumptions, objectives, and methods between scientists and occultists is Brian Vickers, as revealed in an accompanying essay, "On the Function of Analogy in the Occult," ch. 13, pp. 265–92. Cf. Vickers, "Analogy and Identity: the Rejection of Occult Symbolism, 1580–1680," in *Occult and Scientific Mentalities*, ch. 3, pp. 95–163.

135. Anonymous [I.P.S.M.S.], *Alchimia vera* ... (n.p.: 1604), "Theophrastus schreibet an einen seinen guten Freund vom Lapide Philosophico, Anno 1534," p. 58. If we are to believe reports circulating in the seventeenth-century, Trithemius concerned himself in his alchemical operations with more than a crass pursuit of gold. For example, an Oxford ms. (Ashmole 1408, pp. 239–43) furnished on the Internet by Adam McLean (http://www.levity.com/alchemy/everbrn2.html) purports to provide, via his disciple Bartholomeus Korndörffer, two recipes alchemically concocted by Trithemius for devising everburning lights.

136. For the *Chemicus nobilis* see Zetzner, *Theatrum Chemicum*, IV, 663ff; for the *De lapide*, IV, 585ff.; and for the *De spagirico artificio* (see above, ch. 4, note 74), I, 388ff. For excerpts, in French translation, see Chacornac, *Trithème*, pp. 112ff. In conjunction Zetzner oversaw the republication, in a joint binding, of Trithemius's *Polygraphia* and *De septem secundeis* (1600, reprinted 1613). The *Libri experimentorum Johannis Trithemii* still rests in ms. (British National Library, Sloan, cod. 3670). For further examples of specious attributions see Hermann Kopp, *Die Alchemie in Älterer und Neuerer Zeit*, 2 parts (Heidelberg: Carl Winter, 1886; repr., Hildesheim, 1962), I, 226, and Arnold, *Trithemius*, append., pp. 259–60.

137. Mersenne, *Observationes et emendationes ad Francisci Veneti Problemata* (Paris: Sumptibus Sebastiani Cramoisy, 1623), prob. 28, cols. 40–41. Concerning Mersenne's objections to Giorgi see Yates, *Occult Philosophy*, pp. 172–74. For discussions of Mersenne's dispute with Fludd see Thorndike, *Magic*, VII, pp. 439–44; Yates, *Bruno*, pp. 432ff., and *Rosicrucian Enlightenment*, pp. 111–13; Debus, *Chemical Philosophy*, I,. 265–79; and William H. Huffman, *Robert Fludd and the End of the Renaissance* (London: Routledge, 1988), pp. 62ff. For the full title of Fludd's *Macrocosmi et microcosmi historia*, see bibliography. On Fludd's Rosicrucian connections see Yates, *Rosicrucian Enlightenment*, ch. 6, pp. 70ff. and passim. On Fludd's Rosicrucian connections see Yates, *Rosicrucian Enlightenment*, ch. 6, pp. 70ff. and passim.

138. Ibid., col. 41. On the heretic, a certain Aldebert condemned by a Roman Council under Pope Zacharias (741–752), see Thorndike, *Magic*, VI, 551. Mersenne's source for this information, according to Thorndike, was Strozzi Cicogna's *Palagio de gl'incanti* (1605). Concerning this criterion for distinguishing demonic from genuine angelic invocation, by restricting the named angels to three, see Kieckhefer, *Magic*, p. 169.

139. Mersenne, *Quaestiones . . . in Genesim.* . . . (Paris: Sumptibus Sebastiani Cramoisy, 1623), cap. 3, cols. 470–71.

140. For Cartesian interpretations of Mersenne see Thorndike, *Magic*, VII, pp. 426ff.; Yates, *Occult Philosophy*, p. 172, characterizing Mersenne's *Quaestiones in Genesim* as "one of the key works marking the transition out of Renaissance modes of magical thinking into those of the scientific revolution;" and William Hine, "Marin Mersenne: Renaissance Naturalism and Renaissance Magic," in Vickers, ed., *Occult and Scientific Mentalities*, ch. 4, pp. 165–76.

141. Shumaker, *Occult Sciences*, p. 205.

142. Robert Fludd, *Tractatus apologeticus integritatem societatis de Rosea Cruce defendens.* . . . (Leiden: Apud Godefridum Basson, 1617), pars I, cap. 2, pp. 34–35. The previous year Fludd had published from the same press, with a play on his name, an *Apologia compendiaria, Fraternitatem de Rosea Cruce suspicionis et infamiae maculis aspersam, veritatis quasi Fluctibus abluens et abstergens* (Leiden: Apud Godefridum Basson, 1616).

143. Fludd, *Sophiae cum moria certamen.* . . . (Frankfurt: Typis Caspari Rotelii, impensis Wilhelmi Fitzeri, 1629), lib. IV, cap. 3, p. 118. On the Mersenne-Fludd polemic see Thorndike, *Magic*, VII, 439–44, and on the Rosicrucian background for this polemic, Serge Hutin, *Robert Fludd (1574–1637): Alchimiste et Philosophe Rosicrucien* (Paris: Omnium Litéraire, 1971), pt. I, pp. 21ff.; Yates, *Rosicrucian Enlightenment*, pp. 74ff.; and Debus, *Chemical Philosophy*, I, 224ff., and "The Chemical Debates of the Seventeenth Century: The Reaction to Robert Fludd and Jean Baptiste van Helmont," in Righini Bonelli and Shea, eds., *Reason, Experiment and Mysticism*, pp. 19ff., esp. pp. 31ff.

144. Fludd (=Joachim Frizius), *Summum bonum* (Frankfurt: Typis Caspari Rotelii, impensis Wilhelm Fitzeri, 1629), pp. 7–9. On this pseudonymous tract, bound with the Fludd's *Sophiae cum moria certamen* and *Medicina catholica* of the same year, see Yates, *Rosicrucian Enlightenment*, p. 102.

145. Fludd, *Clavis philosophiae et alchymiae Fluddanae* (Frankfurt: Apud Guilhelmum Fitzerum, 1633), memb. 1, p. 5.

146. Ibid., memb. 2, pp. 19–20.

147. Ibid., pp. 19–20.

148. Ibid., p. 20.

149. Ibid., p. 22.

150. Ibid.

151. Thomas Vaughan (=Eugenius Philalethes), *Anthroposophia theomagica.* . . . , in Arthur Edward Waite, ed., *The Works of Thomas Vaughan: Eugenius Philalethes* (Edinburgh/London: Theosophical Publishing House [Neil & Co.], 1919), p. 59. Thomas was a twin to the poet Henry. Emphasizing Trithemius's role in transmitting the precepts of the Hermetic Emerald Table to Vaughan is William Newman, "Thomas Vaughan as an Interpreter of Agrippa von Nettesheim," *Ambix*, 29 (1982): 125–40 (at pp. 128–29). On the campaign to institute occult studies in the English educational curriculum see Mordechai Feingold, "The Occult Tradition in the English Universities of the Renaissance: A Reassessment," in Vickers, ed., *Occult and Scientific Mentalities*, pp. 73–93

152. Vaughan, *Anima Magica Abscondita, or, A Discourse of the Universal Spirit of Nature*, in *Works*, ed. Waite, pp. 90–93.

153. Vaughan, *Magia Adamica, or, The Antiquity of Magic*, in *Works*, pp. 136–37.

154. Henry More, *Conjectura Cabbalistica.* . . . (London: James Flesher for William Morden, 1653). For the intellectual milieu within which More was working see Ernst Cassirer, *The Platonic Renaissance in England*, trans. James P. Pettegrove (Austin: University of Texas Press, 1953), and Randall, *Career of Philosophy: I*, ch. 6: "Reason and British Experience," pp. 460ff. On More's positioning in relation to the problem of magic see A. Rupert Hall, *Henry More: Magic, Religion, and Experiment* (Oxford: Basil Blackwell, 1990), esp. ch. 7, pp. 128ff.

155. More, *Observations Upon Anthroposophia Theomagica and Anima Magica Abscondita* (London: Printed at Parrhesia, but are to be sold by O. Pullen at the Rose in Pauls Churchyard, 1650), p. 63. On the Vaughan-More polemic see Waite's edition of More's *Works*, append. III, pp. 468–73; Arlene Miller Guinsburg, "Henry More, Thomas Vaughan and the Late Renaissance Magical Tradition," *Ambix*, 27 (1980), 36–58; Brann, "The Conflict between Reason and Magic in Seventeenth Century England: A Case Study of the Vaughan-More Debate," *Huntington Library Quarterly*, 43 (1980), 103–26; and, most recently, Daniel Fouke, *The Enthusiastical*

*Concerns of Dr. Henry More: Religious Meaning and the Psychology of Delusion* (Leiden: E. J. Brill, 1997), pp. 50ff.

156. More, *An Antidote against Atheism; or, an Appeal to the Natural Faculties of the Minde of Man, whether there be not a God* (2d ed., London: J. Flesher, 1655), pref., sig. A 5$^{r-v}$. First ed., 1652, repr. 1653. Cf. *Enthusiamus Triumphatus; or, A Discourse of the Nature, Causes, Kinds, and Cure of Enthusiasme. . . .* (London: Printed by J. Flesher for W. Morden Bookseller in Cambridge, 1656). For a summary of Hobbes's key part in this development see Randall, *Career of Philosophy*, pp. 532ff, and for a longer exposition, Samuel I, Mintz, *The Hunting of Leviathan: Seventeenth-Century Reactions to the Materialism and Moral Philosophy of Thomas Hobbes* (Cambridge: Cambridge University Press, 1962).

157. Meric Casaubon, *A Treatise Concerning Enthusiasme. . . .* (London: R.D., 1655), ch. 1, p. 17. On Casaubon's place in this controversy see Paul J. Korshin's introduction to facsimile of 2d ed., 1656 (Gainsville, Fla.: Scholars' Facsimile & Reprints, 1970), pp. v–xxv. Characterizing, with some exaggeration, the father Isaac's prior scholarly achievement as "a watershed separating the Renaissance world from the modern world," is Yates, *Bruno*, p. 398. For a more restrained treatment of Isaac's achievement, placing it in the context of an attack on Cesare Baronio's *Annales ecclesiastici*, see Anthony Grafton, *Defenders of the Text: the Traditions of an Age of Science, 1450–1800* (Cambridge, Mass.: Harvard University Press, 1991), pp. 145ff.

158. Casaubon, *A True and Faithful Relation of What passed for many Years between Dr. John Dee . . . and Some Spirits. . . .* (London: Printed for D. Maxwell, for T. Garthwait, 1659; facsimile, with new introd. by Lon Milo DuQuette, New York: Magickal Childe, 1992), sigs. C 4$^{r-v}$. On Dee's putative anticipation of Rosicrucianism see Yates, *Occult Philosophy*, pp. 88–89.

159. Ibid., sigs. G 2$^{r-v}$.

160. Ibid.

161. John Webster, *The Displaying of Supposed Witchcraft. . . .* (London: J.M., 1677), ch. 1, p. 8. For a summary of the Casaubon-Webster dispute see Thorndike, *Magic*, VIII, 575–80.

162. Webster, *Academiarum Examen, or the Examination of Academies. . . .* (London: Printed for Giles Calvert, 1653), ch. 3, p. 24. Facsimile in Allen G. Debus, *Science and Education in the Seventeenth Century: the Webster-Ward Debate* (London: Macdonald/New York: American Elsevier, 1970), pp. 67ff. (at p. 106).

163. Ibid., ch. 1, pp. 8–9.

164. Casaubon, *Of Credulity and Incredulity in things Natural, Civil, and Divine.*... (London: Printed for T. Garthwait, 1668), p. 35. The second volume appeared two years later under the title *Of Credulity and Incredulity in Things Divine and Spiritual.*... (London: Printed by T.N. for Samuel Lownds, 1670).

165. Gabriel Naudé, *Apologie pour les grands hommes soupçonnez de magie* (Amsterdam: Chez Jean Frederick Bernard, 1712), ch. 2, pp. 21–22. First ed. pub. at Paris in 1625. On this tract see Thorndike, *Magic*, VII, 301–303. Cf. Naudé's *Bibliographia politica, in qua plerique omnes ad civilem prudentiam scriptores qua recensentur qua dijudicantur* (Wittenberg: Impensis Balthasar Mevii, ... typis Johannis Rohneri ..., 1641; first ed: Venice: Apud F. Baba, 1623), pp. 110–11. On Belot's concept see above, pp. 200–201.

166. Ibid., ch. 17, pp. 362–63. For an excerpt from this writing, following up another in support of the abbot from Naudé's *Bibliographia politica* (Venice: Apud F. Baba, 1623), see Espières, *Specimen steganographiae*, sigs. e 1ʳff.

167. Ibid., pp. 363–64. Reference is to the pseudo-Trithemian *Veterum sophorum sigilla et imagines magicae.*... (n.p., 1612; repr., Herrenstadt, 1732, though speciously listed as Pesaro, 1502). Cf. Arnold, *Trithemius*, append.: "spuria," p. 259.

168. Ibid., pp. 364–65.

169. Ibid., pp. 365–66.

170. Jacques Chevanes (=D'Autun), *L'incredulité sçavante et la credulité ignorante* ... (Lyons: Jean Molin, 1671), pp. 1091–92. On Chevanes's cautious approach to the witch persecutions see Robert Mandrou, *Magistrats et Sorciers en France au XVIIᵉSiècle* (Paris: Librairie Plon, 1968), pp. 433–36.

171. Ibid.

172. Ibid., pp. 1092–93.

173. Gerhard Johann Voss (=Vossius), *De arte grammatica libri VII* (Amsterdam: Apud Guilielmum Blaev, 1635), lib. I, cap. 41, p. 141.

174. Casaubon, *True and Faithful Relation.*.., sig. G 2ᵛ.

175. John Wilkins and Seth Ward, *Vindiciae Academiarum conteining, Some briefe Animadversions upon Mr. Websters Book stiled, the Examination of Academies.*... (Oxford: Printed by Leonard Lichfield for Thomas

Robinson, 1654, repr. in Debus, *Science and Education*, pp. 193ff.), introd., p. 5, and text, p. 18 (Debus, pp. 199, 212). For secondary accounts of this debate see, in addition to Debus's assessment introducing the reprint of the Wilkins-Ward tract, his *Chemical Philosophy*, II, 393ff., and Barbara J. Shapiro, *John Wilkins, 1614–1672: An Intellectual Biography* (Berkeley: University of California Press, 1969), pp. 104ff. Cf. Ana Maria Alfonso-Goldfarb, "An 'Older' View about Matter in John Wilkins' 'Modern' Mathematical Magick," in Debus and Walton, eds., *Reading the Book of Nature*, pp. 133–46.

176. John Wilkins, *Mercury, or the Secret and Swift Messenger: Shewing, How a Man May with Privacy and Speed Communicate His Thoughts to a Friend at Any Distance* (London: Printed by I. Norton, for John Maynard and Timothy Wilkins, 1641), with the Trithemius ref. at p. 10. On this tract see Shapiro, *Wilkins*, pp. 30–31 and pp. 46–48.

177. Ibid., pp. 10–11. For the Baconian reference see *The Advancement of Learning*, bk. VI, ch. 1, in *The Advancement of Learning and Novum Organum*, intro. James Edward Creighton (New York: Wiley, 1900), pp. 167–71. With Bacon also pointing the way, Wilkins let it be known, as evidenced by a 1648 work on applied mechanics beginning with the words *Mathematical Magic*, that he was not adverse to accommodating principles of natural magic to his scientific experiments. On this work see Bert Hansen, "Science and Magic," in David C. Lindberg, ed., *Science in the Middle Ages* (Chicago: University of Chicago Press, 1978), pp. 483–506.

178. For the above-stated mandate of the Royal Society see Shapiro, *Wilkins*, p. 192, with the friendship between Wilkins and Hooke further indicated at pp. 194ff. Cf. Ellen Tan Drake, *Restless Genius: Robert Hooke and his Earthly Thought* (Oxford: Oxford University Press, 1996), pp. 12ff. This lecture by Hooke belonged to the Cutlerian series.

179. Robert Hooke, "Of Dr. Dee's Book of Spirits," in *The Posthumous Works* (London: Richard Waller, 1705; repr., New York/London: John Reprint, 1969, with intro. by Richard S. Westfall), p. 205. On this passage see also John Henry, "Robert Hooke, the Incongruous Mechanist," in Michael Hunter and Simon Schaffer, eds., *Robert Hooke: New Studies* (Woodbridge, England: Boydell Press, 1989), pp. 149–80 (at pp. 176–77).

180. Ibid., pp. 203–204.

181. Ibid., p. 205.

182. Ibid., pp. 205–206.

183. See, e.g., Henry, "Robert Hooke . . . ," in Hunter and Schaffer, eds., *Hooke*, pp. 171ff.   *Copyrighted Material*

184. According to Yates, *Rosicrucian Enlightenment*, p. 183: "We have thus here a chain of tradition leading from the Rosicrucian movement to the antecedents of the Royal Society." But for scholarly challenges to Yates see above, ch. 1, note 2. On Newton's arcane interests see Betty Jo Teeter Dobbs, *The Foundations of Newton's Alchemy, or "The Hunting of the Greene Lyon"* (Cambridge: Cambridge University Press, 1975); *The Janus Faces of Genius: The Role of Alchemy in Newton's Thought* (Cambridge: Cambridge University Press, 1991); and "Newton's Alchemy and his Theory of Matter," in Vere Chappell, ed., *Seventeenth Century Natural Scientists* (New York: Garland, 1992), pp. 227–244. See also, in same vol., John Henry, "Occult Qualities and Experimental Philosophy: Active Principles in Pre-Newtonian Matter Theory," pp. 1–47, and P. M. Rattansi, "The Intellectual Origins of the Royal Society," pp. 49–63. Cf. Richard Westfall, "The Role of Alchemy in Newton's Career," in Righini Bonelli and Shea, eds., *Reason, Experiment and Mysticism,* pp. 189–232, and "Newton and Alchemy," in Vickers, ed., *Occult and Scientific Mentalities*, ch. 10, pp. 315–35. This theme has received its most recent attention by Michael White in *Isaac Newton: The Last Sorcerer* (Reading, Mass.: Addison-Wesley, 1997).

185. Francis Bacon, *The Advancement of Learning*, 3d ed. (Oxford: Clarendon Press, 1885), bk. II, vii, 1, p. 111. For treatments of this transition see, e.g., Charles Webster, *From Paracelsus to Newton: Magic and the Making of Modern Science* (Cambridge: Cambridge University Press, 1982); Rossi, *Bacon: From Magic to Science*; and Hansen, "Science and Magic," in Lindberg, ed., *Science in Middle Ages*, esp. pp. 486–87. As extensively illustrated by Easlea, *Witch Hunting, Magic and the New Philosophy*, more than a residue of natural magic persisted beneath this transition from the old to the new philosophy. Also stubbornly persisting were certain prejudices, most notably the presumption of male superiority and dominance over the female. Easlea's thesis (p. 252) is that the scientific revolution, no less than the witch hunts which it helped to terminate, "cannot be understood without reference to the consequences of social stratification."

186. On Wilkins's cryptological interests see above, p. 232–33. Concerning Wilkins's activities in the Royal Society and associated search for a universal scientific language see Shapiro, *Wilkins*, esp. pp. 30ff. and pp. 191ff. Regarding Dalgarno's corresponding quest see pp. 210–13, and Shumaker, *Renaissance Curiosa*, pp. 132ff. Emphasizing Bacon's shift from an esoteric to exoteric methodology is Paolo Rossi, *Francis Bacon: From Magic to Science*, trans. Sacha Rabinovitch (Chicago: University of Chicago Press, 1968), with special attention to his subsequent influence on the Royal Society, introd., p. xiii.

187. Jacob Böhme (=Boehme), *Six Theosophic Points and Other Writings*, trans. John Rolleston Earle (Ann Arbor: University of Michigan Press,

1958), p. 54. For the original German see Böhme, *Sämtliche Schriften*, 11 vols. (facsimile of 1730 ed., Stuttgart: Frommann-Holzboog, 1957), IV, p. 95, no. 23: "Magia ist die beste Theologia; denn in ihr wird der wahre Glaube gegründet, und gefunden." For full-scale biographies of Böhme see Will-Erich Peuckert, *Das Leben Jakob Böhmes* (Jena: Eugen Diederichs, 1924), Hans Grunsky, *Jacob Boehme* (Stuttgart: Frommann-Holzboog, 1956); and most recently, Andrew Weeks, *Boehme: An Intellectual Biography of the Seventeenth-Century Philosopher and Mystic* (Albany: State University of New York Press, 1991). For briefer queries into Böhme's occult interests see Peuckert, *Pansophie*, esp. pp. 434–35; Pierre Deghaye, "Jacob Boehme and His Followers," in Faivre et al., eds., *Modern Esoteric Spirituality*, pp. 210ff.; and Ingrid Merkel, "*Aurora*; or, The Rising Sun of Allegory: Hermetic Imagery in the Work of Jakob Böhme," in Merkel and Debus, eds., *Hermeticism and the Renaissance*, pp. 302ff.

# Chapter 6.  Trithemian Magic in Later Perspective

1. Johann Joseph Hermes, *Über das Leben und die Schriften des Johannes von Trittenheim, genannt Trithemius* (Beilage zum Jahresbericht des Gymnasiums zum Prüm Ostern, 1901), p. 32.

2. Oliver Legipont, *Vita et apologia ven. Joannis Trithemii*, in Ziegelbauer and Legipont, *Historia rei literariae ordinis sancti Benedicti*, pars III, lib. II, pp. 244ff.

3. Collin de Plancy, *Dictionnaire de Science Occultes*, 2 vols. (Migne, ed. *Encyclopédie Théologique*, vols. 48–49) (Paris: Chez l'Editeur aux Ateliers Catholiques du Petit-Montrouge, 1848), II (Migne, vol. 49), "Trithème," col. 757. On this passage see also Shumaker, *Renaissance Curiosa*, p. 98.

4. Pseudo-Trithemius, *Güldenes kleinod, oder Schatzkästlein* . . . On this tract, reputedly trans. by the fifteenth-century monk Basil Valentine, see Kopp, *Die Alchemie*, p. 226.

5. Francis Barrett, *The Magus, or Celestial Intelligencer; being a Complete System of Occult Philosophy.* . . . (London: Printed for Lackington Allen, 1801; repr., New York: University Books, 1967), bk. II, pp. 129–40.

6. Pseudo-Trithemius, *Wunder-Buch von der gottlichen Magie, dem Planeten-jnd Geburtesstunden-Einfluss* (Stuttgart: J. Scheible, 1851, spuriously listed as Passau, 1506).

7. The titles of the genuine writings are *Traité des cause secondes* (Paris: Chamuel, 1897; repr. 1898), and previously indicated (ch. 4, note 28), McLean, ed., *The Steganographia of Johannes Trithemius*.

8. Joscelyn Godwin, Christian Chanel, and John P. Deveney, *The Hermetic Brotherhood of Luxor: Initiatic and Historical Documents of an Order of Practical Occultism* (York Beach, Me.: Samuel Weiser, 1995), p. 175.

9. Dröscher, *Methoden der Geheimschriften*, p. 28.

10. Arnold, *Trithemius*, p. 192. Cf. Couliano, *Eros and Magic*, p. 171. Alternatively, Kahn, *Codebreakers*, p. 130, has assigned the designation "Father of Western Cryptology" to an Italian precursor of Trithemius, Leon Battista Alberti.

11. Fletcher Pratt, *Secret and Urgent: The Story of Codes and Ciphers* (London: Robert Hale, 1939), p. 62.

12. Yates, *Rosicrucian Enlightenment*, p. 108, note 1, and Walker, *Spiritual and Demonic Magic*, p. 89.

13. Arnold, *Trithemius*, pp. 187–88, 190–92. Cf. Couliano, *Eros and Magic*, p. 248, note, terming the Cabalistic system of alphabetical permutations "Temurah."

14. Shumaker, *Renaissance Curiosa*, p. 102.

15. Schneegans, *Trithemius*, p. 186.

16. Peuckert, *Pansophie*, esp. pp. 100ff.

17. Walker, *Spiritual and Demonic Magic*, p. 89.

18. Arnold, *Trithemius*, p. 199.

19. Zambelli, "Scholastic and Humanist Views of Hermeticism and Witchcraft," ch. 6, in Merkel and Debus, *Hermeticism and the Renaissance*, p. 136.

20. Couliano, *Eros and Magic*, p. 162. For the competing Ficinian notion of erotic magic cf. ch. 2, pp. 28ff.

21. Klibansky et al., *Saturn and Melancholy*, pp. 351–52.

22. Franz Friedrich Leitschuh, "Quellen und studien zur Geschichte des Kunst- und Geisteslebens in Franken. I. Trithemius und Dürer," *Archiv des historischen Vereins von Unterfranken und Aschaffenburg*, 44 (1902): 185–95, (at 193). Of the emblems contained in Dürer's engraving pointing to Trithemius for Leitschuh, one is of a dog sleeping at the feet of the melancholic figure, identified with one owned by Trithemius to which Conrad Celtis humorously dedicated an epigram. On this epigram and its background see Arnold, *Trithemius*, p. 79, and Brann, *Trithemius*, p. 243. However, as pointed out by Nauert, *Agrippa*, p. 327, this emblem applied

just as easily to Agrippa, a magician rumored by his enemies to have often been seen in the company of a devil in the form of a black dog. On the commonplace association between melancholy and specifically alchemical magic see my article "Alchemy and Melancholy in Medieval and Renaissance Thought: A Query into the Mystical Basis of Their Relationship," *Ambix*, 32 (1985): 127–48.

23. Thorndike, *Magic*, VIII, 503.

24. The primary text for this identification of the *furor melancholicus* with the *furor divinus*, as extensively demonstrated in Klibansky et al., *Saturn and Melancholy*, and furnished in a dual-column English translation, pp. 18–29, is the Aristotelian *Problemata*, XXX, 1. Ficino it was, according to the authors, who fused the Aristotelian notion of *furor melancholicus* with the Platonic notion of *furor divinus* and (p. 278) conveyed the amalgamated concept to Agrippa.

25. Baron, "Trithemius and Faustus," in Auernheimer and Baron, ed., *Trithemius*, p. 41.

26. Copenhaver, "Astrology and Magic," in Schmitt et al., *Renaissance Philosophy*, p. 285.

27. Baron, as cited above in note 25.

28. See, e.g., Spitz, ch. 4: "Reuchlin: Pythagoras Reborn," in *Religious Renaissance*, pp. 61ff., and Nauert, *Agrippa*, esp. pp. 122–25.

29. Ibid., p. 36.

30. Joscelyn Godwin, *The Theosophical Enlightenment* (Albany: State University of New York Press, 1994). Cf. Christopher McIntosh, *The Rose Cross and the Age of Reason: Eighteenth Century Rosicrucianism in Central Europe and Its Relationship to the Enlightenment*, Studies in Intellectual History, no. 29 (Leiden: E. J. Brill: 1992).

31. Faivre, intro., in Faivre and Needleman, *Modern Esoteric Spirituality*, p. xiv. For further scholarly testaments by Faivre to this belief see his *Access to Western Esotericism* (Albany: State University of New York Press, 1994), and *The Eternal Hermes: From Greek God to Alchemical Magus*, trans. Joscelyn Godwin (Grand Rapids, Mich.: Phanes, 1995).

# Bibliography

## Primary Sources

Agrippa of Nettesheim, Heinrich Cornelius. *Opera.* 2 vols. Lyons: Per Beringos fratres, n.d. [ca. 1600]; facsimile, Hildesheim: Georg Olms, 1970.

———. *De occulta philosophia libri III.* [Cologne], 1533. Facsimile edited by Karl Anton Nowotny. Graz: Akademische Druck u. Verlaganstalt, 1967.

———. *De occulta philosophia libri tres.* Edited by Vittore Perrone Compagni. Studies in the History of Christian Thought, no. 48. Leiden: E. J. Brill, 1992.

———. *Three Books of Occult Philosophy or Magic: Book I—Natural Magic.* Edited by Willis F. Whitehead. London, 1897; repr., Aquarian Press, 1971.

———. *Three Books of Philosophy.* Edited by Donald Tyson, translated by James Freake. St. Paul, Minn.: Llewellyn, 1995.

Agrippa of Nettesheim (pseudo-). *Henry Cornelius Agrippa, his Fourth book of occult pholosophy. Of geomancy by Gerardus Cremonensis. The Nature of Spirits by George Pictorius. Arbatel of Magick.* Translated by Robert Turner. London: Printed by J. C. for J. Harrison, 1655.

———. *Heinrich Cornelius Agrippa's von Nettesheim Magische Werke, sammt den geheimnisvollen Schriften des Petrus von Abano, Pictorius von Villingen, Gerhard von Cremona, Abt Tritheim von Spanheim, dem Buche Arbatel, der sogennanten Heil. Geist-Kunst und verschiedenen anderen.* 5 vols. Berlin: H. Barsdorf, 1921.

Ailly, Pierre d'. *De falsis prophetis.* Append. in Gerson, *Opera omnia,* I. See below: Gerson.

315

Albertus Magnus. *Opera omnia.* Edited by P. Jammy. 21 vols. Leiden: Sumptibus Claudii Prost, 1651.

———. *Opera omnia.* Edited by Bernhard Geyer. Vol. 37. Monasterium Westfalorum: In Aedibus Aschendorff, 1972.

Alexander of Hales. *Summa theologica.* 4 vols. Edited by Bernardin Klumper. Florence: S. Bonaventurae, 1930.

Anonymous [I.P.S.M.S.]. *Alchimia vera, das ist: der wahren und von Gott hochbenedeyten naturgemessen edlen Kunst Alchimia wahre beschreibung.* N.P.: 1604.

Aquinas, St. Thomas. *Basic Writings.* Edited by Anton C. Pegis. 2 vols. New York: Random House, 1945.

Aquinas, St. Thomas [Pseudo- ]. *Aurora consurgans.* Translated by R. F. C. Hull and A. S. B. Glover, edited by Marie-Louise von Franz. New York: Pantheon, 1966.

Argentinus, Ricardus. *De praestigiis et incantationibus daemonum et necromanticorum liber.* Basel: 1568.

August II of Braunschweig-Lüneburg, Duke. See Selenus.

Augustine, St. *The City of God.* Translated by Gerald G. Walsh and Grace Monahan. Vol VII of *Writings of St. Augustine.* New York: Fathers of the Church, 1952.

Aventinus, Johannes. *Sämmtliche Werke.* 6 vols. Munich: Christian Kaiser, 1881-1908.

Bacon, Francis. *The Advancement of Learning and Novum Organum.* Intro. James Edward Creighton. New York: Wiley, 1900.

Bacon, Roger. *Opus majus.* Edited by John Henry Bridges. 2 vols. Oxford: Clarendon Press, 1897.

[Bacon, Roger]. *The Opus majus of Roger Bacon.* Translated by Robert Belle Burke. 2 vols. Philadelphia: University of Pennsylvania Press, 1928.

Barrett, Francis. *The Magus, or Celestial Intelligencer; being a Complete System of Occult Philosophy. In Three Books: Containing the Antient and Modern Practice of the Cabalistic Art, Natural and Celestial Magic, &c. . . .* London: Printed for Lackington Allen, 1801.

Bellarmine, Robert. *De scriptoribus ecclesiasticis liber unus.* Lyons: Sumptibus Horatii Boissat & Georgii Remeus, 1663.

———. *Disputationes . . . de controversiis Christianae fidei, adversus huius temporis haereticos.* 3 vols [in 6 bindings]. Ingolstadt: Ex Typographia Adami Sartorii, 1605.

Belot, Jean. *Les fleurs de la philosophie Chrestienne et morale, ou refutations de Henry Corn. Agrippa & de P. d'Albano en leur philosophie occulte.* Paris: Pour Anthoine du Brueil, 1603.

———. *L'oeuvre de oeuvres, ou le plus parfait des sciences Steganografiques, Paulines, Armadelles et Lullistes.* Rouen: Chez Jean Berthelin, 1669. First ed., Paris: N. Bourdin, 1623.

Bodin, Jean. *De magorum daemonomania, seu detestando lamiarum ac magorum cum Satana commercio libri IV.... Accessit eiusdem opinionum Joannis Wieri confutatio....* Frankfurt: Typis Wolffgangi Richteri, impensis omnium haeredum Nicolai Bassaei, 1603.

Böcking, Eduard, ed. *Ulrichi Hutten equitis operum supplementum: Epistolae obscurorum virorum cum illustrantibus scriptis.* 2 vols. Leipzig: B. G. Teubner, 1870. Repr., Osnabrück, 1966.

Böhme [=Boehme], Jacob. *Sämtliche Werke.* 11 vols. Facsimile of 1730 ed. Stuttgart: Frommann-Holzboog, 1957.

——. *Six Theosophic Points and Other Writings.* Translated by John Rolleston Earle. Ann Arbor: University of Michigan Press, 1958.

[Boissard, Jean-Jacques]. *Tractatus posthumus Jani Jacobi Boissardi vesuntini de divinatione & magicis praestigiis, quarum veritas ac vanitas solide exponitur.* Strassburg/Oppenheim: Johannes Theodorus de Bry, [1615].

Bovillus, Carolus (= Charles de Bouelles). *Liber de intellectu....* Paris: In aedibus Francisci de Hallewin, 1510. Facsimile, Stuttgart-Bad Cannstatt: Friedrich Frommann Verlag [Günther Holzboog], 1970.

Brouwer, Christopher, and Jacob Masen. *Antiquitatum et annalium Treverensium libri XXV.* 2 vols. Liège: Ex officina typographica Jo. Mathiae Hovii, 1670.

Bucelin, Gabriel. *Benedictus redivivus... ab anno Christi M.D. ad praesentem usque aetatem et annos nostros....* Feldkirch: Sumptibus & typis Joannis Hübschlin, 1679.

Butzbach, Johann. *Macrostroma de laudibus tritemianis et commendatione philosophica adversus zoilos et tritemomastigas libri XVI.* Bonn, Universitätsbibliothek, MS no. 357.

Caesarius of Heisterbach. *The Dialogues of Miracles.* Translated by H. Scott and C. C. Swinton Bland. 2 vols. London: G. Routledge, 1929.

Cambihon (=Cambilhom), Johann. *De studiis Jesuitarum abstrusioribus et consiliis eorum sanguinariis* (1608), in Petrus de Wangen *Physiognomonia Jesuitica....* Lyons: 1610.

Caramuel y Lobkowitz, Juan. *Steganographiae nec non claviculae Salomonis germani Joannis Trithemii... genuina facilis, dilucidaque declaratio.* Cologne: Typis Egmondanis, 1635.

Cardano, Girolamo. *De rerum varietate libri XVII.* Basel: Per Henrichum Petri, 1557.

Cartwright, William. *Comedies, Tragi-Comedies with Other Poems.* London: Printed for Humphrey Moseley, 1651.

Casaubon, Meric. *A Treatise Concerning Enthusiasme, As it is an Effect of Nature: but is mistaken by many for either Divine Inspiration, or Diabolical Possession.* London: R.D., 1655. Facsimile of 2d ed. [1656], ed. Paul J. Korshin, Gainesville: Flor[...].

———. *A True and Faithful Relation of What passed for many Years Between Dr. John Dee... and Some Spirits: Tending (had it Succeeded) to a General Alteration of most States and Kingdomes in the World.* London: Printed for D. Maxwell, for T. Garthwait, 1659. Facsimile, with new intro., by Lon Milo DuQuette, New York: Magickal Childe, 1992.

———. *Of Credulity and Incredulity, In things Divine and Spiritual:... Against a late Writer, fully Argued and Disputed.* London: Printed by T.N. for Samuel Lownds, 1670.

———. *Of Credulity and Incredulity in things Natural, Civil, and Divine. Wherein, Among other things, the Sadducism of these times, in denying Spirits, Witches, and Supernatural Operations by pregnant instances and evidences is fully confuted:...* London: Printed for T. Garthwait, 1668.

Cassirer, Ernst, Paul Oskar Kristeller, and John Herman Randall, Jr., eds. *The Renaissance Philosophy of Man.* Chicago: University of Chicago Press [Phoenix], 1948.

*Chartularium Universitatis Parisiensis.* Edited by Henricus Denifle, O.P., and Aemilio Chatelain. 4 vols. Paris: Ex Typis Fratrum Delalain, 1887.

Chevanes, Jacques, d'Autun. *L'incredulité sçavante et la credulité ignorante: au suject des magiciens et de sorciers, avecque la response à un livre intitulé apologie pour tous les grands personages, qui ont este faussement soupçonnés de magie.* Lyons: Jean Moulin, 1671.

Debus, Allen G. *Science and Education in the Seventeenth Century: The Webster-Ward Debate.* London: Macdonald/ New York: American Elsevier, 1970.

Dee, John. Letter to Sir William Cecil, Antwerp, 16 February 1562. Repr. *Philobiblon Society: Bibliographical and Historical Miscellanies.* London: Charles Whittingham, 1854. Vol. I (12): 1–16.

———. *Monas hieroglyphica.* See secondary sources: Josten.

———. *John Dee: Essential Readings.* Edited by Gerald Suster. London: Aquarius, 1986.

Della Porta, Giovanni Battista. *Magiae naturalis libri viginti.* Rouen: Sumptibus Joannis Berthelin, 1650. First ed., 1558.

———. *De furtivis literarum notis vulgo, de ziferis libri IV.* London: Apud Johannem Wolphium, 1591. First ed., Naples, 1563. Repub. as *De occultis literarum notis, seu artis animi sensa occulte aliis significandi, aut ab aliis significata expiscandi enodandique libri quinque.* Strassburg: Impensis Lazari Zetzneri, 1606.

Della Riviera, Cesare. *Il magico mondo degli heroi.* Mantua: Per Francesco Osanna, 1603.

Delrio, Martin. *Disquisitionum magicarum libri sex.* Venice: Apud Vincentium Florinum, 1616. First ed., Louvain: 1599.

[Descartes, Renée]. *Oeuvres de Descartes*. Ed. Victor Cousin. 11 vols. Paris: Chez F. G. Levrault, 1824–1826.

Dieterich, Conrad. *Das buch der weissheit Salomons*. Nuremberg: Wolfgang Endters, 1657.

Duret, Claude. *Thresor de langues de cest univers*. Cologne: Par Matth. Berjon, 1613.

Erasmus, Desiderius. *Opus epistolarum*. Edited by P. S. Allen. 12 vols. Oxford: Oxford University Press, 1910.

Espières, Jean d'. *Specimen steganographiae Joannis Trithemii . . . , quo auctoris ingenuitas demonstratur et opus a superstitione absolvitur, cum vindiciis Trithemianis. . . .* Douai: Apud P. Bellerum, 1641.

Ficino, Marsilio. *Opera omnia*. 2 vols. Basel: Ex officina Henricpetrina, 1576. Facsimile ed., Torino: Bottega d'Erasmo, 1959.

———. *Three Books on Life: A Critical Edition and Translation with Introduction and Notes*. Edited and translated by Carol V. Kaske and John R. Clark. Medieval and Renaissance Texts and Studies, vol 57. Binghamton: State University of New York Press, 1989.

Fludd, Robert. *Apologia compendiaria, Fraternitatem de Rosea Cruce suspicionis et infamiae maculis aspersam, veritatis quasi Fluctibus abluens et abstergens*. Leiden: Apud Godefridum Basson, 1616.

———. *Tractatus apologeticus integritatem societatis de Rosea Cruce defendens, in qua probatur . . . quod admirabilia nobis a Fraternitate R. C. oblata, sine improba Magiae impostura, aut Diaboli praestigiis & illusionibus praestari possint*. Leiden: Apud Godefridum Basson, 1617.

———. *Utriusque cosmi maioris scilicet et minoris metaphysica, physica atque technica historia. . . . Tomus primus, De macrocosmi historia in duos tractatus divisa. Tomus secundus, de supernaturali, naturali, praeternaturali et contranaturali microcosmi historia, in tractatus tres distributa*. Oppenheim: Impensis Johannis Theodori de Bry, typis Hieronymi Galleri, 1617–19.

———. *Sophiae cum moria certamen, in quo Lapis Lydius a falso structore, Fr. Marino Mersenno, monacho reprobatus, celeberrima voluminis sui Babylonici (in Genesim) figmenta accurate examinata*. Frankfurt: Typis Caspari Rotelli, impensis Wilhelmi Fitzeri, 1629.

———. *Clavis philosophiae et alchymiae Fluddanae*. Frankfurt: Apud Guilhelmum Fitzerum, 1633.

Fludd, Robert [=Joachim Frizius]. *Summum bonum*. Frankfurt: Typis Caspari Rotelii, impensis Wilhelm Fitzeri, 1629.

Fritz, Josef, ed. *Das Volksbuch vom Doktor Faust: Nach der um die Erfurter Geschichten vermehrten Fassung*. Halle a/S: Max Niemeyer, 1914 [based on 1596 ed.].

Frizius, Joachim. See Fludd.

Frommann, Johannes Christian. *Tractatus de fascinatione novus et singularis*. Nuremberg: Sumptibus Wolfgangi Mauritii Endteri, & Johannis Andreae Endteri Haeredum, 1675.

Garin, Eugenio et al., eds. *Testi Umanistici su l'Ermetismo: Testi di Ludovico Lazzarelli, F. Giorgio Veneto, Cornelio Agrippa di Nettesheim*. Rome: Fratelli Bocca, 1955.

Gerson, Jean de. *Opera omnia*. Edited by M. Lud. Ellies Du Pin. Antwerp: Sumptibus Societatis, 1706.

Gesner, Conrad. *Bibliotheca universalis, sive catalogus omnium scriptorum locupletissimus, in tribus linguis, Latin, Graeca, & Hebraica*. Zürich: Apud Christophorum Froschoverum, 1545.

———. *Epistolae medicinaliae libri III*. Zürich: Excudebat Christoph Frosch, 1577.

Giorgi, Francesco. *De harmonia mundi totius cantica tria*. Venice: In aedibus Bernardini de Vitalibus Chalcographi, 1525.

Glanvill, Joseph. *A Blow at Modern Sadducism in Some Philosophical Considerations about Witchcraft*. London: Printed by E.C. for James Collins, 1668.

———. *Saducismus Triumphatus: or, Full and Plain Evidence concerning Witches and Apparitions. . . .* London: Printed for S. Lownds, 1689. Facsimile, intro. Coleman O. Parsons, Gainsville, Fla.: Scholars Facsimiles and Reprints, 1966.

Godelmann, Johann Georg. *De magis, veneficis et lamiis recta cognoscendis et puniendis libri III*. Frankfurt: Ex Off. Typ. Nicolai Bassaei, 1591.

Gohory, Jacques [=Leo Suavius]. *De usu et mysteriis notarum liber*. Paris: Apud V. Sertenas, 1550.

———. *Scholia in libros IV Ph. Theoph. Paracelsi de vita longa*. Frankfurt: Christoph Rabb, 1583.

Goltwurm, Caspar [=Goldwurm]. *Wunderzeichen Buch. . . .* Frankfurt: 1567.

Gretser, Jacob. *Opera omnia*. 17 vols. Regensburg: Sumptibus Joannis Conradi Peez, et Felicis Bader Sociorum; ad Pedem Pontis Typis Mariae Apolloniae Hanckin, 1738.

Gropp, Ignatius P., ed. *Collectio novissima scriptorum et rerum Wirceburgensium. . . .* Vol. I, Frankfurt: Ex officina Weldmanniana, 1741.

Hansen, Joseph, ed. *Quellen und Untersuchungen zur Geschichte der Hexenwahns und der Hexenverfolgung im Mittelalter*. Bonn: 1901; Hildesheim: Georg Olms, 1963.

Holkot, Robert. *Phoenix rediviva . . . seu postilla super librum sapientiae Salomonis*. Köln: Apud Arnoldum Metternich, 1689.

Hooke, Robert. *The Posthumous Works*. London: Richard Waller, 1705. Repr., New York/London: John Reprint Corp., 1969, with intro. by Richard S. Westfall.

Hottinga, Dominique de Hottinga (?), *Polygraphie et universelle escriture caballistique . . . utile, convenable & necessaire principalement aux roys, princes, comtes, republiques, & tous amateurs de la subtilitè, industrié, & rarité* (Emden: Chez Halwich Kallenbach, 1620). Plagiarized from Gabriel de Collange's trans., listed below under Trithemius.

Hugo, Hermann. *De prima scribendi origine et universa rei literariae antiquitate.* Antwerp: Ex officina Plantiniana, apud Balthasarem & Joannem Moretos, 1617.

Josten, C. H. "A Translation. . . . " See secondary sources.

Kircher, Athanasius. *Oedipus Aegyptiacus.* 2 vols. Rome: Ex typographia Vitalis Mascardi, 1663.

———. *Polygraphia nova et universalis.* Rome: Ex Typographia Varesii, 1663.

Kors, Alan C., and Edward Peters, eds. *Witchcraft in Europe, 1300-1700: A Documentary History.* Philadelphia: University of Pennsylvania Press, 1972, 1978.

Lactantius. *The Divine Institutes: Books I–VIII.* Translated by Mary Francis McDonald. *Fathers of the Church*, vol. 49. Washington, D.C.: Catholic University of America, 1964.

———. *The Minor Works.* Fathers of the Church, vol. 50. Wash., D.C.: Catholic Univ. Press, 1965.

Lea, Henry Charles. *Materials. . . .* See secondary sources.

Legipont, Oliver. See Ziegelbauer.

Lercheimer, Augustin. see Witekind.

Lilly, William. *The Worlds castrophe, or Europes many Mutations untill 1666 . . . Government of the world under God by the seven planetary Angels; their names, times of government. . . .* London: J. Partridge and H. Blunden, 1647.

Luther, Martin. *Werke: Tischreden.* 6 vols. Weimar: Hermann Böhlaus, 1912-21.

Mallinckrott, Bernhard von. *De natura et usu literarum disceptatio philologica, . . . .* Monasterii Westphaliae: Excudebat Bernardus Raesfelt, 1638.

Manlius, Johannes. *Locorum communium collectanea, a Johanne Manlio . . . ex lectionibus D. Philippi Melanchthonis...excerpta, & nuper in ordinem ab eodem redacta.* Basel: Per Joannem Oporinum, 1563.

Masen, Jacob. See Brouwer.

Mattaire, Michel. *Annales typographici ab artis inventae origine ad annum MDCLXIV.* 5 vols. Vols. I–II: Den Haag: Apud Fratres Vaillart et Nicolaum Prevost, 1719–22; repr., Graz, 1965.

Meisner, Balthasar. *Philosophia sobria.* 3 parts. Jena: Literis Joannis Nisii, 1655.

Mersenne, Marin. *Observationes et emendationes ad Francisci Veneti Problemata.* Paris: Sumptibus Sebastiani Cramoisy, 1623.

———. *Quaestiones celeberrimae in genesim.... Francisci Georgii Veneti cabalistica dogmata fusè refelluntur....* Paris: Sumptibus Sebastiani Cramoisy, 1623.

Migne, Jacques Paul. Ed. *Patrologiae cursus completus.... Series latina.* 222 vols. Paris: Garnier Fratres, 1844-1905.

———. *Patrologiae cursus completus.... Series graeca.* 161 vols. Paris: Garnier Fratres, 1857-1912.

More, Henry [=Alazonomastix Philalethes]. *Observations upon Anthroposophia Theomagica and Anima Magica Abscondita.* London: Printed at Parrhesia, but are to be sold by O. Pullen at the Rose in Pauls Churchyard, 1650.

———. *An Antidote against Atheism; or, An Appeal to the Natural Faculties of the Minde of Man, whether There Be Not a God.* London: J. Flesher, 1655. First ed., 1652; repr. 1653.

———. *Conjectura Cabbalistica; or, A Conjectural Essay of Interpreting the Minde of Moses, According to a Threefold Cabbala: Viz., Literal; Philosophical; Mystical, or Divinely Moral.* London: James Flesher for William Morden, 1653.

———. *Enthusiasmus triumphatus, or, A Discourse of the Nature, Causes, Kinds, and Cure, of Enthusiasme....* London: Printed by J. Flesher for W. Morden Bookseller in Cambridge, 1656. Repr. of 1662 re-edition, ed. M. V. De Porte, Augustan Reprint Society, no. 118. Los Angeles: University of California Press, 1966.

Mutian, Conrad [=Mutianus Rufus]. *Der Briefwechsel.* Edited by Carl Krause. Kassel: A. Freyschmidt, 1885.

Naudé, Gabriel. *Apologie pour les grands hommes soupçonnez de magie.* Amsterdam: Chez Jean Frederick Bernard, 1712.

———. *Bibliographia politica, in qua plerique omnes ad civilem prudentiam scriptores qua recensentur qua dijudicantur.* Wittenberg: Impensis Balthasar Mevii ..., typis Johannis Rohneri ..., 1641. First ed: Venice: Apud F. Baba, 1623.

Origen. *Against Celsus.* Translated by F. Crombie and W. H. Cairns. In *The Ante-Nicene Fathers.* Edited by Alexander Roberts and James Donaldson. New York: Charles Scribner's Sons, 1899.

Palmer, Philip Mason, and Robert Pattison More, eds. *The Sources of the Faust Tradition from Simon Magus to Lessing.* Oxford: Oxford University Press, 1936.

Paracelsus, Theophrastus. *Selected Writings.* Edited by Jolande Jacobi, translated by Norbert Guterman. London: Routledge & Kegan Paul, 1951.

Patrizi, Francesco, da Cherso. *Nova de universis philosophia . . . libri quinquaginta comprehensa.* Ferrara: Apud Benedictum Mammarellum, 1591.

————. *Magia philosophica. . . .* Hamburg: Ex biblioteca Ranzoviana, 1593.

Pereira, Benito. *Adversus fallaces et superstitiosas artes, id est, de magia, de observatione somniorum, et de divinatione astrologica, libri tres.* Ingolstadt: Ex officina typographica Davidis Sartorii, 1591.

Pez, Bernhard. *Thesaurus anecdotorum novissimus.* 6 vols. Augsburg: Sumptibus Philippi Martini, & Joannis Veith Fratrum, 1721.

Pico della Mirandola, Giovanni. *Opera omnia.* 2 vols. Vol. I: Giovanni Pico; Vol. II: Gianfrancesco Pico. Basel: Ex officina Henricpetrina, 1557. Facsimile, Hildesheim: Georg Olms, 1969.

[Pico della Mirandola, Giovanni]. *Pico's 900 Theses: Syncretism in the West.* Edited and translated by Stephen A. Farmer. Binghamton, N.Y.: State University of New York Press. Forthcoming, 1998.

Pictorius, Georg, von Villingen. *De illorum daemonum qui sub lunari collimatio versantur, isagoge . . . quibus accedit de speciebus magiae ceremonialis, quam Goëtiam vocant, epitome . . . an sagae, vel mulieres quas expiactrices nominamus, ignis mulcta sint damnandae, resolutio.* Basel: Per Henricum Petri, 1563.

Pirckheimer, Willibald. *Briefwechsel.* Edited by Emil Reicke. 2 vols. Munich: C. H. Beck, 1956.

Possevino, Antonio, *Apparatus sacer.* 2 vols. Cologne: Apud Joannem Gimnicum sub Monocerote, 1608.

Quevedo-Villegas, Francisco de. *Sueños y discursos de verdades descubridoras de abusos, vicios, y engaños en todos los oficios y estados del mundo.* Valencia: Por Juan Bautista Marçal, junto a San Martin, 1628.

Reuchlin, Johann. *De verbo mirifico.* Printed and bound with *De arte cabalistica,* 1517. Facsimile, Stuttgart-Bad Cannstatt: Friedrich Frommann Verlag, 1964.

Rupprich, Hans. *Humanismus und Renaissance. . . .* See secondary sources.

Scherertzius [=Scherertz], Sigismund. *Libellus consolatorius de spectris, hoc est, apparitionibus et illusionibus daemonum.* Wittenberg: Typis Boreck, sumptibus Pauli Hellwigy, 1621.

Schott, Gaspar. *Magia universalis naturae et artis.* 4 parts. Würzburg: Sumpt. Haeredum Joannis Godefridi Schonwetteri, 1657–1659.

————. *Schola steganographica, in classes octo, distributa.* Nuremberg: Sumptibus Johannis Andreae Endteri, & Wolfgangi Junioris Haered., excudebat Jobus Hertz, 1680. First ed., Nuremberg: 1665.

————. *Physica curiosa aucta & correcta sive mirabilia naturae et artis.* Würzburg: Johannis Andreae Endteri & Wolfgangi, Jun. Haeredum, Excudebat Jobus Hertz, 1667.

Scott, Walter, ed. and trans. *Hermetica*. 4 vols. Oxford: Clarendon Press, 1924.

Selenus, Gustavus [=Duke August II of Braunschweig-Lüneburg]. *Cryptomenytices et cryptographiae libri IX, in quibus & planissima Steganographiae à Johanne Trithemio . . . admirandi ingenii viro, magicè & aenigmatice olim conscriptae, enodatio traditur.* Lüneburg: Excriptum typis & impensis Johannis & Henrici fratrum, 1624.

Sennert, Daniel. *De chymicorum cum Aristotelicis et Galenicis consensu et dissensu liber I.* Wittenberg: Apud Zachariam Schurerum, 1619.

Sigismund of Seeon. *Trithemius sui-ipsius vindex sive Steganographiae . . . apologetica defensio, ex ipso ferè Trithemio collecta et publici juris facta.* Ingolstadt: Ex typographeo Ederiano, apud Elisabetham Angermariam, 1616.

Sprenger, Jacob, and Heinrich Krämer [=Institor]. *Malleus Maleficarum.* Translated and edited by Montague Summers. London: John Rodker, 1928. Repr. 1948; repub. New York: Dover, 1971.

Tanner, Adam, *Astrologia sacra. . . .* Ingolstadt: Ex typographeo Ederiano apud Elisabetham Angermariam, 1615.

Tertullian, *The Apology.* Translated by S. Thelwall. In *Ante-Nicene Fathers*, III. translated and Edited by A. Cleveland Doxe. New York: Charles Scribner's Sons, 1899.

*Theatrum de veneficis.* Frankfurt: Nicolaus Basseus, 1586.

Thevet, André. *Pourtraits et vies des hommes illustres Grecz, Latins, et Payens recueilli de leur tableaux, livres, medales antiques et modernes.* Paris: I. Keruert et Guillaume Chaudiere, 1584.

Tille, Alexander, ed. *Die Faustsplitter in der Literatur des sechzehnten bis achtzehnten Jahrhunderts nach den ältesten Quellen.* Berlin: Emil Felber, 1900.

Trithemius, Johannes. *Opera pia et spiritualia.* Edited by Johannes Busaeus. Mainz: Ex typographeo Ioan. Albini, 1604, 1605.

———. *Opera historica, quotquot hactenus reperiri poteurunt omnia.* 2 parts. Edited by Marquard Freher. Frankfurt: Typis Wechelianis apud Claudium Marnium & haeredes Ioannis Aurbrij, 1601. Facsimile, Frankfurt: Minerva, 1966.

———. *Annales Hirsaugienses.* 2 vols. St. Gall: J. G. Schlegel, 1690.

———. *Nepiachus, ed est, libellus de studiis & scriptis propriis a pueritia repetitis.* In Johann Georg Eccard, *Corpus historicum medii aevi.* 2 vols. Leipzig: Apud Jo. Frid. Gleditschii B. Fil., 1723.

———. *De demonibus* [proemium and chapter headings extant]. In Klaus Arnold, "Additamenta Trithemiana: Nachträge zu Leben und Werk des Johannes Trithemius, insbesondere zur Schrift *De demonibus*," *Würzburger Diözesan Geschichtsblätter* 37–38 (1975), 256–67.

———. *Steganographia, hoc est, ars per occultam scripturam animi sui voluntatem absentibus aperiendi certa.* Frankfurt: Ex officina typographica Matthiae Beckeri, sumptibus Joannis Berneri, 1606, 1608, 1621.

———. *Clavis steganographiae.* Frankfurt: Apud Joannem Bernerum, 1606, 1608, 1621 (annexed to *Steganographia*).

———. *Polygraphiae libri VI.* Basel: M. Furter, 1518. Repub. Cologne: Apud Joannem Birckmannum & Theodorum Baumium, 1571, and Strassburg: Sumptibus Lazari Zetzneri, 1600.

———. *Clavis polygraphiae.* Basel: M. Furter, 1518 (annexed to *Polygraphia*).

———. *De septem secundeis, id est, intelligentiis, sive spiritibus orbes post Deum moventibus libellus sive Chronologia mystica.* Cologne: Apud Ioannem Birckmannum, 1567.

———. *Traite des causes secondes.* Paris: Chamuel, 1897. Repr., 1898.

———. *Von den syben Geysten oder Engeln den God die Hymel zu füre vom Anfang der Welt bevolte hat....* Nuremberg: durch Hieronymum Höltzel in Verlegung und Names des Johan Haselberg, 1522.

———. *Das Wunder Büchlein. Wie die Weldt von Anfang geregiert und erhalten ist....* Speyer: Jakob Schmidt, 1529.

[Trithemius, Johannes]. *Paralipomena opusculorum Petri Blenensis et Ioannis Trithemii.* Edited by Johannes Busaeus. Cologne: Apud Ioannem Wolffraht, 1624.

———. *Antwort Herrn Johann Abts Zu Spanhaim, auft act fragstuck... Hernn Maximilia....* Ingolstadt: durch Alexander unnd Samuel Weyssenhorn gebrüder, 1555.

———. *The Steganographia of Johannes Trithemius.* Translated by Fiona Tait, Christopher Upton and J. W. H. Walden. Edited, with intro., by Adam McLean. Edinburgh: Magnum opus Hermetic sourceworks, 1982.

———. *Polygraphie, et universelle escriture de M. I. Tritheme, abbé,... Avec les tables & figures concernants l'effaict & l'intelligence de l'occulte escriture... Traduicte par Gabriel de Collange.* Paris: I. Kerver, 1561. Repr. 1625.

Trithemius, Johannes, [Pseudo- ]. *Libri experimentorum Johannis Trithemij.* London: British National Library [Sloan], cod. 3670.

———. *De lapide philosophorum.* Halle: 1619.

———. *Veterum sophorum sigilla et imagines magicae... ad stupendos et mirandos effectus... Joa. Trithemii manuscripto erutae prodeunt.* N.p.: 1612; Herrenstadt, 1732, spuriously listed as Pesaro, 1502.

———. *Güldenes kleinod, oder: Schatzkästlein. Aus dem lateinischen, um seiner unschätzbarkeit willen, ins deutsche übers. von fr. Basilio Valentino....* Leipzig: P.G.. Kummer, 1782.

———. *Wunder-Buch von der gottlichen Magie, dem Planeten-und Geburtesstunden-Einfluss.* Stuttgart: J. Scheible, 1851, spuriously listed as Passau, 1506.

Vanini, Giulio Cesare. *Amphitheatrum aeternae providentiae divino-magicum, christiano-physicum, nec non astrologo-catholicum adversus philosophos, atheos, epicureos, peripateticos, et stoicos.* Lyons: Apud Viduam Antonii de Harsy, 1615.

[Vaughan, Thomas.] *The Works of Thomas Vaughan: Eugenius Philalethes.* Edited by Arthur Edward Waite. London/Edinburgh: Theosophical Publishing House (Neill & Co.), 1919.

Vigenère, Blaise de. *Traicté des chiffres, ou secretes manieres descrire.* Paris: Chez Abel L'Angelier, 1586.

Voet, Guisbert. *Selectarum disputationum theologicarum partes III.* 5 vols. Utrecht: Apud Joannem à Waesberge, 1648–1669.

Voss [=Vossius], Gerhard Johann. *De arte grammatica libri VII.* Amsterdam: Apud Guilielmum Blaev, 1635.

Webster, John. *The Displaying of Supposed witchcraft, Wherein is affirmed that there are many sorts of Deceivers and Impostors, and Divers persons under a passive Delusion of Melancholy and Fancy.* London: J.M., 1677.

Weyer [=Wier], Johann. *Opera omnia.* Amsterdam: Apud Petrum Vanden Berge, 1660.

———. *De praestigiis daemonum, incantationibus ac veneficiis libri VI.* Basel: Per Joannem Oporinum, 1563. Repr. 1564, 1566.

———. *Witches, Devils, and Doctors in the Renaissance [De praestigiis daemonum].* Edited by George Mora and Benjamin Kohl, translated by John Shea. Medieval and Renaissance Texts and Studies, vol. 73. Binghamton: State University of New York Press, 1991.

Wilkins, John. *Mercury, or the Secret and Swift Messenger: Shewing, How a Man may with Privacy and Speed communicate his Thoughts to a Friend at any distance.* London: Printed by I. Norton, for John Maynard and Timothy Wilkins, 1641.

Wilkins, John, and Seth Ward. *Vindiciae Academiarum conteining, Some briefe Animadversions upon Mr. Websters Book stiled, the Examination of Academies. . . .* Oxford: Leonard Lichfield for Thomas Robinson, 1654. Repr. in Debus, *Science and Education,* pp. 193ff.

William of Auvergne [=William of Paris]. *Opera omnia.* Edited by B. Le Feron. 2 vols. Orléans: Apud Michalem du-Neuf-Germain, 1674.

Wion, Arnold. *Lignum vitae, ornamentum, et decus ecclesiae, in quinque libros divisum, in quibus totius sanctiss. religionis divi Benedicti initia, viri dignitate, doctrina, sanctitate ac principatu clari describantur.* Venice: Apud G. Angelerium, 1595. German trans.: *Lignum vitae. Baum des Lebens. . . .* Augsburg: In Verlegung Domini Custodis, 1607.

Witekind, Hermann [=Lercheimer, Augustin]. *Christlich bedencken und erinnerung von Zauberey, woher, was, und wie vielfeltig sie sey. . . .* Speyer: Bernhart Albin, 1597. Repr., edited by Carl Binz, Strassburg: Heitz und Mündel, 1885; 2d ed. 1888.

Zara, Antonio. *Anatomia ingeniorum et scientiarum*. Venice: Ambrosii Dei & Fratrum, 1615.

Zetzner, Lazarus. *Theatrum Chemicum*. 6 vols. Strassburg: Lazari Zetzneri, 1613–1661.

Ziegelbauer, Magnoald, and Oliver Legipont. *Historia rei literariae ordinis sancti Benedicti. In iv. partes distributa....* Augsburg/Würgsburg: Sumptibus Martini Veith, 1754.


## Secondary Sources


Anglo, Sidney, ed. *Folie et Déraison à la Renaissance*. Brussels: Editions de l'Université de Bruxelles, 1976.

———, ed. *The Damned Art: Essays in the Literature of Witchcraft*. London: Routledge & Kegan Paul, 1977.

Arnold, Klaus. *Johannes Trithemius (1462-1516)*. Quellen und Forschungen zur Geschichte des Bistums und Hochstifts Würzburg, vol. 23. 2d ed. Würzburg: Kommissionsverlag Ferdinand Schöningh, 1991. First ed.: 1971.

———. "Additamenta Trithemiana...." See primary sources: Trithemius.

Auernheimer, Richard, and Frank Baron, eds. *Johannes Trithemius: Humanismus und Magie im vorreformatorischen Deutschland*. Bad Kreuznacher Symposien I, 1985. Munich: Profil, 1991.

Backes, Martina. *Das literarische Leben am kurpfälzischen Hof zu Heidelberg im 15. Jahrhundert: Ein Beitrug zur Gönnerforschung des Spätmittelalters*. Tübingen: Max Niemeyer, 1992.

Baroja, Julio Caro. *The World of Witches*. Translated by Nigel Glendinning. London: Weidenfeld and Nicolson, 1961, 1964.

Baron, Frank. *Doctor Faustus from History to Legend*. Munich: Wilhelm Fink, 1978.

———. *Faustus. Geschichte, Sage, Dichtung*. Munich: Winkler, 1978.

Barstow, Anne Llewellyn. *Witchcraze: A New History of the European Witch Hunts*. San Francisco/London: HarperCollins [Pandora], 1994.

Beitchman, Philip. *Alchemy of the Word: Cabala of the Renaissance*. Albany: State University of New York Press, 1998.

Bett, Henry. *Joachim of Flora*. London: Methuen, 1931.

Blau, Joseph Leon. *The Christian Interpretation of the Cabala in the Renaissance*. New York: Columbia University Press, 1944.

Bloomfield, Morton W. *The Seven Deadly Sins: An Introduction to the History of a Religious Concept, with Special Reference to Medieval English Literature*. East Lansing: Michigan State College Press, 1952.

Boerner, Peter, and Sidney Johnson, eds. *Faust through Four Centuries: Retrospect and Analysis / Rückblick und Analyse.* Tübingen: Max Niemeyer, 1989.

Borchardt, Frank L. *German Antiquity in Renaissance Myth.* Baltimore: Johns Hopkins Press, 1971.

———. "The *Magus* as Renaissance Man." *Sixteenth Century Journal,* 21 (1990), 57-76.

Brann, Noel L. *The Abbot Trithemius (1462–1516): The Renaissance of Monastic Humanism.* Studies in the History of Christian Thought, vol. 24. Leiden: E. J. Brill, 1981.

———. "The Shift from Mystical to Magical Theology in the Abbot Trithemius (1462–1516)." *Studies in Medieval Culture,* XI. Edited by John R. Sommerfeldt and Thomas H. Seiler. Medieval Institute, Western Michigan University, 1977, 147–59.

———. "A Monastic Dilemma Posed by the Invention of Printing: the Context of the *De laude scriptorum manualium* by Abbot Johann Trithemius." *Visible Language,* 13 (1979): 150–67.

———. "George Ripley and the Abbot Trithemius: An Inquiry into Contrasting Medical Attitudes." *Ambix,* 16 (1979): 212–20.

———. "Is Acedia Melancholy? A Re-examination of This Question in the Light of Fra Battista da Crema's *Della cognitione et vittoria di se stesso* (1531)," *Journal of the History of Medicine and Allied Sciences,* 34 (1979): 180–99.

———. "Was Paracelsus a Disciple of Trithemius?" *Sixteenth Century Journal,* 10 (1979): 70–82.

———. "The Conflict between Reason and Magic in Seventeenth Century England: A Case Study of the Vaughan-More Debate." *Huntington Library Quarterly,* 43 (1980): 103–26.

———. "Pre-Reformation Humanism in Germany and the Papal Monarchy: A Study in Ambivalence." *The Journal of Medieval and Renaissance Studies,* 14 (1984): 159–85.

———. "Alchemy and Melancholy in Medieval and Renaissance Thought: A Query into the Mystical Basis of their Relationship." *Ambix,* 32 (1985): 127–48.

Brown, Peter. *Religion and Society in the Age of Saint Augustine.* London: Faber & Faber; New York: Harper & Row, 1972.

Brückner, Wolfgang, ed. *Volkserzählung und Reformation: Ein Handbuch zur Tradierung und Funktion von Erzählstoffen und Erzählliteratur im Protestantismus.* Berlin: Erich Schmidt Verlag; Druck: A. W. Hayn's Erben, 1974.

Buck, August, ed. *Die okkulten Wissenschaften in der Renaissance.* Wolfenbüttler Wisenchaften in der Renaissance, no. 12. Wiesbaden: Harrassowitz, 1992.

Burkert, Walter. *Lore and Science in Ancient Pythagoreanism.* Translated by E. Minar. Cambridge, Mass.: Harvard University Press, 1972.

Butler, E. M. *The Myth of the Magus.* Cambridge: Cambridge University Press; New York: Macmillan, 1948.

———. *The Fortunes of Faust.* Cambridge: Cambridge University Press, 1952.

Cassirer, Ernst. *The Individual and the Cosmos in Renaissance Philosophy.* Translated by Mario Domandi. New York: Harper, 1963.

———. *The Platonic Renaissance in England.* Translated by James P. Pettegrove. Austin: University of Texas Press, 1953.

Cassirer, Ernst et al. *The Renaissance Philosophy of Man.* See primary sources.

Céard, Jean, ed. *La Curiosité a la Renaissance.* Paris: Société d'Edition d'Enseignement Supérieur, 1986.

Chacornac, Paul. *Grandeur et Adversité de Jean Trithème, Bénédictin Abbé de Spanheim et de Wurtzbourg (1462-1516): la Vie, la legende, l'Oeuvre.* Paris: Editions Traditionelles, 1963.

Chappell, Vere, ed. *Seventeenth Century Natural Scientists.* Vol. 7: *Essays on Early Modern Philosophers from Descartes and Hobbes to Newton and Leibniz.* New York: Garland, 1992.

Clulee, Nicholas H. *John Dee's Natural Philosophy: Between Science and Religion.* London: Routledge, 1988.

Cohn, Norman. *Europe's Inner Demons.* New York: Basic Books, 1975; repr., New American Library [Meridian], 1977. Also, Sussex: Sussex University Press, 1975; London: Paladin, 1976.

Cooperman, Bernard Dov, ed. *Jewish Thought in the Sixteenth Century.* Cambridge, Mass.: Harvard University Press, 1983.

Copenhaver, Brian P. *Symphorien Champier and the Reception of the Occultist Tradition in Renaissance France.* The Hague: Mouton, 1978.

———. "Scholastic Philosophy and Renaissance Magic in the *De vita* of Marsilio Ficino. *Renaissance Quarterly,* 37 (1984): 523-54.

Copenhaver, Brian P., and Charles B. Schmitt. *Renaissance Philosophy.* Oxford: Oxford University Press, 1992.

Couliano, Ioan P. *Eros and Magic in the Renaissance.* Translated by Margaret Cook, with forward by Mircea Eliade. Chicago: University of Chicago Press, 1987.

Culianu, Ioan P. See Couliano.

Deacon, Richard. *John Dee: Scientist, Geographer, Astrologer and Secret Agent to Elizabeth I.* London: Frederick Muller, 1968.

De Bruyn, L. *Women and the Devil in Sixteenth-Century Literature.* Tisbury, Wilts., 1979.

Debus, Allen G., ed. *Science, Medicine and Society in the Renaissance: Essays to Honor Walter Pagel.* 2 vols. New York: Neale Watson, 1972.
———. *The Chemical Philosophy: Paracelsian Science and Medicine in the Sixteenth and Seventeenth Centuries.* New York: Science History Publications, div. of Neale Watson Academic Publications, 1977.
———. *The French Paracelsians: The Chemical Challenge to Medical and Scientific Tradition in Early Modern France.* Cambridge: Cambridge University Press, 1991.
———. *Science and Education in the Seventeenth Century.* ... See primary sources.
Debus, Allen G., and Michael T. Walton, eds. *Reading the Book of Nature: The Other Side of the Scientific Revolution.* Sixteenth Century Essays and Studies, Vol. 41. Kirksville, Mo.: Sixteenth Century Journal Publications, 1998.
Dobbs, Betty Jo Teeter. *The Foundations of Newton's Alchemy; or, "The Hunting of the Greene Lyon."* Cambridge: Cambridge University Press, 1975.
———. *The Janus Faces of Genius: The Role of Alchemy in Newton's Thought.* Cambridge: Cambridge University Press, 1991.
Dodds, E. R. *Pagan and Christian in an Age of Anxiety: Some Aspects of Religious Experience from Marcus Aurelius to Constantine.* New York: Norton, 1965, 1970.
Drake, Ellen Tan. *Restless Genius: Robert Hooke and His Earthly Thought.* Oxford: Oxford University Press, 1996.
Dröscher, Ernst. *Die Methoden der Geheimschriften.* Leipzig: K. F. Koehler, 1921.
Dürrwächter, Anton. "Adam Tanner und die Steganographie des Trithemius." In *Hermann Grauert zur Vollendung des 60. Lebensjahres: Festgabe zur 7. September 1910.* Freiburg im Breisgau: Herdesche Verlagshandlung, 1910.
Dulles, Avery. *Princeps Concordiae: Pico della Mirandola and the Scholastic Tradition.* Cambridge, Mass.: Harvard University Press, 1941.
Easlea, Brian. *Witch Hunting, Magic and the New Philosophy: An Introduction to Debates of the Scientific Revolution, 1450–1750.* Sussex: Harvester Press/Atlantic Highlands, N.J.: Humanities Press, 1980.
Eisenbichler, Konrad, and Olga Zorzi Pugliese, eds. *Ficino and Renaissance Neoplatonism.* University of Toronto Italian Studies, 1. Ottawa: Dovehouse Editions, 1986.
Ernst, Thomas. "Schwarzweisse Magie: Der Schlüssel zum dritten Buch der *Steganographia* des Trithemius." *Daphnis: Zeitschrift für Mittlere Deutsche Literatur,* 25 (1996): 1–205.

Evans, R. J. W. *Rudolf II and his World: A Study in Intellectual History, 1576–1612.* Oxford: Clarendon Press, 1973.

Faivre, Antoine. *Access to Western Esotericism.* Albany: State University of New York Press, 1994.

———. *The Eternal Hermes: From Greek God to Alchemical Magus.* Translated by Joscelyn Godwin. Grand Rapids, Mich.: Phanes, 1995.

Faivre, Antoine, Jacob Needleman, and Karen Voss, eds. *Modern Esoteric Spirituality.* New York: Crossroad, 1992.

Farmer, Stephen A. See primary sources: Pico della Mirandola.

Fleischer, Manfred P., ed. *The Harvest of Humanism in Central Europe: Essays in Honor of Lewis W. Spitz.* St. Louis: Concordia, 1992.

Flint, Valerie I. J. *The Rise of Magic in Early Medieval Europe.* Princeton, N.J.: Princeton University Press, 1991.

Fouke, Daniel. *The Enthusiastical Concerns of Dr. Henry More: Religious Meaning and the Psychology of Delusion.* Leiden: E. J. Brill, 1997.

French, Peter J. *John Dee: The World of an Elizabethan Magus.* London: Routledge & Kegan Paul, 1972.

Galland, Joseph S. *An Historical and Analytical Bibliography of the Literature of Cryptology.* New York: AMS Press, 1945.

Garin, Eugenio. *Giovanni Pico della Mirandola: Vita e Dottrina.* Florence: Felice Le Monnier, 1937.

———. *Astrology in the Renaissance: The Zodiac of Life.* Translated by Carolyn Jackson, June Allen, and Clare Robertson. London: Routledge & Kegan Paul, 1983.

Garin et al., eds. *Testi umanistici su l'ermetismo....* See primary sources.

Geiger, Ludwig. *Johann Reuchlin: Sein Leben und Seine Werke.* Leipzig: Dunker & Humblot, 1871.

Geneva, Ann. *Astrology and the Seventeenth Century Mind: William Lilly and the Language of the Stars.* Manchester: Manchester University Press, 1995.

Gerwalin, H., ed. *500-Jahrfeier Johannes Trithemius 1462–1962 am 11. August 1962 in Trittenheim/Mosel.* Trittenheim: Gemeinde Trittenheim: 1962.

Godwin, Joscelyn. *Athanasius Kircher: A Renaissance Man and the Quest for Lost Knowledge.* London: Thames and Hudson, 1979.

———. *The Theosophical Enlightenment.* Albany: State University of New York Press, 1994.

Godwin, Joscelyn, Christian Chanel, and John P. Deveney. *The Hermetic Brotherhood of Luxor: Initiatic and Historical Documents of an Order of Practical Occultism.* York Beach, Me.: Samuel Weiser, 1995.

Grafton, Anthony. *Defenders of the Text: The Traditions of an Age of Science, 1450–1800.* Cambridge, Mass.: Harvard University Press, 1991.

Grunsky, Hans. *Jacob Boehme*. Stuttgart: Fromman-Holzboog, 1956.

Günther, Mahal, ed. *Der historische Faust: Ein wissenschaftliches Symposium (26./27. September 1980)*. Knittlingen: Publikationen des Faust-Archivs [PFA] ), 1982.

Guinsburg, Arlene Miller. "Henry Moore, Thomas Vaughan and the Late Renaissance Magical Tradition." *Ambix*, 27 (1980): 36–58.

Hall, A. Rupert. *Henry More: Magic, Religion, and Experiment*. Oxford: Basil Blackwell, 1990.

Hansen, Joseph. *Zauberwahn, Inquisition und Hexenprozess im Mittelalter und die Entstehung der Grossen Hexenverfolgung*. Munich: R. Oldenbourg, 1900.

Harmening, Dieter. "Faust und die Renaissance-Magie: zum ältesten Faustzeugnis (Johannes Trithemius an Johannes Virdung, 1507)." *Archiv für Kulturgeschichte*, 55 (1973): 56–79.

Heninger, S. K. *Touches of Sweet Harmony: Pythagorean Cosmology and Renaissance Poetics*. San Marino, Calif.: Huntington Library, 1974.

Hermes, Johann Joseph. *Über das Leben und die Schriften des Johannes von Trittenheim, genannt Trithemius*. Beilage zum Jahresbericht des Gymnasiums zum Prüm Ostern, 1901.

Hopkin, Charles E. *The Share of Thomas Aquinas in the Growth of the Witchcraft Delusion*. Philadelphia: University of Pennsylvania Press, 1940.

Huffman, William H. *Robert Fludd and the End of the Renaissance*. London: Routledge, 1988.

Hughes, Penethorne. *Witchcraft*. London: Longman, Greens, 1952; Penguin, 1965.

Hunter, Michael, and Simon Schaffer, eds. *Robert Hooke: New Studies*. Woodbridge, England: Boydell Press, 1989.

Hutin, Serge. *Robert Fludd (1574–1637): Alchimiste et Philosophe Rosicrucien*. Paris: Omnium Litéraire, 1971.

Joachimsen, Paul. *Geschichtsauffassung und Geschichtschreibung in Deutschland unter dem Einfluss des Humanismus*. Leipzig: B. G. Teubner, 1910.

Josten, C. H. "A Translation of John Dee's Monas Hieroglyphica (Antwerp, 1564), with an Introduction and Annotations." *Ambix*, 12 (1964): 84–220.

Kahn, David. *The Codebreakers: The Story of Secret Writing*. New York: Macmillan, 1967.

Kelly, Henry Ansgar. *The Devil, Demonology, and Witchcraft: The Development of Christian Beliefs in Evil Spirits*. New York: Doubleday, 1968.

Kieckhefer, Richard. *European Witch Trials: Their Foundations in Popular Culture, 1300–1500*. Berkeley: University of California Press, 1976.

———. *Magic in the Middle Ages*. Cambridge: Cambridge University Press, 1989.

Kiesewetter, Karl. *Faust in der Geschichte und Tradition, mit besonderer Berücksichtigung des occulten Phänomenalismus und des mittelalterlichen Zauberwesens*. Hildesheim: Georg Olms, 1963.

Kirsch, Irving. "Demonology and the Rise of Science: An Example of the Misperception of Historical Data." *Journal of the History of the Behavioral Sciences*, 14 (1978), 149–57.

———. "Demonology and Science during the Scientific Revolution," *Journal of the History of the Behavioral Sciences* 16 (1980), 359–68.

Klaits, Joseph. *Servants of Satan: The Age of the Witch Hunts*. Bloomington: Indiana University Press, 1985.

Klibansky, Raymond, Erwin Panofsky, and Fritz Saxl. *Saturn and Melancholy: Studies in the History of Natural Philosophy, Religion, and Art*. New York: Basic Books, 1964. Revised and enlarged ed. of Panofsky and Saxl, *Dürers 'Melencolia I': Eine quellen- und typengeschichtliche Untersuchung*. Studien der Bibliothek Warburg. Leipzig: B. G. Teubner, 1923.

Kopp, Hermann. *Die Alchemie in Älterer und Neuerer Zeit*. 2 parts. Heidelberg: Carl Winter, 1886. Repr., Hildesheim, 1962.

Kors, Alan, and Edward Peters, eds. *Witchcraft in Europe, 1300–1700*.... See primary sources.

Kristeller, Paul Oskar. *Studies in Renaissance Thought and Letters*. Rome: Edizioni di Storia e Letteratura, 1969.

Lea, Henry Charles. *Materials toward a History of Witchcraft*. Edited by Arthur C. Howland. 3 vols. Philadelphia: University of Pennsylvania Press, 1938.

Leitschuh, Franz Friedrich. "Quellen und Studien zur Geschichte des Kunst- und Geisteslebens in Franken. I. Trithemius und Dürer." *Archiv des historischen Vereins von Unterfranken und Aschaffenburg*, 44 (1902): 185–95.

Levack, Brian P. *The Witch-Hunt in Early Modern Europe*. 2d ed. London: Longman, 1995. First ed., 1987.

Lindberg, David C., ed. *Science in the Middle Ages*. Chicago: University of Chicago Press, 1978.

Macfarlane, Alan. *Witchcraft in Tudor and Stuart England*. London: Routledge & Kegan Paul, 1970.

McIntosh, Christopher. *The Rose Cross and the Age of Reason: Eighteenth Century Rosicrucianism in Central Europe and Its Relationship to the Enlightenment*, Studies in Intellectual History, no. 29. Leiden: E. J. Brill: 1992.

McKnight, Stephen A. *The Modern Age and the Recovery of Ancient Wisdom: A Reconsideration of Historical Consciousness, 1450–1650*. Columbia: University of Missouri Press, 1991.

Mahoney, Edward P., ed. *Philosophy and Humanism: Renaissance Essays in Honor of Paul Oskar Kristeller*. New York: Columbia University Press, 1976.

Malinowski, Bronislaw. *Magic, Science, and Religion.* New York: Doubleday-Anchor, 1954.

Mandrou, Robert. *Magistrats et Sorciers en France au XVII$^e$ Siècle.* Paris: Librairie Plon, 1968.

Martin, Ruth. *Witchcraft and the Inquisition in Venice, 1550–1650.* Oxford: Basel Blackwell, 1989.

Maus, Hansjörg. *Faust: Eine Deutsche Legende.* Vienna/Munich: Meyster, 1980.

Meister, Aloys. *Die Anfänge der Modernen Diplomatischen Geheimschrift.* Paderhorn: F. Schöningh, 1902.

Merkel, Ingrid, and Allen G. Debus, eds. *Hermeticism and the Renaissance: Intellectual History and the Occult in Early Modern Europe.* Washington D.C.: Folger Shakespeare Library/London and Toronto: Associated University Presses, 1988.

Midelfort, H. C. Erik. *Witch Hunting in Southwestern Germany, 1562–1684: The Social and Intellectual Foundations.* Stanford, Calif.: Stanford University Press, 1972.

Mintz, Samuel, I. *The Hunting of Leviathan: Seventeenth-Century Reactions to the Materialism and Moral Philosophy of Thomas Hobbes.* Cambridge: Cambridge University Press, 1962.

Molhuysen, P. C. *Cornelius Aurelius: Korte Schets van Zijn Lèven en Werke.* Leiden: S. C. Van Doesburgh, 1902.

Momigliano, Arnaldo, ed. *The Conflict between Paganism and Christianity.* Oxford: Clarendon Press, 1963.

Monter, E. William. *Witchcraft in France and Switzerland: The Borderlands during the Reformation.* Ithaca, N.Y.: Cornell University Press, 1976.

Nauert, Charles G., Jr. *Agrippa and the Crisis of Renaissance Thought.* Illinois Studies in the Social Sciences, no. 55. Urbana: University of Illinois Press, 1965.

Netzhammer, P. Raymund. *Theophrastus Paracelsus: Das Wissenswerteste über dessen Leben, Lehre und Schriften.* Einsiedeln-Waldshut-Köln: Benziger, 1901.

Neusner, Jacob, Ernest S. Frerichs, and Paul Virgil McCracken Flesher, eds. *Religion, Science, and Magic in Concert and in Conflict.* Oxford: Oxford University Press, 1989.

Newman, William. "Thomas Vaughan as an Interpreter of Agrippa von Nettesheim." *Ambix,* 29 (1982): 125–40.

Pachter, Henry M. *Paracelsus: Magic into Science.* New York: Henry Schuman, 1951.

Pächter, Heinz. *Paracelsus: Das Urbild des Doktor Faustus.* Zürich: Büchergilde Gutenberg, 1955.

Pagel, Walter. *Paracelsus: An Introduction to Philosophical Medicine in the Era of the Renaissance*. Basel/New York: S. Karger, 1958.

———. *Das Medizinische Weltbild des Paracelsus: Seine Zusammenhänge mit Neuplatonismus und Gnosis*. Wiesbaden: Franz Steiner, 1962.

———. *The Smiling Spleen: Paracelsianism in Storm and Stress*. Basel: S. Karger, 1984.

Palmer, Philip Mason, and Robert Pattison More. *The Sources of the Faust Tradition from Simon Magus to Lessing*. Oxford: Oxford University Press, 1936.

Panofsky, Erwin, and Fritz Saxl. *Dürers' 'Melencolia I.'* . . . See Klibansky, Panofsky, and Saxl, *Saturn and Melancholy*.

Partington, James Riddick. *A History of Chemistry*. 4 vols. London: Macmillan, 1961.

Peters, Edward. *The Magician, the Witch, and the Law*. Philadelphia: University of Pennsylvania Press, 1978.

Peuckert, Will-Erich. *Das Leben Jakob Böhmes*. Jena: Eugen Diederichs, 1924.

———. *Pansophie: Ein Versuch zur Geschichte der weissen und schwarzen Magie*. Stuttgart: W. Kohlhammer, 1936.

Philip, J. A. *Pythagoras and Early Pythagoreanism*. Toronto: University of Toronto Press, 1968.

Plancy, Collin de. *Dictionnaire de Sciences Occultes*. 2 vols. Vols. 49–50 in Migne, ed. *Encyclopédie Théologique*. Paris: Chez l'Editeur aux Ateliers Catholiques du Petit-Montrouge, 1848.

Pratt, Fletcher. *Secret and Urgent: The Story of Codes and Ciphers*. London: Robert Hale, 1939.

Rabil, Albert, Jr., ed. *Renaissance Humanism: Foundations, Forms, and Legacy*. 3 vols. Philadelphia: University of Pennsylvania Press, 1988, 1991.

Randall, John Herman, Jr. *The Career of Philosophy: Vol. I, From the Middle Ages to the Enlightenment*. New York: Columbia University Press, 1962.

Rattansi, Piyo, and Antonio Clericuzio, eds. *Alchemy and Chemistry in the Sixteenth and Seventeenth Centuries*. International Archives of the History of Ideas, no. 140. Boston/Dordrecht: Kluwer, 1994.

Read, John. *Prelude to Chemistry: An Outline of Alchemy*. London: G. Bell and Sons, 1936. 2d ed., 1939. Repr. Cambridge: Massachussetts Institute of Technology, 1966.

Reeves, Majorie. *The Influence of Prophecy in the Later Middle Ages: A Study in Joachimism*. Oxford: Clarendon Press, 1969.

Renaudet, Augustine. *Préréforme et Humanisme à Paris pendant les Premières Guerres d'Italie (1494–1517)*. 2d ed., Paris: Librairie d'Argences, 1953.

Reusch, Franz Heinrich. *Der Index der Verbotenen Bücher: Ein Beitrag zur Kirchen -und Literaturgeschichte.* 2 vols. Bonn: Max Cohen & Son, 1885.

Righini Bonelli, M. L. and William R. Shea, eds. *Reason, Experiment and Mysticism in the Scientific Revolution.* New York: Science History Publications, 1975.

Robbins, Rossell Hope. *The Encyclopedia of Witchcraft and Demonology.* London: Peter Nevill, 1959.

Roper, Lyndal. *Oedipus and the Devil: Witchcraft, Sexuality and Religion, 1500–1700.* London: Routledge, 1994.

Rossi, Paolo. *Francis Bacon: From Magic to Science.* Translated by Sacha Rabinovitch. Chicago: University of Chicago Press, 1968.

Rupprich, Hans. *Humanismus und Renaissance in den deutschen Städten und an den Universitäten.* Leipzig: P. Reclam jun., 1935. Reprint, Darmstadt: Wissenschaftliche Buchgesellschaft, 1964, 1965.

Ruska, Julius. *Tabula Smaragdina: Ein Beitrag zur Geschichte der Hermetischen Literatur.* Heidelberg: Carl Winter, 1926.

Russell, Jeffrey Burton. *Witchcraft in the Middle Ages.* Ithaca, N.Y.: Cornell University Press, 1972.

———. *The Devil: Perceptions of Evil from Antiquity to Primitive Christianity.* Ithaca, N.Y.: Cornell University Press, 1977.

*Sammler Fürst Gelehrter Herzog August zur Braunschweig und Lüneburg, 1579–1666.* Wölfenbüttel: Herzog August Bibliothek, 1979.

Scarre, Geoffrey. *Witchcraft and Magic in 16th and 17th Century Europe.* Atlantic Highlands, N.J.: Humanities Press International, 1987.

Schleiner, Winfried. *Melancholy, Genius, and Utopia in the Renaissance.* Wiesbaden: Otto Harrassowitz, 1991.

Schmitt, Charles B., Quentin Skinner, Eckhard Kessler, and Jill Kraye, eds. *The Cambridge History of Renaissance Philosophy.* Cambridge: Cambridge University Press, 1988.

Schneegans, Wilhelm. *Abt Johannes Trithemius und Kloster Sponheim.* Kreuznach: Reinhard Schmithals, 1882.

Secret, François. *Les Kabbalistes Chrétiens de la Renaissance.* Paris: Dunod, 1964.

———. "Qui était Libanius Gallus, le maître de Jean Trithème?" *Estudios Lulianos,* 6 (1962): 127–37.

Shapiro, Barbara J. *John Wilkins, 1614–1672: An Intellectual Biography.* Berkeley: University of California Press, 1969.

Sherman, William H. *John Dee: The Politics and Reading and Writing in the English Renaissance.* Amherst: University of Massachusetts Press, 1995.

Shumaker, Wayne. *The Occult Sciences in the Renaissance: A Study in Intellectual Patterns.* Berkeley: University of California Press, 1972.

————. *Renaissance Curiosa: John Dee's Conversations with Angels / Girolamo Cardano's Horoscope of Christ / Johannes Trithemius and Cryptography / George Dalgarno's Universal Language.* Medieval & Renaissance Texts and Studies, Vol. 8. Binghamton: State University of New York Press, 1982.

————. *Natural Magic and Modern Science: Four Treatises, 1590–1657.* Medieval and Renaissance Texts and Studies, Vol. 63, State University of New York Press, 1989.

Silbernagel, Isidor. *Trithemius: Eine Monographie.* Landshut: F. G. Wölfe, 1868. 2d ed., Regensburg: 1885.

Singer, Charles, ed. *Studies in the History and Method of Science.* 2 vols. Oxford: Clarendon Press, 1917.

Singleton, Charles S., ed. *Art, Science, and History in the Renaissance.* Baltimore: Johns Hopkins Press, 1967.

Smeed, John W. *Faust in Literature.* Oxford: Oxford University Press, 1975.

Smith, Charlotte Fell. *John Dee (1527–1608).* London: Constable, 1909.

Spitz, Lewis W. *The Religious Renaissance of the German Humanists.* Cambridge, Mass.: Harvard University Press, 1963.

Stoudt, Debra L. " 'Probatum est per me': The Heidelberg Electors as Practitioners and Patrons of the Medical and Magical Arts." *Cauda Pavonis,* 14 (1995): 12–18.

Strasser, Gerhard H. "The Noblest Cryptologist: Duke August the Younger of Brunswick-Luneburg (Gustavus Selenus) and his Cryptological Activities." *Cryptologia,* 9 (1983): 193–217.

Strauss, Gerald. *Historian in an Age of Crisis: The Life and Work of Johannes Aventinus, 1477–1534.* Cambridge, Mass.: Harvard University Press, 1963.

Sudhoff, Karl. *Paracelsus: Ein deutsches Lebensbild aus den Tagen der Renaissance.* Leipzig: Bibliographisches Institut, 1936.

Thomas, Keith. *Religion and the Decline of Magic: Studies in Popular Beliefs in Sixteenth and Seventeenth Century England.* London: Weidenfeld and Nicolson, 1971.

Thompson, James Westfall, and Saul K. Padover. *Secret Diplomacy, Espionage and Cryptography (1500–1815).* New York: F. Ungar, 1963.

Thorndike, Lynn. *A History of Magic and Experimental Science.* 8 vols. New York: Columbia University Press, 1929–1958.

Telle, Joachim, ed. *Parega Paracelsica: Paracelsus in Vergangenheit und Gegenwart.* Stuttgart: Steiner, 1992.

Tille, Alexander. *Die Faustsplitter. . . .* See primary sources.

Tomlinson, Gary. *Music in Renaissance Magic: Toward a Historiography of Others.* Chicago: University of Chicago Press, 1993.

Trevor-Roper, H. R. *The European Witch-Craze of the Sixteenth and Seventeenth Centuries and Other Essays.* New York: Harper & Row [Torchbook], 1969. Repr. of chs. 1–4, *The Crisis of the Seventeenth Century: Religion, the Reformation and Social Change.* New York: Harper & Row, 1968.

Vickers, Brian, ed. *Occult and Scientific Mentalities in the Renaissance.* Cambridge: Cambridge University Press, 1984.

———. "Frances Yates and the Writing of History." *Journal of Modern History,* 51 (1979): 287–316.

Victor, Joseph M. *Charles de Bouelles, 1479–1533.* Travaux d'Humanisme et Renaissance, no. 161. Geneva: Droz, 1978.

Walker, D. P. *Spiritual and Demonic Magic from Ficino to Campanella.* Studies of the Warburg Institute, vol. 22. London: Warburg Institute, 1958. Repr.: Nendeln/Liechtenstein, 1969.

———. *The Ancient Theology: Studies in Christian Platonism from the Fifteenth to the Eighteenth Century.* London: Duckworth, 1972.

Webster, Charles. *From Paracelsus to Newton: Magic and the Making of Modern Science.* Cambridge: Cambridge University Press, 1982.

Weeks, Andrew. *Boehme: An Intellectual Biography of the Seventeenth-Century Philosopher and Mystic.* Albany: State University of New York Press, 1991.

———. *Paracelsus: Speculative Theory and the Crisis of the Early Reformation.* Albany: State University of New York Press, 1997.

Wenzel, Siegfried. *The Sin of Sloth: Acedia in Medieval Thought and Literature.* Chapel Hill: University of North Carolina Press, 1967.

Westman, Robert S., and J. E. McGuire. *Hermeticism and the Scientific Revolution: Papers Read at a Clark Library Seminar, March 9, 1974.* Los Angeles: University of California Press, 1977.

Whitby, Christopher. *John Dee's Actions with Spirits: 22 December 1581 to 23 May 1583.* 2 vols. New York: Garland, 1988.

White, Michael. *Isaac Newton: The Last Sorcerer.* Reading, Mass.: Addison-Wesley, 1997.

Williams, Gerhild Scholz. *Defining Dominion: The Discourses of Magic and Witchcraft in Early Modern France and Germany.* Ann Arbor: University of Michigan Press, 1995.

Wittkower, Rudolf. *Architectural Principles in the Age of Humanism.* First pub. as vol. 19, *Studies of the Warburg Institute.* Revised ed., London: Alec Tiranti, 1962, 1971.

Wolfe, James Raymond. *Secret Writing: The Craft of the Cryptographer.* New York: 1970.

Yates, Frances. *Giordano Bruno and the Hermetic Tradition.* London: Routledge and Kegan Paul, 1964.

———. *The Art of Memory.* London: Routledge & Kegan Paul, 1966; Harmondsworth, Middlesex: Penguin, 1969.

———. *Theatre of the World*. Chicago: University of Chicago Press, 1969.

———. *The Rosicrucian Enlightenment*. London: Routledge & Kegan Paul, 1972.

———. *The Occult Philosophy in the Elizabethan Age*. London: Routledge & Kegan Paul, 1979.

Zambelli, Paola. "A proposito del *De vanitate scientiarum et artium* di Cornelio Agrippa." *Rivista Critica di Storia della Filosofia*, 2 (1960): 167–81.

Ziegelbauer and Legipont. *Historia rei literariae ordinis sancti Benedicti*. See primary sources.

Zika, Charles. "Reuchlin's *De Verbo Mirifico* and the Magic Debate of the Late Fifteenth Century." *Journal of Warburg and Courtauld Institutes*, 39 (1976), 104–38.

———. "Reuchlin and Erasmus: Humanism and Occult Philosophy." *Journal of Religious History*, 9 (1976–77): 223–46.

Zilboorg, Gregory, and George W. Henry. *A History of Medical Psychology*. New York: W. W. Norton, 1941.

# Index

Abano, Pietro d': as Conciliator, 25; and apocalyptic climate, 25; view of, as sorcerer, 172, 185, 195; Trithemius's ambivalence toward, 68–69; spuriously attributed tracts of, 67; as source of astrological-angelogical system, 25, 68–69, 114, 134, 143

*Abbreviatura*, 205

Abelard, Peter, 20, 21

accidia. *See* demons: accidia

Agrippa of Nettesheim, Heinrich Cornelius: early relationship of, to Trithemius, 152–56; later ambivalence of, 157–61; magical theory of, 3, 152–55; Christianization by, of Hermetic *magnum miraculum*, 155; and divine frenzy (*see* Plato: divine frenzy); relationship to Weyer of (*see* Weyer: Agrippa); magical legend of, 167, 168, 189, 195, 216, 217, 225, 240; as forerunner of Rosicrucians, 220–25; as

reputed mediator for Dürer's *Melencolia I*, 248

Ailly, Pierre d', 26

Alberti, Leon Battista, 312n

Albertus Magnus: and theory of magic, 23–24; role of, as model, 10–11, 91–95, 162; spuriously attributed tracts of, 67; attribution of *Speculum astronomiae* to, 133–34; mentioned, 27, 68, 154, 163, 185, 250

alchemy: illicit forms of, 65, 70–72, 89, 99, 195, 208; licit forms of, 114, 116, 119–20, 126–27, 150, 153, 175–76, 180–81, 210–11, 213; and astrology, 71–72; mystical basis of, 125–30, 181–85; use of, in cryptography, 126, 149–50, 153, 178, 199, 211. *See also* Hermes Trismegistus: Emerald Table, Hermetic movement; magic: natural

Alexander IV, Pope, 16–17

Alexander of Hales, 19–20

Made in the USA
Middletown, DE
08 August 2023

36310601R00215